ESSENTIAL HEALTH BENEFITS

BALANCING COVERAGE AND COST

Cheryl Ulmer, John Ball, Elizabeth McGlynn, and Shadia Bel Hamdounia, *Editors*

Committee on Defining and Revising an Essential Health Benefits Package for Qualified Health Plans

Board on Health Care Services

INSTITUTE OF MEDICINE
OF THE NATIONAL ACADEMIES

THE NATIONAL ACADEMIES PRESS
Washington, D.C.
www.nap.edu

THE NATIONAL ACADEMIES PRESS **500 Fifth Street, N.W.** Washington, DC 20001

NOTICE: The project that is the subject of this report was approved by the Governing Board of the National Research Council, whose members are drawn from the councils of the National Academy of Sciences, the National Academy of Engineering, and the Institute of Medicine.

This study was supported by Contract No. HHSP 23320042509XI, Task Order HHSP23337027T between the National Academy of Sciences and the Assistant Secretary for Planning and Evaluation of the U.S. Department of Health and Human Services. Any opinions, findings, conclusions, or recommendations expressed in this publication are those of the author(s) and do not necessarily reflect the view of the organizations or agencies that provided support for this project.

International Standard Book Number-13: 978-0-309-21914-3
International Standard Book Number-10: 0-309-21914-0

Additional copies of this report are available from the National Academies Press, 500 Fifth Street, N.W., Lockbox 285, Washington, DC 20055; (800) 624-6242 or (202) 334-3313 (in the Washington metropolitan area); Internet, http://www.nap.edu.

For more information about the Institute of Medicine, visit the IOM home page at: **www.iom.edu.**

The serpent has been a symbol of long life, healing, and knowledge among almost all cultures and religions since the beginning of recorded history. The serpent adopted as a logotype by the Institute of Medicine is a relief carving from ancient Greece, now held by the Staatliche Museen in Berlin.

Suggested citation: IOM (Institute of Medicine). 2012. *Essential Health Benefits: Balancing Coverage and Cost.* Washington, DC: The National Academies Press.

"Knowing is not enough; we must apply.
Willing is not enough; we must do."
—Goethe

INSTITUTE OF MEDICINE
OF THE NATIONAL ACADEMIES

Advising the Nation. Improving Health.

THE NATIONAL ACADEMIES
Advisers to the Nation on Science, Engineering, and Medicine

The **National Academy of Sciences** is a private, nonprofit, self-perpetuating society of distinguished scholars engaged in scientific and engineering research, dedicated to the furtherance of science and technology and to their use for the general welfare. Upon the authority of the charter granted to it by the Congress in 1863, the Academy has a mandate that requires it to advise the federal government on scientific and technical matters. Dr. Ralph J. Cicerone is president of the National Academy of Sciences.

The **National Academy of Engineering** was established in 1964, under the charter of the National Academy of Sciences, as a parallel organization of outstanding engineers. It is autonomous in its administration and in the selection of its members, sharing with the National Academy of Sciences the responsibility for advising the federal government. The National Academy of Engineering also sponsors engineering programs aimed at meeting national needs, encourages education and research, and recognizes the superior achievements of engineers. Dr. Charles M. Vest is president of the National Academy of Engineering.

The **Institute of Medicine** was established in 1970 by the National Academy of Sciences to secure the services of eminent members of appropriate professions in the examination of policy matters pertaining to the health of the public. The Institute acts under the responsibility given to the National Academy of Sciences by its congressional charter to be an adviser to the federal government and, upon its own initiative, to identify issues of medical care, research, and education. Dr. Harvey V. Fineberg is president of the Institute of Medicine.

The **National Research Council** was organized by the National Academy of Sciences in 1916 to associate the broad community of science and technology with the Academy's purposes of furthering knowledge and advising the federal government. Functioning in accordance with general policies determined by the Academy, the Council has become the principal operating agency of both the National Academy of Sciences and the National Academy of Engineering in providing services to the government, the public, and the scientific and engineering communities. The Council is administered jointly by both Academies and the Institute of Medicine. Dr. Ralph J. Cicerone and Dr. Charles M. Vest are chair and vice chair, respectively, of the National Research Council.

www.national-academies.org

COMMITTEE ON DEFINING AND REVISING AN ESSENTIAL HEALTH BENEFITS PACKAGE FOR QUALIFIED HEALTH PLANS

JOHN R. BALL (*Chair*), Former Executive Vice President, American Society for Clinical Pathology

MICHAEL S. ABROE, Principal and Consulting Actuary, Milliman, Inc.

MICHAEL E. CHERNEW, Professor of Health Care Policy, Harvard Medical School

PAUL FRONSTIN, Director, Health Research & Education Program, Employee Benefit Research Institute

ROBERT S. GALVIN, Chief Executive Officer, Equity Healthcare, Blackstone Group

MARJORIE GINSBURG, Executive Director, Center for Healthcare Decisions

DAVID S. GUZICK, Senior Vice President for Health Affairs, and President, UF&Shands Health System, University of Florida

SAM HO, Executive Vice President and Chief Medical Officer, UnitedHealthcare

CHRISTOPHER F. KOLLER, Health Insurance Commissioner, State of Rhode Island

ELIZABETH A. McGLYNN, Director, Kaiser Permanente Center for Effectiveness & Safety Research

AMY B. MONAHAN, Associate Professor, University of Minnesota Law School

ALAN R. NELSON, Internist-Endocrinologist

LINDA RANDOLPH, President and Chief Executive Officer, Developing Families Center

JAMES SABIN, Clinical Professor, Departments of Psychiatry and Population Health, Harvard Medical School, and Director, Harvard Pilgrim Health Care Ethics Program

JOHN SANTA, Director of Consumer Reports Health Ratings Center, Consumer Reports

LEONARD D. SCHAEFFER, Judge Robert Maclay Widney Chair and Professor, University of Southern California

JOE V. SELBY, Executive Director, Patient-Centered Outcomes Research Institute

SANDEEP WADHWA, Chief Medical Officer and Vice President of Reimbursement and Payer Markets, 3M Health Information Systems

Study Staff

CHERYL ULMER, Study Director

SHADIA BEL HAMDOUNIA, Research Associate

CASSANDRA L. CACACE, Research Assistant

ASHLEY McWILLIAMS, Senior Program Assistant (through July 2011)

ROGER C. HERDMAN, Director, Board on Health Care Services

Reviewers

This report has been reviewed in draft form by individuals chosen for their diverse perspectives and technical expertise, in accordance with procedures approved by the National Research Council's Report Review Committee. The purpose of this independent review is to provide candid and critical comments that will assist the institution in making its published report as sound as possible and to ensure that the report meets institutional standards for objectivity, evidence, and responsiveness to the study charge. The review comments and draft manuscript remain confidential to protect the integrity of the deliberative process. We wish to thank the following individuals for their review of this report:

Linda Burnes Bolton, Cedars-Sinai Medical Center
Troyen Brennan, CVS Caremark
Jon Gabel, National Opinion Research Center, University of Chicago
Neal Gooch, Utah Insurance Department
Jonathan H. Gruber, Massachusetts Institute of Technology
Gail Gibson Hunt, National Alliance for Caregiving
Michael M. E. Johns, Emory University
Timothy S. Jost, Washington and Lee University School of Law
Robert Krughoff, Center for the Study of Services
Eric Larson, Group Health Research Institute
Jerry Elizabeth Malooley, Benefit Programs and Health Policy for the State of Indiana
Wendy K. Mariner, Boston University School of Public Health
Debra L. Ness, National Partnership for Women and Families
Peter Neumann, Tufts University School of Medicine
Sara Rosenbaum, The George Washington University School of Public Health and Health Services
Alice Rosenblatt, AFR Consulting, LLC
Joshua M. Sharfstein, Department of Health and Mental Hygiene, State of Maryland
Gail Wilensky, Project HOPE
Matthew Wynia, American Medical Association

Although the reviewers listed above have provided many constructive comments and suggestions, they were not asked to endorse the conclusions or recommendations, nor did they see the final draft of the report before its release. The review of this report was overseen by **Christine K. Cassel,** American Board of Internal Medicine and **Donald M. Steinwachs,** Johns Hopkins University. Appointed by the National Research Council and the Institute of Medicine, they were responsible for making certain that an independent examination of this report was carried out in accordance with institutional procedures and that all review comments were carefully considered. Responsibility for the final content of this report rests entirely with the authoring committee and the institution.

Foreword

The Patient Protection and Affordable Care Act marks a milestone on a path toward substantially reducing the number of uninsured and underinsured individuals in this nation. The lack of health insurance is harmful to health, and equity in access to needed health care is one measure of a just society. But in creating the conditions for expanded insurance coverage, how, exactly, should one go about deciding what to include as essential in a health insurance plan?

This Institute of Medicine report *Essential Health Benefits: Balancing Coverage and Cost* answers this question. The Patient Protection and Affordable Care Act sets out parameters and guidance that serve as a point of departure and a constant reference for the committee's deliberations. This report lays out criteria and methods to define and update the essential health benefits package. The committee's recommendations aim at promoting evidence-based practices and prudent stewardship of resources. They encourage innovation and suggest ways to remain sensitive over time to evolving public preferences for coverage. This study was initiated at the request of the Assistant Secretary for Planning and Evaluation at the Department of Health and Human Services, and we sincerely hope the report will prove useful in the implementation of broader insurance coverage.

I am grateful for the support of our sponsors and to the committee, led by John Ball, which grappled with the complexity of balancing coverage needs of individuals and the sustainability of the essential health benefits package. Their work was reinforced by staff working under the direction of Cheryl Ulmer and including Shadia Bel Hamdounia, Cassandra Cacace, and Ashley McWilliams. I commend both committee and staff for this product and believe it provides a sound basis for the defining, and future refining, of an essential health benefits package.

Harvey V. Fineberg, M.D., Ph.D.
President, Institute of Medicine
July 2011

Preface

A critical element of the Patient Protection and Affordable Care Act (ACA) is the set of health benefits—termed "essential health benefits" (EHB)—that must be offered to individuals and small groups in state-based purchasing exchanges and the existing market. If the package of benefits is too narrow, health insurance might be meaningless; if it is too broad, insurance might become too expensive. The Institute of Medicine (IOM) Committee on Defining and Revising an Essential Health Benefits Package for Qualified Health Plans concluded that the major task of the Secretary of the Department of Health and Human Services (HHS) in defining the EHB will be balancing the comprehensiveness of benefits with their cost.

Not surprisingly, the work of this committee drew intense public interest. Opportunity for public input was offered through testimony at two public hearings and through the Web. The presentations at the hearings reinforced for the committee the difficulty of the task of balancing comprehensiveness and affordability. On the one hand, groups representing providers and consumers urged the broadest possible coverage of services. On the other, groups representing both small and large businesses argued for affordability and flexibility. The committee thus viewed its principal task as helping the Secretary navigate these competing goals and preferences in a fair and implementable way.

The ACA sets forth only broad guidance in defining essential health benefits, and that guidance is ambiguous—some would say contradictory. First, the EHB "shall include at least" 10 named categories of health services per Section 1302. Second, the scope of the EHB shall be "equal to the scope of benefits provided under a typical employer plan." Third, there are a set of "required elements for consideration" in establishing the EHB, such as balance and nondiscrimination. Fourth, there are several specific requirements regarding cost sharing, preventive services, proscriptions on limitations on coverage, and the like. Taken together, these provisions complicate the task of designing an EHB package that will be affordable for its principal intended purchasers—individuals and small businesses.

The committee's solution is this: build on what currently exists, learn over time, and make it better. That is, the initial EHB package should be a modification of what small employers are currently offering. All stakeholders should then learn enough over time—during implementation and through experimentation and research—to improve the package. The EHB package should be continuously improved and increasingly specific, with the goal that it is based on evidence of what improves health and that it promotes the appropriate use of limited resources. The committee's recommended modifications to the current small employer benefit package are (1) to take into account the 10 general categories of the ACA; (2) to apply committee-developed criteria to guide aggregate and specific EHB content and the methods to determine the EHB; and (3) to develop an initial package within a premium target.

Defining a premium target, which is a way to address the affordability issue, became a central tenet of the committee. *Why* the Secretary should take cost into account, both in defining the initial EHB package and in updating it, is straightforward: if cost is not taken into account, the EHB package becomes increasingly expensive, and individuals and small businesses will find it increasingly unaffordable. If this occurs, the principal reason for the ACA—enabling people to purchase health insurance and thus covering more of the population—will not be met. At an even more fundamental level, health benefits are a resource, and no resource is unlimited. Defining a premium target in conjunction with developing the EHB package simply acknowledges this fundamental reality. *How* to take cost into account became a major task. The committee's solution in the determination of the initial EHB package is to tie the package to what small employers would have paid, on average, for their current packages of benefits in 2014, the first year the ACA will apply to insurance purchases in and out of the exchanges. This "premium target" should be updated annually, taking into account trends in medical prices, utilization, new technologies, and population characteristics. Since, however, this does little to stem health care cost increases, and since the committee did not believe the HHS Secretary had the authority to mandate premium (or other cost) targets, the committee recommends a concerted and expeditious attempt by all stakeholders to address the problem of health care cost inflation.

An additional task was related to that part of the committee's charge directing it to examine "medical necessity." Medical necessity is a means by which insurers and health plans determine whether it is appropriate to reimburse a specific patient for an eligible benefit. For example, the insurance contract may specify that diabetes care is a covered benefit; whether it is paid for depends on whether that care is medically necessary for the particular patient—whether, for example, the patient has diabetes. The committee believes that medical necessity determinations are both appropriate and necessary and serve as a context within which the EHB package is developed by a health insurer into a specific benefit design and that benefit design is subsequently administered. The committee favors transparency both in the establishment of the rules used in making those determinations and in their application and appeals processes. Indeed, since the design and administration of health benefits rather than the scope of benefits themselves are what appear to differentiate small employer plans from each other and from large employer plans, monitoring benefit design and administration is an important step in the learning process and updating of the EHB.

Further, the committee states that a goal of the updated EHB package is that its content becomes more evidence-based. The committee wishes to emphasize the importance of research about the effectiveness of health services and to emphasize that the results of this research, including costs, should be taken into account in designing the EHB package. New and alternative treatments, in the view of the committee, should meet the standard of providing increased health gains at the same or lower cost.

Since the committee saw balancing comprehensiveness and affordability as the Secretary's major task, it also recognized that any such balancing affected, and was affected by, individual and societal values and preferences. Thus, the committee recommends that both in the determination of the initial EHB package and in its updates, structured public deliberative processes be established to identify the values and priorities of those citizens eligible to purchase insurance through the exchanges, as well as members of the general public. Such processes will enhance both public understanding of the tradeoffs inherent in establishing an EHB package and public acceptance of what emerges.

The committee recommends that the Secretary develop a process that facilitates discovery and implementation of innovative practices over time. A key source for this information will come from what states are observing or enabling in their own exchanges. Moreover, the committee recommends that for states that operate insurance exchanges, requests to adopt alternatives to the federal essential health benefits package be granted only if they are consistent with ACA requirements and the criteria specified in the report and they are not significantly more or less generous than the federal package. State packages also should be supported by meaningful public input.

The committee hopes that its work will be useful in assisting the Secretary of HHS to determine and update the essential health benefits and that its deliberations will be informative to the public. As with most issues of importance, the committee's work involved balancing tradeoffs among competing interests and ideas. We hope this work is a positive step toward effective implementation of a key provision of the ACA.

On a personal note, the chair wishes to thank the committee members for their tireless efforts in the work of the committee. In the chair's experience, the input—extensive and intensive—of the committee members is unprecedented. When qualified people of good intent, of whatever political persuasion, come together for a common purpose, the process is full of learning and enjoyable. Thus it was with this committee, and I thank its members for the experience. In addition, no work of this sort can be done without a highly qualified professional staff. On behalf of the committee, the chair thanks Cheryl Ulmer and her staff for their efforts to capture the substance of the committee's deliberations, their provision of the most detailed background material, and their logistical acumen, especially in designing the public hearings.

John R. Ball
Chair
Committee on Defining and Revising an Essential Health Benefits Package for Qualified Health Plans
September 2011

Acknowledgments

The committee and staff are grateful for many individuals and organizations who contributed to the success of the report. Many thanks go to the numerous individuals to whom staff spoke before and during the study process, as well as those who submitted responses to the committee's online comment form and other materials. In addition, the committee wants to thank those who testified before it during the two public workshops:

Jessica Banthin, Agency for Healthcare Research and Quality
Carmella Bocchino, America's Health Insurance Plans
Meg Booth, Children's Dental Health Project
David Bowen, The Bill & Melinda Gates Foundation
Virginia Calega, BlueCross BlueShield Association
Arnold Cohen, American Congress of Obstetricians and Gynecologists
Rex Cowdry, Maryland Health Care Commission
Helen Darling, National Business Group on Health
Jina Dhillon, National Health Law Program
James Dunnigan, Utah State House of Representatives
Cindy Ehnes, California Department of Managed Health Care
John Falardeau, American Chiropractic Association
Linda Fishman, American Hospital Association
Marty Ford, The Arc and United Cerebral Palsy Disability Policy Coalition
Jean Fraser, San Mateo County Health System
Brian Gallagher, American Pharmacists Association
Alan Garber, Stanford University Center for Health Policy
Andrew George, California Department of Managed Health Care
Jonathan Gruber, Massachusetts Institute of Technology and the National Bureau of Economic Research
Gerald Harmon, American Medical Association
Mark Hayes, Greenberg Taurig, LLP
Leah Hole-Curry, Washington State Health Technology Assessment Program
Carolyn Ingram, Center for Health Care Strategies
Louis Jacques, Centers for Medicare & Medicaid Services

Jeffrey Kang, CIGNA Corporation
Jon Kingsdale, Wakely Consulting
Sharon Levine, The Permanente Medical Group
Jerry Malooley, U.S. Chamber of Commerce
Robert McDonough, Aetna
Maureen McKennan, California Department of Managed Health Care
Sean Morrison, National Palliative Care Research Center
Robert Murphy, American Society of Plastic Surgeons
Samuel Nussbaum, WellPoint
Kavita Patel, University of California, Los Angeles (UCLA) Semel Institute
Susan Philip, California Health Benefits Review Program
Joseph Piacentini, Employee Benefits Security Administration, Department of Labor (DOL)
Andrew Racine, American Academy of Pediatrics
Sara Rosenbaum, George Washington University School of Public Health and Health Services
Somnath Saha, Portland VA Medical Center and Oregon Health Services Commission
Matthew Salo, The National Governors Association
Beth Sammis, Maryland Insurance Administration
Paul Samuels, Legal Action Center and Coalition for Whole Health
Cathy Schoen, The Commonwealth Fund
David Schwartz, Senate Finance Committee
Thomas Sellers, National Coalition for Cancer Survivorship
Jeanene Smith, Office of Oregon Health Policy and Research
Richard Smith, Pharmaceutical Research and Manufacturers of America
Katy Spangler, U.S. Senate Committee on Health, Education, Labor, and Pensions
Stuart Spielman, Autism Speaks
Peter Thomas, Consortium for Citizens with Disabilities
Jeffery Thompson, Washington State Department of Social and Health Services
Michael Turpin, USI Insurance Services
Gary Ulicny, The Shepherd Center
Barbara Warren, Consumers United for Evidence-Based Healthcare
Kenneth B. Wells, David Geffen School of Medicine, UCLA
William Wiatrowski, Bureau of Labor Statistics, DOL
Bruce Wolfe, Obesity Action Coalition
Anthony Wright, Health Access California
Troy Zimmerman, National Kidney Foundation

Funding for this study was provided by the Assistant Secretary for Planning and Evaluation (ASPE). The committee appreciates ASPE's support for this project and would like to especially thank Sherry Glied, Richard Kronick, Carolyn Taplin, Lee Wilson, and Pierre Yong for their expertise and guidance on the project.

Lastly, many individuals within the Institute of Medicine were helpful throughout the study process, including Clyde Behney, Daniel Bethea, Patrick Burke, Marton Cavani, Greta Gorman, Laura Harbold, Abbey Meltzer, Elisabeth Reese, Vilija Teel, Stephanie Tioseco, and Lauren Tobias. We would also like to thank Florence Poillon for assisting in copyediting this report. Christine Stencel of the National Academies' Office of News and Public Information provided substantial support in preparing for the public release of this consensus report and its companion workshop report; Rachel Marcus of the National Academies Press helped facilitate the publication of both manuscripts.

Contents

APPENDIXES

Boxes, Figures, and Tables

Chapter 2

Chapter 3

Chapter 4

Chapter 5

Chapter 6

Chapter 7

Chapter 9

Abstract

The principal intent of the Patient Protection and Affordable Care Act (ACA) is to enable previously uninsured Americans to obtain health insurance. To accomplish this, in part, subsidized plans will be offered to low- and moderate-income individuals and small employers through health insurance exchanges. Plans qualified to be offered through exchanges must at minimum include "essential health benefits" (EHB). The ACA is not very specific on the definition of the EHB, except that such benefits shall include at least 10 enumerated general categories and that the scope of the EHB shall be equal to the scope of benefits provided under a typical employer plan. The ACA requires the Secretary of the Department of Health and Human Services to define the essential health benefits.

The Institute of Medicine (IOM) was asked by the Secretary to make recommendations on the methods for determining and updating the EHB. Notably, the request was to focus on criteria and policy foundations for the determination of the EHB, not to develop the list of benefits. The IOM formed a committee of volunteers with varied perspectives and professional backgrounds; the committee held four face-to-face meetings and numerous conference calls. Broad public input was obtained. In two open workshops, the committee heard from more than 50 witnesses, and 345 comments were received in response to questions posted on the Web. The consensus report then underwent rigorous external review in accordance with procedures established by the Report Review Committee of the National Research Council.

As the committee examined its charge, it saw two main questions for the Secretary: (1) how to determine the initial EHB package and (2) how to update the EHB package.

Defining the initial EHB package. In considering how to determine the initial EHB package, the committee was struck by two compelling facts: (1) if the purpose of the ACA is to provide access to health insurance coverage, then that coverage has to be affordable; and (2) the more expansive the benefit package is, the more it will likely cost and the less affordable it will be. How to balance the competing goals of comprehensiveness of coverage and affordability was key.

The committee concluded that it is best to begin simply by defining the EHB package as reflecting the scope and design of packages offered by small employers today, modified to include the 10 required categories. This package would then be assessed by criteria and within a defined cost target recommended by the committee. The committee considered how four policy domains—economics, ethics, population-based health, and evidence-based practice—could guide the Secretary in determining the EHB package in general. From these policy foundations, the committee recommends: criteria to guide the aggregate EHB package; criteria to guide specific EHB inclusions and exclusions; and criteria to guide methods for defining and updating the EHB.

To ensure affordability and to protect the intent of the ACA, the committee concluded that costs must be considered both in the determination of the initial EHB package and in its updating. Thus, the cost of the initial EHB package resulting from the previous steps should be compared to a premium target, defined by the committee as what small employers would have paid, on average, in 2014. Committee members believe that absent a premium target, there would be no capacity to acknowledge the realities of limited resources and the ongoing need for affordability of the package. The EHB package should be modified as necessary to meet this estimated premium, including using a structured public deliberative process. In addition, the committee recommends that states operating their own exchanges be able to design a variant of the EHB package if certain standards are met.

Updating the EHB package. Both medical science and our understanding of how best to design insurance products will change over time. Thus, the committee recommends creating a framework and infrastructure for collecting data and analyzing implementation of the initial EHB; a National Benefits Advisory Council is recommended to give the Secretary advice on the research plan and on updates to the EHB package. The committee believes that the EHB package should become more fully evidence-based, specific, and value-based over time. In addition, as with the initial package, costs must be taken into account so that any service added to the package should be offset by savings, such as through the elimination of inappropriate or outmoded services.

Finally, the committee noted that even with the use of a premium target, the affordability of the EHB package is threatened by overall rising medical costs in the United States and recommends that the Secretary, in collaboration with others, develop a strategy to reduce health care spending growth across all sectors.

Summary

The Patient Protection and Affordable Care Act (ACA) authorized the largest expansion of health insurance coverage since the development of Medicare and Medicaid. As a result, by 2016, an estimated 30 million individuals, who would otherwise have been uninsured, are expected to obtain insurance through the private health insurance market or state expansion of Medicaid programs. To ensure a consistent level of benefits, the ACA calls for certain types of private and public insurance to incorporate a federally determined essential health benefits (EHB) package. The ACA gives the Secretary of the U.S. Department of Health and Human Services (HHS) sole authority to define the EHB.

HHS asked the Institute of Medicine (IOM) to recommend a process by which the Secretary could define and subsequently update the EHB. As part of its work, the committee sought the views of many experts and stakeholders. Presentations from the committee's two public workshops are available as a separate publication, *Perspectives on Essential Health Benefits: Workshop Report*.[1] Additionally, 10 questions were posted on the IOM website for 6 months to obtain wider public input. The committee developed its recommendations from this information, additional research, and its own deliberations.

WHO IS COVERED BY THE ESSENTIAL HEALTH BENEFITS?

Guidance by the Secretary on the definition of essential health benefits will determine the minimum benefit package that must be offered to individuals and small employers purchasing insurance, and by certain Medicaid expansion plans known as benchmark or benchmark-equivalent plans and state basic insurance plans. More than 68 million people are estimated to obtain insurance that must meet the EHB requirements (Eibner et al., 2010).

MULTIPLE POLICY FOUNDATIONS WERE INTEGRATED TO FRAME THE PROCESS FOR DEVELOPING THE EHB

The Secretary of HHS asked the IOM committee to develop an explicit framework for developing the EHB package that would serve HHS now and in the future (Glied, 2011). Finding that no single policy foundation was

---

[1] The workshop report can be accessed at http://www.iom.edu/EHBperspectives.

sufficient, the committee integrated perspectives from economics, ethics, evidence-based practice, and population health (Figure S-1) to create an overarching framework (Chapter 3).

EXPLICIT CRITERIA WERE DEVELOPED TO GUIDE THE OVERALL PACKAGE, CHOICES OF COMPONENTS, AND THE METHODS FOR UPDATING

The committee used the integrated policy foundations to develop criteria that could guide decisions about the EHB, as the Secretary of HHS requested. As shown in Figure S-2, the committee developed criteria to guide the EHB content in the aggregate and on specific elements. The committee recognized that the process by which the EHB are initially defined and updated is critical to establishing trust in the results. The committee's recommended criteria to guide the processes for establishing and updating the EHB are shown in Figure S-2.

A MULTI-STEP PROCESS IS RECOMMENDED FOR DEVELOPING THE INITIAL EHB

As background, the report reviews the relationships between the benefits that are eligible for coverage, the design of covered benefits, and how benefits are administered, and then discusses various approaches that have been taken by states and private insurers regarding each of these aspects of insurance (Chapter 2). The report also reviews how some of the conflicting or ambiguous issues in the ACA were interpreted by the committee to provide a common understanding from which to develop its recommendations (Chapter 4).

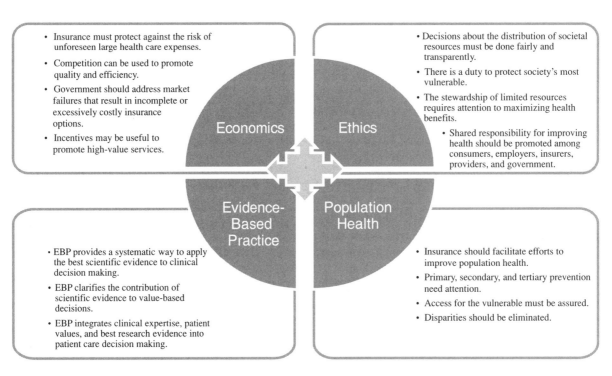

FIGURE S-1 Four policy domains with associated foundational principles for thinking about essential health benefits development and implementation.
NOTE: EBP = evidence-based practice.

Criteria to Guide Content of the Aggregate EHB Package

In the aggregate, the EHB must:
- **Be affordable** for consumers, employers, and taxpayers.
- **Maximize the number of people with insurance coverage.**
- **Protect the most vulnerable** by addressing the particular needs of those patients and populations.
- **Encourage better care practices** by promoting the right care to the right patient in the right setting at the right time.

- **Advance stewardship of resources** by focusing on high value services and reducing use of low value services. Value is defined as outcomes relative to cost.
- **Address the medical concerns of greatest importance** to enrollees in EHB-related plans, as identified through a public deliberative process.
- **Protect against the greatest financial risks** due to catastrophic events or illnesses.

Criteria to Guide EHB Content on Specific Components

The individual service, device, or drug for the EHB must:
- **Be safe**—expected benefits should be greater than expected harms.
- **Be medically effective** and supported by a sufficient evidence base, or in the absence of evidence on effectiveness, a credible standard of care is used.
- **Demonstrate meaningful improvement** in outcomes over current effective services/treatments.
- **Be a medical service**, not serving primarily a social or educational function.

- **Be cost effective**, so that the health gain for individual and population health is sufficient to justify the additional cost to taxpayers and consumers.

Caveats:

Failure to meet any of the criteria should result in exclusion or significant limits on coverage.

Each component would still be subject to the criteria for assembling the aggregate EHB package.

Inclusion does not mean that it is appropriate for every person to receive every component.

Criteria to Guide Methods for Defining and Updating the EHB

Methods for defining, updating, and prioritizing must be:
- **Transparent.** The rationale for all decisions about benefits, benefit design, and changes is made publicly available.
- **Participatory.** Current and future enrollees have a role in helping define the priorities for coverage.
- **Equitable and consistent.** Enrollees should feel confident that benefits will be developed and administered fairly.
- **Sensitive to value.** To be accountable to taxpayers and plan members, the covered service must provide a meaningful health benefit.

- **Responsive to new information.** The EHB will change over time as new scientific information becomes available.
- **Attentive to stewardship.** For judicious use of pooled resources, budgetary constraints are necessary to keep the EHB affordable.
- **Encouraging to innovation.** The EHB should allow for innovation in covered services, service delivery, medical management, and new payment models to improve value.
- **Data-driven.** An evaluation of the care included in the EHB is based on objective clinical evidence and actuarial reviews.

FIGURE S-2 Criteria for assessing content of essential health benefits (EHB) in the aggregate, for specific components, and for methods.

Balancing Coverage and Cost

Congress provided guidance in the ACA to the Secretary about the contents of the EHB by listing 10 categories of care that must be included (Box S-1) and by indicating that coverage should be consistent with the typical employer plan. Given the ACA's focus on providing access to health insurance for workers of small firms and individuals in the first years of the health insurance exchanges, the committee concluded that the EHB should be defined initially by what is typical in the small employer market. The committee noted that the insurance plans offered by small vs. large employers differ primarily in their benefit design and administration rather than in what benefits are covered. The committee also concluded that current state-mandated benefits should not receive any special treatment in the definition of the EHB and should be subject to the same evaluative method as all other parts of the EHB.

The committee's vision for the EHB is that only medically necessary (or appropriate) services for individuals should be covered (Chapter 5). The committee believes that the concepts of individualizing care, ensuring value, and having medical necessity decisions strongly rooted in evidence should be reemphasized in any guidance on medical necessity. Inflexibility in the application of medical necessity, clinical policies, medical management, and limits without consideration of the circumstances of an individual case is undesirable and potentially discriminatory. The committee believes transparency in a rigorous appeals monitoring process is the primary approach to addressing the nondiscrimination provisions in benefit design and implementation, including medical necessity reviews.

Early in its deliberations the committee recognized that to achieve the ACA's goal of improving access to health care services by maximizing the number of people with meaningful health insurance benefits, the cost of the package needs to be included in the definition of the EHB (Chapter 5). As the scope of benefits expands, individuals who are purchasing plans by themselves or through employers face higher premiums. A benefit package that is more expensive also places greater demand on the federal budget to provide subsidies for low-income purchasers and on state budgets to cover some newly eligible Medicaid enrollees.

The EHB can be viewed as a "market basket" of goods and services (i.e., benefit options) that enrollees who need those goods and services are eligible to have covered. The price for access to the services covered by that market basket is the premium. The committee considered two basic approaches the Secretary could take to establish the initial cost of the EHB: select the market basket of benefit options and then estimate what it would cost or set a cost target and determine what could be purchased within that constraint. The committee endorses the latter

---

BOX S-1
Essential Benefits Categories in the Patient Protection
and Affordable Health Care Act

Essential Health Benefits

- Ambulatory patient services
- Emergency services
- Hospitalization
- Maternity and newborn care
- Mental health and substance use disorder services, including behavioral health treatment
- Prescription drugs
- Rehabilitative and habilitative services and devices
- Laboratory services
- Preventive and wellness services and chronic disease management
- Pediatric services, including oral and vision care

SOURCE: §1302(b)(1)(A)-(J).

approach and recommends using as the cost target the estimated national average premium that would have been paid by small employers in 2014 for a silver level–equivalent plan if the ACA had not been enacted.[2] This does not mean that the Secretary is setting a single premium for all silver plans purchased in the country but rather that the estimated average cost of the EHB would not exceed the national average premium for a silver plan. Premiums faced by consumers and employers will vary as they do today by region of the country, design and administration of the insurance plan, whether benefits beyond the EHB are included in the package, and other factors.

Public Input Should Be Obtained to Inform the Tradeoffs Between Covered Elements

The process recommended by the committee to define the EHB explicitly requires that tradeoffs be made between competing elements of the benefit package in order to meet the premium target. Setting priorities among benefit options necessitates integrating scientific evidence about effectiveness with value judgments about relative importance. Thus, the committee recommends that the Secretary undertake a public deliberative process to obtain input on the tradeoffs. The process that the committee supports is described in greater detail in Chapter 6.

Secretarial Guidance Should Be as Explicit as Possible

In examining coverage documents used by insurers today, the committee found that they frequently lacked specificity. The committee further observed that specificity increases the likelihood that consumers will be offered a uniform set of benefits no matter where or from whom they purchase insurance. The committee recommends that the Secretary be as explicit as possible to ensure that the ACA intent of a consistent package of benefits is achieved.

Recommendation 1: By May 1, 2012, the Secretary should establish an initial essential health benefits (EHB) package guided by a national average premium target.

A. **The starting point in establishing the initial EHB package should be the scope of benefits and design provided under a typical small employer plan in today's market. To specify the initial EHB package, this scope of benefits should then be modified to reflect**
   - **The 10 general categories specified in Section 1302(b)(1) of the Affordable Care Act (ACA); and**
   - **The criteria specified in this report for the content of specific elements and aggregate EHB package (see Figure S-2).**

B. **Once a preliminary EHB list is developed as described in (A), the package should be adjusted so that the expected national average premium for a silver plan with the EHB package is actuarially equivalent to the average premium that would have been paid by small employers in 2014 for a comparable population with a typical benefit design.**

C. **The Secretary should sponsor a public deliberative process to assist in determining how the adjustments to the EHB package should be made.**

D. **Initial guidance by the Secretary on the contents of the EHB package should list standard benefit inclusions and exclusions at a level of specificity at least comparable to current best practice in the private and public insurance market.**

---

[2] The ACA establishes four "metal" levels of plans to be offered on exchanges: platinum, gold, silver, and bronze. The plans all must include the EHB. The plans are distinguished by their actuarial value, that is, by the average proportion of eligible expenses that is paid by the plan. The actuarial values for the metal levels are 90 percent for platinum, 80 percent for gold, 70 percent for silver, and 60 percent for bronze. Premium subsidies are calculated based on the average cost of the second lowest premium for a silver plan in a market.

CREATING A FOUNDATION FOR UPDATING
THROUGH MONITORING AND RESEARCH

The committee expects that the EHB will change over time based on a variety of factors and stakeholder input. The Secretary should have a mechanism for learning how the priorities and tradeoffs made by the public are changing, what states are learning about the uptake of new insurance products in the exchanges and reductions in the number of people who are uninsured, what research suggests are the approaches to care delivery and benefit design that improve outcomes, and what innovations in insurance design promote high value care. To make certain that the Secretary can systematically learn from the implementation experience in the exchanges and the changing science base, a process for identifying data needs and developing a coordinated research agenda to support monitoring and updating the EHB should begin immediately (Chapter 7). The committee offers a two-part recommendation regarding a framework for data collection and coordinated research efforts.

A Framework Should Be Developed to Guide Data Collection
for Monitoring Implementation and Updating of the EHB

The state health insurance exchanges will determine which health plans are qualified to operate in the exchange, and can provide information about the progress of implementing the EHB. The ability of the states to provide consistent and usable information to the Secretary will be enhanced if a framework for collecting and analyzing data is developed in advance. The exchanges and other health care–related entities (insurers, providers) will be important sources of data for monitoring and updating the EHB. The committee recommends that the Secretary obtain guidance from expert groups on setting standards for uniform reporting of state-based data.

Recommendation 2a: By January 1, 2013, the Secretary should establish a framework for obtaining and analyzing data necessary for monitoring implementation and updating of the EHB. The framework should account for:

- **Changes related to providers such as payment rates, contracting mechanisms, financial incentives, and scope and organization of practice;**
- **Changes related to patients and consumers such as demographics, health status, disease burden, and problems with access; and**
- **Changes related to health plans such as characteristics of plans (inclusions, exclusions, limitations), cost-sharing practices, patterns of enrollment and disenrollment, network configuration, medical management programs (including medical necessity determination processes), value-based insurance design, types of external appeals, risk selection, solvency, and impact of the ACA-mandated limits on deductibles, co-payments, and out-of-pocket spending on the ability of plans to offer acceptable products.**

A Coordinated Research Agenda Will Enhance Assessments of the EHB

HHS's component agencies, the Department of Labor, and other non-federal organizations routinely collect data that will be pertinent to assessing the EHB over time. In particular, the Secretary should examine how the scope of benefits contributes to expanded coverage and access to quality care, and how the EHB package can be updated to become more evidence-based and value-promoting. The committee recommends that, prior to implementation of the exchanges in 2014, HHS coordinates the development of a research plan to evaluate the implementation of the EHB and identify the data necessary to support this plan. Furthermore, the committee believes that, to the extent patient privacy can be assured, public access to these data for analysis should be enabled, just as HHS has sponsored access to other departmental data (e.g., http://www.health.data.gov).

Recommendation 2b: The Secretary should establish an appropriate infrastructure for implementing this framework that engages and coordinates the efforts of all of the appropriate HHS and other federal agencies

in producing and analyzing the necessary data in a timely manner. These data should be made easily accessible and affordable for public use.

ALLOWANCE FOR STATE-BASED INNOVATION

The committee acknowledges that some flexibility is necessary to encourage innovation. It is the committee's intention that the initial design of the EHB continue to support innovation in the design of insurance products offered (Chapter 8). The ACA is clear that the Secretary of HHS has sole authority to define the EHB. The authority granted to HHS to define EHB does not, however, preclude the Secretary from using that authority to approve state-specific variations of the EHB definition. Those variations must be consistent with the requirements specified in the ACA, should produce a package that is of equivalent comprehensiveness and value, and should have undergone a systematic process for obtaining public input.

Recommendation 3: For states administering their own exchanges that wish to adopt a variant of the federal EHB package, the Secretary should use statutory authority to grant such requests, provided that the state-specific EHB definition is consistent with the requirements of Section 1302 of the ACA and the criteria specified in this report, that they produce a package that is actuarially equivalent to the national package established by the Secretary, and that the request is supported by a process that has included meaningful public input. To best achieve this, the Secretary should encourage a public deliberative process as described in this report and should provide technical assistance to the states for implementing that process.

UPDATING THE EHB

The Secretary asked the IOM to provide guidance on a process for updating the EHB over time. Congress also requires HHS to monitor whether the essential benefits package is being implemented appropriately for all eligible enrollees. As required in Section 1302, the Secretary must periodically update the EHB and provide a report to Congress and the public that addresses the following:

- whether enrollees are facing any difficulty accessing needed services for reasons of coverage or cost;
- whether the EHB needs to be modified or updated to account for changes in medical evidence or scientific advancement;
- how the EHB will be modified to address any such gaps in access or changes in the evidence base; and
- an assessment of the potential of additional or expanded benefits to increase costs and the interactions between the addition or expansion of benefits and reductions in existing benefits to meet actuarial limitations.[3]

The committee recommends that the Secretary undertake an approach to updating the EHB that incorporates the advances in medical science and insurance design within a cost target that is defined by the national average premium for a silver plan offered on the exchanges (Chapter 9). The committee offers a three-part recommendation for the updating process: first, set goals for the updated EHB package; second, propose a method for using costs to frame modifications to the EHB; third, call attention to the need to develop a strategy to address increases in health care spending that threaten the long term integrity of the EHB as a meaningful package.

Goals for Updating the EHB

The committee believes that over time the EHB package should become more explicitly based on evidence of effectiveness and should promote better outcomes for both individuals and the U.S. population relative to the

---

[3] Patient Protection and Affordable Care Act of 2010, Public Law 111-148 as amended by the Health Care and Education Reconciliation Act of 2010. § 1302(b)(4)(H). 111th Cong., 2nd session.

cost of insurance coverage. The committee believes this will require more detailed specification of included and excluded services than will initially characterize the Secretary's guidance. The report provides some examples available today of the desirable level of detail in future EHB definitions (Chapter 9).

Recommendation 4a: Beginning in 2015, for implementation in 2016 and annually thereafter, the Secretary should update the EHB package, with the goals that it becomes more fully evidence-based, specific, and value-promoting.

Incorporating Costs into Updates

The committee considered multiple methods of updating the initial national average premium in Recommendation 1. Based on the current secretarial authority and other factors, the committee recommends that any changes to the EHB result in a package that is no more expensive than the estimated subsequent year cost of the base-year package. This ensures that the EHB will not accelerate the increase in spending for those whose insurance is subject to the EHB. Further, it provides a mechanism for incorporating new categories or services within the cost target (premium), requiring tradeoffs be made explicitly between existing and new elements of coverage.

Recommendation 4b: The Secretary should explicitly incorporate costs into updates to the EHB package.

- **The Secretary should obtain an actuarial estimate of the national average premium for a silver-level plan with the existing EHB package in the next year; the estimate will account for trends in medical prices, utilization, new technologies, and population characteristics.**
- **Any changes to the EHB package should not result in a package that exceeds the actuarially estimated cost of the current package in the next year. A public deliberative process should be used to inform choices about inclusions to or exclusions from the updated package, with specific attention to how inclusion of new benefits could affect the availability of existing covered benefits.**

A Strategy Should Be Developed to Address Rising Costs

From the beginning of its deliberations, the Committee unanimously agreed that if the country does not address the problem of health care costs growing faster than the gross domestic product, it will undermine the ACA's goal of substantially reducing the number of people without health insurance. In Recommendation 4b, the committee endorses allowing the cost of the EHB to increase with the rate of premium increases because that would enhance the likelihood of maintaining the initial level of comprehensiveness established by the Secretary. Unfortunately, this means that the cost of the EHB will likely continue to increase faster than wages and faster than the growth in the economy. In turn, the number of people who will be able to afford to purchase the EHB-defined insurance will decline. As the premiums increase, subsidies will take a larger share of the federal budget. As premiums rise, many more people will choose to enroll in Medicaid rather than a private plan on the exchange, increasing the strain on state budgets. All of these consequences violate one of the criteria established by the committee: the EHB should be affordable for consumers, employers, and taxpayers. The committee further envisioned that the pressure on federal and state budgets might lead to repeal of the EHB requirement. This threat to the long-term integrity of the EHB caused the committee to consider what could be done in order to mitigate these adverse consequences.

Achieving an appropriate balance between comprehensiveness and affordability of the EHB cannot be accomplished through actions taken only on behalf of EHB enrollees or only through the contents of the EHB. Effective efforts to change the rate of increase in health spending require a strategy that addresses all of the drivers of health care costs. The committee considered whether complementary Medicare-only or federal-only approaches to reducing rising health care costs would be sufficient and concluded they would not be. An all stakeholder strategy is required across the public and private sectors. Unless a strategy for containing costs throughout the health care system is adopted, the definition of an essential health benefits package will ultimately fail to achieve congressional intent to establish an appropriate basic package that is affordable.

Recommendation 4c: To ensure over time that EHB-defined packages are affordable and offer reasonable coverage, the Secretary of HHS, working in collaboration with others, should develop a strategy for controlling rates of growth in health care spending across all sectors in line with the rate of growth in the economy.

The committee believes desirable attributes of an approach to developing such a strategy are for it to be non-partisan, include public and private sector collaboration, integrate activities across all sectors, and be able to ensure action on the recommendations. For example, the Secretary could co-convene a commission with a representative of the private sector experienced in purchasing health services to develop and implement meaningful actions to control costs. Because coordinated federal action would increase the likelihood of success in the public sector, the Secretary of HHS could coordinate federal participation in a commission and oversee federal implementation of such a commission's recommendations. The committee considered whether an existing entity could take up this charge, specifically assessing the Independent Payment Advisory Board (IPAB), and decided it was less appropriate for the work envisioned by the committee as IPAB is currently constituted.

While it may appear that addressing the rate of growth in health care spending is beyond the scope of the EHB provisions, the committee views its Recommendations 4b and 4c as necessary complements. The committee's Recommendation 4b is designed to preserve the scope of benefits over time and yet to ensure that the EHB package itself will not accelerate the increase in spending by keeping the package equivalent in content. But without making concerted progress in stemming rising health care costs (Recommendation 4c), it will cost more to purchase the same package of benefits each year, eroding the purchasing power of the estimated 68 million people who will depend on EHB coverage. Eventually, the EHB package will become a hollow promise of coverage. The committee's charge was to develop a viable approach to defining the EHB that would work now and into the future, and this requires a two-pronged approach.

THE SECRETARY SHOULD OBTAIN ONGOING
EXTERNAL ADVICE ON UPDATING THE EHB

Having identified a set of recommendations for updating the EHB and addressing the sector-wide challenges with rising health care costs, the committee next considered whether the Secretary would benefit from forming a new advisory group focused on updates to the EHB. The committee refers to this advisory group as the National Benefits Advisory Council (NBAC).

The committee recommends that the NBAC advise the Secretary on (1) the research framework and scope of the data collection for monitoring implementation (Chapter 7), (2) updates to the overall benefit package and related benefit design issues, (3) changes to the cost target, and (4) appropriate mechanisms for evaluating new interventions. The IOM committee thought that while the NBAC might ideally have a role in defining the initial EHB, it would not be practical to get the NBAC appointed and operational in a timely enough fashion to be useful in this process. However, the public input obtained by the IOM committee and its own deliberations about defining the initial EHB is consistent with what the NBAC will be doing over time.

The NBAC should ensure that the EHB protect the most vulnerable members of society, encourage appropriate use of services, be evidence-based, and encourage cost-effective use of resources. Further, the NBAC is a mechanism to ensure that the process to define and apply decisions about updates to the EHB be fair and transparent.

The committee considered whether an existing entity could fulfill the functions envisioned for the NBAC and specifically considered the U.S. Preventive Services Task Force, the Medicare Evidence Development and Coverage Advisory Committee (MEDCAC), the Patient-Centered Outcomes Research Institute (PCORI), and the Consumer Operated and Oriented Plan (CO-OP) Program Advisory Board. The report describes the current functions of these groups and the extent to which they could undertake the NBAC mission. The committee concluded that none of these entities is designed to or could easily be modified to perform the necessary functions.

Recommendation 5: As soon as is feasible, the Secretary should establish a National Benefits Advisory Council (NBAC), staffed by HHS but appointed through a nonpartisan process, such as the Office of the Comptroller General of the United States. The NBAC should

- **By January 1, 2013, advise the Secretary on a research plan and data requirements for updating the EHB package;**
- **Starting in 2015 for implementation in 2016, make recommendations annually to the Secretary regarding (1) any changes to the EHB package by applying the committee's recommended criteria (see Figure S-2), (2) any changes to the premium target, and (3) any mechanisms that would enhance the evidence base of the EHB package and its potential for promoting value; and**
- **Advise the Secretary on conducting and using the results of a periodic national public deliberative process to inform its recommendations around updates to the EHB.**

CONCLUSION

The ACA establishes an essential health benefits package and defines 10 general categories that must be included in that package. The ACA, however, left considerable discretion to the Secretary of HHS to design this package. The Secretary, in turn, asked the IOM to provide input on the process that might be undertaken to develop the EHB. In its deliberations, the most critical issue identified by the committee is the need to explicitly address the tradeoff between the cost of a benefit package and the comprehensiveness of coverage. If that tradeoff is not addressed, a number of consequences are possible:

- If the benefits are not affordable, fewer people will buy insurance.
- If the benefit design makes access too difficult, people will not get the care they need.
- If health care spending continues to rise faster than gross domestic product (GDP), the value of the EHB is likely to be eroded.

The committee concluded that the benefit package should be designed within the context of financial constraints, using a structured public process to establish priorities. The committee developed a set of criteria to guide the process for designing and updating the EHB. The EHB must be affordable, maximize the number of people with insurance, protect the most vulnerable individuals, protect against the greatest financial risks, promote better care, ensure stewardship of limited financial resources by focusing on high value services of proven effectiveness, promote shared responsibility for improving our health, and address the medical concerns of greatest importance to us all.

REFERENCES

Eibner, C., F. Girosi, C. C. Price, A. Cordova, P. S. Hussey, A. Beckman, and E. A. McGlynn. 2010. *Establishing state health insurance exchanges: Implications for health insurance enrollment, spending, and small businesses.* Santa Monica, CA: RAND Corporation.
Glied, S. 2011. Testimony to the IOM Committee on the Determination of Essential Health Benefits by Sherry Glied, Assistant Secretary for Planning and Evaluation, HHS, Washington, DC, January 13.

1

Introduction

The scope of work for the study is to advise on a process to define and update the essential health benefits (EHB) package, which is a central element in the implementation of current health insurance reform efforts. The EHB will apply to a variety of private and public health insurance programs and will affect 68 million people or more. The content of the EHB will influence insurance product design, take-up rates by individuals and employers, and the comprehensiveness of insurance coverage. Balancing the comprehensiveness of coverage with affordability emerged as a key issue in the committee's deliberation around essential benefits.

The Patient Protection and Affordable Care Act (herein known as the ACA)[1] seeks to reduce the number of uninsured people in this country by providing access to affordable health insurance. As a result of implementation of the ACA, an estimated 30 million currently uninsured individuals are anticipated to obtain insurance through the private health insurance market or state expansion of Medicaid programs.[2] Central to the development of private insurance packages under the ACA is the definition of what the law calls the essential health benefits. In the simplest terms, the EHB are a minimum standard set of benefits that insurers must offer, starting in 2014, in new plans for individual and small group purchasers. Insurers may offer and purchasers may buy plans with additional benefits.

The ACA requires the Secretary of the U.S. Department of Health and Human Services (HHS) to define the EHB. At the request of the Secretary, the Office of the Assistant Secretary for Planning and Evaluation (ASPE) contracted with the Institute of Medicine (IOM) to provide guidance on the methods and criteria by which HHS should establish and update the essential health benefits. This chapter starts with a review of the committee's charge, an overview of key issues that emerged during the public input phase, a description of insurance coverage today and transitions under the ACA, the applicability of the EHB to various forms of public and private insurance, and choices in stakeholders' decisions about participating in the new insurance landscape. Subsequent chapters of this report offer the committee's conclusions and recommendations. The legislative foundation for the EHB is Section 1302 of the ACA, and that guidance is available in Appendix A.

---

[1] Patient Protection and Affordable Care Act of 2010 as amended by the Health Care and Education Reconciliation Act of 2010. 111th Cong., 2d sess. (See http://docs.house.gov/energycommerce/ppacacon.pdf as amended through May 1, 2010; all references to the act reflect this version.)

[2] The Congressional Budget Office estimates vary: 20 million by 2014, 31 million by 2016 (CBO, 2011b), and 30 million by 2016 and 32 million by 2019 (CBO, 2010). RAND projections note, "Relative to the status quo, the reform increases the number of nonelderly people with insurance by 35 million, or 16 percent" by 2016 (Eibner et al., 2010, p. 40).

COMMITTEE CHARGE

Statement of Task

It is important to note that the IOM Committee on Defining and Revising an Essential Health Benefits Package for Qualified Health Plans was not formed to detail the specific services and items that should be included in the EHB package (see Statement of Task in Box 1-1). Instead, the committee was asked to provide guidance on *policy foundations, criteria, and methods* the Secretary should consider in determining and updating the EHB package for qualified health plans, particularly in light of the 10 required categories of care outlined in Section 1302(b)(1) and the requirement in Section 1302(b)(2)(A) for the EHB to be "equal to the scope of benefits provided under a typical employer plan." State-based health insurance exchanges (HIEs) are being established to provide a competitive market through which individuals as well as employees of small businesses will be able to obtain private health insurance coverage. Purchasers are allowed but not obliged to buy their coverage through newly established HIEs; however, subsidies will be available through the exchanges on the basis of a sliding scale for individuals whose incomes are 139-400 percent of the federal poverty level (FPL).[3]

A qualified health plan is a plan that meets the requirements to be sold in an HIE, such as including the EHB, being offered by a licensed insurer that charges the same premium inside and outside the exchange, and other insurance reform elements.[4] Discussions with HHS further indicated that the committee should also recognize the applicability of these benefits to plans beyond the qualified health plans (QHPs) (i.e., Medicaid benchmark, benchmark-equivalent, state basic insurance plans, and certain private plans sold outside the exchanges). The Secretary is expected to issue guidance on the EHB package during 2012 because Section 1321(c) of the ACA requires the Secretary to make an assessment by January 2013 that the states will have operational exchanges by January 1, 2014.[5]

BOX 1-1
Statement of Task for the Institute of Medicine Committee

The Patient Protection and Affordable Care Act (Affordable Care Act) established criteria for qualified health plans (QHPs) to participate in exchanges as defined in Section 1301 of the statute. An ad hoc IOM committee will make recommendations on the methods for determining and updating essential health benefits for QHPs based on examination of the subject matter below.

In so doing, the committee will identify the criteria and policy foundations for determination of the essential health benefits offered by QHPs taking into account benefits as described in Sections 1302(b)(1) and 1302(b)(2)(A), and the committee will assess the methods used by insurers currently to determine medical necessity and will provide guidance on the "required elements for consideration" taking into account those outlined in Section 1302(b)(4)(A-G), including ensuring appropriate balance among the categories of care covered by the essential health benefits, accounting for the health care needs of diverse segments of the population, and preventing discrimination against age, disability, or expected length of life. The committee will also take into account language in Section 1302 on periodic review of essential health benefits, and other sections of the Affordable Care Act: for example, coverage of preventive health services (Section 2713), utilization of uniform explanation of coverage documents and standardized definitions (Section 2715), and other relevant tasks found in the Affordable Care Act for the Secretary of the Department of Health and Human Services (HHS). The committee will provide an opportunity for public comment on the tasks of defining and revising the essential health benefits

---

[3] Individuals whose incomes are at or below 133 percent of the FPL will be eligible for Medicaid, with an additional 5 percent income disregard, effectively raising the income eligibility level to 138 percent of FPL (§ 1004(e), amending § 1902(e)(14) of the Social Security Act).

[4] § 1301.

[5] Personal communication with ASPE staff, October 26, 2010; updated by personal communication with Caroline Taplin, ASPE, June 14, 2011.

Public Comment

Per the last sentence in the statement of task, the public was afforded opportunities to provide advice directly to the committee and then to have that information shared with HHS. The committee began its work by gathering comments in response to a set of 10 online questions derived from its contract with ASPE, which were posted on the IOM project website (Appendix A). This involved a wider group of respondents than could be afforded an opportunity to speak in person with the committee, thus allowing their input to assist the committee in its deliberations and to identify varying perspectives related to the study topics. During the 6 months that the questions were posted, the committee received about 345 online responses from a variety of interested stakeholders, including provider groups, purchasers, insurers, consumer advocates, individual respondents, and government officials. These responses were analyzed and made available to the committee and provided to HHS as submitted. The responses have been open to public review at the IOM through its public access file, as have many other submissions received via e-mail and letters, whose contents were also reviewed by the IOM staff and committee.[6]

Fifty-nine speakers were invited to present at public sessions of the first and second committee meetings, held January 13-14, 2011, in Washington, DC, and March 2, 2011, in Costa Mesa, California. Because of widespread interest in the topic of the EHB, the first workshop was simultaneously audiocast, and audio files were posted on the project website. Initially, a single-day workshop was planned, but additional time was allotted on day 2 of the January meeting and the second workshop was held in March. A companion workshop report summarizes the presentations from the two workshops: *Perspectives on Essential Health Benefits: Workshop Report*.[7] The workshop report is distinct from this consensus report in that it summarizes the individual perspectives of the speakers, rather than includes conclusions or recommendations from the committee. During its deliberations, the committee took into account all of the comments received, not just those received through the workshop venue, as it formulated its approach to identifying and addressing key issues.

MAJOR ISSUES

Learning from the major themes raised in the workshops, other public comment, and additional research, the committee identified key issues surrounding the EHB that required its attention:

- *Setting a balance between comprehensiveness and affordability.* The basic tension was how comprehensive the EHB could be and still be affordable for consumers and payers and sustainable as a program over time (Gruber, 2011).
- *Defining what "typical" should mean in typical employer.* Section 1302 of the ACA requires the EHB to be equal to the scope of benefits provided under a typical employer plan. Congressional staff presented contrasting opinions regarding Congress' intent during the committee's first workshop. One perspective was that the EHB should be a minimum, basic plan affordable for small employers (Hayes, 2011; Spangler, 2011). An alternate perspective was that the EHB should be a more comprehensive plan, more like one that large employers offer, that would still be affordable to all participants in the exchange (Bowen, 2011; Schwartz, 2011). These opposing views were voiced by a variety of other stakeholders.
- *Determining whether state mandates should be included.* The ACA does not require the EHB to include the myriad existing benefits mandated by individual states.[8] Proponents argued for inclusion of particular mandates based on the strength of evidence and/or consideration of popular support for mandates. Opponents noted their potential cumulative additive cost.
- *Considering how specific EHB guidance should be and when variation from state to state might be allowable.* The Secretary is required to define the national EHB package. Specificity in that benefit definition was variously viewed as bringing more uniformity to implementation across states, and more general guidance as promoting flexibility.

---

[6] A request to view the public access file can be made at http://www8.nationalacademies.org/cp/ManageRequest.aspx?key=49299.

[7] The workshop report is available at http://www.iom.edu/EHBperspectives.

[8] § 1311(d)(3)(B).

- *Developing criteria and methods that address calls for the best evidence, patient protection, opportunities for innovation, and fair processes.* Submissions across stakeholder groups emphasized the need for using evidence to make decisions on covered benefits, to determine medical necessity, to set priorities, or to place limits on service. At the same time, there were calls to ensure there would be opportunities for innovation both in medical care and insurance design. The need for fair processes was viewed as applying not only to defining benefits, but also ensuring that patients are able to receive the coverage that is intended.

The committee kept these issues in mind as it developed its recommendations on the criteria and methods for defining and updating the EHB package.

STATUS OF CURRENT HEALTH INSURANCE COVERAGE

Before embarking upon a more detailed discussion of the issues related to the EHB, it is useful to understand what health insurance is, who has and does not have health insurance now, and the transitions in insurance status under health reform. In 2014, each nonelderly individual in the country will be required to have health insurance or face a penalty (with a few exceptions such as experiencing financial hardship)—this is known as the individual mandate.[9] Among the rationales for the individual mandate are that it would broaden the risk pool and seek to stop cost shifting for health care services from the uninsured to those who have insurance (Chandra et al., 2011; McGlynn et al., 2010).

Like other forms of insurance, health insurance is a mechanism for pooling risk—spreading health care costs over many individuals or families (IOM, 2001). Premiums, the dollar amount paid for the insurance package, are collected in advance, and those who get sick and obtain care will be covered from the collected premiums. Baicker and Chandra elaborate: "Uncertainty about when we may fall sick and need more health care is the reason we purchase insurance—not just because health care is expensive (which it is)" (Baicker and Chandra, 2008, p. w534). It is important to recognize that in addition to serving the typical functions of risk insurance, health insurance was developed as a mechanism for financing or pre-paying a variety of health care benefits, including routine preventive services or chronic disease care, whose use is neither rare nor unexpected (IOM, 2001; Mariner, 2010).

Population With and Without Insurance

Insurance coverage in this country for people under 65 years old is primarily employer-sponsored insurance (ESI)—approximately 60 percent of the nonelderly population had this type of coverage in 2010 (Fronstin, 2011b); employer-sponsored insurance figures contain employers in the private market and public sector employers, including those that self-insure rather than purchase insurance. Figure 1-1 shows the 2009 distribution of coverage by type of coverage or uninsurance. According to The Commonwealth Fund's 2010 Biennial Health Insurance Survey, of the 26 million people who bought or tried to obtain private coverage in the individual market during the past 3 years, 19 million faced significant barriers—either they were refused coverage or charged a higher price because of a health problem (9 million), found it very difficult or impossible to find an affordable plan (16 million), or no plan was affordable for their needs (11 million) (Collins et al., 2011). A portion of the uninsured also reflects unemployment during the recent recession (Collins et al., 2011; DeNavas-Walt et al., 2011; Fronstin, 2011a).

Studies reveal that approximately 52 million individuals were uninsured in the United States for some period of time during 2010, up from 38 million in 2001 (Collins et al., 2011).[10] Through a combination of individually purchased policies, employer-based coverage, Medicaid expansion, and federal subsidies, 30 million or more

---

[9] Exemptions will be granted for financial hardship, religious objections, American Indians, those without coverage for less than 3 months, undocumented immigrants, incarcerated individuals, those for whom the lowest-cost plan option exceeds 8 percent of an individual's income, and those with incomes below the tax filing threshold (in 2009 the threshold for taxpayers under age 65 was $9,350 for singles and $18,700 for couples) (§ 1501 and § 10106, adding Internal Revenue Code §5000A(c)).

[10] The U.S. Census Bureau reports 49.9 million without coverage in 2010; although this is a larger number than in 2009, the percentage of the population without insurance remains at 16.3 percent (DeNavas-Walt et al., 2011).

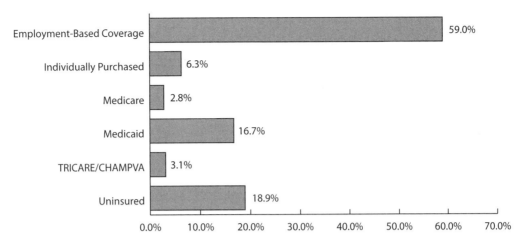

FIGURE 1-1 Nonelderly population with selected sources of health insurance coverage, 2009.
NOTE: Details do not add to 100 percent because individuals may receive coverage from more than one source; analyses are based on Current Population Survey data supplements. S-CHIP is the State Children's Health Insurance Program; TRICARE is administered by the Department of Defense; CHAMPVA is the Civilian Health and Medical Program of the Department of Veterans Affairs.
SOURCE: Fronstin, 2010.

Americans are expected to have insurance than would have in the absence of the law (CBO, 2010, 2011b; Eibner et al., 2010).

Transitions in Insurance Status Under Health Reform

As millions become newly insured and others look for more affordable coverage, people will obtain insurance from new sources. For example, a Kaiser Family Foundation (KFF) study looks at where individual non-group enrollees will transition from, while a RAND microsimulation illustrates the complexity of movement across different forms of insurance or from a state of uninsurance. KFF estimates that the distribution of the Congressional Budget Office's (CBO's) projected 24 million enrolling as individuals in the exchanges in 2019 would be 16 million individuals otherwise uninsured, 3.5 million who lost their ESI, 1.5 million whose previous ESI took more than 9.5 percent of their total family income and are looking for more affordable coverage,[11] 2 million adults above 138 percent of the federal poverty level who lose Medicaid coverage, and 1 million who would have purchased individual coverage anyway (CBO, 2010; KFF, 2011a). Table 1-1 illustrates the outcomes of the RAND microsimulation using 2016 projections and shows movement of about 16 percent of employees into the exchanges from employer insurance, 78 percent of the individual non-group market taking advantage of the exchanges, and the currently uninsured participating in a variety of forms of insurance with the overall result of substantially reducing the number of individuals who would otherwise have been uninsured without health reform.

Accessing Subsidized Health Insurance

Exchanges, functioning as state-based government entities or a nonprofit organization, will be the major conduit for offering subsidized health insurance plans that contain the EHB. However, when a state opts not to open an exchange, the federal government will have the responsibility to operate an exchange directly or through a nonprofit organization. The ACA provides for two types of exchanges, one for individual purchasers (American Health Benefits Exchange) and one for small employers (Small Business Health Options Program [SHOP] Exchanges), but states may combine operations into one exchange (KFF, 2010). Furthermore, the ACA requires

---

[11] Note: These are individuals who are eligible for premium tax credits, because the insurance they are offered by their employers exceeds this affordability threshold.

TABLE 1-1 Transitions from Status Quo Insurance Status to Post-Reform Insurance Status (*N* in millions)

Insurance in the Status Quo (*N*)	Post-Reform Insurance Status					
	ESI: Traditional *(N)*	ESI: Exchanges *(N)*	Individual Exchanges *(N)*	Medicaid *(N)*	Uninsured *(N)*	Other *(N)*
Employer (154)	118	25	4	5	2	0
Medicaid (37)	1	2	0	34	0	0
Non-group (18)	1	3	14	0	0	0
Other (16)	0	0	0	0	0	16
Uninsured (52)	6	6	14	10	16	0
Total (277)	126	36	33	49	18	16

NOTE: Numbers may not total due to rounding. ESI means employer-sponsored insurance. The projections are for the nonelderly population in 2016. The 68 million estimate used in text is based on adding 35.6 million on ESI: Exchanges and 32.7 million in Individual Exchanges and then rounding.
SOURCE: Eibner et al., 2010.

the federal Office of Personnel Management (OPM) to enter into contracts with health insurers to offer at least two multi-state qualified health plans through the exchanges;[12] these are distinct from the Federal Employees Health Benefits Program (FEHBP), which OPM also administers.

IMPACT OF THE EHB ACROSS INSURANCE PROGRAMS

The reach of the EHB is extensive, both in terms of the type of insurance markets and the products it applies to, and ultimately in terms of the projected number of people who would obtain coverage that includes this defined benefit package.

EHB Requirement Applies to Some But Not All Insurance Products

The EHB will be incorporated into a variety of insurance program products—new private health insurance plans offered to individuals and to employers with 100 or fewer employees either inside or outside of the exchange, and certain public programs but not traditional Medicaid (Box 1-2). However, all private plans are not subject to the EHB, including plans offered by any small employer that self-insures, any "grandfathered" plan, and at this time, any plan sponsored by employers in the large group market.[13] Exchanges do not open to larger employers until 2017, and even then it is at a state's option to open the exchange to this segment of the market.[14]

Individual and employer plans in existence at the time of enactment of the ACA (March 23, 2010) qualify for the grandfathered status, whereby the EHB does not apply as long as no changes are made in the plan. For most of these plans, the grandfathered status will not endure; approximately 49-80 percent of small employer plans and 34-64 percent of large employer plans will relinquish grandfather status by the end of 2013 (U.S. Department of the Treasury et al., 2010). Other estimates include a Mercer study projection that 53 percent of firms would lose grandfathered status for one or more plans in 2011 and an additional 48 percent by 2014 (Mercer, 2010), while a Hewitt study estimated that 51 percent of self-insured and 46 percent of fully insured plans would lose grandfathered status in 2011(Hewitt Associates LLC, 2010). HHS estimates that even if a mid-range estimate of plans were to "relinquish" their grandfather status, perhaps as many as 66 percent of small employer plans would

---

[12] § 1334 and § 10104(q).

[13] Self-insured employers are not exempt from the ACA [42 U.S.C. 18054]; its provisions simply do not apply because the self-insured are not insurance companies (by operation of The Employee Retirement Income Security Act [ERISA] §514) and do not offer insurance policies on the exchange.

[14] § 1312(f)(2)(B)(i).

BOX 1-2
Which Programs Incorporate Essential Health Benefits (EHB)?

The EHB Apply to Multiple Insurance Programs, Starting in 2014

Individual Private Market
- Qualified health plans (QHPs) purchased through the exchanges (§ 1301(a)(1)(B) at any of the four actuarial defined "metal" levels [platinum, gold, silver, and bronze] (§ 1302(d)(1)(A)-(D));
- Catastrophic health plans for eligible persons (e.g., persons under age 30 before the beginning of the plan year or for financial hardship when premiums exceed 8 percent of income) purchased in the exchanges (§ 1302(e)(1)-(2));
- Individual and family policies or plans purchased outside the exchange in the individual market (§ 1201, amending § 2707(a) of the Public Health Service Act);
- Plans offered through Interstate Health Care Choice Compact (§ 1333(a)(3)(A));
- Multistate Plans, offered by the federal Office of Personnel Management (OPM) (§ 1334(c)(1)(A)); and
- QHPs offered by Consumer Operated and Oriented Plans (CO-OPs) (nonprofit, member-run health insurance) (§ 1322).

Small Group Private Market
- QHPs for purchase by small firms in the exchanges; a small firm or employer is defined as one with 100 or fewer employees (§ 1304(b)(2)); however, until 2016 states may opt to define small firms as those with 50 or fewer employees (§ 1304(b)(3)), and starting in 2017 exchanges can open to larger firms with 101 or more employees (§ 1312(f)(2)(B)).
- Small employer-sponsored insurance policies or plans purchased outside the exchange (§ 1201, amending § 2707(a) of the Public Health Service Act).
- QHP offered by CO-OPs (nonprofit, member-run health insurance) (§ 1322).

Public Programs Expansions
- Medicaid Benchmark and Benchmark-Equivalent programs, which states may use to provide newly eligible Medicaid beneficiaries with coverage (§ 2001(c), amending § 1937(b) of the Social Security Act). States will also be given the authority to provide certain other groups of Medicaid beneficiaries with this coverage who qualify under existing rules (§ 2001(e), amending § 1902 of the Social Security Act).
- State-Run Basic Health Plans, which provide coverage for persons with incomes between 133 and 200 percent of the federal poverty level (FPL) and for legal resident immigrants who are not eligible for Medicaid; premiums cannot exceed those in the exchanges (§ 1331(a)(1)).

Programs Not Subject to the EHB

- Self-insured employer-sponsored plans
- Grandfathered employer-sponsored plans
- Grandfathered plans in the small group market
- Grandfathered individual plans in the non-group market
- Existing Medicaid plans

be affected. Similarly, grandfathered individual plans would have a high rate of turnover (U.S. Department of the Treasury et al., 2010).

Although not applying to the traditional Medicaid program, the EHB will apply to some public insurance expansion programs for individuals newly eligible for Medicaid. While states will still enroll "categorically" eligible individuals in traditional Medicaid, states may opt to enroll others who are now "financially" eligible in traditional Medicaid or benchmark/benchmark-equivalent programs (CMS, 2010; KFF, 2011b). The Deficit Reduction Act of 2005 permitted states to vary Medicaid benefits to designated populations, often designed to more closely resemble benefits in the private sector. The benefit plans do not need to follow all Medicaid rules and can be modeled on "benchmark" or "benchmark-equivalent" plans in the private sector such as a FEHBP standard plan.[15],[16] These programs will have to include the EHB starting in 2014. State basic health insurance programs are another optional vehicle for states to develop coverage for persons whose income falls between 133 and 200 percent FPL and for low-income legal resident immigrants who are not eligible to receive Medicaid.[17] These expansions will be administered by a state agency but are not necessarily offered through the exchanges.

Millions Affected by the EHB

Estimates vary for the number of persons affected by the implementation of health reform, and thereby the number of persons whose policies incorporate the EHB in 2014 and in later years. By 2016, RAND estimates that 68 million will obtain insurance in the exchanges (35 million through ESI and 33 million purchasing as individuals) and when opened to larger firms with 100 or more employees, exchange participation could grow as high as 139 million (Eibner et al., 2010). In contrast, the CBO projects that 29 million will participate in exchanges in 2019 (24 million individuals and 5 million through employer-sponsored plans) (CBO, 2010). The actual number of affected plans and individuals additionally covered outside the exchange can be influenced by the percentage of plans that have status as grandfathered plans or employers that choose to self-insure.

Medicaid expansion might cover another 17 million persons by 2021 (CBO, 2011a). Because the development of new benchmark, benchmark-equivalent, and state basic health insurance programs—which all incorporate the EHB—is up to each state, it is unclear what the individual reach of those programs might eventually be.

Characteristics of New Individual Purchasers Under the ACA

Although the ACA provides for individual purchase, ESI, and Medicaid options for reducing the number of uninsured, the characteristics of the individual non-group market participants have been most closely studied.[18] KFF expects many persons eligible to be individual (non-group) purchasers in the exchanges to have characteristics of uninsured populations, predicting new exchange enrollees to be "relatively older, less educated, lower income, and more racially diverse" and "in worse health but have fewer diagnosed chronic conditions" (KFF, 2011a, pp. 3-4). The Center for Studying Health System Change (HSC) similarly finds that 40 percent of the uninsured, who are eligible for premium subsidies, have chronic conditions or report fair or poor health status, and another 28 percent report they have experienced problems in accessing care or paying their medical expenses (Cunningham, 2010).

---

[15] Benchmark plans are based on (1) the standard BlueCross BlueShield preferred provider option under the Federal Employee Health Benefit Plan, (2) the HMO (health maintenance organization) plan with the largest commercial, non-Medicaid enrollment in the state, (3) any generally available state employee plan (regardless of whether any state employees select the plan), and (4) any plan that the Secretary of HHS determines to be appropriate. Benchmark-equivalent plans must include inpatient and outpatient hospital services, physician services, laboratory and X-ray services, well-baby and child care (including immunizations), and "other appropriate preventive services" designated by the Secretary of HHS (Deficit Reduction Act of 2005 § 6044 and SSA § 1937). Before the EHB provisions go into effect, CMS provided guidance on interim requirements (CMS, 2010).

[16] Section 2001 of ACA describes the Medicaid expansion. Section 2001(c) stipulates that by January 1, 2014, any benchmark or benchmark-equivalent plan as outlined in Section 1937 of the Social Security Act must offer the EHB package. As of 2009, eight states offered these types of plans.

[17] § 1331.

[18] A study to examine the ESI population is under way by RAND for The Commonwealth Fund, but the results were not available for this report.

STAKEHOLDER DECISIONS WILL RESHAPE HEALTH INSURANCE MARKETS

The ACA lays out a broad set of 10 categories of care for the EHB package in an attempt to rectify deficiencies in some insurance instruments available today[19] and to ensure a broad set of benefits, all while placing caps on premiums and cost sharing to make plans affordable for individual and small employers and eliminating financial barriers to many preventive care services. At present, because the EHB have yet to be defined and implementation does not start until 2014, less is known about what the full scope of covered services or exclusions will be, what premium would be required to obtain coverage of those services, who will choose to enroll in the exchanges, whether employers and insurers will participate or withdraw from the market, and how these and other decisions will determine the sustainability of the program for public funds. The definition of the EHB can ultimately influence each of these areas, particularly with respect to determining the affordability of the package for consumers, employers, and government as well as the adequacy of reimbursement for providers of care.

Figure 1-2 outlines different considerations various stakeholders will take into account for these decisions, and the effects of these decisions can be interactive. Each of these topics is explored in Appendix B, with identification of key financial triggers set in the ACA for eligibility to specific programs and decisions on participation. The cost of premiums, which will be influenced by the comprehensiveness of the EHB package among other benefit design features, compared with the penalty for not purchasing insurance is not strictly a financial one—having health insurance confers an advantage to the consumer whereas paying a penalty does not. Although the impact of some of the choices faced by the various stakeholders are informed by past experience and research simulations, the effect of initial EHB definition on stakeholder response will have to be monitored to inform updates to the EHB package.

The individual consumer is less likely steeped in the details of the ACA than other stakeholder groups and might wonder, "What do the EHB mean for me?"

- *Will the ACA/EHB cover any service I want/need to get?* The EHB will set a minimum set of standard benefits to include in health insurance plans offered initially to individuals and small businesses. Just as in current health insurance practice, plans developed with the EHB will not pay for anything the consumer wants, unless it is a covered benefit and it is medically appropriate for the particular patient. Plans may add additional benefits beyond those in the EHB package, and a consumer could choose to purchase a plan with additional benefits if that best suits his or her needs, although purchasing additional benefits could mean a higher premium.

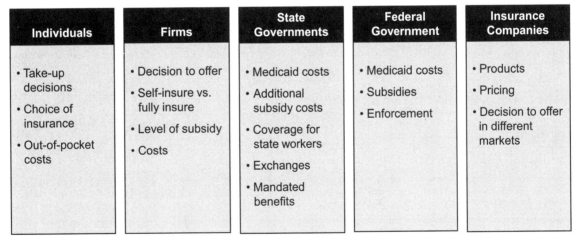

FIGURE 1-2 Different stakeholder considerations during implementation of the Patient Protection and Affordable Care Act (ACA).

---

[19] Deficiencies include, for example, specific disease and fixed-dollar indemnity policies.

- *Will the ACA/EHB provide access to any provider I want to see?* The ACA does not change current practice; which providers the consumer sees will depend on the health insurance purchased. Insurers now offer a variety of options for consumer choice of plans and provider networks. For example, if enrolled in a plan with a *preferred provider network*, the consumer can see those preferred providers and after paying the premium, only be responsible for the deductible and co-payment amounts. The consumer could see an out-of-network provider, but it would cost more than the deductible and usual co-payment share if there is a difference between the provider's bill and the approved level of reimbursement for in-network providers.
- *If the EHB is a standard set of benefits, does that mean that everyone will pay the same premium?* The ACA encourages a variety of plans to be offered in the exchanges so that there will likely be a variety of choices of premiums, deductibles, and co-payment levels, just as there is now. Chapter 2 discusses the topic of benefit design.

ORGANIZATION OF THE REPORT

This report is organized in the following way. This introductory chapter establishes the context for how the EHB, as a new legislative requirement, will significantly impact the health insurance system. Chapter 2 focuses

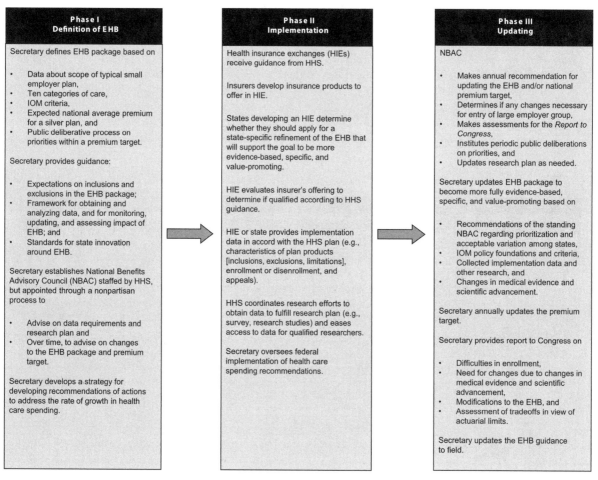

FIGURE 1-3 Learning cycle for defining and revising essential health benefits (EHB).

on approaches to covered benefit definition and design, summarizing a sampling of different approaches that emphasize evidence, priority setting, and value-based insurance design. Chapter 3 provides a set of policy foundations and criteria that the committee used to guide its own deliberations and recommends to the Secretary for use in defining and updating benefits. Chapter 4 presents the committee's conclusions about provisions in the ACA that provide possible conflicting direction for essential benefits, such as the meaning of typical, both in terms of employer size and benefit offerings, and the meaning of essential. These first four chapters provide the background foundation for the committee's recommendations.

The committee organized its thinking about definition and updating as separate phases in a learning cycle, as outlined in Figure 1-3. Chapter 5 provides guidance for the definition of the EHB package and the nature of the Secretary's guidance to insurers and exchanges. Chapter 6 explicates an approach to public deliberation for tradeoffs among benefits. Chapter 7 outlines the importance of not only learning from implementation in Phase II, but also planning in advance for that learning through thoughtful data collection and research with guidance from an appointed National Benefits Advisory Council. Chapter 8 allows for the possibility of alternative ways of defining essential health benefits through a state-initiated process. In Phase III, the learning culminates with updating the EHB. Chapter 9 outlines the updating process, accounting for medical inflation and other factors in the future cost of the EHB package, and a call for action on reducing the growth of health care spending across all payers.

REFERENCES

Baicker, K. and A. Chandra. 2008. Myths and misconceptions about U.S. health insurance. *Health Affairs* 27(6):w534-543.

Bowen, D. 2011. Testimony to the IOM Committee on the Determination of Essential Health Benefits by David Bowen, Deputy Director for Global Health Policy and Advocacy, Gates Foundation, Washington, DC, January 13.

CBO (Congressional Budget Office). 2010. Letter to the Honorable Nancy Pelosi, Speaker, U.S. House of Representatives from Douglas W. Elmendorf, Director, Congressional Budget Office, March 20, 2010.

_____. 2011a. *CBO's analysis of the major health care legislation enacted in March 2010. Statement by Director Douglas W. Elmendorf before the U.S. House of Representatives Subcommittee on Health Committee on Energy and Commerce, March 30, 2011.* Washington, DC: Congressional Budget Office.

_____. 2011b. Letter to the Honorable John Boehner, Speaker of the U.S. House of Representatives from Douglas W. Elmendorf, Director, Congressional Budget Office, February 18, 2011.

Chandra, A., J. Gruber, and R. McKnight. 2011. The importance of the individual mandate—evidence from Massachusetts. *New England Journal of Medicine* 364(4):293-295.

CMS (Centers for Medicare & Medicaid Services). 2010. *Re: Family planning services option and new benefit rules for benchmark plans.* https://www.cms.gov/smdl/downloads/SMD10013.pdf (accessed November 14, 2011).

Collins, S. R., M. M. Doty, R. Robertson, and T. Garber. 2011. *Help on the horizon: How the recession has left millions of workers without health insurance, and how health reform will bring relief. Findings from The Commonwealth Fund Biennial Health Insurance Survey of 2010.* New York: The Commonwealth Fund.

Cunningham, P. J. 2010. *Who are the uninsured eligible for premium subsidies in the health insurance exchanges?* Washington, DC: Center for Studying Health System Change.

DeNavas-Walt, C., B. D. Proctor, and J. C. Smith. 2011. *Income, poverty, and health insurance coverage in the United States: 2010.* Washington, DC: U.S. Census Bureau.

Eibner, C., F. Girosi, C. C. Price, A. Cordova, P. S. Hussey, A. Beckman, and E. A. McGlynn. 2010. *Establishing state health insurance exchanges: Implications for health insurance enrollment, spending, and small businesses.* Santa Monica, CA: RAND Corporation.

Fronstin, P. 2010. *Sources of health insurance and characteristics of the uninsured: Analysis of the March 2010 Current Population Survey. No. 347.* Washington, DC: Employee Benefit Research Institute.

_____. 2011a. *The impact of the 2007-2009 recession on workers' health coverage. No. 356.* Washington, DC: Employee Benefit Research Institute.

_____. 2011b. *Sources of health insurance and characteristics of the uninsured: Analysis of the March 2011 Current Population Survey. Issue brief No. 362.* http://www.ebri.org/pdf/briefspdf/EBRI_IB_09-2011_No362_Uninsured1.pdf (accessed November 14, 2011).

Gruber, J. 2011. *Economic and political considerations in setting essential benefits.* PowerPoint Presentation to the IOM Committee on the Determination of Essential Health Benefits by Jonathan Gruber, Professor of Economics, Massachusetts Institute of Technology, Washington, DC, January 13.

Hayes, M. 2011. *Essential health benefits requirements under section 1302.* PowerPoint Presentation by Mark Hayes, Health & FDA Business Practice Group, Greenberg Traurig, to the IOM Committee on the Determination of Essential Health Benefits, Washington, DC, January 13.

Hewitt Associates LLC. 2010. *Employer reaction to health care reform: Grandfathered status survey.* http://www.aon.com/attachments/02_ER_Reaction_HC_Grandfathered_Survey.pdf (accessed September 7, 2011).

IOM (Institute of Medicine). 2001. *Coverage matters: Insurance and health care.* Washington, DC: National Academy Press.

KFF (Kaiser Family Foundation). 2010. *Explaining health care reform: Questions about health insurance exchanges.* Washington, DC: Kaiser Family Foundation.

———. 2011a. *A profile of health insurance exchange enrollees.* Washington, DC: Kaiser Family Foundation.

———. 2011b. *Medicaid policy options for meeting the needs of adults with mental illness under the Affordable Care Act.* http://www.kff.org/healthreform/upload/8181.pdf (accessed November 14, 2011).

Mariner, W. K. 2010. Health reform: What's insurance got to do with it? Recognizing health insurance as a separate species of insurance. *American Journal of Law & Medicine* 36(2/3):436-451.

McGlynn, E. A., A. Cordova, J. Wasserman, and F. Girosi. 2010. Could we have covered more people at less cost? Technically, yes; politically, probably not. *Health Affairs* 29(6):1142-1146.

Mercer. 2010. *Even as reform pushes up benefit cost, employers will take steps to hold 2011 increase to 5.9%.* http://www.mercer.com/press-releases/1391585 (accessed September 19, 2011).

Schwartz, D. 2011. Testimony to the IOM Committee on the Determination of Essential Health Benefits by David Schwartz, Senate Finance Committee Democratic Staff, U.S. Senate, Washington, DC, January 13.

Spangler, K. 2011. Testimony to the IOM Committee on the Determination of Essential Health Benefits by Katy Spangler, Senior Health Policy Advisor, Senate Health, Education, Labor and Pensions (HELP) Committee, U.S. Senate, Washington, DC, January 13.

U.S. Department of the Treasury, DOL (Department of Labor), and HHS (Department of Health and Human Services). 2010. Group health plans and health insurance coverage relating to status as a grandfathered health plan under the Patient Protection and Affordable Care Act; Interim final rule and proposed rule. *Federal Register* 75(116):34538-34570.

2

Approaches to Determining Covered Benefits and Benefit Design

This chapter reviews approaches to deciding benefit coverage. Insurance terms such as covered benefit, benefit design, utilization management, and medical management are defined and related to the scope of the committee's task. A discussion of the shared responsibility for achieving the goals of ensuring that care is safe, effective, and appropriate, while using resources wisely, sets the stage for a brief overview of the main cost drivers for health care spending and insurance premium growth. Various approaches to insurance design (e.g., use of evidence, prioritization, value-based insurance design) are noted with illustrative applications.

This chapter provides background information on how insurers and employers make decisions about benefit coverage and clinical policies, and highlights several illustrative approaches to making decisions. Key to understanding what constitutes the essential health benefits (EHB) package are the complementary concepts of covered benefits and benefit design. These as well as other insurance terms are defined. Goals for coverage determination and medical necessity decisions are for safe, effective, and appropriate care while using pooled resources wisely. The committee comments on the shared responsibility among insurers, providers of care, and patients for the effective stewardship of shared, limited resources. Finally, the committee highlights some specific approaches to decision making: use of evidence, prioritization practices, and innovation through value-based design. This background material helped to inform the committee's development of policy foundations and criteria in the next chapter.

UNDERSTANDING TERMS

The committee's charge is to advise on the definition and updating of the essential health benefits, and the committee noted that this task incorporates three aspects: the content of the *covered benefits*, the elements of *benefit design*, and the *administration* of those benefits. The committee defines those terms among others (see Box 2-1) and, given the legislative guidance for a typical employer plan, examines how employers and insurers approach development of a benefit package.

Choosing a Policy

When employers offer health insurance coverage to their employees, they begin by outlining to an insurer, insurance broker, or benefit consultant the scope of benefits that they would like to offer. Insurers have standard

BOX 2-1
Understanding Basic Terms Used in This Chapter and Report

Actuarial value. The percentage of charges paid by a health plan, calculated using the medical claims from a standard population, along with a plan's cost-sharing provisions (McDevitt, 2008).

Benefit administration. The insurers' application of the benefit design outlined in the subscriber contract for its subscribers. Elements of benefit administration include subscriber enrollment and disenrollment, processing of claims, making medical necessity decisions, processing appeals of coverage determinations, and application of any federal or state mandates.

Benefit design. Rules governing the terms under which medical care items or services obtained by subscribers are considered covered benefits. Examples include the expected amount of enrollee or member payments for deductibles and other co-payments or co-insurance, the network of providers a subscriber may see, and the nature and extent of medical management (e.g., prior authorization or primary care physician referral requirements).

Categories of care. Ten categories listed in Section 1302 of the Patient Protection and Affordable Care Act (ACA): ambulatory patient services; emergency services; hospitalization; maternity and newborn care; mental health and substance use disorder services, including behavioral health treatment; prescription drugs; rehabilitative and habilitative services and devices; laboratory services; preventive and wellness services and chronic disease management; and pediatric services, including oral and vision care.

Coverage determination. The decision on whether a medical care item or service obtained by a subscriber is a covered benefit. Coverage determinations may be appealed by the subscriber under rules set forth by state law and ACA.

Covered benefits. The medical care items or services obtained by a subscriber that a health insurance plan agrees to pay for, under certain terms and limitations. Covered benefits and excluded services, and the terms and limitations of coverage, are defined in the health insurance plan's coverage documents or the subscriber contract.

Deductible. The amount you must pay for covered care before your health insurance begins to pay. Insurers apply and structure deductibles differently.

Exclusions. Lists of specific medical items or services or general circumstance (e.g., not medically necessary) in a subscriber contract that are not covered benefits.

Health insurance. A method of pooling risk of financial loss across a group or population, in which a contract or policy under which a third party (i.e., an insurer) agrees to assume the financial risk for the costs of a set of services defined in the contract in return for a premium.

plans, which they can customize to employer needs and the requirements of specific markets (e.g., state mandates for inclusion of specific benefits). The benefit package has to meet what the employer considers an affordable premium for the company and the employees. The overall premium will reflect which services are included, included but with limits, or excluded; deductible and co-payment levels or co-insurance requirements; the network of providers; the insured group's risk profile; the degree of medical management in the policy; and health plan administrative expenses, overhead, and profits. A plan with more excluded services, a narrower network of providers, more restrictive visit limits, and higher employee deductible and cost sharing will tend to have a less expensive premium for a comparable set of covered benefits.

Inclusions. Lists of specific covered benefits in subscriber contracts.

Medical management systems. Systems designed to ensure that members receive appropriate [covered] health care services. Medical management systems include, but are not limited to, utilization management, quality improvement, case management, and complaint resolution (NCQA, 2007).*

Medical necessity determination. A specific type of coverage determination about whether a medical item or service, which is a covered benefit, is medically necessary for an individual patient's circumstances, and thus a covered benefit. Typically, this determination is made by the insurer.

Medically necessary. A condition of benefit coverage frequently found in subscriber contracts. Under the terms of most subscriber contracts, the receipt of a medical care item or service does not in and of itself indicate that the item or service was medically necessary (see Chapter 5 for additional discussion).

Out-of-Pocket Cost. Your expenses for medical care that are not reimbursed by insurance. These include: deductibles, co-insurance, and co-payments for covered services in addition to all costs for non-covered services.

Premium. The dollar amount paid for an insurance policy. Premiums can be paid by employers, unions, employees or individuals or shared among different payers.

Qualified health plan. Under the ACA, starting in 2014, an insurance plan that is certified by an exchange, provides essential health benefits, follows established limits on cost sharing (e.g., deductibles, co-payments, out-of-pocket maximum amounts), and meets other requirements. A qualified health plan will have a certification by each exchange in which it is sold (HHS, 2010b).

Subscriber. A person and his or her dependents for which a premium has been paid to a health insurer. Also called an enrollee.

Utilization management. The process of evaluating and determining coverage for and appropriateness of medical care services, as well as providing needed assistance to clinician or patient, in cooperation with other parties, to ensure appropriate use of resources (NCQA, 2007).

Utilization review. A formal evaluation (preservice, concurrent, or post-service) of the coverage, medical necessity, efficiency, or appropriateness of health care services and treatment plans (NCQA, 2007). Terms such as retrospective and prospective review are often used.

---

* [covered] added for clarification to the National Committee for Quality Assurance (NCQA) definition.

What Does It Mean?

Covered Benefits

The scope of *covered benefits* is outlined in an insurance contract or explanation of coverage document (alternately, called evidence of coverage or summary of benefits). Documents differ in the level of detail used to describe the services and items that are covered and may include general categories of care, specific items and services, or circumstances under which benefits are included or expressly excluded. One usual contract exclusion is of any service not considered *medically necessary* by the payer. Section 1302 of the Patient Protection and Affordable

Care Act (ACA) guides the Secretary of the Department of Health and Human Services (HHS) to define the EHB to include at least 10 specific categories of care (Box 2-1) and to be equal to the scope of benefits provided under a typical employer plan. Although this Institute of Medicine (IOM) committee is not requested to specify the detailed inclusions and exclusions in the EHB package, the committee examined legislative guidance for different programs and numerous sample plan documents to learn about the level of detail in them and the implications these might hold for secretarial guidance on the EHB (see Chapters 4 and 5).

Benefit Design

Benefit design sets out the parameters by which patients can obtain services and their financial liability for deductibles and co-payments or co-insurance. The ACA eliminates some past benefit design options, specifically the use of annual and lifetime dollar limits; puts in place some boundaries on how high deductibles and cost sharing can be; requires that provider networks be adequate; and requires that the design be nondiscriminatory. The ACA permits the use of other benefit design options, specifically utilization management techniques commonly employed as of the date of passage of the act.[1] These practices help hold down premiums, as do choices of higher levels of deductibles and cost sharing.

Research on insurance-induced use shows that covered services will be provided at higher rates than those that are not covered (Card et al., 2008, 2009; Dafny and Gruber, 2005); this can result in improved access to care as well as the potential increased utilization of unnecessary services. As a result, for example, insurers may put prior authorization requirements or limits on the number of visits for certain services (Flynn et al., 2002; Wickizer and Lessler, 2002). By the same token, services that can potentially lead to reduced costs as well as better patient outcomes, such as some preventive care and early interventions, lead some plans to adopt medical management programs to encourage use of these services (e.g., some value-based insurance design plans).

Benefit design will have a significant impact on what can be included in the EHB package at a given premium level, so the committee found that benefit design was not readily separable from the contents of the benefits and considered it within the scope of study. Indeed, Dr. Sherry Glied, Assistant Secretary for Planning and Evaluation (ASPE), in her presentation before the committee said that when the Chief Actuary of the Centers for Medicare & Medicaid Services (CMS) certifies the EHB package, the actuary will look at both the content of benefits and the benefit design "in practice in the world and make estimates on that basis" (Glied, 2011).

Most readers will have some general understanding, through their own experience with health insurance, of the basic terms in Box 2-1, but they are likely less familiar with the terms—actuarial estimate, actuarial value, and actuarial equivalence. Understanding the difference in the meaning of these terms and how they relate to benefit design will become important to understanding some aspects of the committee's recommendations:

- *Actuarial estimates* project the expected cost of each individual benefit category or service for a standard population. Knowing these expected costs, an insurer can estimate the impact on premium. Then purchasers—whether individuals, employers, state governments, or the federal process of defining the EHB—can look at the actuarial estimate for certain benefits to determine if they are a priority for inclusion for the premium price that will need to be paid. As noted above, employers might start by looking at an insurer's standard or typical plan offering and then decide to customize by adding or subtracting benefits, and/or by applying benefit design choices such as requiring more stringent limits rather than cut a benefit category out (e.g., limit to 10 versus 20 physical therapy visits).
- *Actuarial value* is the percentage of covered expenses that a plan is likely to pay *on average* for a standard population rather than being paid out-of-pocket by the consumer. In the health insurance exchanges, a range of plans will be offered, and the ACA provides a way to ease comparisons among them—the use of Actuarial Value[2] (AV) to provide a sense of the relative protection offered by plans. Four tiers or levels of coverage are differentiated in the ACA based on a specified actuarial value percentage: platinum: 90 percent, gold: 80 percent, silver: 70 percent, and bronze: 60 percent. Plans at each actuarial level will

---

[1] Patient Protection and Affordable Care Act of 2010 as amended. § 1563(d)(1), 111th Cong., 2d sess.
[2] § 1302(d)(1)(A)-(D).

contain the EHB, but the plans will be differentiated by benefit design choices. Insurers are not required to offer all four "metal" levels, but are required to offer at least one plan at each of the silver and gold levels of coverage (excluding dental-only plans).[3] Under the ACA, premium subsidies for low-income individuals are linked to the second lowest priced silver plan available in their exchange. Thus, the silver plan is likely to be the dominant plan sold. To re-emphasize, the actuarial value is an average. Within any insured population group, there will individuals, in for example the silver plan (on average 70 percent actuarial value) whose percentage of return could be from 0 to 100 percent. For example, a person who never spends more than is required by his or her deductible will have a low percentage return, while a very sick person who uses many services will have a higher return rate.

- *Actuarial equivalence* is a not a concept for consumers to use in deciding which plan to buy even though "actuarial equivalence calculations provide a means to compare the relative generosity of different benefit packages" (AAA, 2009). Furthermore, plans can be actuarially equivalent and still have different premiums because premiums will take into account the health status and utilization patterns of the local population to be enrolled, payments negotiated with providers, breadth of provider network, various degrees of medical management, administrative costs and company profits. The concept of actuarial equivalence, however, will be useful for the CMS Actuary to apply to determine if the EHB are equal in scope to the typical employer plan, and for the Secretary to determine if any state-specified package is equivalent to the nationally defined EHB package. Actuarial equivalence calculations generally consider covered benefits, cost-sharing requirements (deductibles, co-insurance, co-payments [including by service type], out-of-pocket cost limits, and benefit limits) as applicable to an in-network benefit level, but the committee's interest is mainly in benefit equivalence when comparing the EHB to the scope of typical employers (Chapter 5) and possible state variations to the national EHB.

The committee offers an example of the type of benefit design data that would inform the monitoring and updating of the EHB as well as provide more detail to inform consumers about their plans. Chapter 7 further discusses the need for data collection such as in Box 2-2.

Benefit design and its subsequent *administration* can be instrumental in addressing the cost and quality of services and care delivered. Insurers and employers are experimenting with an array of medical management and cost-sharing designs (e.g., value-based insurance design). The committee believes the intent of the ACA was to view utilization management (UM) in a broader *medical management* context to ensure appropriateness and quality and not simply to limit access to care. The National Committee for Quality Assurance (NCQA) defines UM as a "process of evaluating and determining coverage for and appropriateness of medical care services, as well as providing needed assistance to clinician or patient, in cooperation with other parties, to ensure appropriate use of resources" (NCQA, 2007, p. 364). URAC, another accreditation body, uses a similar definition and cites the continued need for traditional utilization management techniques (e.g., pre-certification, concurrent review) as tools for controlling costs (URAC, 2011).

About 15 years ago, Milstein wrote, "UM and the reduced volume of health care services it typically fosters have struck a nerve" feeling that it "may be jeopardizing patients' well-being" (Milstein, 1997, p. 87). He called for better evidence-based utilization standards for decision making and accreditation standards and certification for UM programs such as those that URAC and NCQA now provide, among other things. Today, purchasers and insurers, while still using UM often with more sophisticated claims analytics, employ a broader array of techniques called *medical management* to seek to improve quality and cost of care through designation of high-performing networks, patient and provider supports, and more transparent evidence-based clinical policies (Figure 2-1). However, despite this progress, much work remains to be done to ensure the appropriateness of care.

Benefit Administration

Elements of *benefit administration* also fall into the committee's purview because the statement of task specifically calls for the committee to assess implementation-related issues such as medical necessity, safeguards for

---

[3] § 1301(a)(1)(C)(ii).

BOX 2-2
Description of Benefit Design

Benefit design includes

1. A description of the covered benefits: services, drugs, devices

    a. Identification of those covered services, drugs, and devices that are variably covered (tiering)
    b. Identification of those covered services, drugs, and devices that are limited in quantity, frequency, or some other way

2. A description of the cost-sharing process

    a. Specific definition of and dollar amounts related to deductibles, co-payment, co-insurance, and out-of-pocket maximum
    b. Specific identification of any covered services, drugs, or devices having no cost sharing
    c. Specific definition of any covered services, drugs, or devices in which cost sharing does not accrue to the out-of-pocket maximum
    d. Specific definition of those services, drugs, or devices whose cost is not included in the out-of-pocket maximum when they are not covered
    e. The actuarial value

3. A list of coverage exclusions

4. Definitions of key terms affecting coverage, including whether the definition is consistent with an external standard

    a. Definition of medical service
    b. Medical necessity
    c. Experimental, investigational
    d. Cosmetic
    e. Dental

5. Identification of benefit design innovations

    a. Value-based insurance designs that align cost sharing with value

nondiscrimination (which can entail appeals processes), and making choices that are understandable to consumers. The contents of the EHB and the benefit design limits placed upon them can enhance or impede access to care, as well as encourage or discourage enrollment in a plan. Chapter 7 also speaks to assessment of the impact of the EHB on implementation.

Deciding Covered Benefits vs. Medical Necessity Determination

During a presentation to the committee, Dr. Alan Garber distinguished a coverage decision (i.e., what an insurer decides to offer in a plan as a covered general benefit category or specific service for a particular price) from a medical necessity determination (i.e., whether the care is deemed appropriate for a particular person for a particular condition and circumstance) (Garber, 2011). Although physicians may make an initial recommendation of service for the patient, its necessity is subject to review and approval by the payer. Insurers indicated that these

6. Identification of provider networks, incentives, and care delivery options

    a. Incentives and disincentives for providers at individual and organizational levels
    b. Network design: types of networks (e.g., narrow networks, tiered or concentric networks, broad networks) and level of care or site of service for specific procedures or conditions within networks
    c. Centers of excellence (without any out-of-network coverage for specific conditions)
    d. Identification of delivery arrangements that could affect care
        i. Medical homes
        ii. Disease management
        iii. Care coordination
        iv. Specialty referral requirements

7. Identification of approaches designed to influence the use of services, including specific services that need to be authorized prior to provision, to be provided in specific sites (such as surgery in an ambulatory surgery center), or to be provided at a specific level of care (such as "skilled" services in a nursing home)

8. Identification of medical policies that could affect coverage including an explicit statement that these policies may apply to all covered services on an individual patient basis

    a. Access to specific medical policies affecting coverage
    b. A description of the process for administering these policies including complaint, request for review, and appeal processes

9. Medical management and/or utilization management programs (e.g., when prior authorization is required for specific services; site of service, level of care, or preferred providers)

10. Payment policies that affect coverage or cost sharing.

    a. Hold-harmless arrangements
    b. Pricing arrangements that may affect cost sharing and out-of-pocket maximums
    c. Reference pricing for drugs and medical or surgical services

11. Quality and cost transparency reports on variation by provider, condition, procedure, facility, and geography

12. Overall description of how benefits are administered, including description of the complaint, request for review, and appeals processes

decisions are based on specific established criteria, such as safety, clinical evidence, relative cost of services with comparable outcomes (Kaminiski, 2007; Singer et al., 1999), and compliance with state or federal laws, as applicable. Before the committee, Dr. Garber stated that if payment changes put more financial risk on the shoulders of providers, then providers "will have more of a stake in ensuring that only effective care and necessary care is delivered, so medical necessity decision making may turn out to play a lesser role." The nation is, however, "years off from the time when medical necessity decisions will be unnecessary or much less prominent in determining which care is delivered" (Garber, 2011).

From the practitioner and patient perspectives, a significant issue has been that these determinations are opaque and knowledge of decisions overturned is not always accessible, and further that these determinations may reflect a clinical policy that the health insurer feels is most appropriate (i.e., the treatment they feel is most appropriate for a given condition) rather than taking into account the individual patient. Their perspectives are that these determinations are not always evidence-driven, but could also be driven by attempts to raise barriers to payment

Provider-Focused Tools

- Pre-service / Concurrent / Retrospective Review and Physician Education
- Outpatient, Inpatient, and Pharmacy Utilization Review
- Physician and Hospital Performance Measurement
- Physician and Hospital Quality Improvement Programs
- Value-based Provider Payments

- High-performance Networks, incl. Centers of Excellence
- Delivery System Innovation, such as Patient-Centered Medical Homes and ACOs
- Electronic Medical Records, apply Meaningful Use
- Electronic Prescribing
- Health Information Exchanges

Core Tools
Benefit Plan Design ■ Medical Necessity Clinical Guidelines and Medical Policies ■ Coverage Determination Guidelines ■ Appeals and Grievances for Members and for Providers ■ Medical Technology Assessment

Member-Focused Tools
- Health and Wellness Programs
- Case Management
- Disease Management
- Care Coordination
- Transparency of Physician and Hospital Performance Assessments
- Consumer-directed Incentives for Healthier Behavior
- Value-based Insurance Designs, including Tiered Benefits

Provider- and Member-Focused Tools
- Health Care Information Technology
- Sophisticated Clinical Analytics to Identify Gaps in Care and in Affordability
- Collaborative Measurement Projects, using Multi-Payer Claims Databases
- Administrative Simplification through Automation

FIGURE 2-1 Illustration of multiple medical management tools used by UnitedHealthcare.
NOTE: ACO = Accountable Care Organization.
SOURCE: Sam Ho, UnitedHealthcare.

for covered care while a medical necessity determination should most importantly take into account the individual patient's condition and needs. This contributes to the problem patients have in comprehending why some things their physician recommends are not reimbursable. The well-documented public backlash against managed care in the 1990s was driven by patient, provider, and public concern that insurers were not applying their conditions fairly. Speakers before the committee related stories about denials of care, with Anthony Wright, executive director of Health Access California, noting consumers' fear of the fine print of insurance contracts (Wright, 2011).

The committee concludes that medical management techniques, with appropriate checks and balances, are necessary to ensure that the EHB package can be delivered at the most affordable cost. However, a fair and reasonable appeals process for adverse determinations—including independent medical review will be implemented under the ACA, and the results should be monitored to inform the updating of the EHB.[4] The committee reviews insurers' medical necessity definitions and clinical policy guidelines and advises on possible secretarial guidance in Chapter 5 and the need to monitor appeals in Chapter 7.

UNDERSTANDING CONTRIBUTORS TO COSTS

Goals for coverage decisions and medical necessity determinations are for safe, effective, and appropriate care while using resources wisely. Despite such lofty goals, we know, for example, that unnecessary care is delivered (NEHI, 2008; Schuster et al., 2005), recommended care for adults is delivered just 55 percent of the time (McGlynn et al., 2003), and some care when delivered inappropriately can actually be unsafe (Brenner and Hall, 2007; Rosen,

---

[4] It is important to note that under the ACA, contested medical necessity determinations can be appealed to an independent external appeals review.

2010; Simpson, 2010). Furthermore, major drivers for health care costs include our growing chronic disease burden and demand for the newest technologies, even if they do not produce greater value than existing less costly technologies. Insurers, providers of care, and patients all have a shared responsibility for appropriate utilization of shared health care resources. Although individuals have the right to spend their own resources as they see fit, spending from a shared pool of funds confers a degree of accountability for effective stewardship of those funds.

Shared Responsibility

Ideally, insurers make their coverage decisions based on evidence, are consistent in the application of evidence, provide meaningful benefits with an acceptable level of risk, and discourage the use of unnecessary or even harmful services. For example, one study suggests that perhaps one-third of computed tomography (CT) scans are unnecessary and could be replaced by alternative approaches or avoided altogether (Brenner and Hall, 2007). CT scans have a radiation dose about 50 times that of conventional X-rays and are implicated in the development of cancers that could have been avoided without this treatment (Brenner and Hall, 2007). On discovering a 25 to 35 percent annual increase in the utilization of advanced imaging tests (including variations in prescribing and duplicative tests with the potential exposure of patients to unnecessary radiation), Highmark Blue Cross Blue Shield established an advanced imaging program to better manage the appropriate utilization of these tests, a privileging program requiring providers to meet quality and safety standards, and a prior authorization program for patients. These were implemented with the aim of reducing duplicate tests and enhancing adherence to safety standards (Highmark Blue Cross Blue Shield, 2011).

Multiple insurers indicated to the committee that they were committed to applying standards of evidence in making benefit coverage decisions and in developing clinical policies (Calega, 2011; Levine, 2011; McDonough, 2011; Nussbaum, 2011). At the same time, they acknowledged that there are often gaps in available evidence. Furthermore, it is "very difficult" to remove coverage unless there is documentation that a service is no longer of value, and there is a need for the nation to devote funding to develop more evidence to support coverage decisions (Calega, 2011). Other examples of inappropriate—not only unnecessary but also potentially harmful—use, cited by others, include inappropriate use of cardiac catheterization (Ko et al., 2010) or single-photon emission computed tomography (SPECT) cardiac scans (Hendel et al., 2010), which themselves not only add unnecessary costs but also can lead to further unnecessary and potentially dangerous surgery for patients; unnecessary diagnostic testing such as $3,000 BRCA-1 genetic tests in patients for whom such testing is not clinically indicated (White et al., 2008); and inappropriate treatment for breast cancer patients (e.g., autologous bone marrow transplant) (Jacobson et al., 2007).

Ideally, physicians also make decisions about necessary care based on evidence; however, there is often significant geographic practice variation (Wennberg, 2011). Unwarranted differences in *effective care*—that is, "interventions for which the benefits far outweigh the risks"—can reflect underuse of guideline-supported care. *Preference- and supply-sensitive care* variations reflect differences in professional opinion and response to the capacity of the health care system, resulting in low utilization in some areas and overuse in others. Uncertainty plays a role in variation; when in doubt, there is a tendency to perform a procedure, and the incentives are certainly in place to do so. According to Eddy, "The losers are patients, consumers, and taxpayers—anyone who has to undergo a valueless procedure or pay the bill" (Eddy, 1984, p. 86).

Ideally, patients also make decisions in their own best interests, but this is not always the case. The process for deciding among "preference-sensitive" options must be based on informed understanding of treatment alternatives, an element that is sorely lacking in many situations (Baker et al., 2010). To engage consumers in informed decision making, more insurers and employers are encouraging the use of specialized decisions aids (O'Connor et al., 2007; Stacey et al., 2011).

Evolution of Insurance Coverage and Cost Drivers

The contents of health insurance policies today reflect their historical development, but health insurance is not static and is adapting to today's health burdens, emerging evidence, and cost drivers in the market. Health insurance grew out of a movement to protect against disability due to accidents or catastrophic illnesses; over time, hospital pre-payment insurance policies developed and then policies developed to protect against other types of medical expenses (Abraham, 1986; IOM, 1993; Rosenblatt et al, 1997). More recently, coverage for preventive health care services and prescription drugs has emerged—emphasizing ongoing care, not just acute or emergency situations. Indeed, Medicare did not add prescription drug coverage until Part D went into effect in 2006, 41 years after the Medicare program was established.

Major Expenditure Categories

Health care expenditures for persons under 65 years can be categorized into three major expense categories: hospital inpatient, ambulatory care services (e.g., physician office services, hospital outpatient services), and prescription drugs, comprising about 84 percent of health care spending for nonelderly adults and about 70 percent for children (note that this is all spending, not just insurance) (Kashihara and Carper, 2010). Among those under 65 who are privately insured, about 10 percent of the population accounts for 60 percent of all health care spending (Yu and Ezzati-Rice, 2005). The growth in overall inflation-adjusted spending for all ages in these categories over time is shown in Figure 2-2.

Cost Drivers

The major drivers of health care costs are recognized as new technologies, more intensive testing, growing chronic disease burden, increased utilization (growing and aging population), and consumer or provider demand for state-of-the-art care (Table 2-1) (KFF, 2010; PwC Health Research Institute, 2011). Unit price increases for medical care—that is, price per unit of service—are another driver, with one recent estimate attributing 5-19 percent of the annual growth rate between 1960 and 2007 to unit price increases (Smith et al., 2009). Unit prices for a new service vary dramatically by geographic region and volume. Accordingly, all of these cost drivers have implications for the cost of purchasing health insurance as well as benefit design and administration. Health insurance premiums are also affected by federal and state mandates requiring the addition of specific types of benefits; however, the degree of that effect depends on various factors, such as size of the population affected, utilization, and the contents of existing coverage.

Innovation has helped advance medical science and prolong lives, but the Congressional Budget Office (CBO) estimates that the addition of new technologies accounts for about half of the per capita growth in health care spending (Table 2-1) (CBO, 2008). The CBO further notes that some of those advances can be very costly, while others, although relatively inexpensive, can drive up spending because their use becomes widespread, and finally some may reduce aggregate costs (CBO, 2008). A more recent study finds lower estimates of medical technology's

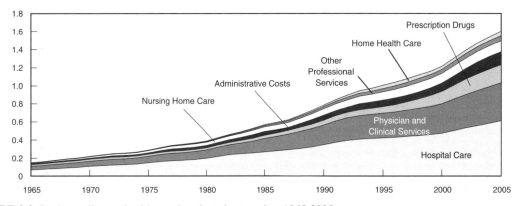

FIGURE 2-2 Real spending on health care in selected categories, 1965-2005.
NOTE: Spending amounts are adjusted for inflation using the gross domestic product implicit price deflator from the Bureau of Economic Analysis.
SOURCE: CBO, 2008.

TABLE 2-1 Estimated Contributions of Selected Factors to Growth in Real Health Care Spending per Capita, 1940 to 1990

Percentage	Smith et al. (2000)[a]	Cutler (1995)[b]	Newhouse (1992)[c]
Aging of the population	2	2	2[d]
Changes in third-party payment	10	13	10[e]
Personal income growth	11-18	5	<23
Prices in the health care sector	11-22	19	*
Administrative costs	3-10	13	*
Defensive medicine and supplier-induced demand	0	*	0
Technology-related changes in medical practice	38-62	49	>65

NOTE: Amounts in the table represent the estimated percentage share of long term growth that each factor accounts for. < = less than; > = greater than; * = not estimated.

[a] Congressional Budget Office based on Sheila D. Smith, Stephen K. Heffler, and Mark S. Freeland, 2000, "The Impact of Technological Change on Health Care Cost Increases: An Evaluation of the Literature" (working paper).

[b] David M. Cutler, 1995, "Technology, Health Costs, and the NIH" (paper prepared for the National Institutes of Health Economics Roundtable on Biomedical Research, September 1995).

[c] Joseph P. Newhouse, 1992, Medical Care Costs: How Much Welfare Loss? *Journal of Economic Perspectives* 6(3)Summer:3-21.

[d] Represents data for 1950 to 1987.

[e] Represents data for 1950 to 1980.

SOURCE: CBO, 2008.

contribution, 27-48 percent of the annual growth rate (average 4.8 percent annually) from 1960 to 2007, and a similar level of 29-43 percent attributable to aggregate income (real per capita gross domestic product [GDP]) (Smith et al., 2009). Emerging technologies such as personalized medicine and biologics will continue to have an impact on spending and insurance premiums. Although there is not a desire to stifle innovation in medical science, rising costs will affect the affordability of coverage in the private sector and in public programs, including subsidization of insurance in the health insurance exchanges. As new technologies become available, important questions are not only whether something is safe and effective, but also whether it will provide benefits beyond comparable treatments and which patients will benefit. Another question to consider will be how best to stimulate the development and dissemination of technologies that may reduce costs.

The huge but often preventable chronic disease burden in this country calls for a greater emphasis on prevention, given that about half of all deaths in the United States are considered attributable to modifiable health behaviors (Mokdad et al., 2004, 2005). The change in handling of preventive health services in the ACA is illustrative of evolving insurance policy, realigning incentives, and making positive use of medical management to promote preventive services and disease management programs to improve care and maintain a healthy workforce (Nussbaum, 2011).

As noted in Table 2-1, administrative costs, including profits for insurers and their shareholders, contribute to premium costs. The ACA has new provisions for the medical-loss ratio, which sets the minimum percentage of premiums that insurers may spend on actual medical care (e.g., 80 percent for individuals and small group insurance and 85 percent for larger group insurance).[5]

ILLUSTRATIVE APPROACHES TO COVERAGE DECISIONS

Benefit design is "an iterative process," taking into account what employers and consumers in the marketplace want and are willing to pay for. Thus, what is typical in the market today becomes a base for consideration of the EHB package. Similarly, any insurer benefit package tends to build on what is already covered. In updating packages, insurers told the committee they might conduct focus groups, hold field satisfaction surveys, and receive feedback from insurance brokers on market demand as well as survey advances in medical technology.

---

[5] § 1001, amending § 2718 of the Public Health Service Act [42 U.S.C. 300 gg–18].

The committee heard from numerous stakeholders about ways of making coverage decisions; most of the methods presented deal with assessing whether an individual technology should be included for coverage or is necessary for a specific individual rather than looking at the package of benefits as a whole. The committee presents three general approaches that reflect a range of current practices: (1) use of evidence for adding individual technologies to the benefit package, (2) prioritization among benefits, and (3) value-based insurance design. Illustrative examples are given.

Evidence-Based Approaches

Examples of the criteria and methods insurers use to develop their evidence base for covered benefit and medical management decisions follow. Insurers seek to apply the best standard of evidence available. In some cases, for example, Medicare allows coverage in conjunction with evidence development in clinical trials, and Washington state has shown some flexibility in cases where a rare condition is less likely to have a sufficiently developed evidence base.

Receiving and Analyzing Multiple Sources of Input

Insurers keep abreast of medical trends, clinical practice guidelines, approvals by CMS and the Food and Drug Administration (FDA) of new technologies and pharmaceuticals, and evidence-based reviews from the BlueCross BlueShield Association's Technology Evaluation Center (TEC) and others. From these various inputs and internal analyses, insurers examine whether this information should lead to changes in covered benefits and development of clinical policies applied in medical necessity determinations, as illustrated for WellPoint's process in Figure 2-3.

Aetna similarly selects new and existing technologies for detailed review based on contextual considerations including the quantity of use and the importance of questions that have arisen regarding the specific medical technology; the potential impact of the technology on the company and its members; the availability of evidence in the peer-reviewed literature, guidelines, and consensus statements; changes in regulatory status; whether the technology relates to a rare condition; or other information that is material to the status of the medical technology (McDonough, 2011). Through this process, the need for medical management (e.g., whether the service might best be performed in centers of excellence) is determined. Thus, rather than exclude a specific service, a clinical policy could define under what circumstances it would be covered. Like WellPoint, Aetna's clinical coverage criteria are derived in part from the BlueCross BlueShield Association's TEC (Box 2-3). In addition to these criteria, Aetna considers indications in major drug compendia recognized by CMS, the approval status of technologies from relevant government regulatory bodies (e.g., CMS, FDA), and technology assessments from other reliable sources of information such as the California Technology Assessment Forum and Health Technology Assessment International.

Medicare established the Medicare Evidence Development & Coverage Advisory Committee (MEDCAC) in 1998 to provide CMS with independent guidance and expert advice, "based upon the reasoned application of scientific evidence" on specific clinical topics, including issues relevant to coverage policy development (HHS, 2010a). Service-level assessments have included things such as assessing the strength of the evidence for multifactorial, noninvasive, "lifestyle" modifying interventions to treat cardiac disease and clarifying what constitutes the standard of care in wound therapy (HHS, 2010a). Pre-meeting materials considered include external health technology assessment(s) (TAs) conducted by the Agency for Healthcare Research and Quality or an Evidence-Based Practice Center under contract with that agency; any other relevant TAs; an evidence summary prepared by CMS staff; and copies of relevant articles reviewed by CMS.

Applying a Hierarchy of Evidence

UnitedHealthcare uses processes similar to the insurers above, applying a hierarchy of criteria and evidence for coverage determination; a first step is consideration of mandatory requirements from federal or state sources and then application of a hierarchical standard for evidence to potential interventions considered for coverage (Box 2-4).

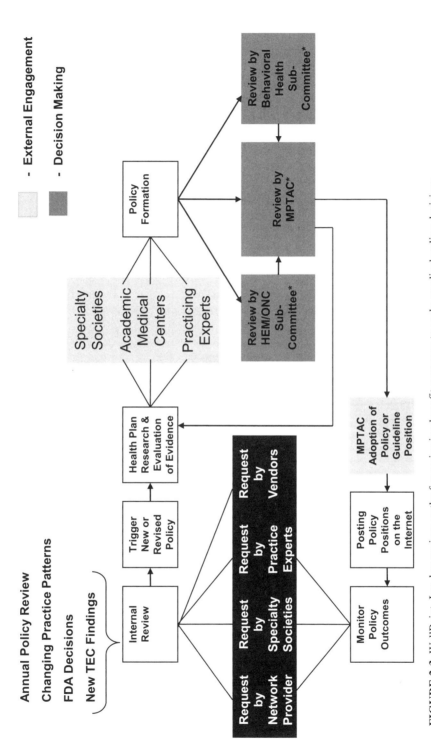

FIGURE 2-3 WellPoint, Inc. has various paths for reviewing benefit coverage to make medical policy decisions.

*Depending on the subject, different review committees will be engaged. This illustration includes the Hematology/Oncology Committee (HEM/ONC), the Medical Policy & Technology Assessment Committee (MPTAC), and the Behavioral Health subcommittee; each of these includes external physician representation.

SOURCE: Nussbaum, 2011.

BOX 2-3
The BlueCross and BlueShield Association Technology Evaluation Center's
Clinical Coverage Criteria

The following criteria are considered in evaluating a medical technology:

- The technology must have final approval from the appropriate governmental regulatory bodies (when required).
- The scientific evidence must permit conclusions concerning the effect of the technology on health outcomes.
- The technology must improve net health outcome.
- The technology must be as beneficial as any established alternatives.
- The improvement must be attainable outside investigational settings.

SOURCE: BCBSA, 2011.

BOX 2-4
UnitedHealthcare's Hierarchy of Criteria for Benefit or Coverage Determination

Federal and state mandates (e.g., Centers for Medicare & Medicaid Services [CMS] National Coverage Decisions [NCDs] are the highest criteria for Medicare beneficiaries).

Standards of Evidence:

- Statistically robust, well-designed randomized controlled trials
- Statistically robust, well-designed cohort studies
- Large, multisite observational studies
- Single-site observational studies
- In the absence of incontrovertible scientific evidence, medical policies may be based upon national consensus statements by recognized authorities. The following stratification describes the hierarchy of use of medical policies and clinical guidelines within UnitedHealthcare:

  o National guidelines and consensus statements (e.g., U.S. Preventive Services Task Force [USPSTF], National Institutes of Health [NIH] clinical statements, Agency for Healthcare Research and Quality [AHRQ] clinical statements)
  o Evidence-based nationally recognized clinical guidelines
  o CMS NCDs
  o Clinical position papers of professional specialty societies (e.g., American College of Physicians [ACP], American College of Cardiology [ACC], American College of Chest Physicians [ACCP]) when their statements are based on referenced clinical evidence

- Expert opinion using Cochrane grading
- Particularly for new or emerging medical technologies, no health service will be deemed unproven solely on the basis of a lack of randomized controlled trials. Similarly, UnitedHealthcare will develop no medical policies based solely on expert opinion.

SOURCE: Personal communication with committee member Sam Ho, UnitedHealthcare, 2011.

Washington State similarly uses a hierarchy of evidence (Box 2-5), embedded in its administrative code,[6] to define benefits across the state's coverage programs (i.e., Medicaid, state employee benefit program, and state basic health plan [a coverage program for lower-income populations not eligible for Medicaid]). The key principles for the design process—with many stakeholders participating including legislators, providers, and beneficiaries—are consistency of decisions, transparency, hierarchy of decision criteria, evidence basis, and focus on patient safety. These benefits use "the best evidence of proven value to the population, while respecting the appropriateness of services and the authority of the treating provider" (Thompson, 2011).

This hierarchy of evidence and its application are used to define covered benefits and to establish the basis for medical necessity decisions. In testimony before the committee, Dr. Jeffery Thompson, chief medical officer, State of Washington Medicaid Program, illustrated changes in coverage and improvements in care and outcomes using this evidence-based approach. Before the introduction of evidence-based benefit design, cardiac rehabilitation was not a covered benefit; but once reviewed, A-level evidence revealed this service contributed to avoiding further surgery, hospitalization, and recurrence of events—so the benefit is now covered (Thompson, 2011). Similarly, bariatric surgery was previously covered for numerous indications, but the mortality rate reached 40 percent at some hospitals. Review of the evidence revealed that surgery is indicated for this program in some instances (e.g., BMI >35 with diabetes and/or joint replacement) but not all. By limiting coverage to specific evidence-based indications and use of centers of excellence, the department self-reports that it has reduced case costs by half ($36,000 to $17,000) and improved outcomes—no bariatric surgery–related death in seven years among individuals enrolled in state-covered plans (Thompson, 2011).

Although the department generally approves benefits supported by A- and B-level evidence, it does not necessarily reject benefits with only C- and D-level evidence. For example, if a provider can prove that a service supported by inconsistent, C-level evidence is "less costly, less risky, and is the next step in reasonable care," then coverage may be considered. For example, a PET (positron emission tomography) scan for cancer diagnosis may have limited or no outcome studies but in special cases can reduce the costs and risks of a surgical procedure. Additionally, recognizing that certain rare conditions may never have A-level studies, state-covered plans have been willing to cover some experimental D-level treatments.[7] Washington state's evidence hierarchy has also been extended to pharmaceutical benefits in developing a tiered formulary, with the state's basic health plan having a $10 co-payment for drugs "above the line" (e.g., omeprazole) and a 50 percent co-payment for drugs "below the line" (e.g., Prevacid) (Thompson, 2011).

Prioritization Approach

Individuals and employers have budgets that limit what they are willing to pay, leading to the exclusion of certain benefits and the adoption of multiple benefit design options discussed earlier. Whether private or public funds are spent, questions arise about what people think shared resources should be spent on. To date, insurers and purchasers have made some decisions on which things should be excluded, such as no coverage of medical procedures solely for cosmetic purposes (e.g., surgery or other procedures performed solely for beautification or to improve appearance) (see Appendix F for information on typical exclusions). The State of Oregon has gone a step further to define in much more detail which services are included and excluded, and setting priorities among them so that as budget levels change, it is transparent which things are covered.

Oregon determines a detailed list of prioritized condition-treatment pairs for its Medicaid program, known as the Oregon Health Plan (Box 2-6); these originally totaled more than 700 and are at 679 for 2011 (Oregon Health Services Commission, 2011b). Services necessary to determine a diagnosis are covered. Ancillary services such as prescription drugs and durable medical equipment (DME) are covered for conditions in the funded region. In 2006, the commission revised its methodology to have a population focus. "Greater emphasis is [now] placed on preventive services and chronic disease management, reflecting the fact that providing health care before reaching

---

[6] Washington Administrative Code, 388-501-0165 (1994).

[7] Provided the treatment is approved by an internal review board (IRB), the treating physician is in a study, and the patient has provided informed consent.

BOX 2-5
Hierarchy of Evidence Employed by Washington State

Definition: (a) The hierarchy (in descending order with Type I given the greatest weight) is:

(i)   *Type I:* Meta-analysis done with multiple, well-designed controlled studies;
(ii)   *Type II:* One or more well-designed experimental studies;
(iii)   *Type III:* Well-designed, quasi-experimental studies such as nonrandomized controlled, single group pre-post, cohort, time series, or matched case-controlled studies;
(iv)   *Type IV:* Well-designed, nonexperimental studies, such as comparative and correlation descriptive, and case studies (uncontrolled); and
(v)   Type V: Credible evidence submitted by the provider.

Classification: (b) Based on the quality of available evidence, the department determines if the requested service is effective and safe for the client by classifying it as an "A," "B," "C," or "D" level of evidence:

(i)   *"A" level evidence:* Shows the requested service or equipment is a proven benefit to the client's condition by strong scientific literature and well-designed clinical trials such as Type I evidence or multiple Type II evidence or combinations of Type II, III, or IV evidence with consistent results (an "A" rating cannot be based on Type III or Type IV evidence alone).

(ii)   *"B" level evidence:* Shows the requested service or equipment has some proven benefit supported by:

    (A) Multiple Type II or III evidence or combinations of Type II, III, or IV evidence with generally consistent findings of effectiveness and safety (a "B" rating cannot be based on Type IV evidence alone); or
    (B) Singular Type II, III, or IV evidence in combination with department-recognized:
        (I)   Clinical guidelines; or
        (II) Treatment pathways; or
        (III) Other guidelines that use the hierarchy of evidence in establishing the rationale for existing standards.

crisis mode will prevent avoidable morbidity and mortality" (DiPrete and Coffman, 2007, p. 5). The following five impact measures are considered: (1) *healthy life-years,* (2) *suffering,* (3) *population effects,* (4) *vulnerability of population,* and (5) *tertiary prevention,* combined with the two factors of effectiveness and need for medical service under the current formula (DiPrete and Coffman, 2007).

The resulting prioritized list is used by the legislature to allocate funding for Medicaid and the State Children's Health Insurance Program (SCHIP), but the legislature cannot change the priorities set by the independent Health Services Commission (DiPrete and Coffman, 2007). Rather, the legislature "draws a line" on the list beyond which it cannot pay—in 2011 at line 502 (Oregon Health Services Commission, 2011a)—based on the cumulative actuarial estimates of the cost for each condition-treatment pair for the covered population. Approximately 75 percent of the more than 679 condition-treatment pairs are funded (Table 2-2). The list is updated every 6 months to account for changes in medical coding and to make technical corrections, then is reviewed every 2 years for any changes in priority rankings. This process of prioritization is frequently cited as being too time- and labor-intensive for

(iii) *"C" level evidence:* Shows only weak and inconclusive evidence regarding safety and/or efficacy such as:

   (A) Type II, III, or IV evidence with inconsistent findings; or
   (B) Only Type V evidence is available.

(iv) *"D" level evidence:* Is not supported by any evidence regarding its safety and efficacy, for example that which is considered investigational or experimental.

Application: (c) After classifying the available evidence, the department:

(i) Approves "A" and "B" rated requests if the service or equipment:

   (A) Does not place the client at a greater risk of mortality or morbidity than an equally effective alternative treatment; and
   (B) Is not more costly than an equally effective alternative treatment.

(ii) Approves a "C" rated request only if the provider shows the requested service is the optimal intervention for meeting the client's specific condition or treatment needs, and:

   (A) Does not place the client at a greater risk of mortality or morbidity than an equally effective alternative treatment; and
   (B) Is less costly to the department than an equally effective alternative treatment; and
   (C) Is the next reasonable step for the client in a well-documented tried-and-failed attempt at evidence-based care.

(iii) Denies "D" rated requests unless:

   (A) The requested service or equipment has a humanitarian device exemption from the Food and Drug Administration (FDA); or
   (B) There is a local institutional review board (IRB) protocol addressing issues of efficacy and safety of the requested service that satisfies both the department and the requesting provider.

SOURCE: Washington Administrative Code, 388-501-0165.

---

wider adoption, yet this is done by a staff of four in Oregon.[8] Approximately one-third of the state has benefited from the expanded access made possible by setting explicit health service priorities (DiPrete and Coffman, 2007).

Value-Based Insurance Design Approach

Value-based insurance design (VBID) seeks to align patient cost sharing with the value of clinical services, including how they are provided (e.g., most appropriate setting and health care provider). VBID identifies those services whose benefits relative to their costs represent an efficient use of resources for patients, comparing the cost-effectiveness of one intervention to alternatives, including no intervention (Fendrick et al., 2010). The use of these services is then incentivized, traditionally through two mechanisms: (1) minimal cost barriers and (2) financial incentives. Approaches to VBID call for lowering cost sharing for high-value services and raising

---

[8] Personal communication with Mark Gibson, Center for Evidence-Based Policy, Oregon Health and Science University, February 9, 2011.

BOX 2-6
Oregon Treatment-Condition Pair Examples

Line: 10
Condition: Type I diabetes mellitus
Treatment: medical therapy
ICD-9: 250.01,250.03,250.11,250.13,250.21,250.23,250.31,250.33,250.51,250.53,
250.61,250.63,250.71,250.73,250.91,250.93,251.3,V53.91,V65.46
CPT: 49435,49436,90935-90947,90989-90997,92002-2014,92227,95250,95251,
96150-96154,97802-97804,98966-8969,99051,99060,99070,99078,
99201-99360,99366,99374,99375,99379-99444,99468-99480,99605-99607
HCPCS: G0245,G0246,G0406-G0408,G0425-G0427,S0270-S0274,S9145,S9353

Line: 118
Condition: Fracture of ribs and sternum, open
Treatment: Medical and surgical treatment
ICD-9: 807.1,807.3,V54.19,V54.29
CPT: 11010-11012,21805,21810,21825,97602,98966-98969,99051,99060,99070,99078,
99201-99360,99366,99374,99375,99379-99444,99468-99480,99605-99607
HCPCS: G0406-G0408,G0425-G0427,S0270-S0274

Line: 573
Condition: Allergic rhinitis and conjunctivitis, chronic rhinitis
Treatment: Medical therapy
ICD-9: 372.01-372.06,372.14,372.54,372.56,472,477,995.3,V07.1
CPT: 30420,86486,92002-92060,92070-92226,92230-92313,92325-92353,92358-
92371,95004,95010,95015-95180,98966-98969,99051,99060,99070,99078,
99201-99360,99366,99374,99375,99379-99444,99468-99480,99605-99607
HCPCS: G0406-G0408,G0425-G0427,S0270-S0274

SOURCE: Oregon Health Services Commission, 2011a.
NOTE: CPT = Current Procedural Terminology; HCPCS = Healthcare Common Procedure Coding System; ICD = International Statistical Classification of Diseases and Related Health Problems.

TABLE 2-2 The State of Oregon Uses a Prioritized List of Services to Make Coverage Decisions

Line Number	Examples of Services	Coverage
1	Maternity care	Covered
101	Medical treatment of acute lymphocytic leukemia	
201	Surgical treatment of brain hemorrhage	
301	Treatment for rheumatic heart disease	
401	Laser therapy to prevent retinal tear	
501	Treatment for noninflammatory vaginal disorders	
551	Treatment for back pain without neurologic impairment	Not Covered
651	Treatment for calcium deposits	

SOURCE: Oregon Health Services Commission, 2011b.

costs through higher co-payments on services with low value (Choudhry et al., 2010b). Other mechanisms by which VBID programs can impact spending include designating in- and out-of-network providers based on high performance value, not just price, and/or providing incentives for enrollees to adopt more healthful behaviors and/or to achieve better biometric results, such as blood pressure, cholesterol, blood sugar levels, or body mass index (MedPAC, 2011). One challenge is that as one seeks to align coverage with more specific cost-effective services and health outcomes, the more complex benefit design and implementation can become. Although barriers to each VBID approach exist, they all have the potential to improve the efficiency of the health care system. Given the differences across approaches, it is suggested that regulators allow for flexibility when designing such programs (Chernew et al., 2010).

Consequently, innovative programs to improve health and lower long term costs have been developed and studied to determine the benefits of VBID. For example, one study comparing results in the context of identical disease management programs found that when one employer reduced co-payments for five classes of drugs, adherence increased in four classes and overall nonadherence was reduced by 7 to 14 percent (Chernew et al., 2008). Similarly, Choudhry et al. (2010a) found when a large employer, Pitney Bowes, eliminated co-payments for statins, adherence was 2.8 percent greater than for those still paying co-payments, and when it reduced co-payments for medication inhibiting blood clotting, patient adherence was 4 percent greater. Similarly, Maciejewski et al. (2010) also found that adherence to diabetes, hypertension, hyperlipidemia, and congestive heart failure medications was improved between 2 and 4 percent when employees were offered the medications at a reduced cost (no co-payments for generic and reduced co-payment for brand name medications), compared to employees not offered that option.

Assessing the financial impacts of VBID implementation can be challenging, because many programs are new and "even if a strategy is effective, how that translates into costs or savings may vary from one organization to another" (MedPAC, 2011, p. 88). This lack of generalizability requires an individualized analysis of programs. The state of Minnesota reported a savings of 7 percent after instituting an incentive program in 2002 for enrollees to see efficient providers; primary care clinics are ranked annually on overall claims-based cost and divided into four tiers, with patients facing higher cost sharing when utilizing clinics with the highest overall costs (MedPAC, 2011). Also, actuarial modeling of an Oregon value-based plan suggests "the potential to produce savings of 3 percent to 5 percent initially" when applied in the state's Oregon Educators Board plan (MedPAC, 2011, p. 85; Smith and Saha, 2011). By these indications, VBID is an approach to control health care spending—with a focus on *value*, using co-payment rates that are based on the value of clinical services (benefits and costs), rather than solely on the costs of delivering those services (Fendrick et al., 2001).

BOX 2-7
Inclusion Criteria for Oregon's Value-Based Services (VBS)

- Ambulatory services (i.e., outpatient), including medications, diagnostic tests, procedures, and some office visits
- Primarily offered in the medical home
- Primarily focused on chronic illness management, preventive care, and/or maternity care
- Of clear benefit, strongly supported by evidence
- Cost-effective
- Reduce hospitalizations or emergency department visits, reduce future exacerbations or illness progression, or improve quality of life
- Low cost up front
- High utilization desired
- Low risk of inappropriate utilization

SOURCE: Oregon Health Services Commission, 2011c.

Oregon has a long history of incorporating value into its decisions about health coverage, having rank-ordered its benefits since 1989 as discussed previously. It is now translating lessons learned from its Medicaid program to the private sector. Identifying over time, per inclusion criteria (Box 2-7), a set of 20 value-based services (VBS) applicable to a set of diagnoses, the Health Services Commission determined that these should be promoted and hence offered at no or minimal cost sharing with a waived deductible in the state's Medicaid program (e.g., the provision of diagnostic spirometry and medications according to the National Institute for Health and Clinical Excellence 2008 stepwise treatment protocol for asthma) (Oregon Health Services Commission, 2010). Finding that many Medicaid recipients already receive these services with little or no cost sharing, the expectation is that this will have a more significant effect when adopted in the private sector. Importantly for the continued role of VBS, the Health Services Commission plans to update this list annually to ensure that the most current high-quality supporting evidence (such as Cochrane systematic reviews of randomized controlled clinical trials and evidence-based guidelines) is used for designing coverage (Oregon Health Services Commission, 2011c).

One additional proposal for a state-specific essential benefits package to cover *all* Oregonians, since sidelined in anticipation of federal guidance on the EHB, was slated to include among its VBS offered with 0-5 percent cost sharing the following: routine vaccinations, prenatal care, chronic illness management, and smoking cessation treatment. Less effective care and care for minor injury and self-limited illness (e.g., chronic back pain, viral sore throat, seasonal allergies, and acne) would have the highest cost sharing (Saha et al., 2010). Currently, a separate effort through the Oregon Health Leadership Council (OHLC), an organization of business leaders, health plans, and providers seeking to reduce the rate of increase of health care costs, is actively leading efforts to incorporate value-based design in the private sector. With an estimated 8-12 percent premium reduction, the OHLC proposed a benefit package with three tiers of service, in which the middle one—level 2—resembles most traditional plans with a deductible and co-insurance for most services, but the level 1 tier would cover prescription drugs, some lab, imaging, and other ancillary services related to six chronic conditions—*coronary disease, congestive heart failure, chronic obstructive pulmonary disease, diabetes, asthma, and depression*—with minimal or no cost sharing. On the other hand, several types of surgeries (for example, coronary artery bypass grafting [CABG] and angioplasty) have significant cost sharing. OHLC originally wanted to include primary care visits in the tier without cost sharing; however, administrative barriers, such as the inability of billing systems to distinguish primary care visits from those for a specific chronic condition, may not make it feasible for all insurers (MedPAC, 2011).

As of January 1, 2011, a plan based on the VBS model, which includes no cost sharing for cholesterol and blood pressure medications, is being offered to employees of Evraz, Inc., which operates steel mills in Oregon and Delaware. Furthermore, while some workers have the option of staying in their current plan, the company is waiving the employee premium contribution for individuals who opt for the value-based plan. Finally, a similar plan has been rolled out to the employees of the health insurer ODS, further indicating that value-based insurance design is being recognized as an attractive approach to plan design.

Summary

This chapter provides the committee's review of considerations in benefit choices, benefit design, cost drivers, and a sample of illustrative approaches to deciding benefit coverage and its application in clinical policies—setting the stage for developing the policy foundations and criteria for designing the EHB package in the next chapter.

REFERENCES

AAA (American Academy of Actuaries). 2009. *Critical issues in health reform: Actuarial equivalence.* http://www.actuary.org/pdf/health/equivalence_may09.pdf (accessed September 22, 2011).

Abraham, K. 1986. *Distributing risk: Insurance, legal theory, and public policy.* New Haven, CT: Yale University Press.

Baker, N., J. W. Whittington, R. K. Resar, F. A. Griffin, and K. M. Nolan. 2010. *Reducing costs through the appropriate use of specialty services.* Cambridge, MA: Institute of Healthcare Improvement.

BCBSA (BlueCross BlueShield Association). 2011. *Technology Evaluation Center criteria.* http://www.bcbs.com/blueresources/tec/tec-criteria.html (accessed June 15, 2011).

Brenner, D. J., and E. J. Hall. 2007. Computed tomography—an increasing source of radiation exposure. *New England Journal of Medicine* 357(22):2277-2284.

Calega, V. 2011. Comments to the IOM Committee on the Determination of Essential Health Benefits by Virginia Calega, Vice President, Medical Management and Policy, Highmark BlueCross BlueShield, Washington, DC, January 13.

Card, D., C. Dobkin, and N. Maestas. 2008. The impact of nearly universal insurance coverage on health care utilization: Evidence from Medicare. *The American Economic Review* 98(5):2242-2258.

_____. 2009. Does Medicare save lives? *The Quarterly Journal of Economics* 124(2):597-636.

CBO (Congressional Budget Office). 2008. *Technological change and the growth of health care spending.* Washington, DC: Congressional Budget Office.

Chernew, M. E., M. R. Shah, A. Wegh, S. N. Rosenberg, I. A. Juster, A. B. Rosen, M. C. Sokol, K. Yu-Isenberg, and A. M. Fendrick. 2008. Impact of decreasing copayments on medication adherence within a disease management environment. *Health Affairs* 27(1):103-112.

Chernew, M. E., I. A. Juster, M. Shah, A. Wegh, S. Rosenberg, A. B. Rosen, M. C. Sokol, K. Yu-Isenberg, and A. M. Fendrick. 2010. Evidence that value-based insurance can be effective. *Health Affairs* 29(3):530-536.

Choudhry, N. K., M. A. Fischer, J. Avorn, S. Schneeweiss, D. H. Solomon, C. Berman, S. Jan, J. Liu, J. Lii, M. A. Brookhart, J. J. Mahoney, and W. H. Shrank. 2010a. At Pitney Bowes, value-based insurance design cut copayments and increased drug adherence. *Health Affairs* 29(11):1995-2001.

Choudhry, N. K., M. B. Rosenthal, and A. Milstein. 2010b. Assessing the evidence for value-based insurance design. *Health Affairs* 29(11):1988-1994.

Cutler, D. M. 1995. *Technology, health costs, and the NIH.* Paper prepared for the National Institutes of Health Economics Roundtable on Biomedical Research. http://www.economics.harvard.edu/faculty/cutler/files/Technology,%20Health%20Costs%20and%20the%20NIH.pdf (accessed September 12, 2011).

Dafny, L., and J. Gruber. 2005. Public insurance and child hospitalizations: Access and efficiency effects. *Journal of Public Economics* 89:109-129.

DiPrete, B., and D. Coffman. 2007. *A brief history of health services prioritization in Oregon.* http://www.oregon.gov/OHA/OHPR/HSC/docs/PrioritizationHistory.pdf?ga=t (accessed May 19, 2011).

Eddy, D. M. 1984. Variations in physician practice: The role of uncertainty. *Health Affairs* 3(2):74-89.

Fendrick, A. M., D. G. Smith, M. E. Chernew, and S. N. Shah. 2001. A benefit-based copay for prescription drugs: Patient contribution based on total benefits, not drug acquisition cost. *American Journal of Managed Care* 7(9):861-867.

Fendrick, A. M., D. G. Smith, and M. E. Chernew. 2010. Applying value-based insurance design to low-value health services. *Health Affairs* 29(11):2017-2021.

Flynn, K. E., M. A. Smith, and M. K. Davis. 2002. From physician to consumer: The effectiveness of strategies to manage health care utilization. *Medical Care Research and Review* 59(4):455-481.

Garber, A. M. 2011. *Medical necessity, coverage policy, and evidence based medicine.* PowerPoint Presentation to the IOM Committee on the Determination of Essential Health Benefits by Alan Garber, Stanford University, Washington, DC, January 13.

Glied, S. 2011. Testimony to the IOM Committee on the Determination of Essential Health Benefits by Sherry Glied, Assistant Secretary for Planning and Evaluation, U.S. Department of Health and Human Services, Washington, DC, January 13.

Hendel, R. C., M. Cerqueira, P. S. Douglas, K. C. Caruth, J. M. Allen, N. C. Jensen, W. Pan, R. Brindis, and M. Wolk. 2010. A multicenter assessment of the use of single-photon emission computed tomography myocardial perfusion imaging with appropriateness criteria. *Journal of the American College of Cardiology* 55(2):156-162.

HHS (Department of Health and Human Services). 2010a. *Charter: Medicare Evidence Development & Coverage Advisory Committee.* Washington, DC: U.S. Department of Health and Human Services.

_____. 2010b. *Glossary.* http://www.healthcare.gov/glossary (accessed November 7, 2010).

Highmark Blue Cross Blue Shield. 2011. *Provider Resource Center: Highmark Radiology Management Program.* https://prc.highmarkblueshield.com/rscprc/faces/prcMainPage.jsp (accessed April 19, 2011).

IOM (Institute of Medicine). 1993. *Employment and health benefits.* Washington, DC: National Academy Press.

Jacobson, P. D., R. A. Rettig, and W. M. Aubry. 2007. Litigating the science of breast cancer treatment. *Journal of Health Politics, Policy and Law* 32(5):785-818.

Kaminski, J. L. 2007. *Defining medical necessity.* http://www.cga.ct.gov/2007/rpt/2007-r-0055.htm (accessed April 20, 2011).

Kashihara, D., and K. Carper. 2010. *Statistical brief #301: National health care expenses in the U.S. civilian noninstitutionalized population, 2008.* http://www.meps.ahrq.gov/mepsweb/data_files/publications/st301/stat301.shtml (accessed June 26, 2011).

KFF (Kaiser Family Foundation). 2010. *U.S. health care costs.* http://www.kaiseredu.org/Issue-Modules/US-Health-Care-Costs/Background-Brief.aspx (accessed June 26, 2011).

Ko, D. T., J. S. Ross, Y. Wang, and H. M. Krumholz. 2010. Determinants of cardiac catheterization use in older Medicare patients with acute myocardial infarction. *Circulation: Cardiovascular Quality and Outcomes* 3(1):54-62.

Levine, S. 2011. PowerPoint Presentation to the IOM Committee on the Determination of Essential Health Benefits by Sharon Levine, Associate Executive Medical Director, The Permanente Medical Group, Costa Mesa, CA, March 2.

Maciejewski, M. L., J. F. Farley, J. Parker, and D. Wansink. 2010. Copayment reductions generate greater medication adherence in targeted patients. *Health Affairs* 29(11):2002-2008.

McDevitt, R. 2008. *Actuarial value: A method for comparing health plan benefits.* Oakland, CA: California Healthcare Foundation.

McDonough, R. 2011. *Determination of essential health benefits.* PowerPoint Presentation to the IOM Committee on the Determination of Essential Health Benefits by Robert McDonough, Director, Clinical Policy Research and Development, Aetna, Washington, DC, January 13.

McGlynn, E. A., S. M. Asch, J. Adams, J. Keesey, J. Hicks, A. DeCristofaro, and E. A. Kerr. 2003. The quality of health care delivered to adults in the United States. *New England Journal of Medicine* 348(26):2635-2645.

MedPAC (Medicare Payment Advisory Commission). 2011. *June 2011 report to the Congress: Medicare and the health care delivery system.* Washington, DC: Medicare Payment Advisory Commission.

Milstein, A. 1997. Managing utilization management: A purchaser's view. *Health Affairs* 16(3):87-90.

Mokdad, A. H., J. S. Marks, D. F. Stroup, and J. L. Gerberding. 2004. Actual causes of death in the United States, 2000. *Journal of the American Medical Association* 291(10):1238-1245.

_____. 2005. Correction: Actual causes of death in the United States, 2000. *Journal of the American Medical Association* 293(3):293-294.

NCQA (National Committee for Quality Assurance). 2007. *Special needs plan (SNP) phase 1—draft stucture and process requirements glossary.* http://www.ncqa.org/portals/0/publiccomment/SNP/SNP_Glossary.pdf (accessed June 26, 2011).

NEHI (New England Healthcare Institute). 2008. *How many more studies will it take?* Cambridge, MA: New England Healthcare Institute.

Newhouse, J. P. 1992. Medical care costs: How much welfare loss? *Journal of Economic Perspectives* 6(3):3-21.

Nussbaum, S. 2011. *Health insurance plan variance in coverage (inclusions, exclusions, networks) and benefit design for quality improvement.* PowerPoint Presentation to the IOM Committee on the Determination of Essential Health Benefits by Sam Nussbaum, Executive Vice-President, Clinical Policy and Chief Medical Officer, Wellpoint, Inc., Costa Mesa, CA, March 2.

Oregon Health Services Commission. 2010. *Value-based services: Proposed "barrier-free" services for use within a value-based benefit package.* http://www.oregon.gov/OHA/OHPR/HSC/docs/VBS.pdf (accessed August 4, 2011).

_____. 2011a. *The prioritized list.* http://www.oregon.gov/OHA/healthplan/priorlist/main.shtml (accessed June 27, 2011).

_____. 2011b. *Prioritized list of health services: April 1, 2011.* http://www.oregon.gov/OHA/OHPR/HSC/docs/L/Apr11List.pdf (accessed May 10, 2011).

_____. 2011c. *Value-based services.* http://www.oregon.gov/OHA/OHPR/HSC/VBS.shtml (accessed June 26, 2011).

PwC (PricewaterhouseCoopers) Health Research Institute. 2011. *Behind the numbers: Medical cost trends for 2012.* New York: PricewaterhouseCoopers.

Rosen, A. K. 2010. *Are we getting better at measuring patient safety?* http://www.webmm.ahrq.gov/perspective.aspx?perspectiveID=94 (accessed June 26, 2011).

Rosenblatt, R., S.A. Law, and S. Rosenbaum. 1997. *Law & the American health care system.* New York: Foundation Press.

Saha, S., D. D. Coffman, and A. K. Smits. 2010. Giving teeth to comparative-effectiveness research—the Oregon experience. *New England Journal of Medicine* 362(7):e18.

Schuster, M. A., E. A. McGlynn, and R. H. Brook. 2005. How good is the quality of health care in the United States? *Milbank Quarterly* 83(4):843-895.

Simpson, K. R. 2010. Reconsideration of the costs of convenience: Quality, operational, and fiscal strategies to minimize elective labor induction. *Journal of Perinatal & Neonatal Nursing* 24(1):43-52.

Singer, S., L. Bergthold, C. Vorhaus, S. Olson, I. Mutchnick, Y. Y. Goh, S. Zimmerman, and A. Enthoven. 1999. Decreasing variation in medical necessity decision making. Appendix B. Model language developed at the "Decreasing Variation in Medical Necessity Decision Making" Decision Maker Workshop in Sacramento, CA, March 11-13, 1999.

Smith, J., and S. Saha. 2011. *Oregon's value based benefits package.* PowerPoint Presentation to the IOM Committee on the Determination of Essential Health Benefits by Jeanene Smith, Administrator, Office for Oregon Health Policy and Research and Somnath Saha, Staff Physician, Portland VA Medical Center and Chair, Oregon Health Services Commission, Costa Mesa, CA, March 2.

Smith, S. D., S. K. Heffler, and M. S. Freeland. 2000. *The impact of technological change on health care cost spending: An evaluation of the literature.* https://www.cms.gov/NationalHealthExpendData/downloads/tech_2000_0810.pdf (accessed September 12, 2011).

Smith, S., J. P. Newhouse, and M. S. Freeland. 2009. Income, insurance, and technology: Why does health spending outpace economic growth? *Health Affairs* 28(5):1276-1284.

Stacey, D., C. L. Bennett, M. J. Barry, N. F. Col, K. B. Eden, M. Holmes-Rouner, H. Llewellyn-Thomas, A. Lyddiatt, F. Légaré, and R. Thomson. 2011. Decision aids for people facing health treatment or screening decisions. *Cochrane Database of Systematic Reviews* (10):CD001431.

Thompson, J. 2011. *Health care that works: Evidence-based Medicaid.* PowerPoint Presentation to the IOM Committee on the Determination of Essential Health Benefits by Jeffery Thompson, Chief Medical Officer, Washington Medicaid Program, Washington State Department of Social and Health Services, Costa Mesa, CA, March 2.

URAC. 2011. *What is care management?* http://www.urac.org/resources/careManagement.aspx (accessed June 26, 2011).

Wennberg, J. E. 2011. Time to tackle unwarranted variations in practice. *British Medical Journal* 342:687-690.

White, D. B., V. L. Bonham, J. Jenkins, N. Stevens, and C. M. McBride. 2008. Too many referrals of low-risk women for BRCA1/2 genetic services by family physicians. *Cancer Epidemiology Biomarkers & Prevention* 17(11):2980-2986.

Wickizer, T. M., and D. Lessler. 2002. Utilization management: Issues, effects, and future prospects. *Annual Review of Public Health* 23:233-254.

Wright, A. 2011. Testimony to the IOM Committee on the Determination of Essential Health Benefits by Anthony Wright, Executive Director, Health Access California, Costa Mesa, CA, March 2.

Yu, W. W., and T. M. Ezzati-Rice. 2005. *Statistical brief #81: Concentration of health care expenditures in the U.S. civilian noninstitutionalized population.* http://www.meps.ahrq.gov/mepsweb/data_files/publications/st81/stat81.shtml (accessed June 26, 2011).

3

Policy Foundations and Criteria for the EHB

The Institute of Medicine committee was tasked with developing a framework for the Secretary to use when explicitly defining and revising the essential health benefits (EHB). Upon integrating its research and public input from its workshop and online public comment form, the committee established four policy foundations to guide its work: economics, ethics, evidence-based practice, and population health. Related criteria are outlined for three purposes: (1) assessment of the aggregate EHB package, (2) evaluation of individual services to be included in the EHB package, and (3) guidance on fair processes.

The Secretary asked the Institute of Medicine (IOM) committee to develop an explicit framework for considering the EHB package that would serve the Department of Health and Human Services (HHS) now and in the future (Glied, 2011). This chapter outlines the resulting framework, including the specific policy foundations and criteria that the committee used to guide its own work. The committee later recommends that the Secretary use this framework when defining the EHB package and updating it in the years to come (see Chapters 5 and 9).

The committee specifically queried the public via its online public comment form about what principles, criteria, and processes the Secretary might use for defining and revising the EHB. The many suggestions made, as well as information gleaned from the committee's research, could be classified into four main policy foundation domains: *economics, ethics, evidence-based medical practice, and population health*. What follows is a general discussion of these domains, principles associated with these domains, and a list of criteria that emerged common to these policy areas to direct evaluation of the aggregate EHB package, to assess individual technologies for inclusion, and to establish appropriate characteristics of processes. The committee's framework of policy foundations and related criteria is consistent with the goals of the Patient Protection and Affordable Care Act (ACA) and those initiatives contained within it, such as HHS's National Quality Strategy[1]—to expand access to health insurance, to improve the quality of care, to improve the health of individuals and communities, and to reduce the cost of care. It also reflects previous IOM work related to improving the quality of care, such as *Crossing the Quality Chasm*'s six aims[2] (IOM, 2001).

---

[1] Patient Protection and Affordable Care Act of 2010 as amended. § 3011, 111th Cong., 2d sess. The current version of the National Quality Strategy is available at http://www.healthcare.gov/center/reports/quality03212011a.html#na (accessed June 27, 2011); it adopts the Institute for Healthcare Improvement's "Triple Aim" (Berwick et al., 2008).

[2] The IOM's six quality aims are safe, effective, patient-centered, timely, efficient, and equitable (IOM, 2001).

POLICY FOUNDATIONS

The committee finds that no single policy lens is sufficient or comprehensive enough for explicitly framing decisions about the EHB. Figure 3-1 graphically illustrates the four domains and principles associated with those domains. Each of these distinct perspectives—complementary in some cases, overlapping in others, conflicting at times—influences how we think about what health insurance should cover and how it should be implemented.

Economics

A benefit design framework rooted in economics primarily conceives of coverage as *insurance*—protecting individuals and their families against the risk of unforeseen health care needs, particularly those associated with large expenses (Santerre and Neun, 2010). An economics approach uses markets to promote value and efficiency, relying heavily on these markets to find the equilibrium between price and demand. With respect to the ACA, new markets are being developed for health insurance products that will include the EHB. Decisions about the scope of coverage in the EHB package and product benefit design will affect its success in the market—both whether it can be sustained with private and public funds over time and whether a sufficient number of insurers will participate in the exchange, or otherwise opt to exclusively sell plans not subject to the EHB (e.g., those with a grandfathered status, or self-insured in the large employer market). Insufficient participation of willing purchasers or willing suppliers of insurance products may affect competitiveness as well as require government intervention in the content of packages offered or their price. Ideally, insurers will compete for the estimated 68 million EHB-related purchasers and will do so in a way that provides multiple insurance options at competitive prices.

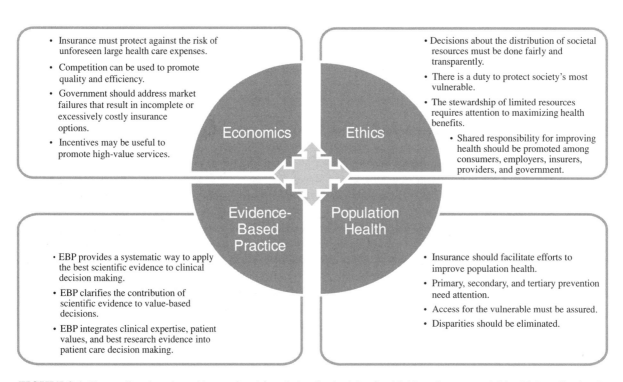

FIGURE 3-1 Four policy domains with associated foundational principles for thinking about essential health benefits development and implementation.
NOTE: EBP = evidence-based practice.

While markets reflect the preferences of purchasers, economists recognize the risks of moral hazard and adverse selection. Moral hazard refers to the situation in which consumers alter their behavior when provided with health insurance (Santerre and Neun, 2010) such as in the case of *insurance-induced use* in which individuals with insurance seek more care—both appropriate and inappropriate—than they otherwise would (Pauly, 1968). An insurance market is hard to sustain when induced use exceeds premium income, particularly when the benefits do not justify the costs. To remedy this, insurers have implemented cost sharing, but this often reduces appropriate and inappropriate use equally (Siu et al., 1986), or they may opt for managed care arrangements. Yet if the moral hazard is too great, and the cost of mitigating it too high for a given service, private insurers may drop the service from coverage because customers do not want to pay for the moral hazard in a higher premium.

Nonrandom enrollment can result from both adverse selection and risk selection. Benefit choice and design elements by insurers can result in these consequences; consumer choice to enroll or not enroll similarly affects the pool of purchasers and the potential to spread financial risk across a broader-based population. For example, *adverse selection* occurs "when individuals at greater risk of high health spending are more likely to need and seek coverage, while low-risk individuals are more likely to opt out of coverage" (AAA, 2011, p. 2). A premium spiral typically ensues as the average insured risk increases and results in higher premiums, which, in turn, "may lead to more low-risk individuals opting out of coverage, which would result in even higher premiums. Avoiding such spirals requires minimizing adverse selection and instead attracting a broad base of low-risk individuals, over which the costs of high-risk individuals can be spread" (AAA, 2011, p. 2). The individual mandate was envisioned as the most effective means to maximally broaden the insured population base to help address the current state of cross-subsidization of the uninsured by the insured and minimize adverse selection, while also gaining insurance industry acceptance for the insurance reforms contained in the ACA (Chandra et al., 2011; McGlynn et al., 2010). Furthermore, the ACA also provides three risk-adjustment programs to help address risk selection:[3]

- Temporary *reinsurance*,[4] which reimburses insurers for the cost of individuals who have unusually high claims;
- Temporary *risk corridors*,[5] which "mitigate the pricing risk that insurers face, when their data on health spending for potential enrollees are limited," by providing "a government subsidy if insurer losses exceed a certain threshold"—set at 3 percent in this case (conversely, excess gains are also limited with the requirement for plans to pay the government if their gains exceed this threshold); and
- A permanent risk-adjustment program that requires a transfer of funds between health plans that disproportionately enroll low-risk individuals to those that enroll a greater percentage of high-risk individuals, thus eliminating any incentive for competing plans to avoid enrolling these (AAA, 2011, pp. 3-4).

Notably, while risk adjustment reduces the effects of adverse selection between plans based on the relative risk of their enrollees, "it cannot, however, mitigate the effects of adverse selection against the market as a whole if a disproportionate share of low-risk individuals choose not to purchase coverage from any health plan" (AAA, 2011, p. 3). Without a large pool of enrollees, all health costs cannot be fairly distributed or amortized across an entire population.

Risk selection (aka "cherry picking" or "cream skimming"), in contrast to patient-driven adverse selection, is insurer-driven and refers to the use of benefit package design (or other tools) to disproportionately attract healthy individuals. This can result in greater profits for insurers and the potential for insufficient access for the sick in the non-guaranteed issue market; the ACA addresses this potential by incorporating consumer protections (such as,

---

[3] § 1343.

[4] Beginning in 2014 and ending in 2016 (§ 1341).

[5] Beginning in 2014 and ending in 2016 (§ 1342).

no preexisting condition exclusions,[6] guaranteed issue,[7] and limiting the medical loss ratio[8]) and prohibiting the Secretary from making any coverage decisions or designing benefits for the EHB in a way that would discriminate against individuals because of their age, disability, or expected length of life. Implementation bears watching to ensure that benefit design at the plan level does not inadvertently breach these nondiscrimination provisions or create barriers to accessing care.

A variety of benefit design approaches and value-based incentives are being used, as noted in Chapter 2. Cautions have been raised to ensure that incentives have their intended consequences. For example, *cost sharing* is a means for insurers to involve enrollees in the cost burden of their care and seeks to align incentives with purchase price. *Network tiering* is a method that encourages enrollees to seek care from designated "high-value" providers, with a lower corresponding co-payment than for "out-of-network" care. Network tiering can increase health disparities if the number of designated high-value providers cannot accommodate the patient load (i.e., they do not accept new patients) or if lack of proximity (in rural areas especially) creates an unreasonable travel burden (Tackett et al., 2011). A similar mechanism applying to pharmaceutical use is *formulary tiering.* A three-tier plan, for example, could have three co-payment levels; the lowest for generic drugs, the next for formulary (preferred) drugs, and the highest for nonformulary brand name drugs (Joyce et al., 2002). However, if the tiers are based on price alone, it is not a value-based design. In a variant pharmaceutical benefit design called *reference pricing,* insurers cover "only the prices of low-cost, benchmark drugs in therapeutic clusters that are deemed to be close substitutes for one another in treating specific illnesses. Patients who desire a higher-price substitute in a cluster must then pay the full difference between the retail price of that drug and the reference price covered by the insurer" (Kanavos and Reinhardt, 2003, p. 16). Similarly, such a pricing model is being considered to put the burden on offerers of new technologies to convey why any price increases would be justified over currently available technologies in terms of better outcomes for patients.

Porter remarks, "If value improves, patients, payers, providers, and suppliers can all benefit while the economic sustainability of the health care system increases. . . . Cost reduction without regard to the outcomes achieved is dangerous and self-defeating, leading to false 'savings' and potentially limiting effective care" (Porter, 2010, p. 2477). The committee defines *value* as *outcomes relative to costs.* In Chapter 2, there is a brief overview of cost drivers for health care spending and insurance premium growth, as well as discussion of unwarranted preference and supply-sensitive variations in care. Market pressures can lead to unnecessary utilization of high-cost services and items without a commensurate benefit—for example, marketing by vendors directly to patients of profitable services that have low health gains over alternatives (e.g., virtual physical exams, high-cost pharmaceuticals). Similarly, interest groups can be potent in trying to force through benefits that evidence does not support. Comparative effectiveness and cost-effectiveness analyses are tools that can be used to compare relative outcomes.

Ethics

A framework rooted in ethics recognizes that no set of metrics can provide a guarantee of ethical *actions,* but promotes theoretical reflection and conceptual analysis in support of adherence to "ethical norms." Public examination of clinical effectiveness and priority setting among benefits, combined with the use of ethically guided benefit management processes, will contribute to preserving access to benefits that are the safest and most effective, all while eliminating interventions that have been proven to be ineffective or even harmful. Thus, an ethical framework requires consideration of stewardship of shared population-wide resources and, at the same time, fidelity to the needs of the individual (Daniels and Sabin, 1997, 2008). Stewardship is not just a matter of living within a budget, but of having a broader obligation for the judicious use of resources so that they are available when people who contribute to the resource pool most need them.

The American Medical Assocation's (AMA's) Ethical Force Program proposed five content areas directly related to the fairness of a health benefits design and subsequent administration, stating that health care coverage

---

[6] § 1201, amending § 2704 of the Public Health Service Act.

[7] § 1201, amending § 2702 of the Public Health Service Act.

[8] The medical loss ratio informs consumers and regulators about the percentage of the premium being spent on fees, administration, and profits. The ACA requires insurance companies to spend at least 80 percent or 85 percent of premium dollars on medical care depending on market segment. § 1001, amending § 2718 of the Public Health Service Act [42 U.S.C. 300gg–18].

decisions should be (1) transparent, (2) participatory, (3) equitable and consistent, (4) sensitive to value, and (5) compassionate (Box 3-1). Of note, these are not listed in order of importance, but rather in the logical order in which they may be considered in the decision-making process (AMA, 2004).

The five areas suggested are to be advocated for because

1. **Transparency** is necessary for market accountability;
2. **Participatory** processes ensure that public concerns are understood and considered, foster a heightened sense of fairness and legitimacy among stakeholders, and additionally promote quality improvement by drawing attention to grievances;
3. **Equity and consistency** safeguard against inappropriate discrimination (both for legal reasons in setting and enforcing precedents and for promoting public acceptability of a system);
4. **Sensitivity to value** is rooted in the consequentialist approach of promoting the greatest good; and
5. **Compassion** is consistent with the health insurance function of protecting against an imbalance in individual risk, requiring that health care resource allocation transcend the formulaic by incorporating flexibility and responsiveness to extraordinary individual circumstances and informing itself on such individual variations (AMA, 2004).

The five areas identified by the AMA represent aspirational targets. They are not easy to achieve in full measure. With transparency, it is not possible to convey all information (particularly with regard to additions or revisions) to all people; participatory processes are often skewed to those who are already empowered, so attention must be placed on minorities (such as those with rare diseases) who may have been heard less often. A focus on consistency requires meticulous record-keeping, which can be challenging and should not hinder progress in incorporating developments when previous decisions are determined to be incorrect or new circumstances are encountered. Sensitivity to value requires a modality for assessment that must ensure the intended effect of the service is considered. Finally, beyond the

---

BOX 3-1
The American Medical Association's (AMA's) Ethical Force
Program Five Content Areas for Performance Measurement
in Designing and Administering Health Benefits

Transparency: The processes for designing and administering health benefits should be fully transparent to those affected by these processes.

Participatory: Organizations[a] should purposefully and meaningfully involve all stakeholders in creating and overseeing the processes for designing and administering health benefits.

Equity and consistency: Processes for designing and administering health benefits should result in similar decisions under similar circumstances.

Sensitivity to value: Processes for designing and administering health benefits should take into account the net health outcomes of services or technologies under consideration and the resources required to achieve these outcomes.

Compassion: The design and administration of health benefits should be flexible, responsive to individual values and priorities, and attentive to the most vulnerable individuals and those with critical needs.

---

[a] For example, health insurance exchanges.
SOURCE: AMA, 2004.

difficulty of gauging compassion lies the challenge of balancing individual need with stewardship of societal resources, while avoiding inequity in the distribution of those resources (AMA, 2004). The IOM committee concluded that in a large, pluralistic society like the United States, there are no shared principles by which to assign fixed weights to the values the AMA identified. For that reason, as discussed in Chapter 6, the committee posited a central role for a fair process to guide EHB design and administration, and described the role of public deliberation and "accountability for reasonableness" (Daniels and Sabin, 2008) in creating that process.

Evidence-Based Practice

Evidence drives the evolution of medical practice—from its origins rooted in mythology, to observation, randomized trial, systematic review, and large-scale personalized modeling. In directing this move from the "usual and customary" and "standard of practice" to mixed models of evidence- or expert-based practice, evidence-based medical practice improves the quality of clinical decision making. In addition to positively impacting the health of the population, there is also the potential to "reduce the use of marginal services and control some of the variation in utilization among providers" (Santa and Gibson, 2006, p. 3). Yet current incentives in the health care system—whether related to physician behavior, patient behavior, hospital behavior, or manufacturer behavior—are not necessarily aligned with evidence-based practice (Jacques, 2011), contributing to unexplained and/or unintended variation in medical and health care quality.

Evidence-based practice (EBP) could be fostered through EHB design. In practice, "evidence based medicine is the conscientious, explicit, and judicious use of current best evidence in making decisions about the care of individual patients" (Sackett et al., 1996, p. 71). The use of evidence helps both to define coverage and to determine medical necessity for individual patients. The IOM has published a number of studies stressing the "imperative for change" to improve the quality of health care through the use of evidence and incentives to support its use in practice—noting unsustainable rates of increase in costs, unwarranted variation in the use of services, shortcomings in the health care system's ability to translate knowledge into practice, and too frequent lapses in applying new technology safely and appropriately (IOM, 2001, 2008, 2011a,b). Numerous studies support findings that unnecessary care is delivered (NEHI, 2008; Schuster et al., 2005), recommended care is not (McGlynn et al., 2003), and that care when delivered inappropriately can be unsafe (Brenner and Hall, 2007; Rosen, 2010; Simpson, 2010).

Recognizable gaps in the evidence base and in the strength of evidence mean that uncertainty remains around decision making for numerous services. Opportunities for coverage with evidence development, as Medicare does (e.g., pancreatic islet cell transplantation), can help if there is a mechanism to collect rigorous treatment and outcomes data. The expected technological explosion from multiple fields may fuel growth in what is known as personalized medicine, and this will add further challenges to applying EBP as the tension between studies based on populations and treatment decisions at the individual level increases. As important as evidence is, care must be taken to ensure that the absence of evidence (different from negative evidence) does not have more impact on specific groups. For example, given the directive to "take into account the health care needs of diverse segments of the population," if evidence gaps selectively disadvantage particular groups, such as children, disabled persons, minorities or women, special effort should be taken to avoid discrimination.

EBP is understood by clinicians, but has variable acceptability among the general public on a conceptual level, with one study finding "many of these consumers' beliefs, values, and knowledge to be at odds with what policy makers prescribe as evidence-based health care" (Carman et al., 2010, p. 1400). Furthermore, "When science or the evidence flies in the face of people's desires or their personal health beliefs," there can be a backlash from both medical professionals and patients (Good, 2010). However, evidence should help clarify decisions in a more transparent way to the public; in the context of making tradeoffs among benefits, when the choice is living within evidence-based guidelines vs. paying more, or giving up a covered category, people accept the guidelines (Ginsburg et al., 2006). Furthermore, aligning coverage with scientific evidence can be a safeguard against inappropriate discrimination (Rosenbaum, 2011) in the practice of individualized, condition-specific care.

Given the broad range of EBP's potential applications, it is important to consider how evidence is currently used for decision making within health care (Table 3-1). As noted by Clancy and Cronin (2005), "Increasing the relevance of scientific evidence to clinical and policy decisions relies on both a transparent approach to evaluating

TABLE 3-1 Uses of Evidence for Decision Making

Type of Decision	Decision Maker	Role of Evidence
Product approval	FDA	Level I
Product purchasing, for example, formulary selection	Health plans, PBMs	Level II
Clinical decisions		
Practice guidelines	Clinicians	Level II
Shared decisions	Clinicians, patients	Level III
Assess and improve health care quality		
Internal improvement	Health care organizations	Level II
Public reporting	Payers/purchasers; states	Level II
Pay for performance[a]	Payers/purchasers	Level II
Choice of plans or providers	Consumers; employers	Level III
Select benefits and coverage	Insurers; employers	Levels II-III
Organizational and management decisions	Health care organization leaders	Level IV
Care options[b]	Individuals; patient and disease groups	Levels III-IV

NOTES: Level I: rigorous evidence required (absolute requirement); level II: evidence is predominant input when available, supplemented by expert judgment; level III: available evidence is one but not the only input to decisions; level IV: available evidence is limited, other considerations are important. FDA = U.S. Food and Drug Administration; PBM = pharmacy benefit manager.

[a] Pilot programs.

[b] Emerging focus.

SOURCE: Clancy and Cronin, 2005. Copyrighted and published by ProjectHOPE/*Health Affairs* as Clancy and Cronin, Evidence-based decision making: Global evidence, local decisions. *Health Aff* (*Millwood*) 1(24):151-162.

the quality of scientific studies and a broad debate about the interpretation of scientific findings and their optimal application" (Clancy and Cronin, 2005, p. 152). One research area of considerable interest is the question of "appropriate use"—because it is possible to establish that a service has credible evidence for efficacy, with *conditions* of coverage (e.g., higher vs. lower cost sharing, participation in research to generate evidence) as opposed to considering benefits independently, absolutely, and unconditionally covered.

Obstacles to increased use of evidence in health benefits design include a perceived lack of sufficient evidence, inability to communicate—with credibility and transparency—to consumers the rationale behind perceived limitations on coverage, inadequate benefit design description, financial and administrative considerations, and resistance to change among providers, vendors, and consumers (Bernstein, 2010; Santa and Gibson, 2006). Among these, lack of adequate information—either because the issue has not been studied or because no positive results have been found—is the most significant challenge encountered in EBP. Evidence-based medical practice is an ever-evolving effort that requires analysis—which can be costly—to develop standards that will guide clinical decision making—often through one or a number of entities charged with reviewing and analyzing evidence (e.g., U.S. Preventive Services Task Force, Cochrane, Agency for Healthcare Research and Quality [AHRQ]).

A related difficulty that arises is in the interpretation of the information available, particularly with regard to cases where there is conflicting evidence, treatment heterogeneity (variable response based on some other factor[9]), or no consensus about relative effectiveness among services. Indeed, the quality of all evidence must be evaluated—for risk of bias, consistency, precision, directness, and reporting bias. In 2011, the IOM published *Clinical Practice Guidelines We Can Trust* and *Finding What Works in Health Care: Standards for Systematic Reviews,* which set standards to improve the quality of clinical practice guidelines (CPG) and systematic reviews (SR), respectively. When the Secretary of HHS and insurers use evidence to make benefit design decisions, they will be working in an evidence environment that is far from ideal, but they should use the best evidence available (IOM, 2011a,b).

Population Health

The IOM has long highlighted the need for a greater focus on population health alongside individual health (IOM, 1988, 2002). The committee agrees that it is necessary to consider the needs of both the individual and the

---

[9] For example, co-morbid condition, gender, or metabolic ability.

overall population when setting priorities (Sabin, 1998) and acknowledges the tension this places on policy makers when making coverage decisions. Population health focuses on improving the *overall* health status of a community, thus departing from the predominant late 20th century medical care model of focusing interventions only on the individual (Kindig, 2007). The function of health insurance, in this framework, is to encourage access to health-promoting care services, through primary and secondary prevention (e.g., immunizations to reduce transmission of communicable diseases; screenings for conditions such as high blood pressure, type 2 diabetes mellitus, or certain cancers, in which a delay in the initiation of treatment is associated with increased mortality).

The ACA changes the paradigm for preventive health services, because preventive and wellness services (including chronic disease management) are 1 of the 10 categories of care required for the EHB. Furthermore, services that have been rated highly effective by the U.S. Preventive Services Task Force must be offered without patient cost sharing[10] (currently 45 preventive services have received a high evidence grade of A or B) (USPSTF, 2010; HHS, 2010).

In 2006, in anticipation of efforts to develop an essential benefits package, Oregon's Health Services Commission changed its prioritized list's ranking methodology (discussed in Chapter 2) to incorporate a population focus, moving certain preventive services higher on the list (MedPAC, 2011). Additionally, one study by Thornton and Rice (2008) suggests that population health can be improved when health insurance coverage is extended to the uninsured (a 10 percent increase in insurance coverage of a state's population was estimated to reduce mortality by 1.69-1.92 percent). Such an effect may not be seen in national statistics if the proportion of the population becoming newly insured is small or the extension of life is minimal, but the expansion of health coverage under the ACA and the insureds' response to care provide an opportunity to study these effects. Finally, efforts to identify and then eliminate the disparities experienced while accessing health care must accompany any population health approach.

A few states also explicitly assess the impact on the health of their overall population when considering whether certain health benefits should be mandated for insurance packages. Among these, California, by law, undertakes a public health impact analysis of proposed mandated health benefits by collecting data from state registries, state-specific population-based surveys, and national surveys to determine disease prevalence and incidence, impact of benefit coverage on health outcomes (including morbidity, mortality, disability, and quality of life), health care utilization, and how it will reduce premature health and economic loss (CHBRP, 2011; McMenamin et al., 2006). Furthermore, a focus on and improvement of population health is considered to positively influence economic growth (Bloom and Canning, 2000; Mirvis and Bloom, 2008), while having the potential to save money in the long term (Murphy and Topel, 2003).

CRITERIA

After considering these policy foundations for explicitly designing coverage, the committee derived criteria for determination of the EHB as the Secretary of HHS requested. Individual criteria go across multiple policy domains—for example, the concept of stewardship is as much of an ethical as an economic criterion. A need for distinction among criteria for three purposes became apparent: first, criteria for assessing the EHB package's *content* in the aggregate; second, criteria for assessing individual services for possible inclusion or exclusion in the package; finally, separate criteria for the *methods* employed in deliberations over composition, whether employed by the Secretary, states, any advisory body, or the public. These criteria promote responsible oversight of the EHB.

Guidance on Content

Figure 3-2 lists the criteria for the aggregate package and individual service assessments for the EHB. These criteria are part of the process, defined by the committee, to define the initial EHB package (Recommendation 1 in Chapter 5) and updating the package (Recommendation 5 in Chapter 9).

With respect to the application of criteria for the overall package, the committee acknowledges that the expected effects for each of these criteria can be along a continuum and multiple metrics could be applied to

---

[10] Only when these services are delivered by a network provider.

Criteria to Guide Content of the Aggregate EHB Package

In the aggregate, the EHB must:

- **Be affordable** for consumers, employers, and taxpayers.

- **Maximize the number of people with insurance coverage.**

- **Protect the most vulnerable** by addressing the particular needs of those patients and populations.

- **Encourage better care practices** by promoting the right care to the right patient in the right setting at the right time.

- **Advance stewardship of resources** by focusing on high value services and reducing use of low value services. Value is defined as outcomes relative to cost.

- **Address the medical concerns of greatest importance** to enrollees in EHB-related plans, as identified through a public deliberative process.

- **Protect against the greatest financial risks** due to catastrophic events or illnesses.

Criteria to Guide EHB Content on Specific Components

The individual service, device, or drug for the EHB must:

- **Be safe**—expected benefits should be greater than expected harms.

- **Be medically effective** and supported by a sufficient evidence base, or in the absence of evidence on effectiveness, a credible standard of care is used.

- **Demonstrate meaningful improvement** in outcomes over current effective services/treatments.

- **Be a medical service**, not serving primarily a social or educational function.

- **Be cost effective**, so that the health gain for individual and population health is sufficient to justify the additional cost to taxpayers and consumers.

Caveats:

Failure to meet any of the criteria should result in exclusion or significant limits on coverage.

Each component would still be subject to the criteria for assembling the aggregate EHB package.

Inclusion does not mean that it is appropriate for every person to receive every component.

FIGURE 3-2 Criteria for assessing content of essential health benefits (EHB) as a whole and for specific components.

measure that effect. For example, estimates by the Congressional Budget Office (CBO), RAND, and others give guidance on expected enrollment numbers, reductions in the uninsured, and changes in average premium prices (CBO, 2011a,b; Eibner et al., 2010; KFF, 2011), which, along with actuarial estimates of specific benefit categories, can be applied in estimating the impact of the contents of various benefit package options. The committee was acutely aware that the affordability of the EHB package would affect market response and has more to say in Chapter 5 on how a projected national average premium can guide EHB package development. The committee recognizes the intent of the ACA to maximize the number of people who are meaningfully insured and thereby the implicit goal embedded in the CBO scoring of the health reform bill for the potential reduction in the number of uninsured and take up of coverage through private means. Monitoring of implementation will inform these and other metrics. The committee recommends development of a monitoring and research agenda in Chapter 7, which should include identification of metrics to monitor the criteria.

The ACA and HHS's National Quality Strategy underline the need for better care practices. The committee believes that decisions on covered benefits and benefit design choices can support better care practices. The committee supports an evidence-based and value-based approach to coverage of health services as desirable to maximize the health gains of such services as well as provide patients with the best choice of safe and effective treatments. This argues for development of a shared EHB evidence base, monitoring of access to designated EHB coverage so that benefits supported by evidence are available to those who need them, and being encouraging to new modes of delivery or insurance design that foster value. How one evaluates an entire package or even 1 of the 10 categories of care as being fully evidence-based will be challenging but also argues for more detail in benefit specification (see Chapters 5 and 9) and improvement in the quality of evidence over time. Currently, each insurer, whether public or private, is making decisions on effectiveness of services separately, at times duplicating efforts that might be better directed in cooperative evaluation of research and establishment of clinical policies.

Insurance is a method of pooling the risk of financial loss across a group or a population. This prompts the question, "Which medical services should be paid for using a limited pool of shared funds?" Insurance policies exclude certain benefits; HHS will certainly have to exclude benefits that might be important to certain stakeholders, and these may even be services that have an evidence base that shows at some level they are effective. Most of us will be paying into insurance pools, directly through purchasing insurance and/or indirectly through taxes. Thus, we all depend on the possibility of spending from these shared pools and should want financial protection against catastrophic illnesses and conditions and assurances that care paid for out of shared resources is medically necessary. In contrast to other policy foundations, an insurance/economic frame emphasizes mitigation of short-term risk. Thus, relying on this frame alone is insufficient for establishing the EHB; coverage of prevention services, which are often relatively low cost and whose use can be anticipated, would tend not to be covered under an insurance frame solely.

The ACA puts an emphasis on prevention, and it will be necessary to invest in effective prevention and treatment practices for leading causes of morbidity and mortality to advance population health. In setting that as a goal, however, there must always be, as the ACA requires, attention to diverse segments of society and a spectrum of needs throughout the lifecycle and across a variety of conditions to prevent discrimination in the choice of benefits.

The committee criteria on evaluating individual components reflect current practice of evaluating such services as discussed in Chapter 2. There are many existing groups that evaluate specific services (e.g., BlueCross BlueShield Association's Technology Evaluation Center, AHRQ Evidence-Based Practice Centers) for effectiveness, although not always using cost and comparative effectiveness as the committee endorses. The committee also emphasizes that the EHB package should focus on medical services (Chapter 4), but that some nonmedical services may add value (i.e., promote health gain for the cost) and are supported by an evidence base of effectiveness. Several caveats are added to this list of criteria; services that fail to meet all of the criteria might be subject to restriction if they are included, for example, through the setting of limits on their duration and scope. Services that meet all of the criteria must still be subject to review as part of a package of benefits. And even when included as a covered benefit, if it is not medically necessary for an individual, then it should not be covered (Chapter 5).

Criteria to Guide the Methods

Repeatedly emphasized to the committee was the importance of having a trustworthy method for defining and updating the EHB. In developing these criteria, the committee identifies the following as key (Figure 3-3)—that the methods be transparent, participatory, equitable and consistent, sensitive to value, responsive to new information, attentive to stewardship, encouraging to innovation, and data-driven. These attributes of methods can apply at many levels, not only the national definition of the EHB, but also how states may make decisions about benefits in their states (Chapter 8 on innovation) and insurer decisions on medical necessity and any subsequent appeals.

The transparency of the EHB process at the national level extends to making the rationale behind choices made for the EHB package public (Chapter 5). Participation can take many forms, but in the context of making tradeoffs among benefits, the committee recommends going beyond usual stakeholder public comment to have formalized deliberation on tradeoffs (Chapters 5, 6, and 9). Equity and consistency are particularly important to ensure that medical necessity decisions are conducted fairly and with transparency, at a minimum, in external appeals (Chapters 5 and 7).

Criteria to Guide Methods for Defining and Updating the EHB

Methods for defining, updating, and prioritizing must be:

- **Transparent.** The rationale for all decisions about benefits, benefit design, and changes is made publicly available.
- **Participatory.** Current and future enrollees have a role in helping define the priorities for coverage.
- **Equitable and consistent.** Enrollees should feel confident that benefits will be developed and administered fairly.
- **Sensitive to value.** To be accountable to taxpayers and plan members, the covered service must provide a meaningful health benefit.

- **Responsive to new information.** The EHB will change over time as new scientific information becomes available.
- **Attentive to stewardship.** For judicious use of pooled resources, budgetary constraints are necessary to keep the EHB affordable.
- **Encouraging to innovation.** The EHB should allow for innovation in covered services, service delivery, medical management, and new payment models to improve value.
- **Data-driven.** An evaluation of the care included in the EHB is based on objective clinical evidence and actuarial reviews.

FIGURE 3-3 Criteria to guide methods for defining and updating the essential health benefits (EHB).

Together, these policy foundations, principles, and criteria comprise the committee's framework for defining and revising the EHB package, in a manner consistent with the ACA.

REFERENCES

AAA (American Academy of Actuaries). 2011. *Risk adjustment and other risk-sharing provisions in the Affordable Care Act.* http://www.actuary.org/pdf/Risk_Adjustment_IB_FINAL_060811.pdf (accessed July 8, 2011).

AMA (American Medical Association). 2004. *Ensuring fairness in health care coverage decisions: A consensus report on the ethical design and administration of health care benefit packages.* Chicago, IL: American Medical Association.

Bernstein, J. 2010. *Using evidence to design benefits.* Washington, DC: Academy Health.

Berwick, D. M., T. W. Nolan, and J. Whittington. 2008. The triple aim: Care, health, and cost. *Health Affairs* 27(3):759-769.

Bloom, D. E., and D. Canning. 2000. The health and wealth of nations. *Science* 287(5456):1207-1209.

Brenner, D. J., and E. J. Hall. 2007. Computed tomography—an increasing source of radiation exposure. *New England Journal of Medicine* 357(22):2277-2284.

Carman, K., M. Maurer, J. M. Yegian, P. Dardess, J. McGee, M. Evers, and K. Marlo. 2010. Evidence that consumers are skeptical about evidence-based health care. *Health Affairs* 29(7):1400-1406.

CBO (Congressional Budget Office). 2011a. *Additional information about CBO's baseline projections of federal subsidies for health insurance provided through exchanges.* Washington, DC: Congressional Budget Office.

_____. 2011b. *CBO's March 2011 baseline: Health insurance exchanges.* http://www.cbo.gov/budget/factsheets/2011b/HealthInsuranceExchanges.pdf (accessed June 30, 2011).

Chandra, A., J. Gruber, and R. McKnight. 2011. The importance of the individual mandate—evidence from Massachusetts. *New England Journal of Medicine* 364(4):293-295.

CHBRP (California Health Benefits Review Program). 2011. *Public health impact analysis.* http://chbrp.org/pubhealth.html (accessed September 22, 2011).

Clancy, C. M., and K. Cronin. 2005. Evidence-based decision making: Global evidence, local decisions. *Health Affairs* 1(24):151-162.

Daniels, N., and J. Sabin. 1997. Limits to health care: Fair procedures, democratic deliberation, and the legitimacy problem for insurers. *Philosophy & Public Affairs* 26(4):303-350.

_____. 2008. *Setting limits fairly: Learning to share resources for health.* 2nd ed. New York: Oxford University Press.

Eibner, C., F. Girosi, C. C. Price, A. Cordova, P. S. Hussey, A. Beckman, and E. A. McGlynn. 2010. *Establishing state health insurance exchanges: Implications for health insurance enrollment, spending, and small businesses.* Santa Monica, CA: RAND Corporation.

Ginsburg, M., S. D. Goold, and M. Danis. 2006. (De)constructing basic benefits: Citizens define the limits of coverage. *Health Affairs* 25(6):1648-1655.

Glied, S. 2011. Testimony to the IOM Committee on the Determination of Essential Health Benefits by Sherry Glied, Assistant Secretary for Planning and Evaluation, HHS, Washington, DC, January 13.

Good, L. B. 2010. *Breast cancer screening USPSTF update: An interview with Miriam Alexander, MD, MPH, ACPM President-elect.* http://www.medscape.com/viewarticle/714497 (accessed September 22, 2011).

HHS (Department of Health and Human Services). 2010. *Preventive services covered under the Affordable Care Act.* http://www.healthcare.gov/law/about/provisions/services/lists.html (accessed June 14, 2011).

IOM (Institute of Medicine). 1988. *The future of public health.* Washington, DC: National Academy Press.

———. 2001. *Crossing the quality chasm: A new health system for the 21st century.* Washington, DC: National Academy Press.

———. 2002. *The future of the public's health in the 21st century.* Washington, DC: The National Academy Press.

———. 2008. *Knowing what works in health care: A roadmap for the nation.* Washington, DC: The National Academies Press.

———. 2011a. *Clinical practice guidelines we can trust.* Washington, DC: The National Academies Press.

———. 2011b. *Finding what works in health care: Standards for systematic reviews.* Washington, DC: The National Academies Press.

Jacques, L. 2011. *Coverage policy: Aligning an insurance benefit with evolving evidence.* PowerPoint Presentation to the IOM Committee on the Determination of Essential Health Benefits by Louis Jacques, Director of Coverage and Analysis Group, Centers for Medicare & Medicaid Services, Washington, DC, January 13.

Joyce, G. F., J. J. Escarce, M. D. Solomon, and D. P. Goldman. 2002. Employer drug benefit plans and spending on prescription drugs. *Journal of the American Medical Association* 288(14):1733-1739.

Kanavos, P., and U. Reinhardt. 2003. Reference pricing for drugs: Is it compatible with U.S. health care? *Health Affairs* 22(3):16-30.

KFF (Kaiser Family Foundation). 2011. *A profile of health insurance exchange enrollees.* Washington, DC: Kaiser Family Foundation.

Kindig, D. A. 2007. Understanding population health terminology. *Milbank Quarterly* 85(1):139-161.

McGlynn, E. A., S. M. Asch, J. Adams, J. Keesey, J. Hicks, A. DeCristofaro, and E. A. Kerr. 2003. The quality of health care delivered to adults in the United States. *New England Journal of Medicine* 348(26):2635-2645.

McGlynn, E. A., A. Cordova, J. Wasserman, and F. Girosi. 2010. Could we have covered more people at less cost? Technically, yes; politically, probably not. *Health Affairs* 29(6):1142-1146.

McMenamin, S. B., H. A. Halpin, and T. G. Ganiats. 2006. Assessing the public health impact of state health benefit mandates. *Health Services Research* 41(3p2):1045-1060.

MedPAC (Medicare Payment Advisory Commission). 2011. *June 2011 report to the Congress: Medicare and the health care delivery system.* Washington, DC: Medicare Payment Advisory Commission.

Mirvis, D. M., and D. E. Bloom. 2008. Population health and economic development in the United States. *Journal of the American Medical Association* 300(1):93-95.

Murphy, K., and R. Topel. 2003. Diminishing returns? The costs and benefits of improving health. *Perspectives in Biology and Medicine* 46(3 Suppl):S108-128.

NEHI (New England Healthcare Institute). 2008. *How many more studies will it take?* Cambridge, MA: New England Healthcare Institute.

Pauly, M. V. 1968. The economics of moral hazard: Comment. *The American Economic Review* 58(3):531-537.

Porter, M. E. 2010. What is value in health care? *New England Journal of Medicine* 363(26):2477-2481.

Rosen, A. K. 2010. *Are we getting better at measuring patient safety?* http://www.webmm.ahrq.gov/perspective.aspx?perspectiveID=94 (accessed June 26, 2011).

Rosenbaum, S. 2011. Statement to the IOM Committee on the Determination of Essential Health Benefits by Sara Rosenbaum, Hirsh Professor and Chair, Department of Health Policy and Health Services, School of Public Health, The George Washington University, Washington, DC, January 13.

Sabin, J. E. 1998. The second phase of priority setting. Fairness as a problem of love and the heart: A clinician's perspective on priority setting. *British Medical Journal* 317(7164):1002-1004.

Sackett, D. L., W. M. C. Rosenberg, J. A. M. Gray, R. B. Haynes, and W. S. Richardson. 1996. Evidence based medicine: What it is and what it isn't. *British Medical Journal* 312(7023):71-72.

Santa, J., and M. Gibson. 2006. *Designing benefits with evidence in mind.* Washington, DC: Employee Benefit Research Institute.

Santerre, R. E., and S. P. Neun. 2010. The demand for medical insurance: Traditional and managed care coverage. In *Health economics: Theory, insights, and industry studies.* Mason, OH: South-Western, Cengage Learning.

Schuster, M. A., E. A. McGlynn, and R. H. Brook. 2005. How good is the quality of health care in the United States? *Milbank Quarterly* 83(4):843-895.

Simpson, K. R. 2010. Reconsideration of the costs of convenience: Quality, operational, and fiscal strategies to minimize elective labor induction. *Journal of Perinatal & Neonatal Nursing* 24(1):43-52.

Siu, A. L., F. A. Sonnenberg, W. G. Manning, G. A. Goldberg, E. S. Bloomfield, J. P. Newhouse, and R. H. Brook. 1986. Inappropriate use of hospitals in a randomized trial of health insurance plans. *New England Journal of Medicine* 315(20):1259-1266.

Tackett, S., C. Stelzner, E. McGlynn, and A. Mehrotra. 2011. The impact of health plan physician-tiering on access to care. *Journal of General Internal Medicine* 26(4):440-445.

Thornton, J. A., and J. L. Rice. 2008. Does extending health insurance coverage to the uninsured improve population health outcomes? *Applied Health Economics and Health Policy* 6(4):217-230.

USPSTF (U.S. Preventive Services Task Force). 2010. *USPSTF A and B Recommendations.* http://www.uspreventiveservicestaskforce.org/uspstf/uspsabrecs.htm (accessed June 14, 2011).

4

Resolving ACA Intent

At times, provisions in the Patient Protection and Affordable Care Act (ACA) send conflicting signals, requiring the committee members to come to a common understanding about what these provisions should mean for the essential health benefits (EHB). Specifically, the committee reached the following conclusions before offering recommendations in subsequent chapters: (1) the EHB package should first be constructed as a basic plan that meets statutory requirements before additions, and any addition should be subject to the same evaluative process the committee recommends; (2) every service or item that might be classified within the 10 categories or a typical employer plan is not essential; (3) due to data limitations on offered benefits, the scope of typical employer benefits needs to be thought of as equivalent to a typical premium and the EHB package should be built up to fit within such a predefined premium target; (4) initial secretarial definition of the benefits should be as detailed as data permit; (5) typical employer should be defined as small firms, and the constraints they face taken into account; (6) state mandates should not receive special treatment but should be subject to the same inclusion criteria as any other service or item; and (7) benefits should be focused on medical ones.

Through an array of statutory provisions involving the 10 categories of care, the typical employer plan, consideration of state mandates, and various other requirements, the ACA provides legislative guidance for the contents of the EHB. Yet the committee's review of this language revealed some conflicting and ambiguous direction with respect to the definition of the EHB. Furthermore, presentations during the committee's public workshops and responses to its public comment form revealed a spectrum of views on foundational issues that needed resolution.

The foundational areas explored in this chapter involve the following questions:

- Does essential mean a basic or very expansive package?
- Are the 10 categories of care covered in typical employer plans?
- Is everything within the 10 categories of care or a typical employer plan essential?
- Within what boundaries, if any, are the covered benefits meant to be defined?
- How specific should the Secretary be when defining the package?
- What is a typical employer in the context of the ACA?
- How should state mandates be considered?
- Should medical and nonmedical services be distinguished in the context of the EHB?

Thus, the committee thought it wise to step back from the details of the statutory language to consider elaborating on the underpinnings of the approach that the Department of Health and Human Services (HHS) should take in determining what, in fact, is an essential benefit. After all, this is the package of benefits that many individuals will be required to purchase, and the meaning of essential can take on different connotations and result in benefit packages of diverse degrees of comprehensiveness and affordability.

FINDING THE MEANING OF ESSENTIAL

To many, essential in common parlance means basic, a minimum "floor" of benefits, yet others differ, seeing the intent of the ACA for the EHB package to be to provide a robust and comprehensive coverage. To complicate matters, the word essential was often used interchangeably by people providing comments to the committee, but to mean different things.

For example, at the committee's first workshop, presentations by a bipartisan panel of former and current Senate staff members expressed some disagreement about what the ultimate package would look like—whether the desire was to create a "robust" benefit package vs. a "minimum" benefit package. Mr. David Schwartz said that Congress intended the EHB package to be "meaningful" and comprehensive and thus linked it to the benefits of a typical large employer plan as did Dr. David Bowen (Bowen, 2011; Schwartz, 2011). In contrast, Mr. Mark Hayes pointed out that the ACA uses the term essential because the legislature intended these to be basic, not comprehensive benefits, affordable for small employers (Hayes, 2011). Although the ACA lays out a more comprehensive set of benefits than does the Federal Employees Health Benefits Program (FEHBP) statute, Ms. Katy Spangler emphasized that the committee should "look at the least robust version of the benefit package as meeting" the standard of minimum essential coverage; otherwise, she said, fewer people will be able to afford coverage, thus defeating the purpose of the ACA to expand coverage to those who cannot now afford it (Spangler, 2011). Other presenters and commentators similarly presented diverse visions of the EHB package.[1]

Previous mandatory coverage requirements have similarly been couched in terms such as "minimum" or "basic," and these provided floors that could be supplemented at the individual, employer, or plan option. For example, the 1973 Health Maintenance Organization (HMO) Act required "a comprehensive package of basic benefits, including essential preventive services, along with a list of supplemental benefits for which the enrollees would make an extra payment" (The American Presidency Project, 2011; Bergthold, 2010). In 1990, the American Medical Association (AMA) put forward a proposal for a *minimum health care benefit package* that would have required employers to offer insurance coverage that included a limited set of covered benefits (for example, including no more than a specific number of doctor visits per year), the result of making what the AMA described as difficult choices to provide a degree of benefits to those who previously had no coverage.[2] In 1993 with the objective of providing small employers access to affordable health insurance and thus be better able to compete with larger employers, the State of Maryland set standards for all insurance carriers participating in the small employer market, establishing a "*floor*"—actuarial equivalency to the minimum benefits required to be offered by federally qualified HMOs—and a "*ceiling*"—the average premium for the standard benefit plan could not exceed 12 percent of Maryland's average annual wage. Subsequently, this amount was reduced to 10 percent. Approximately 98 percent of those participating in that market add benefits, "buying up" from the basic plan (MHCC, 2007; Sammis, 2011; Wicks, 2002).[3] Utah NetCare, which is Utah's "version of an EHB package," was designed to be a third less expensive than the average employer-based premium in that market. Although the basic benefit package is currently available and being purchased, "most people purchase benefit packages in excess of the basic requirements."[4] Others pointed to the basic mandatory vs. optional services under Medicaid as an example of

---

[1] See the committee's workshop publication for further discussion, *Perspectives on Essential Health Benefits.*

[2] This benefit package idea was rescinded as AMA policy in 2005.

[3] The Maryland Insurance Association also surveyed the largest carriers in 2008 regarding the top five benefit plans sold to small employers. These results were not published.

[4] According to Utah's largest commercial insurer with about 50 percent of the market, the enrollment or uptake of the minimum NetCare package among their members represents about 0.005 percent of the overall market. Personal communication with James Dunnigan, Utah State Legislature, May 4, 2011.

differentiating between levels of basic and enriched service choices in benefit packages. Section 1302 of the ACA specifically allows health plans to add benefits beyond whatever is defined as the essential health benefit package; however, individuals accessing coverage by virtue of exchange subsidies may not be able to afford supplementary coverage beyond what is offered in the exchange plan.

Having as many benefits incorporated in a plan as possible provides consumers protection for unforeseen expenditures, but it does so at the risk of raising the overall premium substantially, constituting an initial barrier to obtaining coverage for many and raising the total amount of federal subsidization. On the other hand, if the benefit package is not comprehensive enough or deductibles and co-payments are too high, patients may be underinsured. The major issue confronting the committee was how to balance the expansiveness of the benefit package with its affordability, while preserving the intent of the ACA to expand coverage to millions.

10 CATEGORIES OF CARE VS. TYPICAL

The 10 categories of care designated in Section 1302 for inclusion in the EHB package are a mix of condition-specific care (maternity and newborn care), types of services (laboratory services), facility-based care (hospitalization), and age-based services (pediatric services).[5] Consequently, some categories overlap; for example, if maternity care was not a separate category, those services could be classified among the others. Section 1302 requires that the EHB include "at least" the following:

- Ambulatory patient services
- Emergency services
- Hospitalization
- Laboratory services
- Maternity and newborn care
- Mental health and substance use disorder services, including behavioral health treatment
- Pediatric services, including oral and vision care
- Preventive and wellness services and chronic disease management
- Prescription drugs
- Rehabilitative and habilitative services and devices

Congress sought to remediate what it saw as shortcomings in current coverage by pulling out certain categories to ensure that they were covered, such as maternity services, mental health and substance abuse disorder services, and habilitative services. Coverage of maternity care has frequently not been a standard offering in the individual market; instead, until the ACA requirement goes into effect, it often must be purchased as an additional policy rider that is frequently "expensive and limited in scope" (NWLC, 2008). Habilitative services are distinct from rehabilitation, in that they are designed to help a person first attain a particular function vs. restoring a function. As was remarked during one of the committee's workshops, a separate listing of mental health and substance abuse disorder services would not be required if parity had truly been achieved.

The EHB are to reflect typical employer plans, and the U.S. Department of Labor (DOL) conducted a review of plan documents in fulfillment of the ACA's requirement for a survey of employer-sponsored coverage to determine the benefits typically covered by employers. The results of the "survey" can best be characterized as a survey of plan documents and their degree of specificity, which does not fully reflect whether plans actually offer a specific benefit. For example, the DOL reports 67 percent of workers have plans that list coverage of durable medical equipment, while one Mercer survey (2011) suggests that 97 percent of employers actually cover this benefit to some degree.

Although most of the broader categories of the ACA are in typical plans, it is less clear whether habilitation, wellness and chronic disease management programs, and pediatric oral and vision are, and even if they are, what services are affected. The committee asked three insurers to report on whether they covered these and other categories and services in the small group market (Appendix C, Tables C-2 to C-4).

---

[5] The ACA as amended expressly prohibits listing abortion as an essential health benefit (§ 1303(b)(1)(A)(i)).

- Habilitation was not covered by two of the three insurers reporting, with the third including habilitation in most plans but with coverage criteria determined by state mandates; early intervention services were not covered by one plan but were by the others in response to state mandates.
- Case management and diabetes care management,[6] possible components of wellness and chronic disease management, were "available" from two insurers with the other responding that these were not covered benefits.
- Full pediatric oral and vision care have not been standard benefits, but are typically available as riders.[7]
- Depending on the particular mental health and substance abuse disorder service, coverage was indicated as almost universal, although some services such as inpatient or outpatient substance abuse detoxification was less frequently covered. Coverage may have been in response to state mandates or had specific policy limitations.[8]

The plans offered by large employers are considered the most inclusive of benefits, yet even in these plans, services such as wellness services and pediatric oral and vision services may only be available as supplements to a standard medical plan and habilitation is not specifically designated as a covered benefit (Kang, 2011; Mercer, 2011). How these categories, and the services within them, are defined may change insurer response about whether they are currently covered services or not. Nonetheless, it appears the typical employer plan will have to be expanded to accommodate the 10 categories of care.

The statute permits the Secretary to add more categories, by saying the EHB package must include "at least" the 10 broad categories of care. It was beyond the committee's charge to specify the addition of specific categories and services, but the committee wanted to conceptually explore how to think about inclusions as the Secretary would have to do. As Congress did in drafting the legislation, the committee examined legislative guidance for other health insurance programs (e.g., FEHBP, Medicare, Medicaid, private plans) to see what other categories are required under those programs. For example, hospice and home health care are separately designated services for inclusion under Medicare Part A.[9] Home care is "mandatory" under Medicaid (Appendix D). But neither is specifically drawn out in the FEHBP statute, or the Massachusetts creditable coverage requirements, although they are required in Maryland's small business products (MHCC, 2011). Next, the committee explored whether they might be considered typical benefits. For hospice care, the DOL's Bureau of Labor Statistics' National Compensation Survey found it to be available to 67 percent of workers enrolled in plans (BLS, 2009), Mercer reported 91 percent of employers were offering this benefit, and the three insurers polled by the committee indicated it was covered. For home health care, the DOL found that 73 percent of workers have plans that mention coverage, Mercer found that 93 percent of employers offer such coverage, and the three polled insurers indicated that it was covered (Appendix C). For both services, coverage was subject to certain criteria and limits. Thus, the typical employer plan is likely to have to add additional services to meet the statutorily required 10 categories as well as likely already to have some categories or services that might be considered beyond those 10 categories.

Conclusion: The committee concludes that the contents of the EHB package should first be constructed as a basic plan that will meet the statutory requirements of typical employer plan and its expansion to the 10 categories before considering any other additions. Adding more benefits would necessitate raising premiums and/or further modifying benefit design and administration factors, such as network design and medical management criteria and programs. As a result, the committee does not recommend specific additions to the 10 categories of care at the outset but would require any additions to be considered within the broader

---

[6] The DOL report indicated that diabetes care management was listed in 27 percent of workers' plan documents reviewed, but 73 percent do not have plans that mention coverage (see Appendix C).

[7] Mercer reported that 46 percent of all employers offer plans that provide pediatric dental and 44 percent provide pediatric vision coverage (see Appendix C).

[8] The DOL report found less frequent mention of some services in plan documents with respect to substance abuse services. The services reported on in the IOM committee's request to the insurers were primarily limited to those listed in the DOL survey. (See Appendix C.)

[9] Social Security Act, Title XVIII § 1812 [42 U.S.C. 1395(d)].

evaluative process outlined in this report's Recommendation 1 for defining essential health benefits (see Recommendation 1 in Chapter 5).

ESSENTIAL VS. NONESSENTIAL

The decision about what is essential or nonessential is likely more complex than a binary one of determining whether a benefit is essential or not, but of being more or less essential, thus requiring an element of prioritization in the definition of essential benefits. Employers and insurers already deem some things excluded from coverage based solely on the impact on premiums or because offering such coverage would expose the insurer to the risk of adverse selection. Other times a decision is made according to a "social insurance test": is it reasonable to ask others in the risk pool to subsidize the cost of providing the benefit (Levine, 2011)? Section 1302 states that the EHB shall include the 10 general categories and "the items and services covered within the categories." However, within these 10 general categories, as well as in typical employer plans, there are services and items that should be excluded or limited in coverage because they can be deemed less effective and thereby less essential. Additionally, there may be services that have been excluded in the past that should be reconsidered.

Conclusion: The committee concludes that the Section 1302 language that says "the items and services covered within the categories" should not be construed to mean that every service that is within 1 of the 10 categories or is covered by a typical employer plan should automatically be included in the definition of the EHB.

BOUNDARIES OR NOT

The ACA provides further guidance that suggests that the EHB cannot be approached with an open wallet, but must fall within a cost range that is affordable for likely purchasers and sustainable by the government. The exchange products are to be based on a typical employer model. Employers buy insurance products on behalf of their employees and under budgetary constraints, and they are acutely aware of the fact that each dollar spent on health insurance premiums is a dollar that cannot be allocated to wages or other benefits (Emanuel and Fuchs, 2008). Therefore, operating under a budget and considering tradeoffs among inclusion and exclusion of benefits as well as benefit design options is typical among employers.

Before passage of the ACA, the Congressional Budget Office (CBO) scored the impact of the bill's provisions on the federal budget and on premiums for individuals and small employers, using as a starting point the average employer premium from the Medical Expenditure Panel Survey (MEPS) but with subsequent adjustment based on consideration of the Kaiser Family Foundation (KFF)/Health Research & Educational Trust (HRET) employer benefit survey and consultation with benefit consultants on premium trends. The scope of benefits was considered to be reflected in the scope of the average employer plan premium (with the average weighted by enrollment). Thus, the average employer premium was factored into the calculations used in assessing the ultimate cost impact of health reform on individuals, small business, and the federal government (CBO, 2009a,b).[10] Finally, the ACA requires a report to Congress on updating the EHB, which is to specifically assess the impact of any additions to benefits that might increase costs and identify corresponding reductions to meet the actuarial limitation of the scope of a typical employer plan.

The legislative language can be interpreted to mean that the EHB will not be more costly than "typical" employer-based insurance, and this provides a fiscal restraint on the expansiveness of the EHB package and its cost,[11] and by extension, the federal subsidy amount paid over time. The lack of specificity in available data about benefit inclusions also argues for the scope of the benefit package to be thought about in dollar terms reflecting

---

[10] Personal communication with Phil Ellis, Congressional Budget Office, February 11, 2011.

[11] Former legislative staff conveyed to the IOM committee that the typical employer language in Section 1302 was considered to be a reasonable restraint on the expansiveness of benefits. Personal communication with Yvette Fontenot, formerly with the Senate Committee on Finance, December 6, 2010.

what a plan subscriber is typically paying. The reference to "scope of benefits" in Section 1302 may, therefore, have to be interpreted as equivalent to what can be obtained by a typical premium amount.

Conclusion: The committee concludes that scope of benefits of a typical employer plan needs to be thought of not only as the listing of benefits but also as what is paid by the subscriber for those benefits. Without some constraint on the size of the EHB package, the premium prices faced by individuals seeking to obtain coverage both inside and outside of the exchanges in the individual and small business market may prove unaffordable to the target population and diminish access to health insurance coverage. The committee concludes that the EHB should be defined as a package that will fall under a predefined cost target rather than building a package and then finding out what it would cost.

UNDERSTANDING TYPICAL SPECIFICITY IN SCOPE OF BENEFITS

The study sponsor asked the Institute of Medicine how best to reconcile a federal standard for benefits coverage under the EHB package with state and regional variations in practices and benefits coverage patterns (Glied, 2011). The statute guides EHB definition to include at least 10 broad benefit categories of care and be equal in scope to the benefits provided under a typical employer plan. The committee considered how much variance could be permissible across the country with regard to the defining and implementation of the EHB—and consequently how specific secretarial guidance should be to states and insurers.

Specificity of Inclusions in Existing Documents

Several reports have sought to identify covered benefit inclusions to describe the scope of a typical employer plan, each one variously reporting by the portion of workers covered, the portion of employers providing coverage, or whether the benefits are standard or not. National data remain limited in specificity regardless of source.

Insurance policies vary in the degree of specificity with which they describe covered benefits; some health plan documents are very general while others are more highly detailed. The DOL, for its legislatively required "survey" of employer-sponsored coverage, examined 3,200 plan documents and found it difficult to describe with much precision the benefits of typical employer plans. Attempts were made to abstract 19 types of services or items from plans—finding, depending on the service, that from 9 to 73 percent of workers' plans do not mention whether the service is included; for example, 9 percent of workers' plans do not specifically list coverage of emergency room visits, while 73 percent of workers' plans do not specifically list coverage of kidney dialysis or diabetes care management (DOL, 2011). Thus, the usefulness of plan documents, as the DOL and the IOM committee in similar exercises found, is limited in informing about whether a benefit is covered as a typical benefit (Appendix C, Table C-1, column 2). It is unusual for every possible service to be explicitly listed as included; Oregon's prioritized list for Medicaid, including each of the condition-treatment pairs that are covered, was the most specific list encountered (Oregon Health Services Commission, 2011).

Conclusion: As a result of the finding of lack of specificity, the committee believes that if a requested medical service can reasonably be construed to fall within 1 of the 10 covered benefit categories[12] and is not expressly excluded, then it should be considered eligible for coverage as long as it is judged medically necessary for a particular patient.

For example, radiation therapy for cancer treatment might not be listed explicitly as a covered service but could reasonably be considered to fall within the general category of ambulatory patient services and, therefore, covered if judged medically necessary. The medical necessity of a particular treatment would be based on the specific type and state of the patient's cancer, as well as previous treatments applied to the individual's diagnosis.

---

[12] This conclusion references the 10 categories because they are identified by the law; the conclusion could be extended to benefit categories once identified by the Secretary as part of the EHB.

However, greater specificity within plan documents listing which classes of services are covered (e.g., listing of radiation therapy) would provide greater clarity and consistency across plan documents.

Balancing Flexibility and Specificity in Guidance

The committee considered whether only using the 10 broad categories of care in Section 1302 would be sufficient for secretarial guidance for the inclusion content of the EHB or if the 10 categories alone would result in too much state-by-state variation in what is considered essential. If more specificity is desired, then how detailed should the benefits list be? With increasing specificity comes greater uniformity in the EHB, and with this the advantages of standardization: clarification of price differences among plan options, for greater consumer confidence in picking plans with lower costs; minimization of adverse selection; ease in risk adjustment; and help in ensuring the adequacy of the lowest-cost plan (Bergthold, 1993). It might also be implied from HHS' request to the DOL to examine specific services that HHS expects to include some additional specificity beyond the 10 required categories.

If specificity has these advantages, what degree of regional or local variation in EHB definition should be allowable? In testimony to the committee, the director of the California Department of Managed Health Care cautioned, based on experience with state requirements for managed care, that very broad categories in the authorizing Knox-Keene Act left too much undetermined and thus resulted in many state mandates to clarify intent (DMHC, 2011). Conversely, the National Governors Association, among other proponents of secretarial guidance promoting a high degree of flexibility, felt that generality would better enable market competition and innovation (Salo, 2011).

The committee examined the legislative guidance for a number of programs and the plan documentation that resulted in those programs (e.g., FEHBP, the Massachusetts and Utah exchanges, managed health care in California, the Maryland plan for the small group market). The committee finds that the legislative guidance for these programs at least outlines broad general categories of care as does the ACA but may go beyond general categories to list more discrete services (e.g., coverage for transplants in Maryland's requirements for its small business Comprehensive Standard Health Benefit Plan) (Appendix D). Regardless of statutory descriptions, resulting plans, as reflected in evidence of coverage documents that consumers receive, generally go on to specify services in greater detail. However, plans even under the same legislative authority can vary in their degree of specificity within the same state. Moreover, in each of these programs (whether a state-specific program or the FEHBP), there is one entity providing oversight, while the EHB package will be administered across the 50 states by many different bodies. Individual states are opting for differing structures (i.e., quasi-governmental structure, nonprofit corporation, state government operated) and modes of contracting; some states will be active purchasers and will selectively decide which plans may participate in the exchange, while others will take a clearinghouse approach, accepting all comers (KFF, 2011). This multi-jurisdictional approach increases the likelihood that use of broad categories by the Secretary would result in variation even within local markets, compromising consumer protections unless there was increased specification beyond the 10 categories of care in the ACA.

Conclusion: To ensure better national comparability, the committee concludes that initial secretarial guidance should include as much specificity as can be developed from current best practices in plan documentation. More specificity is needed than the 10 categories outlined in the ACA because implementation of the EHB program will be disseminated across multiple jurisdictions, each with its own individual state-based oversight bodies.

TYPICAL EMPLOYER: SMALL VS. LARGE

Several questions arise with respect to typical employer. First, how should typical employer be defined? Sherry Glied, Assistant Secretary for Planning and Evaluation, indicated that she would welcome the committee's advice on the meaning of typical (Glied, 2011). As noted above, there were different perspectives on whether the benefit plan should reflect that of the small- or large-sized employer. Consequently, the committee wanted to review the landscape of employer sponsorship of insurance and examine different attributes of plans offered by small and large employers:

- What is a typical employer in general and in the context of the ACA?
- What are the typical cost of premiums, amount of employee cost sharing, and trends in plan type by employers of different sizes?
- What benefit differences are there for employers of different sizes?

What Is a Typical Employer?

Several approaches can be taken to defining typical employer, and they may lead to different results in terms of benefit coverage and design. If based on the number of firms or employers, then a typical employer looks more like a small employer (98 percent of all employer firms in the United States are classified as small) (U.S. Census Bureau, 2008),[13] and if based on the number of covered employees, a typical employer looks more like a large employer (65 percent of all employees in the country) (U.S. Census Bureau, 2008). Beyond this simple distinction are more nuanced differences in the degree to which employers offer health insurance coverage, whether the EHB package will apply to the plans offered by firms of different sizes, and the degree of uninsurance among their employees, all of which can be important to defining typical in the context of health insurance expansion under the ACA.

In 2011, just 60 percent of employers nationwide offered health insurance, including 99 percent of large firms (with 200 or more employees) and 59 percent of small firms (with 3 to 199 employees). Smaller firms, particularly those with less than 10 workers (48 percent offered in 2011) and those with 10-24 workers (71 percent), are less likely to offer health insurance coverage (KFF and HRET, 2011) (see Table 4-1). Thus, the workers of these smaller firms are a target of health reform coverage.

Employers might obtain insurance through insurance brokers, directly from insurers, or decide to self-insure; understanding the extent of self-insurance in small and large firms is of interest because self-insured plans are not required to incorporate the EHB. Self-insured means that the employer acts as its own insurer and accepts the associated risk; "fully insured" arrangements means the employer and employee pay a per capita premium to an insurance company that accepts the risk. In 2010, 16 percent of workers in smaller firms (3-199 employees) were in self-insured arrangements;[14] there is also a type of insurance that is a blend of insurance and self-insurance, in which some small employers choose insurance plans that have very high deductibles, such as $5,000, and the employer might self-fund the deductible amount. In contrast to the significantly lower percentage of small firms that are currently self-insured, 58 percent of workers in firms with 200-999 workers are self-insured, 80 percent in firms with 1,000-4,900 workers, and 93 percent in firms with more than 5,000 workers (KFF and HRET,

TABLE 4-1 Percentage of Firms Offering Health Benefits, by Firm Size, 1999-2011

Firm Size	1999	2000	2001	2002	2003	2004	2005	2006	2007	2008	2009	2010	2011
3-9 Workers	55	57	58	58	55	52	47	49	45	50	47	59[a]	48[a]
10-24 Workers	74	80	77	70[a]	76[a]	74	72	73	76	78	72	76	71
25-49 Workers	88	91	90	87	84	87	87	87	83	90[a]	87	92	85[a]
50-199 Workers	97	97	96	95	95	92	93	92	94	94	95	95	93
All small firms (3-199 Workers)	65	68	67	65	65	62	59	60	59	62	59	68[a]	59[a]
All large firms (200 or More Workers)	99	99	99	98[a]	97	98	97	98	99	99	98	99	99
All firms	66	68	68	66	66	63	60	61	59	63	59	69[a]	60[a]

NOTE: These results are from the Kaiser-HRET Survey of Employer-Sponsored Health Benefits, 1999-2011. Results based on sample of both firms that completed the entire survey and those that answered just one question regarding whether they offered health insurance.
[a] Estimate is statistically different from estimate for the previous year shown ($p < .05$).
SOURCE: KFF and HRET, 2011. Reprinted with permission by Gary Claxton, Vice President and Director of the Health Care Marketplace Project, Kaiser Family Foundation.

---

[13] Note: The number of nonemployer firms (21,351,320) is much greater than employer firms (5,930,132); nonemployer firms have no payroll.

[14] The KFF and HRET survey uses the terms self-funded and fully funded rather than self-insured and fully insured.

2010a). Thus, workers in smaller firms are more likely to obtain health insurance that would include the EHB package, whether they access it through the exchange or not. The insurance landscape, however, is in flux, with more small employers considering whether to self-insure to avoid requirements to provide an EHB package if it is more expansive than they desire or, alternately, provide employees with a fixed dollar contribution to have them purchase plans as individuals (Eibner et al., 2011).

Uninsured workers are a prime target for insurance expansion; substantial numbers of workers are uninsured and need affordable insurance. Among the 29.3 million uninsured workers in 2009, 48 percent worked in firms with fewer than 100 employees and an additional 13 percent were self-employed (KFF, 2009).[15] Furthermore, the rates of small firms offering insurance are much lower for worker populations at or below the 25th percentile in hourly wages compared with small firms having higher wage workforce (Blumberg and McMorrow, 2009). Others emphasize that the portion of uninsured or "underinsured" in small firms of fewer than 50 workers is greater than in larger firms—that is, more than half of those at small firms vs. about a quarter of those in large firms (Collins et al., 2010). Although often employed by large firms, these uninsured low-income workers would need an affordable benefit package, and their needs are likely more similar to employees in small firms.

What Are Typical Premiums, Deductibles, and Plan Types?

The main reasons given for smaller firms not offering insurance are primarily economic: the employer cannot afford it, the employee share would be too high, employees prefer the monetary benefit in terms of wages, and the benefit is not needed to retain employees. In the 2010 KFF and HRET Annual Employer Health Benefits Annual Survey, more than half of the respondents cited cost of health insurance being too high as the reason for not offering it (Holve et al., 2003; KFF and HRET, 2010a). Because employers are making purchasing decisions on behalf of their employees and health benefits offered by employers represent a tradeoff between benefits and wages for employees, employees too have an interest in the level of expenditures. Increases in health insurance premiums, in general, have been implicated in decreased coverage rates (Chernew et al., 2005). The committee explored whether there were differences in premiums, deductibles, and plan types between small and large employers.

Premiums

It is useful to understand similarities and differences in the premiums paid by employers and workers in small and large firms, particularly if premium equivalence is used in defining a scope of benefits because of a lack of definitiveness in plan documents. Unadjusted premium data show little difference by employer size; however, an often-cited article indicates that in 2002, small employers paid 18 percent more, on average, for the same benefits as those offered by the largest firms (Gabel et al., 2006; Miller, 2011).[16] The amount was 25 percent higher for indemnity plans and 18 percent higher for preferred provider organization (PPO) arrangements. Assuming similar health status and demographics between the small and large employers studied, higher premiums for smaller firms vs. larger ones could be attributed to higher insurance broker commissions, a smaller population base over which to spread administrative costs, insurer profit/risk charges, and weaker market power of individual and small group purchasing on their own (Executive Office of the President Council of Economic Advisors, 2009; Gabel et al., 2006). More up-to-date adjusted figures were not available to the committee, but the ACA medical loss ratio (MLR) provisions should help address some of these issues. The MLR informs consumers and regulators about the percentage of the premium being spent on fees, administration, and profits.[17]

---

[15] About one-third of the uninsured are in firms with fewer than 100 workers.

[16] Gabel et al. (2006) find this difference when comparing the smallest firm size of 1 to 9 workers compared with firms with 1,000 or more workers.

[17] Small group must meet a medical loss ratio of at least 80 percent and large group must meet a loss ratio of at least 85 percent, or rebates must be paid (§ 1001, amending § 2718 of the Public Health Service Act) [42 U.S.C. 300gg–18]. "These requirements, effective on January 1, 2011, are designed to make sure that 85 cents on the dollar is spent on claims costs, while the remaining 15 cents are allocated to administrative expenses in the large group market. In the small group and individual markets, 80 cents on the dollar are spent on claims cost, while the remaining 20 cents are allocated to administrative expenses. If a carrier fails to meet this benchmark, a portion of the premium must be refunded to subscribers" (McGraw Wentworth, 2011, p. 1).

A consistent relationship of firm size to premium price is not apparent across single and family coverage. MEP-IC (MEPS-insurance component) data define a small firm as one with 50 employee full-time equivalents (FTEs); starting in 2014, the ACA requires state exchanges to serve businesses with 50 or fewer employees, leaving it to the state to decide whether to open the exchange market to employers of 100 or fewer individuals. Data on 2009 private sector premiums do not show much difference in premiums for individual policies ($4,652 for small firms under 50 vs. $4,674 for larger firms), and for a family of four, larger firms pay more ($12,041 for small firms vs. $13,210 for large) (Branscome and Davis, 2011; Davis and Branscome, 2011). Older MEPS data for 2006 show that private sector small firms paid 4.5 percent more than larger firms for single coverage policies, but 3.0 percent less for family policies (Branscome, 2008).[18] Premiums for "plus 1" policies in 2009 show a higher premium for small firms ($9,124 for small vs. $9,042 for large) (Crimmel, 2010).

Employers have to determine what portion of the premium the employer and the employee will contribute. Some employers do not require employees to contribute (AHRQ, 2009a). On average, employee contributions in the private sector are 20.5 percent of individual policy premiums and 26.7 percent for family policies, with 2009 MEPS-IC data showing that employees of small firms contributed a lower percentage than those of larger firms for individual policies, but the reverse relationship for family policies (Branscome and Davis, 2011; Crimmel, 2011; Davis and Branscome, 2011). Although employer contributions have an apparent impact on the premium cost seen by an individual employee, in fact, the entire cost of health insurance premiums—like all other employee benefits—are ultimately taken from employee wages. Thus, both employers and employees have a strong interest in ensuring restrained premium growth.

Deductibles

Differentials in deductible levels suggest that benefits purchased by employees of small firms already require greater out-of-pocket payment for deductibles, raising the question of how much more emphasis could be placed on the benefit design factor of deductibles vs. other approaches to balance the breadth of EHB coverage with an affordable premium. For example, the 2009 total average deductible for an employee-only policy in a larger firm is $822 compared with $1,283 for firms of fewer than 50 employees, and for families the difference is $1,610 vs. $2,652, respectively (AHRQ, 2009b,c). Workers in small firms have seen deductibles increase much faster than workers in large firms. The average deductible for employee-only PPO coverage increased from $469 to $1,146 between 2005 and 2010 among workers in firms with 3-199 workers, compared to $254 to $460 among larger firms (KFF and HRET, 2005, 2010). Moreover, 46 percent of covered workers in small firms had deductibles of $1,000 or more compared with 17 percent of covered workers in large firms for single coverage (KFF and HRET, 2010a). Little variation by firm size is now observed in the percentage of workers enrolled in a plan with a deductible, with an average for all plans of 73.8 percent (AHRQ, 2009a). This is in contrast to the practice in 2002 when larger firms were less likely to have a deductible.

Plan Types

The majority of firms offer only one type of plan, with only 15 percent of small firms and 44 percent of large ones offering more choice (KFF and HRET, 2010a).[19] Gabel's study found that benefits were less comprehensive for small firms, regardless of their enrollment in indemnity or PPO plans (Gabel et al., 2006).

Different plan types have more or less stringent medical management to administer benefits, and regardless of firm size there has been tendency over time for an increasing degree of medical management as shown by data about plan types (KFF and HRET, 2010b). At opposite ends of the spectrum are the traditional fee-for-service indemnity plan, with no managed care elements, and the staff model HMO, with the most. Between these two extremes lie PPOs, HMOs that permit greater choice of physicians, and *point-of-service* (POS) plans that combine

---

[18] For premium per enrolled employee, $4,260 for small firms (less than 50 employees) and $4,077 for large. For employee plus one, $8,105 and $7,969, respectively, and for family coverage, $11,095 and $11,438, respectively.

[19] Note: This survey defines small as 3-199 workers and large as 200 or more.

elements of the HMO and PPO in an attempt to balance freedom of choice for the employee and financial control for the employer. *Indemnity plans* have virtually disappeared, while there is growth in PPO arrangements and different forms of managed care. *Consumer-driven health plans* or *high-deductible health plans with a savings account option (HDHP/SO)* have been introduced to better engage individuals in their own health care choices. These plans are typically offered through a PPO, but enrollment data are often shown separately because of the distinct nature of the cost-sharing arrangement.

DOL data only report on percentage use of fee-for-service (FFS) and HMO arrangements, and recent data do not show a difference by firm size (BLS, 2011), but this may be attributed in part to the fact that DOL FFS data include both PPO and POS data. KFF and HRET (2010a) data suggest a gradient of less participation in PPO FFS arrangements from larger firms to small but increasing participation in POS plans (a type of managed care arrangement); there is a less clear pattern for choice of a high-deductible health plan, although workers in very large firms are electing these at the highest rate of all groupings.

What Benefits Are Offered by the Typical Employer?

Attempts to distinguish differences in benefits by employer size met data limitations beyond that experienced by the DOL's survey of plan documents, but what data are available show little difference in the scope of benefits by firm size; instead benefit design factors play a larger role. The DOL Bureau of Labor Statistics' National Compensation Survey, collected from a sample of 3,900 employers, was able to yield data on coverage of 10 different services by employer size—outpatient and inpatient surgery, physician office visits, hospital room and board, chiropractic, home health care, skilled nursing facility, hospice care, biofeedback, and homeopathy (BLS, 2009); in most instances, the frequency with which the employer pool offers each of these benefits is very similar regardless of the size of the employer (Appendix C, Table C-1 columns 3 and 4). For example, outpatient surgery is offered to 97 and 98 percent of large and small employers workers, respectively, and hospice is offered by 66 and 69 percent, respectively. Other data from the 2009 Mercer National Survey of Employer-Sponsored Health Plans are not reported by the most relevant firm size in the context of the ACA (Mercer, 2009) but show that employers with fewer than 500 workers are less likely to cover some specific services such as alternative medicine therapies (e.g., acupuncture, chiropractic) and infertility services (Table C-1 columns 5 and 6).

Because of the limitations of the DOL survey of plan documents in revealing the contents of employer plans to inform a typical profile of benefits, the committee obtained data from three major health insurers—CIGNA, UnitedHealthcare, and WellPoint—on the benefits that they offer in the small employer and individual markets (see earlier discussion of the likely benefit enhancements that small employer plans will have to make to meet the 10 category requirement in the ACA). The profile of services covered by all of their standard plans, covered by some due to state mandates, or excluded is very similar for the small group market across these insurers (Appendixes C and F). The committee does not have a basis to assert that these plans are "typical" of all insurers, but finds that they are potentially informative to HHS for developing a preliminary list of services and actuarial estimates to consider when defining the EHB in accordance with the steps in the committee's Recommendation 1 (Chapter 5).

Both WellPoint and UnitedHealthcare report that little of the variation in customizing coverage in either the large and small group market is due to differences in covered benefits as opposed to benefit design options. Employers and insurers told the committee that tighter provider networks and tighter medical management are a feature of products selected in the smaller firm market (Calega, 2011; Turpin, 2011). WellPoint conveyed that its small group market is very standardized, and even in the large group market, only 5 percent of customization requests relate to adding coverage and 2 percent to removing coverage (e.g., when an employer becomes self-insured and does not want to include a state mandate), with the remainder of customization requests pertaining to adjusting cost sharing or limit setting (Appendix E). WellPoint reported in detail on the benefits covered by 99.7 percent of its small group products through Anthem Blue Standard Coverage Plans (small group = 1 or 2 to 50 employees); only a very small percentage of plans (0.3 percent) excluded specific services such as allergy testing and injections, cardiac and pulmonary rehabilitation, and durable medical equipment (Appendix E).

To further illustrate the influence of benefit design as opposed to differences in covered benefits, United-Healthcare offered a comparison of covered benefits in the large and small firm markets, using plans offered in

Plan Features	FEHB High Option VA	VA– Small Business Higher Actuarial Value	→		Lower Actuarial Value
Covered Services: Infertility	Limited Coverage	Not covered			
Cost Difference	N/A	-1.6%			
Cost Sharing:					
Deductible	$0	$0	$1,000	$2,000	$5,000
Member Co-insurance	0%	0%	0%	20%	20%
Out-of-Pocket Max	$1,800	$1,500	$1,000	$4,000	$10,000
PCP/Specialist Co-pays	$25/$35	$20/$40	$25/$50	$25/$50	$30/$60
Estimate of Actuarial Value	84%	85%	75%	64%	55%
Total Cost Difference vs. FEHB Plan		0%	-12%	-25%	-35%

- The majority of the cost difference is the result of Deductible, Coinsurance, and Out-of-pocket Max benefit levels.

FIGURE 4-1 Comparison of UnitedHealthcare (UHC) Federal Employee Health Benefit (FEHB) program plan offered in Virginia (VA) vs. other UHC small business plans offered in the state.
NOTE: N/A = not applicable; PCP = primary care provider.
SOURCE: Sam Ho, UnitedHealthcare.

Virginia—a low-mandate state—as an example (Figure 4-1). The single covered benefit difference is that FEHBP has limited coverage of infertility services, while none of the small business products include infertility services. The resulting cost difference based on that service alone is a 1.6 percent lower price in the small group market. However, the major differential in pricing comes from benefit design choices, including the level of deductible, cost sharing, and out-of-pocket maximums desired—a 12 to 35 percent lower price—not differences in covered services.

Benefit profiles are also very similar between the small group and individual markets according to these three insurers; the primary differences, reported by CIGNA, UnitedHealthcare, and WellPoint, have been: (1) maternity care has not been a feature of the individual plans unless purchased as a rider or mandated by the state, but the ACA requires its inclusion, (2) coverage for mental health and substance abuse services in individual plans has varied more than the small group market plans, with coverage being more limited and sometimes excluded unless required by state mandates (Appendix C, Tables C-2 to C-4).

In summary, health insurance premiums are determined by a number of factors including the population covered by a plan, the expansiveness of coverage, the benefit design, and underlying medical and insurance prices depending on the competitiveness of the local market. Based on available data, small and large employers offering insurance, on average, are paying similar premiums, yet small employers appear to have more cost-sharing limits on coverage. For example, employees of smaller firms are paying higher deductibles. Thus, benefit design considerations have been an important factor in what coverage is available to small firms and at what price. An advantage of exchange participation is that it will bring the purchasing power of larger groups to the marketplace and, ideally, offer more comprehensive coverage for what small employers are now paying, and through subsidies, allow additional persons to obtain coverage that they could not afford previously. Notably, when the state-based health insurance exchanges begin operations in 2014, the focus will be on serving individual purchasers and firms with fewer than 100 employees. Beginning in 2017, states can choose to allow those in the large group market (100+ employees) to purchase coverage in the exchanges.[20]

---

[20] § 1312(f)(2)(B).

Conclusion: Available data suggest the profile of covered benefits among large and small employers and the average premium paid is often not great; benefit design choices play a greater role. Given the ACA's focus on providing access to health insurance for workers of small firms and individuals in the opening years of the health insurance exchanges, the committee concludes that the initial focus of the EHB definition should be one that would be typical in the small employer market. Thus, when there is sufficient information to inform a choice between the scope of benefits between small and large employers (whether specified in service type, premium amount, or limits on services), the emphasis should be on the choice that would reflect the typical small employer market as long as that is consistent with meeting the statutory requirements (e.g., 10 categories).

STATE MANDATES

An extension of thinking about what is essential is consideration of the disposition of state mandates and how they fit within an EHB package. The term "state-mandated health benefits" (also referred to simply as "mandates," "state mandates," or "mandated benefit laws") refers to state laws that require health insurance contracts to cover specific treatments or services or medically necessary care provided by a specific type of provider.[21] Prior to the passage of the ACA, states were the primary regulators of the content of health insurance policies. The committee was asked to consider what role, if any, existing state mandates should play in defining essential health benefits. The ACA obligates each state to subsidize the benefits it mandates above and beyond EHB requirements.[22]

Applicability of State Mandates

Although all states have some mandates in place, they differ dramatically with respect to the total number in each state. Estimates of the number of existing mandates vary significantly, in part because they vary in terms of what they define as a "mandate" and also whether they count multiple laws requiring the same type of coverage in different market segments as distinct mandates. The Council for Affordable Health Insurance (CAHI) found an average of 42 mandates per state, with a high of 69 in Rhode Island and a low of 13 in Idaho (Bunce and Wieske, 2010). These numbers include, however, not only treatment and provider mandates, but also "population" mandates (requirements to cover specific populations such as newborns or grandchildren) and "offer" mandates (requirements simply to offer certain coverage for purchase). Other studies have found much lower numbers. For example, a 2007 study found an average of 18 mandates per state, with a high of 35 in California and a low of 2 in Idaho. These numbers do not include offer mandates, but do include population mandates (Monahan, 2007). Analysis of the number and type of state mandates by the BlueCross BlueShield Association tends to find fewer mandates than the CAHI numbers (Cauchi, 2011; Laudicino et al., 2010). Mandates proliferated particularly during the past 10-20 years (Bellows et al., 2006). Certain types of mandates are very common. For example in 2010, 50 states require coverage for mammography screening, 47 states currently have mandates requiring coverage for diabetes-related supplies, 45 require coverage for treatment in an emergency room, and 36 require coverage for off-label drug use (Bunce and Wieske, 2010); some are less frequent: congenital defect (1 state), early intervention services (7), and hospice care (12). With respect to provider mandates, 44 states require coverage for the services of chiropractors, 44 require coverage for the services of psychologists, and 41 require coverage for the services of optometrists, while 19 states mandate speech/hearing therapists, 12 mandate acupuncturists, and 7 mandate drug abuse counselors (Bunce and Wieske, 2010).

State mandates do not apply to every type of health insurance arrangement or type of market product. For example, the General Accountability Office (GAO) found the median number of mandates that were commonly applicable to the large employer, small employer, and individual market in 2002 to be 17 (GAO, 2003).[23] Impor-

---

[21] Some states also have laws requiring health insurers to *offer* coverage for certain types of benefits or providers. Those laws are omitted from this discussion.

[22] § 1311(d)(3)(B).

[23] The GAO report reviewed benefit requirements in eight states (Alabama, Colorado, Georgia, Idaho, Illinois, Maryland, Nevada, and Vermont) (GAO, 2003).

tantly, they do not apply to any employer-provided health plans that are self-insured by the employer. Given the high rates of self-insurance among larger employers, the result is that more than half (59 percent) of the individuals with employer-provided coverage are covered by plans that are not subject to state regulation, including state mandates (KFF and HRET, 2010a) and the proportion is higher among very large firms (MacDonald, 2009). Whether mandates apply to state Medicaid programs, or other state programs designed to provide coverage to low-income individuals, depends on the particular statute enacting the mandate. Legislatures may include such programs within a mandate, but often they do not (Hyman, 2000). Typically the greatest impact of mandates is on privately financed health insurance sold through the individual and small group markets within a state. Additionally, the FEHBP national fee-for-service plans do not have to incorporate state mandates, but can pick up state mandates as a negotiated benefit.

Debate Over State Mandates

State mandates have been a controversial element of health insurance regulation. Proponents of mandates argue that there are situations in which market intervention, in the form of mandates, is necessary to meet various health policy goals or to correct market failure. For example, mandates can be used to make coverage available that insurance companies would not voluntarily offer because of concerns about adverse selection. Additionally, mandates can be used to increase utilization of effective medical services, thereby improving population health. Mandates can also be used to enforce principles of justice or fairness by requiring the risk of loss due to certain medical conditions be shared within an insured community.

Critics of mandates tend to focus on two distinct issues. The first is the restraint that mandates place on the ability of two willing parties to contract freely. The objection based on freedom to contract is a normative argument based on the position that individuals should have the right to choose which risks they want to insure against and which they do not, and that it is unfair to require individuals to purchase coverage they do not value or desire.

The second primary critique of mandated benefit laws is that they increase the cost of health insurance and therefore lead to fewer individuals being able to afford insurance. Essentially, the argument is that it is unjust to increase the cost of coverage by requiring coverage for a broad range of services when it results in some individuals being unable to afford and purchase basic insurance coverage. There is, however, no consensus regarding the price impact of mandates or the effect that any price increase has on coverage rates.

Finally, concerns have been expressed that mandates are not evidence-based and do not always reflect clinical best practices. Thirty-two states have authorized some type of benefit review procedure to be put in place, and 27 states have in place some "systematic approach" to evaluating financial impact (CHBRP, 2009). However, very few of these laws actually *require* prospective, expert analysis of evidence for a mandate before it can be voted on by the legislature. Even in states with robust review procedures, there is little evidence that the review procedure leads to evidenced-based mandates that significantly improve health outcomes. One recent study of the mandate processes in Connecticut and California concluded that "without a specific structure in place to provide legislators with appropriate data (e.g., on costs, medical effectiveness) very little evidence is provided to legislators. And even when there is a structure in place to ensure such data are available, those data appear to have only a modest impact on bill passage"; as a result, "even where there is an independent, expert commission providing robust data on proposed regulation, bills with virtually no impact on either health insurance coverage or treatment utilization are passed" (Monahan, 2012).

These concerns were echoed in comments the committee received, including numerous arguments that state mandates are not evidence-based, increase variability across states, and contribute to increasing insurance premiums (Bocchino, 2010; Darling, 2011; Malooley, 2011). Indeed, well-known examples among several mandates of questionable clinical value that have been passed prematurely include those requiring coverage for high dose chemotherapy and autologous bone marrow transplant for breast cancer and for hormone replacement therapy (Jacobson, 2008; Jacobson et al., 2007). Others were concerned that "benefit mandate choices [should be] kept outside the purview of elected officials" (Jones, 2010) and that, after passage, state mandates may crowd out the introduction of alternative services, while remaining "static" (Stoss, 2010). The consumer advocate group Health Access said that although it supports some mandates (such as mental health parity and coverage of prenatal care in the individual market), it does not regularly endorse benefit mandates because they are often related to specific drugs, devices, or tests and do not tend to evolve as treatments change (Wright, 2011). Others argued that HHS should view state mandates "as informed judgments of what is needed by populations" (Spielman, 2011).

Options Considered by the Committee

The committee was asked to consider what role, if any, existing state mandates should play in defining essential health benefits. The committee considered several different options, discussed below.

1. *Incorporate all existing state mandates into the definition of "essential health benefits" that apply to a particular state.*

One option considered by the committee was to recommend that in defining the EHB the Secretary should incorporate all state mandates that were in effect on March 23, 2010, in a particular state. The advantage of this approach is that it would preserve the coverage requirements that a state had in place prior to the passage of the ACA, without requiring the state to bear any increased cost that might otherwise result from mandating a benefit not included in the definition of essential health benefits. However, doing so may be seen as being contrary to the ACA's statutory language, which clearly contemplates requiring states to pay the increased premium cost that results from state mandates that exceed essential health benefit requirements. It would also result in drastically unequal definitions of essential health benefits among the states and would essentially require the federal government to subsidize state policy choices.

2. *Incorporate mandates that exist in a majority or supermajority of states into the definition of essential health benefits that applies in all states.*

Another option considered by the committee was to recommend that in defining the EHB, the Secretary include coverage for any treatments or services that are required to be covered by either a majority or a supermajority of the states. Doing so would allow for a uniform definition of essential health benefits, but would also subject minority states to the legislative actions of the majority states and would likely drive up the cost of coverage in states without many existing mandates. As above, the federal government would be forced to subsidize state policy decisions, although under this option only those decisions made by a majority of states. In addition, because very few states have legislative decision-making processes that reliably incorporate evidence, the committee was concerned that incorporating even supermajority mandates would undercut the overall approach to the EHB advocated by the committee, and as set forth in this report, by potentially including mandates that could not be justified under the committee's framework.

3. *Do not explicitly incorporate existing state mandates into the essential health benefits framework, but rather subject coverage for all types of treatments and services to the same framework, principles, criteria, and methods used to determine essential health benefits generally.*

Finally, the committee considered giving no special preference to existing state mandates, but rather requiring the potential coverage of any treatment or service to be governed by the same criteria, with none receiving special consideration by virtue of its status as a state mandate. This option would result in states' being required to pay the increased costs associated with any mandates that exceed the EHB requirements. While disadvantageous to states, the result is clearly contemplated by the statutory language of the ACA. This approach also has the significant advantage of allowing for consistency in all EHB coverage decisions and in providing federal uniformity. Given the lack of evidence that existing state mandates result from a sound evidence-based process, the committee concludes that this third option is the most desirable alternative.

Conclusion: Because state mandates are not typically subjected to a rigorous evidence-based review or cost analysis, cornerstones of the committee's criteria, the committee does not believe that state-mandated

benefits should receive any special treatment in the definition of the EHB and should be subject to the same evaluative method (see Recommendation 1 in Chapter 5). This interpretation is consistent with the language in the ACA regarding state mandates; that is, Congress did not require their inclusion.

MEDICAL VS. NONMEDICAL

At the committee's first meeting, the Assistant Secretary for Planning and Evaluation (ASPE) asked the committee to consider the corollary question of what distinguishes a medical service from a nonmedical service and how that distinction might apply in the context of defining what is essential. The propensity has been not to define what a medical service is specifically, but to say what is not covered because it is nonmedical (e.g., custodial care is not considered a medical service), is provided by a non–health care provider, or requires an assessment of whether a service is medically necessary. The committee explored various ways of defining: (1) by provider, (2) by specific services, and (3) by medical necessity determination.

Defining medical services as those delivered only by physicians, nurses, and physician assistants is more restrictive than most employer policies. A broader range of health services provided by other types of health professionals (e.g., physical therapy, speech therapy, occupational therapy) is often included in employer policies. Some plans both in the United States and elsewhere, however, limit the providers they include as covered—for example, requiring a supplementary policy be purchased to have access to physical therapy services rather than as part of a basic policy (British Columbia Ministry of Health, 2011). The inclusion of rehabilitation and habilitation in the 10 required categories suggests that such health professionals would provide "medical" services relevant to the EHB (Ford, 2011; Thomas, 2011). Acupuncturists and naturopaths are frequently excluded provider categories in standard insurance policies, on the basis that their practice falls into a "nonmedical" category, except in states where there is state-mandated coverage inclusion. The ACA prohibits insurers from discriminating on the basis of type of provider as long as the provider is operating within its scope of practice; however, this is a separate issue from defining specific types of services as being part of the EHB package.[24]

Insurers make distinctions about whether services or specific items are nonmedical and whether that alone is a sufficient reason for exclusion. For example, while interventions such as the teaching of Braille and American Sign Language can improve functioning and productivity in persons who are blind or hearing impaired, they have been classified as primarily educational and not part of health care delivery. Similarly, exercise-related services and items (e.g., exercycles, gym memberships, personal trainers) are beneficial to health, but insurers reach different conclusions about whether to support such services (e.g., certain Medicare Advantage plans support gym memberships, while Kaiser Permanente does not) (Empire Blue Cross Blue Shield, 2011; Levine, 2011). However, some educational services such as diabetes or asthma self-management training are covered services by insurers because they are directly related to a medical condition and improve clinical outcomes, plus they are time limited. The introduction of habilitation as a category for the EHB raises questions about where to draw the line between habilitation and social/educational services that is not easily resolvable.

Other presenters and online questionnaire respondents advocated for inclusion of the full spectrum of Early and Periodic Screening, Diagnosis, and Treatment (EPSDT) program services, such as the Medicaid optional service of primary care case management and any treatments needed to address conditions found as a result of the preventive services covered (Booth, 2011; Courselle, 2011; Jezek, 2010; KFF, 2005; Maves, 2010), or given the large turnover factor from Medicaid to the exchanges, for inclusion of other types of support services offered in federally qualified health centers to ensure patient access to care (some of these services are included by insurers as part of medical management, but others such as transportation may not be). For tax purposes, the Internal Revenue Service (IRS) takes a broad view of expenditures that could be included as allowable deductible medical expenses (Harmon, 2011; Pratt, 2004),[25] but this seems less applicable to the context of defining the EHB given that the IRS definition goes well beyond the kinds of expenses that are typically covered by any type of private health insurance plan.

---

[24] § 1201, amending § 2706(a) of the Public Health Service Act [42 U.S.C. 300gg–5].

[25] 26 U.S.C. § 213 defines the allowable deductible expenses under the tax code.

As one of its criteria for the EHB, the committee concludes that inclusions in the EHB be based on being a medical service, not serving primarily a social or educational function. Because the boundaries of what is medical and nonmedical are not always distinct, the committee acknowledges that the decision of what is medical and nonmedical will for the time being need to rest at the health plan level with oversight by state regulators and HHS to document what services are offered or excluded, particularly in the area of habilitation. Many insurers are engaging in innovative programs to improve care practices and the appropriateness of services for individuals, and these might include some components that might be considered nonmedical yet they better help patients achieve medical goals, often in a less costly way. Thus, they may serve other committee criteria to be cost-effective and to support innovation. In Chapter 5, the committee reviews components of medical necessity definitions.

Conclusion: As one of its criteria for the EHB, the committee concludes that included benefits should be a *medical* service or item, not serving primarily a social or educational function. This conclusion does not preclude coverage of some educational or support services with that and the other committee criteria in mind (e.g., supported by a sufficient evidence base of effectiveness and promoting a health gain to justify the cost). However, like other services and items to be included as an essential health benefit, such service must meet the test of Recommendation 1 (see Chapter 5).

The next chapter outlines a process for defining the initial EHB set that builds on the conclusions reached in this chapter.

REFERENCES

AHRQ (Agency for Healthcare Research and Quality). 2009a. *Table 1.F.1 (2009) percent of private sector employees enrolled in a health insurance plan that had a deductible by firm size and selected characteristics: United States, 2009.* http://meps.ahrq.gov/mepsweb/data_stats/ summ_tables/insr/national/series_1/2009/tif1.htm (accessed July 11, 2011).

_____. 2009b. *Table 1.F.2 (2009). Average individual deductible (in dollars) per employee enrolled with single coverage in a health insurance plan that had a deductible at private-sector establishment by firm size and selected characteristics: United States, 2009.* http://meps.ahrq. gov/mepsweb/data_stats/summ_tables/insr/national/series_1/2009/tif2.htm (accessed July 11, 2011).

_____. 2009c. *Table 1.F.3. Average family deductible (in dollars) per employee enrolled with family coverage in a health insurance plan that had a deductible at private-sector establishments by firm size and selected characteristics: United States, 2009.* http://meps.ahrq.gov/ mepsweb/data_stats/summ_tables/insr/national/series_1/2009/tif3.htm (accessed July 11, 2011).

The American Presidency Project. 2011. *376—statement on signing the Health Maintenance Organization Act of 1973: December 29, 1973.* http://www.presidency.ucsb.edu/ws/index.php?pid=4092#axzz1S653ScBM (accessed June 28, 2011).

Bellows, N. M., H. A. Halpin, and S. B. McMenamin. 2006. State-mandated benefit review laws. *Health Services Research* 41(3 Pt 2):1104-1123.

Bergthold, L. 1993. Benefit design choices under managed competition. *Health Affairs* 12:99-109.

_____. 2010. *What is an "essential benefit"?* http://healthaffairs.org/blog/2010/10/29/what-is-an-essential-benefit/ (accessed November 1, 2010).

BLS (Bureau of Labor Statistics). 2009. *Table 14. Medical care benefits: Coverage for selected services, private industry workers, National Compensation Survey, 2008. In National Compensation Survey: Health plan provisions in private industry in the United States, 2008.* Washington, DC: U.S. Bureau of Labor Statistics.

_____. 2011. *Table 1. Hospital room and board: Type of coverage, private industry workers, National Compensation Survey.* http://www.bls. gov/ncs/ebs/sp/selmedbensreport.pdf (accessed July 11, 2011).

Blumberg, L. J., and S. McMorrow. 2009. *What would health reform mean for small employers and their workers.* http://www.urban.org/url. cfm?ID=411997 (accessed July 6, 2011).

Bocchino, C. 2010. Online questionnaire responses submitted by Carmella Bocchino, Executive Vice President, America's Health Insurance Plans to the IOM Committee on the Determination of Essential Health Benefits, December 6.

Booth, M. 2011. Testimony to the IOM Committee on the Determination of Essential Health Benefits by Meg Booth, Deputy Director, Children's Dental Health Project, Washington, DC, January 14.

Bowen, D. 2011. Testimony to the IOM Committee on the Determination of Essential Health Benefits by David Bowen, Deputy Director for Global Health Policy and Advocacy, Gates Foundation, Washington, DC, January 13.

Branscome, J. M. 2008. *Statistical brief #207: Employer-sponsored single, employee-plus-one, and family health insurance coverage: Selection and cost, 2006.* http://www.meps.ahrq.gov/mepsweb/data_files/publications/st207/stat207.shtml (accessed July 7, 2011).

Branscome, J. M., and K. E. Davis. 2011. *Statistical brief #321: Employer-sponsored health insurance for small employers in the private sector, by industry classification, 2009.* http://www.meps.ahrq.gov/mepsweb/data_files/publications/st321/stat321.shtml (accessed July 6, 2011).

British Columbia Ministry of Health. 2011. *Medical and health care benefits.* http://www.health.gov.bc.ca/msp/infoben/benefits.html (accessed June 30, 2011).

Bunce, V. C., and J. P. Wieske. 2010. *Health insurance mandates in the states 2010.* http://www.cahi.org/cahi_contents/resources/pdf/MandatesintheStates2010.pdf (accessed May 4, 2011).

Calega, V. 2011. Comments to the IOM Committee on the Determination of Essential Health Benefits by Virginia Calega, Vice President, Medical Management and Policy, Highmark Blue Cross Blue Shield, Washington, DC, January 13.

Cauchi, R. 2011. *State health insurance mandates and the ACA* essential benefits provisions.* http://www.ncsl.org/default.aspx?tabid=14227 (accessed November 8, 2011).

CBO (Congressional Budget Office). 2009a. Letter to the Honorable Evan Bayh, U.S. Senate from Douglas W. Elmendorf, Director, Congressional Budget Office, November 30, 2009.

_____. 2009b. Letter to the Honorable Harry Reid, Senate Majority Leader from Douglas W. Elmendorf, Director, Congressional Budget Office, December 19, 2009.

CHBRP (California Health Benefits Review Program). 2009. *Appendix 22: Other states' health benefit review programs, 2009.* Oakland, CA: California Health Benefits Review Program.

Chernew, M., D. M. Cutler, and P. S. Keenan. 2005. Increasing health insurance costs and the decline in insurance coverage. *Health Services Research* 40(4):1021-1039.

Collins, S. R., K. Davis, J. L. Nicholson, and K. Stremikis. 2010. *Realizing health reform's potential: Small businesses and the Affordable Care Act of 2010.* New York, NY: The Commonwealth Fund.

Courselle, A. 2011. Online questionnaire responses submitted by Abigail Coursolle, Greenberg Traurig Equal Justice Works Staff Attorney, Western Center on Law & Poverty to the IOM Committee on the Determination of Essential Health Benefits, March 11.

Crimmel, B. L. 2010. *Statistical brief #285: Employer-sponsored single, employee-plus-one, and family health insurance coverage: Selection and cost, 2009.* http://www.meps.ahrq.gov/mepsweb/data_files/publications/st285/stat285.pdf (accessed November 8, 2011).

_____. 2011. *Statistical brief #325: Changes in premiums and employee contributions for employer-sponsored health insurance, Private industry, 2001-2009.* http://www.meps.ahrq.gov/mepsweb/data_files/publications/st325/stat325.shtml (accessed November 8, 2011).

Darling, H. 2011. *Recommendations on criteria and methods for defining and updating individual mandates and packages: Purchaser perspectives.* PowerPoint Presentation to the IOM Committee on the Determination of Essential Health Benefits by Helen Darling, President and CEO, National Business Group on Health, Washington, DC, January 13.

Davis, K., and J. M. Branscome. 2011. *Statistical brief #322: Employer-sponsored health insurance for large employers in the private sector, by industry classification, 2009.* http://www.meps.ahrq.gov/mepsweb/data_files/publications/st322/stat322.shtml (accessed July 6, 2011).

DMHC (California Department of Managed Health Care). 2011. *Independent state review processes.* PowerPoint Presentation to the IOM Committee on the Determination of Essential Health Benefits by Cindy Ehnes, Director, Maureen McKennan, Acting Deputy Director for Plan and Provider Relations, and Andrew George, Assistant Deputy Director, Help Center, Department of Managed Health Care, Costa Mesa, CA, March 2.

DOL (Department of Labor). 2011. *Selected medical benefits: A report from the Department of Labor to the Department of Health and Human Services.* http://www.bls.gov/ncs/ebs/sp/selmedbensreport.pdf (accessed June 13, 2011).

Eibner, C., F. Girosi, A. R. Miller, A. Cordova, E. A. McGlynn, N. M. Pace, C. C. Price, R. Vardavas, and C. R. Gresenz. 2011. *Employer self-insurance decisions and the implications of the Patient Protection and Affordable Care Act as modified by the Health Care and Education Reconciliation Act of 2010 (ACA).* Santa Monica, CA: RAND Corporation.

Emanuel, E. J., and V. R. Fuchs. 2008. Who really pays for health care? The myth of "shared responsibility." *Journal of the American Medical Association* 299(9):1057-1059.

Empire Blue Cross Blue Shield. 2011. *2010 services and programs for Medicare Advantage members.* http://www.empireblue.com/wps/portal/ehpmember?content_path=member/noapplication/f0/s0/t0/pw_b136007.htm&label=2010%20Services%20and%20Programs%20for%20Medicare%20Advantage%20Members&rootLevel=2&label=Member%20Services (accessed July 13, 2011).

Executive Office of the President Council of Economic Advisors. 2009. *The economic effects of health care reform on small businesses and their employees.* http://www.whitehouse.gov/assets/documents/CEA-smallbusiness-july24.pdf (accessed July 13, 2011).

Ford, M. 2011. Testimony to the IOM Committee on the Determination of Essential Health Benefits by Marty Ford, Director of Legal Advocacy, The Arc and United Cerebral Palsy Disability Policy Collaboration, Washington, DC, January 13.

Gabel, J., R. McDevitt, L. Gandolfo, J. Pickreign, S. Hawkins, and C. Fahlman. 2006. Generosity and adjusted premiums in job-based insurance: Hawaii is up, Wyoming is down. *Health Affairs* 25(3):832-843.

GAO (Government Accountability Office). 2003. *Private health insurance: Federal and state requirements affecting coverage offered by small businesses.* Washington, DC: U.S. Government Accountability Office.

Glied, S. 2011. Testimony to the IOM Committee on the Determination of Essential Health Benefits by Sherry Glied, Assistant Secretary for Planning and Evaluation, HHS, Washington, DC, January 13.

Harmon, G. 2011. Statement to the IOM Committee on the Determination of Essential Health Benefits by Gerald Harmon, Retired Major General U.S. Air Force and Member, Council on Medical Service, American Medical Association, Washington, DC, January 14.

Hayes, M. 2011. *Essential health benefits requirements under Section 1302.* PowerPoint Presentation to the IOM Committee on the Determination of Essential Health Benefit by Mark Hayes, Health & FDA Business Practice Group, Greenberg Traurig, Washington, DC, January 13.

Holve, E., M. Brodie, and L. Levitt. 2003. Small business executives and health insurance: Findings from a national survey of very small firms. *Managed Care Interface* 16(9):19-24.

Hyman, D. A. 2000. Regulating managed care: What's wrong with a patient bill of rights. *Southern California Law Review* 73(2):221-275.

Jacobson, P. D. 2008. Transforming clinical practice guidelines into legislative mandates. *JAMA: Journal of the American Medical Association* 299(2):208-210.

Jacobson, P. D., R. A. Rettig, W. M. Aubry. 2007. Litigating the science of breast cancer treatment. *Journal of Health Politics, Policy and Law* 32(5):785-818.

Jezek, A. 2010. Online questionnaire responses submitted by Amanda Jezek, Deputy Director, Federal Affairs, March of Dimes to the IOM Committee on the Determination of Essential Health Benefits, December 6.

Jones, D. 2010. Online questionnaire responses submitted by Daniel Jones, Director, Government Affairs, National Small Business Association to the IOM Committee on the Determination of Essential Health Benefits, December 6.

Kang, J. 2011. Statement by Jeffrey Kang, Chief Medical Officer, CIGNA to the IOM Committee on the Determination of Essential Health Benefits, Washington, DC, January 13.

KFF (Kaiser Family Foundation). 2005. *Medicaid: An overview of spending on "mandatory" vs. "optional" populations and services.* http://www.kff.org/medicaid/upload/Medicaid-An-Overview-of-Spending-on.pdf (accessed November 8, 2011).

_____. 2009. *Health insurance coverage in America, 2009.* http://facts.kff.org/chart.aspx?cb=60&sctn=174&ch=1914 (accessed November 8, 2011).

_____. 2011. *Establishing health insurance exchanges: An update on state efforts.* Washington, DC: Kaiser Family Foundation.

KFF and HRET (Health Research and Education Trust). 2005. *Employee Health Benefits 2005 Annual Survey.* Menlo Park, CA and Chicago, IL: Kaiser Family Foundation and Health Research and Education Trust.

_____. 2010a. *Employer Health Benefits 2010 Annual Survey.* Menlo Park, CA and Chicago, IL: Kaiser Family Foundation and Health Research and Education Trust.

_____. 2010b. *Survey of employer health benefits 2010.* http://ehbs.kff.org/pdf/2010/EHBS%202010%20Chartpack.pdf (accessed November 8, 2011).

_____. 2011. *Employer Health Benefits 2010 Annual Survey.* Menlo Park, CA and Chicago, IL: Kaiser Family Foundation and Health Research and Education Trust.

Laudicina, S. S., J. M. Gardner, and A. M. Crawford. 2010. *State legislative healthcare and insurance issues.* Washington, DC: BlueCross BlueShield Association.

Levine, S. 2011. PowerPoint Presentation to the IOM Committee on the Determination of Essential Health Benefits by Sharon Levine, Associate Executive Medical Director, The Permanente Medical Group, Costa Mesa, CA, March 2.

MacDonald, J. 2009. *Health plan differences: Fully-insured vs. self-insured. EBRI fast facts No. 114.* http://www.ebri.org/pdf/FFE114.11Feb09.Final.pdf (accessed July 12, 2011).

Malooley, J. 2011. *Purchaser decision-making on benefit design.* PowerPoint Presentation to the IOM Committee on the Determination of Essential Health Benefits by Jerry Malooley, Director, Benefit Programs Health Policy, State of Indiana, Personnel Department, and Member, U.S. Chamber of Commerce, Washington, DC, January 13.

Maves, M. 2010. Online questionnaire responses submitted by Michael Maves, Chief Executive Officer and Executive Vice President, American Medical Association to the IOM Committee on the Determination of Essential Health Benefits, December 20.

McGraw Wentworth. 2011. *Reform update.* http://www.mcgrawwentworth.com/Reform_Update/2011/Reform_Update_23.pdf (accessed September 23, 2011).

Mercer. 2009. *National survey of employer-sponsored health plans.* New York: Mercer, Inc.

_____. 2011. *Health care reform: The question of essential benefits.* http://www.mercer.com/press-releases/1416845 (accessed June 29, 2011).

MHCC (Maryland Health Care Commission). 2007. *Options available to reform the Comprehensive Standard Health Benefit Plan (CSHBP) as required under HB 579 (2007).* Baltimore, MD: Maryland Health Care Commission.

_____. 2011. *Maryland's comprehensive standard benefit plan for small businesses.* http://mhcc.maryland.gov/smallgroup/cshbp_brochure.htm (accessed November 7, 2011).

Miller, E. A. 2011. Affordability of health insurance to small business: Implications of the Patient Protection and Affordable Care Act. *Journal of Health Politics Policy and Law* 36(3):539-546.

Monahan, A. 2007. Federalism, federal regulation, or free market? An examination of mandated health benefit reform. *University of Illinois Law Review* 2007(5):1361-1416.

_____. 2012. Fairness versus welfare in health insurance content regulation. *University of Illinois Law Review,* 2012(1).

NWLC (National Women's Law Center). 2008. *Nowhere to turn: How the individual health insurance market fails women.* Washington, DC: National Women's Law Center.

Oregon Health Services Commission. 2011. *Prioritized list of health services: April 1, 2011.* http://www.oregon.gov/OHA/OHPR/HSC/docs/L/Apr11List. pdf (accessed May 10, 2011).

Pratt, K. 2004. Inconceivable? Deducting the costs of fertility treatment. *Cornell Law Review* 89(5):1121-1200.

Salo, M. 2011. Comments to the IOM Committee on the Determination of Essential Health Benefits by Matthew Salo, Director, Health & Human Services Committee, National Governor's Association, Washington, DC, January 13.

Sammis, B. 2011. *Maryland: Development of Comprehensive Standard Health Benefit Plan.* PowerPoint Presentation to the IOM Committee on the Determination of Essential Health Benefits by Beth Sammis, Acting Insurance Commissioner, Maryland Insurance Administration, Washington, DC, January 13.

Schwartz, D. 2011. Testimony to the IOM Committee on the Determination of Essential Health Benefits by David Schwartz, Senate Finance Committee Democratic Staff, U.S. Senate, Washiangton, DC, January 13.

Spangler, K. 2011. Testimony to the IOM Committee on the Determination of Essential Health Benefits by Katy Spangler, Senior Health Policy Advisor, Senate Health, Education, Labor, and Pensions (HELP) Committee, U.S. Senate, Washington, DC, January 13.

Spielman, S. 2011. *Autism and the determination of essential health benefits.* Powerpoint Presentation to the IOM Committee on the Determination of Essential Health Benefits by Stuart Spielman, Senior Policy Advisor and Counsel, Autism Speaks, Washington, DC, January 14.

Stoss, J. 2010. Online questionnaire responses submitted by Julie Stoss, Vice President, Government Relations, Kaiser Permanente to the IOM Committee on the Determination of Essential Health Benefits, December 6.

Thomas, P. W. 2011. Testimony to the IOM Committee on the Determination of Essential Health Benefits by Peter W. Thomas, Co-Chair Health Taskforce, Consortium for Citizens for Disabilities, Washington, DC, January 13.

Turpin, M. 2011. *Building affordable and sustainable essential benefits.* PowerPoint Presentation to the IOM Committee on the Determination of Essential Health Benefits by Michael Turpin, Executive Vice President and National Health and Benefits Practice Leader, USI Insurance Services, Washington, DC, January 13.

U.S. Census Bureau. 2008. *Statistics about business size (including small business) from the U. S. Census Bureau.* http://www.census.gov/econ/smallbus.html (accessed July 6, 2011).

Wicks, E. K. 2002. *Assessment of the performance of small-group health insurance market reforms in Maryland.* Washington, DC: Health Management Associates.

Wright, A. 2011. Testimony to the IOM Committee on the Determination of Essential Health Benefits by Anthony Wright, Executive Director, Health Access California, Costa Mesa, CA, March 2.

5

Defining the EHB

The Secretary is charged to define the essential health benefits (EHB) and asked the Institute of Medicine (IOM) for advice on a process for this task. The committee outlines steps and criteria to achieve the initial EHB set: first, building from the statutory requirements of a typical employer plan (with the committee recommending that small employer be used to define what is typical) and 10 categories of care; next, applying the committee's recommended criteria to assess the package as a whole and for individual components (Figure S-2 in the Summary); and then, adjusting the content so that it could be accommodated under the expected national average premium for a silver plan for a small employer in 2014. The final adjustments should be informed by a public deliberative process that advises on preferences in making tradeoffs. The committee's advice for the Secretary's guidance to insurers and the exchanges on the content of the EHB is to give the greatest degree of specificity that current national data and best practices in subscriber (enrollee) contracts allow. Additionally, the committee offers suggestions for secretarial guidance with respect to the required elements for consideration and medical necessity.

Before insurance products that are required to incorporate the essential health benefits (EHB) can be developed, the Secretary of the Department of Health and Human Services (HHS) must define which benefits constitute the EHB package. The Patient Protection and Affordable Care Act (ACA) directs that the scope of this package should reflect benefits offered in typical employer plans and the 10 broad categories of care listed in Section 1302 of the act. In the previous chapter, the committee reached several conclusions related to the legislative language:

- The scope of a typical employer plan should be based on what is typically offered by small employers.
- Because the specificity of national data on covered benefits in the small employer market is limited, scope should also be interpreted to mean equal financial value to a typical small employer premium.
- Every service or item that might be classified within the 10 categories or the typical employer plan is not essential.
- To ensure a more consistent national benefit package, initial secretarial guidance should include as much specificity as can be developed from current best practices in plan documentation because the EHB will be implemented in policies and programs across multiple jurisdictions each with its own state-based oversight body.

These conclusions and the committee's previously listed criteria frame the process, outlined in this chapter, by which this IOM committee recommends that the Secretary define the EHB. The process starts with the content and structure of the typical small employer plan and then broadens the coverage to incorporate ACA-required categories that are not usually found in those packages (Box 5-1). Because the package must be affordable to individual purchasers, employees of small firms, and public funders, the committee recommends balancing the comprehensiveness of the package offered against its potential cost and explores several options for incorporating costs into the EHB definition before recommending a specific approach. Additionally, the committee comments on the issue of secretarial guidance regarding the specificity of the EHB package, "required elements for consideration" as stipulated by Section 1302(b)(4)(A) through (E), and definitions of medical necessity.

STEP 1: DEVELOP THE STARTING POINT

Typical Small Employer Policy

The ACA calls for the scope of benefits to reflect those typical of employers today; the committee recommends that the small employer market define what is typical at the outset. The level of specificity in benefit definition varies across insurance plan documents, often making it difficult to assess if a benefit is covered or simply not listed in a plan document. Given the paucity of data to determine typical benefits, the Secretary will likely have to be guided by the contents of plans that provide more detailed coverage information. To make concrete the level of coverage that characterizes current contracts covering millions of employees working for small firms, the committee collected information provided from three major insurers to illustrate which covered benefit inclusions are national in scope and which are covered only in some states because of market conditions and state mandates (Appendix C). The committee was not able to assess whether these are "typical" of the entire small group market, but this plan coverage detail provides a starting point for developing a list of EHB content that can be refined by both additions and deletions during the following steps.

BOX 5-1
Steps in Recommended Process for Defining
an Essential Health Benefits (EHB) Package

1. Develop the Starting Point for the EHB
   a. Start with a typical small employer plan based on available knowledge
   b. Develop preliminary service list (with inclusions and exclusions) to fulfill 10 categories
   c. Apply the committee-developed criteria and adjust the preliminary list as necessary

2. Incorporate Cost into the Development of the Initial EHB
   a. Assess the cost of the package developed in the first step
   b. Develop a target budget for the EHB (e.g., national premium target based on typical small employer plan)

3. Reconcile Preliminary List to the Premium Target
   a. Publicly identify actuarial expenditures for components for possible tradeoffs
   b. Receive guidance on priorities from public deliberation processes and other public participatory processes
   c. Review final list by reapplying IOM committee criteria to evaluate the aggregate package

4. Issue Guidance on Inclusions and Permissible Exclusions

Meeting the 10-Category Requirement

The committee noted that the typical employer plan in either the small or large group market does not include all of the 10 categories of care specified in the ACA; therefore, the Secretary must next identify the gaps. In its review, the committee found that some areas—habilitation, mental health and substance use disorder services, some wellness services and chronic disease management, and pediatric oral and vision care—appear less likely to be covered in *standard* commercial subscriber contracts. Pediatric oral and vision care have been available as policy riders, and the contents of those policies can be examined. Habilitation and much of mental health, substance abuse, and behavioral services have largely been left to the public sector. The committee is guided by the unambiguous direction of Section 1302 to start with a commercial health insurance benefit; however, it suggests that the Secretary compare, in particular, how Medicaid plan benefits for habilitation and mental health and substance abuse services compare with commercial plans that currently include such services. For example, Maryland has requirements to cover habilitative services in children under the age of 19 in its Comprehensive Standard Benefit Plan for Small Businesses although the small business products are not subject to all state-mandated benefits (Maryland Insurance Administration, 2009; MHCC, 2011). On the basis of this review, the Secretary would add selected services to the preliminary list to fulfill the 10-category requirement.

Consistency between the exchange-defined benefits and traditional Medicaid program benefits would reduce the benefit gaps experienced by the large number of people who move between the two types of insurance (Sommers and Rosenbaum, 2011). The testimony received by the committee was mixed as to whether such consistency should occur by making exchange benefits look like Medicaid or by changing Medicaid to look like the new exchange policies. The EHB requirement, however, only applies to the Medicaid expansion benchmark and benchmark-equivalent programs, which are designed to more closely resemble private sector plans, not traditional Medicaid.

The committee did not recommend specific service expansions beyond the 10 categories required by the ACA because these, together with the requirement for the scope of services of typical employers, were seen as sufficiently broad and adding categories beyond these, although not precluded, might prove difficult under the committee process that requires consideration of the overall cost of the package.

Applying Committee Criteria

The committee expects that at this point in the process the Secretary will have a long and varied list of potential categories and specific services for inclusion. The description will in all likelihood be a mix of services, conditions, and treatments that range in level of specificity. This heterogeneity reflects current practice, but the committee recommends that the definitions of covered services become more specific over time, as HHS monitors implementation (Chapter 7) and updates the EHB (Chapter 9).

The committee recommends a set of criteria for evaluating both the specific elements for inclusion and the overall package, as well as criteria to guide the process by which the overall package and its elements are defined (see Figure S-2 in the Summary). Specifically, in considering whether particular categories or services are included, the committee recommends evaluating each to determine whether it is safe, effective, likely to enhance patient outcomes when compared with available alternatives, and that the cost is justified by the health gain. Included elements should perform acceptably on all of these criteria. The committee also recommends evaluating the overall set of benefits to determine whether the package is affordable, likely to maximize the number of people with insurance, able to protect the most vulnerable, likely to encourage best practices, consistent with the principle of advancing stewardship of finite resources, likely to protect people against the greatest financial risks, and addresses the medical concerns of greatest importance for the eligible populations.

To accomplish the initial evaluation in the timeframe required for implementation, the committee recognizes that a formal value-based analysis cannot be conducted for each possible service in each benefit category. However, resources are available that can help the Secretary in assessing the relative merits of potential categories or services. Some of these have been used by states in building benefit structures for existing public insurance programs, by insurance companies in developing clinical policies, and in the research literature. For example, in Chapter 2, the committee reviews how the state of Washington applies graded evidence to its decisions on service inclusions for insurance benefits in its public programs (e.g., insurance coverage for state employees) (CMS, 2010; Thompson,

2011). Value-based insurance design and the Oregon prioritized list, as now being adapted for the commercial sector, provide other examples of how the relative values of different services have been evaluated (Kapowich, 2010; Oregon Health Services Commission, 2011; Saha et al., 2010; Smith and Saha, 2011). Using existing assessments, where available, will facilitate the evaluation of categories and services for initial prioritization for inclusion in or exclusion from the EHB package based on available evidence.

STEP 2: INCORPORATE COST INTO THE DEVELOPMENT OF THE INITIAL EHB

Early in its deliberations, the committee concluded that the costs associated with offering the EHB would materially affect the likelihood that the ACA would achieve its goal of significantly reducing the number of people without health insurance. The committee, therefore, incorporates into its recommended process, consideration of overall costs to frame choices about what would ultimately be included in the EHB package. This section examines the committee's rationale for including cost as a criterion and the various approaches considered before arriving at its recommended approach.

Rationale for Incorporating Costs into the Definition of Essential Health Benefits

The committee had a series of robust conversations about whether to incorporate cost considerations into the definition of essential health benefits and ultimately decided that costs were a critical component of the definition for five reasons.

First, and most importantly, cost provides a useful mechanism to help frame tradeoffs between competing options for inclusion in a benefit package. In fact, the law makes clear that the essential health benefits should reflect the scope of a typical employer plan, and typical employers commonly use premiums as a key element in deciding on the benefit package they will offer employees. For employers, establishing a budget creates one way to explicitly consider benefit package tradeoffs when resources are limited.

Second, in examining the legislative history of the ACA and in testimony received from congressional staff involved in the development of the law, it is clear that improving access to care by expanding the number of people with health insurance was the primary goal of the legislation. Because one important determinant of the number of people who have health insurance is the cost of obtaining coverage (Abraham and Feldman, 2010), the price of the EHB package will influence the ability to achieve the law's goal.

Third, the committee observed that the cost estimates developed by the Congressional Budget Office (CBO) for the ACA were a key element in its ultimate passage. Those cost projections incorporated an estimate of the average premium price of health insurance to be purchased on the exchanges, which in turn affected the total cost of the subsidy and the cost of the federal portion of Medicaid.

Fourth, the committee reflected on the current concern around the deficit and the impact of existing open-ended entitlements, such as Medicare, on the manageability of the federal budget. From a pragmatic viewpoint, requiring a benefit package that was more expensive than typical packages was not regarded by the committee as consistent with today's fiscal realities.

Fifth, the idea of having an explicit budget has been recognized as both an ethical and practical precondition for expanding access to care in medicine (Levine et al., 2007). The committee recommends three cost-related criteria—affordability of insurance, stewardship of resources and maximizing access to care—for the Secretary to use to assess the overall EHB package.

For all of these reasons, the committee concluded that the Secretary must use cost to provide guidance in developing the essential health benefits package.

Sources and Approaches to Setting the Initial Cost Target

The committee examined different sources and approaches that the Secretary might use in setting the initial cost target, including (1) CBO's estimate of premium prices that was used in evaluating the overall cost of the legislation; (2) an analysis done by the RAND Corporation for the Department of Labor (DOL) that evaluated the effect of design choices in the exchanges on premiums in the individual and small group markets; and (3) a competitive bidding process such as is currently used for Part D in Medicare. These are discussed below to illustrate how the Secretary can incorporate costs into the definition of the EHB.

Fixed Target Approach Based on CBO Estimates for the ACA

The CBO, in a letter to Senator Bayh on November 30, 2009, noted that premiums are set to cover the average amount the insurer expects to pay for services that are eligible for coverage under a plan, plus an amount for administrative expenses, overhead, and profit (CBO, 2009). The costs for covered services reflect the following:

- The scope of covered benefits (the essential health benefits)
- Cost-sharing requirements (deductibles, co-payments)
- The health status of the covered population and the propensity of that population to use health services
- Provider payment rates
- Degree of medical management

These factors interact with one another. For example, research has demonstrated that cost sharing can affect the propensity of people to use services (Newhouse et al., 1981; Rosenthal et al., 2009; Rowe et al., 2008). Provider payment rates may affect both the mix and volume of services offered (Buntin et al., 2009).

The CBO then considered the effect of the proposed legislation on changes to premiums in the small group market and identified differences in three major areas: (1) the amount (e.g., comprehensiveness of benefits, level of cost sharing) of insurance purchased due to changes in the scope of benefits; (2) the price for a specific amount of coverage for a particular group of enrollees; and (3) the characteristics of people obtaining coverage. Table 5-1 shows the CBO-estimated effect on premiums, compared to projected premiums without the law, in the small group market from each of these factors before accounting for subsidies or small business tax credits. The committee noted that the average aggregate effect on premiums in the small group market was small.

Although the committee selects the small group market as the basis for establishing the essential health benefits, it is worth noting that the EHB definition will also apply to policies in the individual market. Based on its microsimulation model, the CBO also estimated the effects of the law on premiums for individual policies, as shown in Table 5-2. The expanded scope of benefits in the individual market, coupled with reduced patient cost sharing, is the main factor contributing to higher premiums in that market under the new law compared to projections of premiums that would have prevailed had the law not been enacted. The committee noted that the effect on premiums in the individual market is much larger than for the small group market.

For illustrative purposes, the committee converted the CBO estimates, which were presented in 2016 dollars, to 2014 dollars because that is the year the EHB policy will take effect. The resulting premiums, compared to premiums if the law had not passed, show little to no change in the small group market but an increase in the individual market premiums (Table 5-3).

TABLE 5-1 Congressional Budget Office (CBO) Estimates of the Effect of the Law on Premiums in the Small Group Market, in November 2009 Letter to Senator Bayh

Component Affecting Premiums	Expected Difference Between Premiums in Small Group Market After the Law Compared to Premiums Projected Without the Law
Difference in amount of coverage[a]	0 to +3%
Difference in price paid for a given amount of insurance coverage[b]	−1 to −4%
Differences in characteristics of insured	−1 to +2%
Total (before subsidies)	−2 to +1%

[a] This includes both the expanded scope of benefits and lower cost sharing.
[b] This takes into account both lower administrative costs and higher fees.
SOURCE: CBO, 2009.

TABLE 5-2 Congressional Budget Office (CBO) Estimates of the Effect of the Law on Premiums in the Individual Market, in November 2009 Letter to Senator Bayh

Component Affecting Premiums	Expected Difference Between Premiums in Non-group Market After the Law Compared to Premiums Projected Without the Law
Difference in amount of coverage[a]	+27 to +30%
Difference in price paid for a given amount of insurance coverage[b]	−7 to −10%
Differences in characteristics of insured	−7 to −10%
Total (before subsidies)	+10 to +13%

[a] This includes both the expanded scope of benefits and lower cost sharing.
[b] This takes into account both lower administrative costs and higher fees.
SOURCE: CBO, 2009.

TABLE 5-3 Congressional Budget Office (CBO) Estimated Premiums for Individual and Family Policies in Exchange Markets, in Letter to Senator Bayh, Converted to 2014 Dollars

Type of Policy	Premiums in the Absence of the ACA (2014 $)	Premiums After Implementation of the ACA (2014 $)
Small Group Market		
Individual	6,933	6,933
Family	17,156	17,067
Individual Market		
Individual	4,889	5,156
Family	11,645	13,511

NOTE: ACA = Patient Protection and Affordable Care Act.

Fixed Target Approach Based on RAND Estimates in Department of Labor Study

RAND conducted a study for the Department of Labor examining, among other issues, how some of the design features of the exchanges might affect coverage, health care spending, and choice of insurance (Eibner et al., 2010). The RAND study, which utilized microsimulation modeling, also took a more detailed approach to defining and projecting the behavior of the small group market than had previously been undertaken by any research group. Table 5-4 shows the premiums used in the RAND analysis (which generates premiums within the model rather than using an externally selected price).[1] Unlike the CBO analysis, which used a single national average premium, the RAND analysis provides premiums by precious metal tier,[2] which demonstrates the effect of the cost-sharing element on the premium. The committee also converted the RAND estimates from 2010 dollars to 2014 dollars because that is the year the EHB policy will take effect.

In designing their exchanges, states have the option to either keep the individual and small group markets in separate risk pools or combine them into a single risk pool. Table 5-5 shows the difference in premiums if the risk pools are separated.[3] Because people who are enrolled in the exchanges as individuals tend to be less healthy than those who are enrolled through an employer, the premiums for the individually enrolled population are about 40 percent higher. RAND found that if the risk pools were combined, fewer small employers would offer coverage and many of those who would have otherwise been covered through employer-sponsored insurance (ESI) would choose to enroll in Medicaid.

This analysis suggests that the Secretary may have to take into account some of the design choices being made by states in incorporating costs into the determination of essential health benefits. It also suggests that an estimated

---

[1] This enables an explicit accounting for health status and change in utilization as a result of newly acquiring insurance.

[2] ACA Section 1302(d)(1)(A)-(D) describes four "precious" metal tiers of actuarial value (AV): bronze, silver, gold, and platinum; see Chapter 2 for further description of actuarial value and the metal tiers. The EHB are required in each metal tier.

[3] Regardless of risk pool, each metal level contains the EHB.

TABLE 5-4 Premiums for Single Coverage in the Exchange Market in the Absence of the Patient Protection and Affordable Care Act (ACA) Compared with After Implementation of the ACA (in 2014 dollars)[a]

Market	Premiums in the Absence of the ACA (2014 $)	Premiums Projected After Implementation of the ACA (2014 $)
Employer-sponsored insurance[b]	7,022	6,902
Exchange bronze	N/A	4,600
Exchange silver[c]	N/A	5,474
Exchange gold	N/A	6,831
Exchange platinum	N/A	7,323
Non-group (individual market)	7,426	N/A

[a] Assumes combined individual and small group market risk pools, employers with fewer than 100 full-time equivalent employees able to enroll, 12 percent administrative load.
[b] Includes both small and large group markets.
[c] Subsidy connected to premium of this plan.

TABLE 5-5 Individual and Small Group Premiums in Exchange Markets When Risk Pools Are Split or Combined (in 2014 dollars)

	Split Risk Pools (2014 $)		Combined Risk Pool (2014 $)
	Individual	Small Group	
Bronze	5,379	3,855	4,600
Silver	6,401	4,588	5,474
Gold	7,462	5,348	6,381
Platinum	8,561	6,138	7,323

national average premium price for a particular metal level, such as the silver plan, would be reasonable because this is the premium price that is used to determine the amount of subsidy for which an individual is eligible.

Competitive Bidding Approach

Rather than the fixed-target approaches described above, the committee also considered a competitive bidding approach similar to that being used for Medicare Part D (prescription drug coverage). Under Medicare Part D, the broad elements of the basic benefit package design are established (e.g., the amount of the deductible, the cost-sharing portion, the level at which catastrophic coverage begins). Plans may offer alternative coverage structures as long as the alternative is actuarially equivalent to the standard plan. Plans may also offer coverage that goes beyond the basic benefit package, but such supplemental coverage is not subsidized by Medicare.

The Centers for Medicare & Medicaid Services (CMS) obtains bids annually from plans wishing to offer coverage in this program. The bids are based on covering a standard Medicare population. CMS calculates a national average premium based on the bids received. Enrollees pay a base premium plus any difference between the bid of the plan they enroll in and the national average. Those electing more expensive plans pay higher-than-average premiums, while those electing less expensive plans pay lower-than-average premiums.

A competitive approach in the context of the exchanges would have to be administered at the state level, and the committee believes that considerable variability exists in the ability of states to execute this function. On the one hand, states are already responsible for reviewing many aspects of plan operations, so this requirement would increase the burden on states that do not have an adequate infrastructure in place to review bids. On the other hand, many states are already involved with competitive bidding in Medicaid managed care programs and Medicaid pharmacy programs, so the existing infrastructure may be available for this option. Given the considerable pressure on state budgets, variability in the states' infrastructure necessary to support reviews of competitive bids, and the relatively tight timeframe for implementation of the EHB, the committee concluded that this approach was likely not feasible in all states and thus was not an approach the committee recommends to the Secretary.

How Costs Could Be Incorporated into Determining the Essential Health Benefits Package

The committee considered how the Secretary might use the sources of data above to set the initial essential health benefits package within a target cost. Table 5-6 illustrates the steps in the process.

Conceptually as envisioned by the committee, the Secretary would start with a figure like the aggregate CBO estimate for the small group market ($6,933 for an individual policy) or the RAND estimate for a silver plan ($5,474 for an exchange policy in which the risk pools are combined). Because these base estimates were arrived at before the ACA was finalized,[4] the CMS Chief Actuary would need to update the "starting amount" for 2014 taking into account the provisions of the ACA that have already taken effect. Because neither the RAND nor the CBO analyses considered in any detail the potential effect of the required 10 categories of coverage on the premiums for those policies, the Secretary would also need to obtain estimates of the incremental costs of expanding the scope of benefits for a typical small group plan from the CMS Chief Actuary. The committee discussed this approach with an actuarial expert and determined that it was a feasible approach.[5] Then, the Secretary could obtain estimates from the CMS Chief Actuary on the incremental costs of all other potentially included elements. The Secretary will also have to make some assumptions about the degree to which benefit design, on average, is currently operationalized as a mechanism in controlling premium costs; those assumptions should be made public. The premium target is created as a mechanism for bounding decisions about what will be included in the EHB. It establishes a nationwide budget mechanism for the Secretary to work within when defining the EHB package.

The alternative approach, rejected by the committee, would have been to define the EHB without considering the cost of the resulting package. The committee does not intend for the premium target to be used to specify the premiums that can be established by qualified health plans. In fact, the committee does not believe that the Secretary has the authority to specify a premium for any plan. The premiums set by plans in the market that offer the EHB will vary as they do today. The distribution of resulting premium prices in different locales will reflect the other elements that determine the cost of health insurance: health status of enrollees, propensity to use services, provider payment rates, network design, and medical management. However, the committee's guidance to the Secretary is to establish the initial package of essential health benefits that are actuarially equivalent to a national average

TABLE 5-6 Sample Approach to Incorporating Costs into the Definition of Essential Health Benefits

Process	Result from Step	Updated Result
Starting amount from fixed target sources estimated to reflect a silver plan	$5,474-$6,933	$5,474-$6,933
Change due to expanding scope of benefits to any of the required 10 categories not included in small employer plans today	+$168	$5,642-$7,101
Obtain actuarial estimates of the incremental cost of each proposed additional element in the scope of benefits	Dollar amounts by individual areas of coverage	Components of overall premium price provided as an actuarial "price list"
Conduct public deliberative process to set priorities	Package selected to fall within budgeted range	Final description of the scope of essential health benefits eligible for coverage
Final result: benefit package with a estimated national average premium		$5,474-$6,933

---

[4] Note: The modeling by the CBO and RAND does not typically discriminate the inclusion or exclusion of specific small service categories; deductibles and co-payments are the main drivers of the premium prices observed and/or generated in these models.

[5] For example, these estimates could be expressed either as a percentage of current premiums or as a dollar amount per member per month. Overall, the expert estimated for illustrative purposes that under one assumption about expanded scope, premiums might increase by approximately $130 per member per year in 2014 dollars. Removing limits that exist today (lifetime and annual dollar amounts) might increase premiums by $40 per member per year in 2014 dollars. Similar estimates could be obtained by the Secretary from an actuarial consultant.

premium estimate. Each exchange will then set the mechanisms by which it evaluates whether qualified plans are offering the EHB and whether the premiums proposed by the plans within a particular state are reasonable.

STEP 3: RECONCILE INITIAL LIST TO THE PREMIUM TARGET

The central debate in constructing the EHB package has been balancing the comprehensiveness of benefits with their costs so as to promote value. This is not an academic exercise but one that has real repercussions for how many people will be able to afford the premium—because the essential health benefits apply to individual and small group policies both inside and outside the exchanges. Furthermore, it will have an impact on state and federal budgets through subsidies and whether people are able to obtain commercial insurance or need to remain fully on public programs. The committee envisions that the Secretary will be able to calculate the estimated national average premium, as well as obtain the actuarial estimates for the categories and services that comprise the list of potential benefits. These may then be compared to reconcile the list to ensure that the incremental cost of all of the proposed benefits will fit within the premium target.

From an ethical standpoint, if constraints are real and must be acknowledged, this should occur in as fair and just a fashion as possible per the committee's criteria on methods (see Figure S-2 in the Summary). In evaluating the individual components of the EHB and the overall package, the committee encourages the Secretary to engage in public processes that are transparent, participatory, equitable and consistent, sensitive to value, responsive to new information, attentive to stewardship, encouraging of innovation, and data-driven.

The use of a public deliberative process for setting priorities, as described in Chapter 6, provides an effective method for meeting many of these requirements. Thus, the committee recommends, in this stage of the process, that structured, public deliberation sessions be conducted to set priorities within the concept of a budgetary constraint. Actuarial estimates of different components of benefits and choices in benefit design should be publicly available for consideration in the context of public processes. Recognizing the time limitations for development of implementation guidance to the states and insurers, the committee envisions that a total of 10-15 of these small group meetings could be conducted in different areas of the country by a nongovernmental organization funded by HHS or through philanthropic means. Although the results of this process are advisory only, they must be well structured to permit full dialogue and consideration of possible tradeoffs. These deliberations differ from simply receiving comments through stakeholder meetings, in which individuals or groups promote particular benefits. The deliberations will also serve an important public education function, allowing the public to see the cost tradeoffs among benefits as well as the impact of different co-insurance and co-payment structures. A national public deliberation effort, even with a limited number of participants, can serve as a model for states that wish to replicate the process. The Secretary should additionally seek public comment through the publication of a notice of proposed options for inclusion in the EHB and actuarial estimates associated with those options simultaneously with the public deliberation exercise. The availability of actuarial information will enrich the content of public input through both mechanisms.

Although the committee believes there should be sufficient time to conduct these public deliberations before finalizing an EHB package by May 2012, the committee is also aware that time pressures may preclude the design and execution of a credible process prior to HHS issuing initial EHB details. If so, then the Secretary should arrange for the national public deliberation process to be conducted within the first year following the release of the initial EHB design.

The Secretary is ultimately responsible for the final definition of the EHB. Before finalizing the list, the Secretary should reassess how well it conforms to the committee's criteria for the contents of the aggregate package (see Figure S-2). The Secretary should publicly identify the rationale behind choices in the final package of EHB that emerges for plans in 2014.

STEP 4: ISSUE GUIDANCE ON INCLUSIONS AND PERMISSIBLE EXCLUSIONS

Once the final EHB package has been determined, the Secretary must communicate these decisions in the form of guidance and/or regulation. Again, the committee recommends a pragmatic approach, acknowledging the reality of mixed methodologies that currently exist in coverage descriptions and working to improve them over time. Ideally, a description of a benefits package should provide clear and consistent guidance to consumers, providers, and insurers, resulting in fair, consistent, and easily understood coverage decisions. As discussed in Chapters 4 and 9, the reality falls well short of this ideal. The committee notes that when guidance lacks specificity, considerable variation will result. The committee urges the Secretary to be as specific as best practices, data, and time allow.

Defining Inclusions and Permissible Exclusions

Consistent with the structure of employer policies, guidance from the Secretary on the EHB must contain explicit direction about categories and services that must be included and those that it is "permissible to exclude." The categories and services included in the EHB are the only ones that count toward limits on deductibles and co-payments and the only ones to which annual and lifetime dollar limits can be applied. In the absence of specific secretarial guidance on coverage, the resulting packages offered in exchanges will likely vary considerably with respect to what is considered an essential benefit. In contrast, benefit design considerations (e.g., provider network arrangements, medical management, deductibles) will vary and are expected to under the ACA's metal levels. Although insurers may offer additional benefits in their packages and states may mandate additional benefits, those are not subject to all of the ACA limitations.

The HHS guidance on inclusions and permissible exclusions should be designed to achieve consistent benefit interpretations by qualified health plans, exchange authorities, state-based regulators, medical care providers, and patients. In anticipation of the EHB definitions being issued by the Secretary, various insurers today are coming to different conclusions about what might be excluded as nonessential (Anthem, 2011; UnitedHealthcare, 2011). Plan documents vary in how insurers address exclusions as well as listed inclusions. For example, exclusions might be defined as specific services (e.g., a plan does not cover cosmetic surgery, bariatric surgery, infertility services, or orthodontic care for temporomandibular joint syndrome) or more generally stated (e.g., no coverage for services, drugs, or supplies that are not medically necessary; no coverage for services, drugs, or supplies not required according to accepted standards of medical, dental, or psychiatric practice in the United States; no coverage for services not specifically listed as covered).[6] Appendix E presents exclusions in the small group market for one insurer; Appendix F lists exclusions from a broader spectrum of plans.

At the outset, the committee does not expect that the Secretary's list will delineate every service that is covered, because this would require annotation with the medical condition and perhaps circumstances in which it would be appropriate for use (i.e., deemed medically necessary). However, the Secretary will need to identify permissible exclusions. Exchanges need to know if it is permissible to exclude certain services when qualifying a health plan. Guidance should provide the most comprehensive description possible that makes such variables clear and permits reasonable judgments (both substantive and actuarial) of what is covered. As noted previously, even if a service is listed as permissible to exclude from the minimum set of benefits that constitute the EHB and the related EHB limits, an insurer could offer the benefit in one of an array of plans they develop for the market.

The state exchanges and state regulators have an important role in monitoring submitted plan documents to ensure that they do not contain outlier practices that would undermine the intent of EHB coverage; although external appeals data and patient satisfaction surveys will provide important after-the-fact detail, this initial review and comparison of plans seeking to become qualified is critical and knowledge of what has been typical in the state should inform what detail is missing from the national list for most categories of care.

In Chapter 7, the committee discusses the degree of ambiguity in classifying different services and whether certain services are part of the 10 categories or fall outside. There will be considerable pressure on HHS from many stakeholders to have services classified as falling within the 10 categories of care as well as in being part of typical small employer plans. Although the committee's process allows for inclusion of services that are beyond the 10 categories of care or the typical employer plan, realistically, the premium constraint may not allow additions.

---

[6] The committee is not recommending specific exclusions, which was outside its task; these are illustrative of exclusions in existing plans listed in the Appendixes.

The committee's direction on specificity in secretarial guidance and movement toward more uniformity is focused on what is *covered* or *permissibly excluded* by a plan, not on the level and features of deductibles, co-payments, co-insurance, and out-of-pocket maximums other than those set by the ACA. Some states are considering limits on the number of plans that could be offered in an exchange. It was outside the committee's task to comment on whether exchanges should be allowed to limit the number of plan selections offered in an exchange.

Presenting General Exclusionary Language

Besides listing service-specific and general exclusions in plan evidence of coverage documents, the committee found the idea of having a standard set of general exclusions attractive so that the simplified six-page documents for consumer comparisons of plans on the exchanges could list whether a plan adopted or varied from a standard set of general exclusions. General exclusion language is often too voluminous to fit in the small space allotted on those consumer documents; for example, the committee found plan documents with seven pages of exclusions. Box 5-2 lists the general exclusions set out by the Office of Personnel Management (OPM) for fee-for-service plans operating within the Federal Employees Health Benefits Program (FEHBP). Plans are allowed to add to the list of general exclusions. For example, the Blue Cross and Blue Shield Service Benefit Plan expands the OPM general exclusions list to contain 30 general and specific exclusions. OPM offers a similar but slightly different set for health maintenance organization (HMO) plans.

BOX 5-2
General Exclusions: Federal Employee Health
Benefit Program Fee-for-Service Option

- Services, drugs, or supplies you receive while you are not enrolled in this plan;
- Services, drugs, or supplies not medically necessary;
- Services, drugs, or supplies not required according to accepted standards of medical, dental, or psychiatric practice;
- Experimental or investigational procedures, treatments, drugs, or devices;
- Services, drugs, or supplies related to abortions, except when the life of the mother would be endangered if the fetus were carried to term, or when the pregnancy is the result of an act of rape or incest;
- Services, drugs, or supplies related to sex transformations;
- Services, drugs, or supplies you receive from a provider or facility barred from the FEHB Program;
- Services, drugs, or supplies you receive without charge while in active military service;
- Services or supplies for which no charge would be made if the covered individual had no health insurance coverage;
- Services or supplies furnished by immediate relatives or household members, such as spouse, parents, children, brothers or sisters by blood, marriage or adoption;
- Services or supplies furnished or billed by a non-covered facility, except that medically necessary prescription drugs and physical, speech, and occupational therapy rendered by a qualified professional therapist on an outpatient basis are covered subject to plan limits; and
- Charges that the enrollee or plan has no legal obligation to pay, such as excess charges for an annuitant age 65 or older who is not covered by Medicare Parts A and/or B, doctor's charges exceeding the amount specified by the Department of Health and Human Services when benefits are payable under Medicare, or state premium taxes however applied.

SOURCE: Personal communication with Dean Schleicher, Office of Personnel and Management, July 15, 2011.

Because it was not the committee's charge to define the EHB, the purpose of Box 5-2 is to illustrate the types of general exclusions that are common today. Under "Required Elements for Consideration" later in this chapter, the committee raises issues surrounding nondiscrimination and exclusionary language in plans.

COMMITTEE RECOMMENDATION ON DEFINING THE EHB

In summary, the process for defining the aggregate EHB package must derive from its legislative foundations. In designing the EHB package, the committee recommends that the Secretary be guided by the offerings of the small group market, and then modify the package to take into account the more expansive 10 categories of care in the ACA. To balance the comprehensiveness of the total package against its cost, the Secretary will have to evaluate whether the package as a whole meets the committee's criteria, reflects public priorities, and can be accommodated within the budgetary constraint defined by an estimated national average silver plan premium. As noted earlier, premiums are not based solely on the contents of the package, but reflect other elements of benefit design and administration. The Secretary will have to be explicit about the assumptions about benefit design and administration that should be used in developing the national average premium. These assumptions will influence the content of the benefit package consistent with the premium target level that the committee recommends—tying the target to the silver plan level because this is the premium price level that is used in calculating federal subsidies for plans purchased in the exchanges.

Recommendation 1: By May 1, 2012, the Secretary should establish an initial essential health benefits (EHB) package guided by a national average premium target.

    A.   **The starting point in establishing the initial EHB package should be the scope of benefits and design provided under a typical small employer plan in today's market. To specify the initial EHB package, this scope of benefits should then be modified to reflect**

- **The 10 general categories specified in Section 1302(b)(1) of the Affordable Care Act (ACA); and**
- **The criteria specified in this report for the content of specific elements and aggregate EHB package (see Figure S-2 in the Summary).**

    B.   **Once a preliminary EHB list is developed as described in (A), the package should be adjusted so that the expected national average premium for a silver plan with the EHB package is actuarially equivalent to the average premium that would have been paid by small employers in 2014 for a comparable population with a typical benefit design.**

    C.   **The Secretary should sponsor a public deliberative process to assist in determining how the adjustments to the EHB package should be made.**

    D.   **Initial guidance by the Secretary on the contents of the EHB package should list standard benefit inclusions and exclusions at a level of specificity at least comparable to current best practice in the private and public insurance market.**

The committee's criteria on methods should apply to the overall process of defining the package. When the Secretary decides something should or should not be covered, those specific determinations should be transparent and the rationale made public. Whether the goal of balancing coverage and costs is met through initial definition of the EHB will ultimately be tested during implementation: for example, are projected reductions in the number of uninsured, participation rates in the exchanges, and increased access to appropriate care achieved? In the meantime, the average premium amount serves as a proxy against which benefit coverage is assessed.

OTHER AREAS FOR THE SECRETARIAL GUIDANCE RELATED TO THE EHB

This section discusses the required "elements for consideration" (balance, nondiscrimination) and determination of medical necessity. Toward this end, the committee considered in what areas the Secretary could provide additional guidance at the outset beyond the definition of the EHB to help exchanges protect at-risk groups and ensure the adequacy of plans. Although secretarial guidance will be informative, it is monitoring implementation that is the key feature to protect against untoward consequences related to these provisions.

Required Elements for Consideration

The "required elements for consideration" provisions of Section 1302 are designed to address the issue of insurer discretion to design benefits, make coverage decisions, determine reimbursement rates, and establish incentive programs in ways that could potentially discriminate against certain conditions, degrees of illness, or population groups. Per its charge, the committee examined the first four of the required elements for consideration in Section 1302, finding that (1) "balance among categories" and taking "into account the health care needs of diverse segments of the population" require the EHB package to have a focus on population rather than individual needs (e.g., including traditionally underserved populations), while (2) the references to nondiscrimination and to individual wishes focus on individual needs (Box 5-3). If the Secretary defines the EHB in accordance with committee's policy foundations (Chapter 3), these dual interests will be accounted for, but during implementation at the state level, monitoring will be necessary to ensure that practice meets principles.

Balance Across Categories and Diverse Segments

"The Secretary is to ensure that the EHB reflect an appropriate balance among the categories … so that benefits are not unduly weighted toward any category." The committee concluded that there is no simple way to address this element. The EHB should incorporate a spectrum of care that meets the evidence-based needs of the varied medical conditions and services that a diverse population of patients requires.

In response to the committee's online query about balance and diversity, various approaches to assessing performance on these dimensions were suggested.[7] Both employers and insurers tended to support having balance across categories defined by a marketplace norm of typical employer plans. The committee believes this is a reasonable approach at the outset, and any information the Secretary has obtained that describes such norms regarding limits and cost-sharing practices would likely be informational not regulatory. Another suggestion, provided by both WellPoint and the American Medical Association (Maves, 2010), was that the goal of balance should be to ensure parity in access to health care services—for example, by having "equal access to providers in each of the 10 categories, as determined by network adequacy standards" (Walter-Dumm, 2010).

Utilization patterns were most often offered as a way to measure and set norms of practice and identify diverse patient needs (Sacco, 2010; Sandstrom, 2010; Wojcik, 2010). This information may be helpful in actuarial estimation, but there are limits to the utility of this approach given the ACA's addition of new service categories to the standard benefit package. Consumers and providers that provided input to the committee were often wary of depending solely on existing utilization and coverage patterns to assess balance (Kotch, 2010; Touschner, 2010). They argued that current utilization data or even the experience in typical employer plans cannot identify previously unaddressed needs related to some of the 10 categories of care, such as habilitation, mental health and substance abuse parity, and expanded access to preventive services. Others raised the problem of using utilization patterns to identify appropriate multidisciplinary or specialized care (Rice, 2010). Arguments were also presented against traditional "utilization" determinants for pediatric populations, pointing out that this population typically has consumed fewer resources than adults and that investing in preventive services for children presents an opportunity for life-long impact (Racine, 2011). Nevertheless, the committee supports measures of use as one approach to guide and assess balance considerations. For example, if enrollees of a given plan were systemically not using

---

[7] Illustrative responses of the hundreds received are cited.

BOX 5-3
Selected Required Elements for Consideration

Section 1302 (b) (4) REQUIRED ELEMENTS FOR CONSIDERATION.—In defining the essential health benefits under paragraph (1), the Secretary shall—

(A) ensure that such essential health benefits reflect an appropriate balance among the categories described in such subsection, so that benefits are not unduly weighted toward any category;

(B) not make coverage decisions, determine reimbursement rates, establish incentive programs, or design benefits in ways that discriminate against individuals because of their age, disability, or expected length of life;

(C) take into account the health care needs of diverse segments of the population, including women, children, persons with disabilities, and other groups;

(D) ensure that health benefits established as essential not be subject to denial to individuals against their wishes on the basis of the individuals' age or expected length of life or of the individuals' present or predicted disability, degree of medical dependency, or quality of life;

(E) provide that a qualified health plan shall not be treated as providing coverage for the essential health benefits described in paragraph (1) unless the plan provides that—

(i) coverage for emergency department services will be provided without imposing any requirement under the plan for prior authorization of services or any limitation on coverage where the provider of services does not have a contractual relationship with the plan for the providing of services that is more restrictive than the requirements or limitations that apply to emergency department services received from providers who do have such a contractual relationship with the plan; and
(ii) if such services are provided out-of-network, the cost-sharing requirement (expressed as a co-payment amount or coinsurance rate) is the same requirement that would apply if such services were provided in-network;

SOURCE: § 1302(b)(4)(A)-(E).

---

services considered high value (e.g., not managing their chronic disease adequately), the Secretary might examine the benefit offerings or design for evidence of inappropriate "imbalance."

The concern raised by the diverse segments clause is that benefit packages could be established that would, in effect, enable plans to attract the healthiest enrollees ("cherry picking") (Monahan, 2010; Sacco, 2010). This might happen through benefit design, for example, by having a provider network that did not include specific specialists, primary care physicians in certain geographic locations, or selected medications. Respondents to the committee's online question about diverse segments of the population frequently interpreted the provision as addressing the question of disparities in access across racial, ethnic, language, and socioeconomic lines. If a plan failed to attract a reasonable number of beneficiaries in a given clinical or demographic group, it might be evidence of an imbalance in benefit design.

Nondiscrimination Provisions

Congressional guidance to safeguard against the potential for discrimination based on age, disability, or expected length of life, as stipulated through Section 1302(b)(4)(B) and (D), reflects concern about past practices by some insurers. One interpretation of this portion of the law provided in testimony to the committee was that "what Congress is trying to get at is the notion … if there is no objective evidence, if we have an absence of clinical evidence to suggest that the treatment does not work for persons with certain disabilities, then the [condition-specific] limitation should not stand" (Rosenbaum, 2011b). The committee interprets the congressional intent of these provisions as primarily to ensure that insurers do not make arbitrary and discriminatory decisions based on certain characteristics of people rather than assessing the individuality of each case when making medical necessity decisions and applying clinical policies.

Effect of benefits' exclusionary language and required elements for consideration. The committee examined the scope of exclusions considered typical across the industry (Appendix F). Among those deemed to be "industry typical," the committee questioned whether some would be considered to discriminate by disability. The committee did not have the time or resources to research the legal repercussions, nor was it tasked with addressing specific services; as a result, it does not take a position with respect to any of the items listed below or others on the expanded list (Appendix F). The committee brings the following illustrative examples to the Secretary's attention as perhaps needing further evaluation to see if they should be allowable; for example, exclusions encompassed

- Any disease or injury resulting from a war, declared or not, … or any release of nuclear energy;
- Treatment of injuries sustained while committing a crime; a voluntary participant in disorderly conduct, riot, or other breach of the peace;
- Treatment of dementia, except for treatment of psychological symptoms;
- Nutritional supplements and formulas needed for the treatment of inborn errors; and
- Sexual reassignment surgery.[8]

The first two items might be considered situational exclusions, not disability-based exclusions. Should it be allowable for a plan to deny treatment if a person was exposed to environmental radiation?[9] Should it be allowable for a plan to deny treatment to a person who needed treatment incident to a crime; what if the individual was considered involved in the crime due to exceeding a legal limit on blood alcohol level? The committee was advised during its first workshop that intoxication exclusionary clauses, once prevalent when alcoholism was considered a behavioral choice rather than a medical condition (Rosenbaum, 2011b; Rosenbaum et al., 2004), are less common today. Still the committee found exclusionary language in one plan, for example, that a person would not be covered if injured while intoxicated above a certain blood alcohol level and driving a car, scooter, or off-road vehicle.[10]

The remaining items raise debatable points about whether people are being denied treatment based on a disability as opposed to a decision made about the design of benefits—that is, the service is not elected to be among the priorities to be paid for out of shared resources.

Setting benefit limits. Could benefit limits also be discriminatory? Respondents to the committee's online question about the issue of setting limits on benefit categories could be simplistically split into two groups: those in favor of benefit limits and those against benefit limits. Those in favor of limits noted that they are an important component of value-based benefit design and are necessary to ensure quality and affordability. Benefit limits are often cited as an effective means of lowering premium costs. Those who did not support limits frequently expressed concern that nonmonetary medical management limits (e.g., step therapy, visit limits, prior authorization) would increasingly be utilized by insurers as a "loophole" to get around the prohibition against lifetime and annual dollar limits. The National Partnership for Women and Families stated that "non-dollar service limits can be just as detrimental [as lifetime and annual limits] as insurers can simply substitute non-dollar limits, like annual service limits, nullifying the effect of this important consumer protection" (Monahan, 2010). Specifically, the following were raised as areas of most concern:

---

[8] Sexual reassignment surgery is a frequent exclusion in plans; of note in FEHBP plans, it is considered a procedure-based exclusion rather than a condition-based one. Personal communication with Dean Schleicher, U.S. Office of Personnel Management, July 13, 2011.

[9] Subrogation clauses allow insurers to recoup medical expenses the insurer paid from third parties who are legally responsible for an injury.

[10] Personal communication with Tanji Northrup, Health Division Director, Utah Insurance Department, February, 23, 2011.

- Generic-only drug coverage, because certain drugs are not available in a generic-only formulary, leaving patients liable for needed high-priced pharmaceuticals and perhaps affecting their adherence to drug regimens (Fung et al., 2008)
- Condition-specific restrictions[11]
- Dollar or visit limits on specific benefit categories, services, or drug classes (e.g., therapy caps) even though the ACA prohibits annual and lifetime dollar limits
- Nonnormative limits such as very low numbers of allowed inpatient hospital days or coverage of the second day of hospitalization but not the first

The committee notes that there is a balance between setting arbitrary limits and those that reflect best practices and/or scientific evidence. Others have pointed out that limits, when undisclosed and not scientifically based, are problematic: "These normative, undisclosed, and fixed limits on treatment do not allow for any deviation based on underlying condition … are often not based on evidence; they are simply conclusory statements by actuarial firms" (Rosenbaum, 2011a, p. 8-5). The committee affirms its desire for evidence-based limits and medical necessity assessments considering the individuality of the particular case. This needs to be coupled with protections for vulnerable patients, such that any limit should have the right of appeal.

Conclusion: With respect to the required elements for consideration, the committee concludes that congressional and secretarial direction on the contents of the 10 categories of care and the scope of the typical small employer plan provides the best *a priori* guidance. One supplementary *a priori* approach that the Secretary could employ would be to require that contracts submitted to an exchange to become a qualified health plan (QHP) include an attestation in its subscriber contracts that the plan will abide by the required elements for consideration in Section 1302(b)(4)(A)-(D) or incorporate the required elements language fully in the contracts. As all small group and individual coverage, not just QHPs, is subject to the EHB, this approach could also be applied by state insurance commissioners to non-exchange plans.

It is impossible that HHS guidance will anticipate every circumstance that might be a possible violation of the required elements. It is the job of the exchanges and state insurance commissioners to identify insurer practices that will not provide meaningful coverage and consumer protection. Because states are on the frontline of review, they are likely sources to identify practices that are either problematic or possibly innovative through monitoring (see Chapter 7). Having a systematic way to communicate those findings across the exchanges and states in real time could help other states.

Chapter 7 outlines the importance of planning for data collection on benefits, benefit design, limits imposed, and monitoring implementation. At the outset, state health exchanges and state regulators will be able to compare what is being typically offered in their states under the EHB requirements and identify outlier practices for covered benefits, exclusions, and benefit design limits and networks. Over time, evaluation of these elements, appeals, and utilization patterns can help identify if any areas need further evaluation to determine if they are out of balance, do not serve diverse population segments, discriminate, or reflect desirable innovative practices. The purpose of well-developed internal and external appeals processes as required by the ACA is to allow consistency in benefit interpretation across insurers to emerge from the review of specific cases yet recognize individual circumstances when warranted. The right to appeal provides only a limited check on contract benefit limits and exclusions, because any external review will generally be bound by coverage limits imposed by the insurance policy. Although, in some appeals cases, medical necessity may "trump" a visit limit, medical necessity may not apply to some strict benefit design limitations in commercial insurers and some Medicare provisions.

---

[11] An interim final rule related to limits was issued on June 28, 2010, and explicitly stated that "the rules of this section do not prevent a group health plan, or a health insurance issuer offering group health insurance coverage, from excluding all benefits for a condition" (U.S. Department of the Treasury et al., 2010, p. 37223). Additional guidance on limits can be found on the Center for Consumer Information and Insurance Oversight (CCIIO) website: http://cciio.cms.gov/resources/regulations/index.html#alw.

Emergency Room Coverage

The fifth required element has very specific language related to accessing emergency room services (Box 5-3[E]), and a prohibition against a plan being qualified unless it follows the outlined practices.

Conclusion: The secretarial guidance could require that the legislative language of the fifth required element be incorporated directly into contract provisions in order to participate as a qualified health plan. Similarly, state insurance commissioners could require this for plans outside the exchange that incorporate the EHB.

Medical Necessity

Medical necessity is a condition of benefit coverage usually found in insurance contracts, allowing health insurers to review the appropriateness of any intervention a patient receives. In evidence of coverage contract documents, there will be services listed that the enrollee is eligible to receive and that qualify for coverage contingent on a finding of medical necessity for the individual patient. Moreover, there will be non-listed services that are medically necessary, based on the patient's specific condition, and unless expressly excluded in the plan documents, insurance coverage for the services will be determined by medical necessity review. Therefore, determination of medical necessity is used to ensure that each individual patient receives the most appropriate care; this is particularly important when every "inclusion" and "exclusion" is not listed, and as medical science changes, it allows for flexibility before lists can be updated.

Per the committee's Statement of Task to "assess the methods used by insurers currently to determine 'medical necessity,'" the committee undertook an analysis of existing definitions and stakeholders concerns, and examined the use of evidence in the application of medical necessity and the related issue of clinical policy determination. Opportunity for public input—particularly on the advantages or disadvantages of current definitions, the need (if any) for secretarial guidance on medical necessity, and approaches to help formulate such guidance—was provided through the committee's online questionnaire. Based on these public findings, additional testimony, and committee research into various options, the committee identified the following major issues:

- The term "necessity" can lead to misunderstandings—with patients asking how something their provider prescribes could not be considered necessary or physicians inquiring how an insurer can question their judgment. Such responses imply that the medical necessity process is established to deny coverage, rather than being built on a scientific evidence base, according to the National Business Group on Health (Wojcik, 2010). In insurance practice, the insurer makes the final assessment of medical necessity for uncontested cases; patients and providers have the right to an independent external appeal under many current policies and more will under the ACA.[12]
- Multiple definitions of medical necessity exist, and respondents were split in their views about whether the IOM or HHS should establish a national standard definition of medical necessity. Responses from consumers and providers tended to support a national definition, particularly emphasizing individualization of care and not inflexible clinical policies (Baker, 2010; Gascho, 2010; Morgan, 2010; Sacco, 2010; Smith, 2010; Zollar and Kendrick, 2010), and insurers tended to be opposed saying medical necessity is not a "tool for determining what items and services should make up a benefit package," which they viewed as the task assigned to the Secretary (Fox, 2010). Furthermore, they noted that Section 1563 of the ACA allows insurers flexibility to employ appropriate medical review and determination of medical necessity (Bocchino, 2010; Calega, 2011; Walter-Dumm, 2010).
- Safeguards in the application of medical necessity may be needed, particularly for special populations (e.g., children; individuals with disabilities, mental illness, or rare diseases) both in the definition of what medical necessity means and in monitoring its implementation.

---

[12] 29 CFR 2590.715-2719(c)(2)(i).

Some commented that they preferred the term medical appropriateness, but the committee acknowledges that the term medical necessity is widespread in the vernacular and in regulatory guidance. Medical necessity has been historically and continually referenced in federal and state statute, and it is a familiar term in commercial medical insurance products. The committee believes the Secretary has the opportunity through the EHB definition process to educate the public on the meaning of medical necessity—why it is consistent with individualized assessments of the appropriateness of care, with keeping coverage affordable, and with ensuring patients' rights of appeal if they view care as inappropriately denied (see additional discussion in Chapter 2 of medical management, of which medical necessity is one element).

Key Elements in Definitions

The committee considered multiple definitions of medical necessity across Medicare, in sample Medicaid programs, and in use by private insurers (Appendix G). In the late 1990s, a research team at Stanford developed a more "evidence-based" definition of medical necessity that has now been incorporated in a number of contracts of insurers and state Medicaid programs (e.g., Hawaii, Kansas, Blue Cross Blue Shield of Arkansas) (Coding Institute, 2000).[13] Key elements were that an intervention could be considered medically necessary if first recommended by the treating physician and then determined by the insurer to have met conditions pertaining to each of the following elements: *medical purpose, scope, evidence,* and *value* (as illustrated in Table 5-7 and outlined in more detail in Appendix G). These five categories were identified as those into which most existing and proposed criteria at the time fell from the Stanford workshop members' analysis. Notably, it was pointed out at the time that "it was clear that most definitions have criteria that address purpose and scope, and closely following those criteria in frequency are criteria about authority and evidence. [At the time], few definitions addressed value or cost effectiveness" (Singer et al., 1999, p. 57).

Similarly, a major national legal settlement between insurers (e.g., CIGNA, Health Net, Prudential, Anthem/WellPoint, Humana) and 900,000 physicians created a standard followed by many in the insurance industry.[14] Starting with a "prudent physician" standard (the primary component of the American Medical Association [AMA] definition of medical necessity), the settlement contains the five elements of the Stanford definition. A separate Second Circuit Court of Appeals case directs that if "the plan administrator presents sufficient evidence that a treatment is not necessary in the usual case it is up to the patient and his or her physician to show that this individual patient is different from the usual in ways that make the treatment medically necessary for him or her" (Kaminski, 2007, p. 2). As in the Stanford definition, authority, purpose, scope, evidence, and value are part of defining what constitutes medical necessity in the national settlement (Table 5-7).

Additionally, the National Association of Insurance Commissioners, as part of its effort to define consumer-friendly insurance terms, conveyed to HHS a number of sample medical necessity definitions from subscriber contracts in six states (NAIC, 2010). Most of those samples reference prudent physician judgment, clinically appropriate care and best practice, and a scientific evidence base. Few sample definitions explicitly mention individualizing care or addressing value, efficiency, or cost-effectiveness of care, but those elements could be encompassed within the construct of delivering clinically appropriate care depending on how the definition is applied in practice.

The committee observed, based on the definitions from plans from these six states as well as plans in other states, that individual states do not require health insurers operating within a single state to have a uniform definition of medical necessity. Nor does the Federal Employee Health Benefits Program require participating plans to have a single definition.[15]

---

[13] Personal communication with Linda Bergthold, health policy consultant, November 19, 2010.

[14] Kaminski reports that if a "state-enacted definition is more expansive than the settlement's definition, the state law will control. But if the settlement's definition is more expansive, it will control with respect to the parties subject to the settlement" (Kaminski, 2007, p. 2).

[15] Personal communication with Dean Schleicher, U.S. Office of Personnel Management, July 13, 2011.

TABLE 5-7 Key Elements in Definitions of Medical Necessity

Terms Under	Stanford Definition[a]	National Legal Settlement[b]
Authority	An intervention is medically necessary if, as recommended by the treating physician and determined by the health plan's medical director or physician designee	Health care services that a physician, exercising prudent clinical judgment, would provide to a patient
Medical purpose	A health intervention for the purpose of treating a medical condition (i.e., to *treat* meaning to prevent, diagnose, detect, treat, or palliate) or to maintain or restore functional ability	Health care services for the purpose of preventing, evaluating, diagnosing, or treating an illness, injury, disease, or its symptoms
Scope	The most appropriate supply or level of service, considering potential benefits and harms to the patient	Clinically appropriate, in terms of type, frequency, extent, site, and duration and considered effective for the patient's illness, injury, or disease
Evidence	Known to be effective in improving health outcomes. For new interventions, effectiveness is determined by scientific evidence. For existing interventions, effectiveness is determined first by scientific evidence, then by professional standards, then by expert opinion	Generally accepted standards of medical practice—meaning standards that are based on credible scientific evidence published in peer-reviewed medical literature, generally recognized by the relevant medical community, or otherwise consistent with standards of clinical judgment
Value	Cost-effective for this condition compared to alternative interventions, including no intervention, with application of the cost-effectiveness criterion in the case of the individual patient being determinative	Intervention should not be more costly than an alternative service or sequence of services at least as likely to produce equivalent therapeutic or diagnostic results

[a] Singer et al., 1999. [Note: See full definition in Appendix G.]
[b] Kaminiski, 2007.

Medical Purpose

Additionally, in light of the importance of medical necessity determinations during implementation of the EHB package and concerns about inappropriate denials of care, the committee examined the element of "medical purpose of the intervention," which had been raised as particularly problematic because its phrasing in medical necessity definitions and, more importantly, in its interpretation as applied to patient cases can result in limitations of care. Although the committee heard anecdotal accounts of denials of care based on narrow interpretations of the wording of definitions of medical necessity, the extent of the problem was not well documented. Illustrative examples of medical necessity approvals confined to interventions that only "cure" a person's condition or only "restore" their function were presented as discriminatory against conditions for which there may be no recovery (e.g., multiple sclerosis for which maintenance of function or prevention of worsening of infirmity is more pertinent) or conditions whose initial lack of attainment of developmentally appropriate functioning would effectively preclude the concept of such restoration (e.g., an individual with developmental disabilities who has never attained speech or movement) (Ford, 2011; Rosenbaum, 2011b).

A congressional floor statement called attention to having a broadly based interpretation for the category of rehabilitative and habilitative services and devices, including "items and services used to restore functional capacity, minimize limitations on physical and cognitive functions, and maintain or prevent deterioration of functioning."[16]

---

[16] Floor statement of the Honorable Bill Pascrell, Jr., (NJ) in the U.S. House of Representatives. Congressional Record—House Extension of Remarks (March 21, 2010). Congressman Pascrell, a co-chair of the Congressional Brain Injury Task Force, included the following in his House floor statement: "The term rehabilitative and habilitative services includes items and services used to restore functional capacity, minimize limitations on physical and cognitive functions, and maintain or prevent deterioration of functioning as a result of an illness, injury, disorder or other health condition. Such services also include training of individuals with mental and physical disabilities to enhance functional development" (Pascrell, 2010).

Advocates for children, such as the American Academy of Pediatrics, suggested modeling medical necessity requirements after early and periodic screening, diagnosis, and treatment (EPSDT) coverage rules,[17] stating that a disadvantage of typical insurance approaches is that they do not take into account developmental stages or the need for habilitative services that do not treat a disease but rather allow a child to accommodate to a condition and reach his or her highest level of functioning (American Academy of Pediatrics, 2005; Racine, 2011). On the other hand, concern has been raised that the Medicaid EPSDT requirement to address any diagnosed condition and its approach to defining medical necessity were far more extensive than any typical employer insurance plan; at the same time, others have noted that Medicaid is more likely to enroll and be responsive to the needs of children with special health care needs (The Commonwealth Fund and The George Washington University 2005; DHS, 2011; Jezek, 2010; Koyanagi, 2010; O'Connell and Watson, 2001).

Evaluations of medical necessity will have to comply with inclusion of the 10 categories of care as well as prohibitions against discrimination based on age, disability, and expected length of life in the ACA and secretarial guidance. As noted in testimony to the committee with regard to potential discrimination in the application of medical necessity to persons with disabilities, "The central question is whether the treatment is medical in nature and whether the individual can be expected to medically benefit from it" (Rosenbaum, 2011a, p. 8-3).

Clinical Policies

Insurers' clinical policies help address ambiguity about coverage that is not specifically addressed in listings of included and excluded services, and are often applied in medical necessity decision making. Chapter 2 presents sample hierarchies of medical evidence that are used in developing coverage decisions and clinical policies; most services do not have randomized controlled trials to support them, and clinical policies are designed to identify the most objective, credible, and scientifically based heuristic or hierarchy of medical evidence.

Clinical policies are not available for all conditions but are usually developed in areas where additional clarity is needed, a high volume of services might be anticipated, the services have associated high expenditures, and/or medical benefit for patients is found only under certain limited clinical scenarios. For example, the Massachusetts Medicaid program publishes 16 separate guidelines for determination of medical necessity that are specific to different kinds of services (e.g., organ transplant, bariatric surgery). In the instance of organ transplant, the guidelines indicate the possibility for coverage in the case of a congenital maldevelopment, primary malignancy, and failure of vital organ function, among others, but do not "ordinarily" consider transplants necessary under certain circumstances, such as when a patient has ongoing systematic bacterial infection or presence of an irreversible disease (Massachusetts Department of Health, 2011). Many commercial plans similarly publish their clinical policies; Aetna, once unique in doing so, publishes hundreds of clinical policies online (Aetna, 2011). The "vast majority" of technologies is not selected for evaluation and is not subject to utilization management (e.g., pre-authorization, limits on visits) (McDonough, 2011).

Medical necessity reviews are where the tough decisions on coverage are made, and having more light shed on clinical policies and review criteria would enhance understanding of whether EHB coverage needs to be updated and if there are areas potentially subverting the intentions of the required elements for consideration. It was beyond the committee's time and resources to mount a systematic examination of available clinical policies, but such an evaluation could reveal similarities and differences in clinical policies for specific conditions, and thereby interpretations of the strength of the evidence basis. This could inform where evidence supports additional specificity on EHB inclusions, as well as could reveal whether specific limits on services are rooted in evidence and should not be considered discriminatory based on age, disability, and expected length of life.

Secretarial Guidance on Medical Necessity

The committee believes that medical necessity evaluation is an important part of benefit design, with the potential to enhance appropriateness of care for individuals and through that mechanism to enhance the value and

---

[17] "Screening and diagnostic services to determine physical or mental defects in recipients under age 21; and health care, treatment, and other measures to correct or ameliorate any defects and chronic conditions discovered" (42 CFR 440.40(b)(1)-(2)).

affordability of care. The committee considered that any definition of medical necessity is but one aspect of help-ing to ensure access to appropriate care and that promoting transparency in medical necessity definitions, clinical policies, and appeals monitoring would further understanding.

Conclusion: The committee's vision for the EHB is that only medically necessary (or appropriate) services for individuals should be covered. The committee believes that the concepts of individualizing care, ensuring value, and having medical necessity decisions strongly rooted in evidence should be reemphasized in any guidance on medical necessity. Inflexibility in the application of medical necessity, clinical policies, medical management, and limits without consideration of the circumstances of an individual case is undesirable and potentially discriminatory. The committee believes transparency in a rigorous appeals monitoring process is the primary approach to addressing the nondiscrimination provisions in benefit design and implementation, including medical necessity reviews.

Rather than requiring a uniform national definition of medical necessity, the committee suggests the following areas for guidance to states and health plans:

- A requirement for transparency in its medical necessity definition in all plans containing the EHB, and the disposition of at least external review case data; and
- The components of the Stanford and national settlement definitions address areas that should be considered part of medical necessity definitions and criteria for application (i.e., authority, medical purpose, scope, evidence and value). Secretarial guidance should inform the breadth of the medical purposes of interventions possible under the EHB; interpretation of the *medical purpose* of interventions must be broad enough to address the services encompassed in the 10 categories of care—including services such as habilitation, rehabilitation, and prevention. Specifically, the criteria used for medically necessary services or services that conform to medical necessity are medical services that are (1) clinically appropriate for the individual patient; (2) based on the best scientific evidence, taking into account the available hierarchy of medical evidence; and (3) likely to produce incremental health benefits relative to the next best alternative that justify any added cost. In some cases, the next best alternative may be no treatment at all.[18]

These elements for the definition of medical necessity are consistent with best practices and supported by legal precedent (Kaminiski, 2007). The committee also encourages the development of new evidence; the Stanford definition language "known to be effective in improving health outcomes" should not preclude opportunities for innovation such as coverage with evidence development.

The committee view is that there can be variation in the wording of medical necessity definitions, but it is the interpretation of the definitions that is most important. The new national requirement for an independent external review is an important step in protecting the rights of patients; external review will begin *de novo* and will be binding on the insurer. Thus, in contested cases, external reviewers will ultimately make the final medical necessity determination. Because monitoring and learning from implementation are important, the committee further suggests

- Standardized data collection and evaluation of appeals (see Chapter 7 discussion of planning for such data collection);
- Examination of clinical policies (see Chapter 7 discussion of data collection and research the committee supports); and
- Transparency and disclosure of data and rationale on these decisions, while protecting individual confidentiality.

---

[18] For example, in Washington State's administrative code (WAC 388-500-0005), medically necessary "is a term for describing a requested service which is reasonably calculated to prevent, diagnose, correct, cure, alleviate or prevent worsening of conditions in the client that endanger life, or cause suffering or pain, or result in an illness or infirmity, or threaten to cause or aggravate a handicap, or cause physical deformity or malfunction. There is no other equally effective, more conservative or substantially less costly course of treatment available or suitable for the client requesting the service. For the purpose of this section, 'course of treatment' may include mere observation or, where appropriate, no treatment at all" (MRSC, 2011).

In Chapter 9, the committee recommends the establishment of a National Benefits Advisory Council (NBAC) to advise the Secretary on updating the EHB; as one of its functions, the NBAC should evaluate the nature of appeals to understand if more specific guidance is required on particular services.

REFERENCES

Abraham, J. M., and R. Feldman. 2010. Taking up or turning down: New estimates of household demand for employer-sponsored health insurance. *Inquiry* 47(1):17-32.

Aetna. 2011. *Clinical policy bulletins alphabetical list*. http://www.aetna.com/healthcare-professionals/policies-guidelines/cpb_alpha.html (accessed August 1, 2011).

American Academy of Pediatrics. 2005. Model contractual language for medical necessity for children. *Pediatrics* 116(1):261-262.

Anthem. 2011. *Update regarding essential health benefits—February 2011*. http://www.anthem.com/provider/noapplication/f1/s0/t0/pw_b157997.pdf?refer=ahpprovider&state=me (accessed June 28, 2011).

Baker, K. 2010. Online questionnaire responses submitted by Kellan Baker, Senior Policy Associate, National Coalition for LGBT Health to the IOM Committee on the Determination of Essential Health Benefits, December 6.

Bocchino, C. 2010. Online questionnaire responses submitted by Carmella Bocchino, Executive Vice President, America's Health Insurance Plans to the IOM Committee on the Determination of Essential Health Benefits, December 6.

Buntin, M. B., C. H. Colla, and J. J. Escarce. 2009. Effects of payment changes on trends in post-acute care. *Health Services Research* 44(4):1188-1210.

Calega, V. 2011. Comments to the IOM Committee on the Determination of Essential Health Benefits by Virginia Calega, Vice President, Medical Management and Policy, Highmark Blue Cross Blue Shield, Washington, DC, January 13.

CBO (Congressional Budget Office). 2009. Letter to the Honorable Evan Bayh, U.S. Senate from Douglas W. Elmendorf, Director, Congressional Budget Office, November 30, 2009.

CMS (Centers for Medicare & Medicaid Services). 2010. *Medicaid and CHIP promising practices: Details for access*. http://www.cms.gov/medicaidchipqualprac/mcppdl/itemdetail.asp?itemid=CMS1227590 (accessed September 14, 2010).

Coding Institute. 2000. *Fewer denials with the new medical-necessity definition*. http://www.supercoder.com/articles/articles-alerts/onc/fewer-denials-with-the-new-medical-necessity-definition/ (accessed August 1, 2011).

The Commonwealth Fund and The George Washington University. 2005. *Comparing EPSDT and commercial insurance benefits*. http://www.allhealth.org/briefingmaterials/03EPSDTvscommercial-173.pdf (accessed November 7, 2011).

DHS (State of Wisconsin Department of Health Services). 2011. *2011-2013 Medicaid efficiencies: Alternative benchmark plan*. http://www.dhs.wisconsin.gov/mareform/alt-bm/AltBenchmark.pdf (accessed November 7, 2011).

Eibner, C., F. Girosi, C. C. Price, A. Cordova, P. S. Hussey, A. Beckman, and E. A. McGlynn. 2010. *Establishing state health insurance exchanges: Implications for health insurance enrollment, spending, and small businesses*. Santa Monica, CA: RAND Corporation.

Ford, M. 2011. Testimony to the IOM Committee on the Determination of Essential Health Benefits by Marty Ford, Director of Legal Advocacy, The Arc and United Cerebral Palsy Disability Policy Collaboration, Washington, DC, January 13.

Fox, A. 2010. Online questionnaire responses submitted by Alissa Fox, Senior Vice President, Blue Cross and Blue Shield Association to the IOM Committee on the Determination of Essential Health Benefits, December 6.

Fung, V., I. Tager, R. Brand, J. Newhouse, and J. Hsu. 2008. The impact of generic-only drug benefits on patients' use of inhaled corticosteroids in a Medicare population with asthma. *BMC Health Services Research* 8(1):151.

Gascho, E. 2010. Online questionnaire responses submitted by Eric Gascho, Manager, Federal Government Relations, National Health Council to the IOM Committee on the Determination of Essential Health Benefits, December 6.

Jezek, A. 2010. Online questionnaire responses submitted by Amanda Jezek, Deputy Director, Federal Affairs, March of Dimes to the IOM Committee on the Determination of Essential Health Benefits, December 6.

Kaminiski, J. L. 2007. *Defining medical necessity*. http://www.cga.ct.gov/2007/rpt/2007-r-0055.htm (accessed April 20, 2011).

Kapowich, J. M. 2010. Oregon's test of value-based insurance design in coverage for state workers. *Health Affairs* 29(11):2028-2032.

Kotch, J. 2010. Online questionnaire responses submitted by Jonathan Kotch, Professor, UNC Gillings School of Global Public Health to the IOM Committee on the Determination of Essential Health Benefits, November 29.

Koyanagi, C. 2010. Online questionnaire responses submitted by Chris Koyagni, Policy Director, The Bazelon Center for Mental Health Law to the IOM Committee on the Determination of Essential Health Benefits, November 29.

Levine, M. A., M. K. Wynia, P. M. Schyve, J. R. Teagarden, D. A. Fleming, S. K. Donohue, R. J. Anderson, J. Sabin, and E. J. Emanuel. 2007. Improving access to health care: A consensus ethical framework to guide proposals of reform. *The Hastings Center Report* 37(5):14-19.

Maryland Insurance Administration. 2009. *Maryland's mandated benefits*. http://www.mdinsurance.state.md.us/sa/documents/MarylandMandatedBenefits09-09rev.pdf (accessed April 24, 2011).

Massachusetts Department of Health. 2011. *Guidelines for medical necessity determination*. http://www.mass.gov/?pageID=eohhs2terminal&L=6&L0=Home&L1=Provider&L2=Insurance+%28including+MassHealth%29&L3=MassHealth&L4=Guidelines+for+Clinical+Treatment&L5=Guidelines+for+Medical+Necessity+Determination&sid=Eeohhs2&b=terminalcontent&f=masshealth_provider_guidelines_mnd_guidelines_organtransplants&csid=Eeohhs2 (accessed August 5, 2011).

Maves, M. A. 2010. Online questionnaire responses submitted by Michael Maves, CEO and Executive Vice President, American Medical Association, to the IOM Committee on the Determination of Essential Health Benefits, December 20.

McDonough, R. 2011. *Determination of essential health benefits.* PowerPoint Presentation to the IOM Committee on the Determination of Essential Health Benefits by Robert McDonough, Director, Clinical Policy Research and Development, Aetna, Washington, DC, January 13.

MHCC (Maryland Health Care Commission). 2011. *Maryland's comprehensive standard benefit plan for small businesses.* http://mhcc.maryland.gov/smallgroup/cshbp_brochure.htm (accessed November 7, 2011).

Monahan, C. 2010. Online questionnaire responses submitted by Christine Monahan, Health Policy Advisor, National Partnership for Women & Families to the IOM Committee on the Determination of Essential Health Benefits, December 6.

Morgan, T. 2010. Online questionnaire responses submitted by Theresa Morgan, Coalition to Preserve Rehabilitation to the IOM Committee on the Determination of Essential Health Benefits, December 6.

MRSC (Municipal Research and Services Center of Washington). 2011. *Medical definitions.* http://www.mrsc.org/mc/wac/WAC%20388%20%20TITLE/WAC%20388%20-500%20%20CHAPTER/WAC%20388%20-500%20-0005.HTM (accessed September 27, 2011).

NAIC (National Association of Insurance Commissioners). 2010. http://www.naic.org/documents/committees_b_consumer_information_ppaca_final_materials.pdf (accessed July 29, 2011).

Newhouse, J. P., W. G. Manning, C. N. Morris, L. L. Orr, N. Duan, E. B. Keeler, A. Leibowitz, K. H. Marquis, M. S. Marquis, C. E. Phelps, and R. H. Brook. 1981. Some interim results from a controlled trial of cost sharing in health insurance. *New England Journal of Medicine* 305(25):1501-1507.

O'Connell, M., and S. Watson. 2001. *Medicaid and EPSDT.* http://www.nls.org/conf/epsdt.htm (accessed July 29, 2011).

Oregon Health Services Commission. 2011. *Prioritized list of health services: April 1, 2011.* http://www.oregon.gov/OHA/OHPR/HSC/docs/L/Apr11List.pdf (accessed May 10, 2011).

Pascrell, Jr., B. 2010. Floor statement by Representative Bill Pascrell, Jr. to the U.S. House of Representatives. *Congressional Record:* 156(45):E462.

Racine, A. 2011. Testimony to the IOM Committee on the Determination of Essential Health Benefits by Andrew Racine, American Academy of Pediatrics, Washington, DC, January 14.

Rice, M. 2010. Online questionnaire responses submitted by Michelle Rice, Regional Director of Chapter Services, National Hemophilia Foundation to the IOM Committee on the Determination of Essential Health Benefits, December 6.

Rosenbaum, S. 2011a. Non-discrimination in the required elements for consideration. In *Perspectives on essential health benefits.* Washington, DC: The National Academies Press.

_____. 2011b. Statement to the IOM Committee on the Determination of Essential Health Benefits by Sara Rosenbaum, Hirsh Professor and Chair, Department of Health Policy and Health Services, School of Public Health, The George Washington University, Washington, DC, January 13.

Rosenbaum, S., H. Van Dyck, M. Bartoshesky, and J. Teitelbaum. 2004. *SAMHSA policy brief. Analysis of state laws permitting intoxication exclusions in insurance contracts and their judicial enforcement.* http://www.gwumc.edu/sphhs/departments/healthpolicy/dhp_publications/pub_uploads/dhpPublication_3626D84B-5056-9D20-3DE5C10098AB28B8.pdf (accessed May 4, 2011).

Rosenthal, M. B., Z. Li, and A. Milstein. 2009. Do patients continue to see physicians who are removed from a PPO network? *American Journal of Managed Care* 15(10):713-719.

Rowe, J. W., T. Brown-Stevenson, R. L. Downey, and J. P. Newhouse. 2008. The effect of consumer-directed health plans on the use of preventive and chronic illness services. *Health Affairs* 27(1):113-120.

Sacco, R. 2010. Online questionnaire responses submitted by Ralph Sacco, President, American Heart Association to the IOM Committee on the Determination of Essential Health Benefits, December 21.

Saha, S., D. D. Coffman, and A. K. Smits. 2010. Giving teeth to comparative-effectiveness research—the Oregon experience. *New England Journal of Medicine* 362(7):e18.

Sandstrom, R. 2010. Online questionnaire responses submitted by Robert Sandstrom, Associate Professor, Department of Physical Therapy, Creighton University to the IOM Committee on the Determination of Essential Health Benefits, December 6.

Singer, S., L. Bergthold, C. Vorhaus, S. Olson, I. Mutchnick, Y. Y. Goh, S. Zimmerman, and A. Enthoven. 1999. Decreasing variation in medical necessity decision making. Appendix E. Model language developed at the "Decreasing Variation in Medical Necessity Decision Making" Decision Maker Workshop in Sacramento, CA, March 11-13, 1999.

Smith, J., and S. Saha. 2011. *Oregon's value based benefits package.* PowerPoint Presentation to the IOM Committee on the Determination of Essential Health Benefits by Jeanene Smith, Administrator, Office for Oregon Health Policy and Research and Somnath Saha, Staff Physician, Portland VA Medical Center and Chair, Oregon Health Services Commission, Costa Mesa, CA, March 2.

Smith, K. C. 2010. Online questionnaire responses submitted by K. Conwell Smith, Vice President, Legislation, Federation of American Hospitals to the IOM Committee on the Determination of Essential Health Benefits, December 6.

Sommers, B. D., and S. Rosenbaum. 2011. Issues in health reform: How changes in eligibility may move millions back and forth between Medicaid and insurance exchanges. *Health Affairs* 30(2):228-236.

Thompson, J. 2011. *Health care that works: Evidence-based Medicaid.* PowerPoint Presentation to the IOM Committee on the Determination of Essential Health Benefits by Jeffery Thompson, Chief Medical Officer, Washington Medicaid Program, Washington State Department of Social and Health Services, Costa Mesa, CA, March 2.

Touschner, J. 2010. Online questionnaire responses submitted by Joe Touschner, State Health Policy Analyst, Georgetown Center for Children and Families to the IOM Committee on the Determination of Essential Health Benefits, December 6.

UnitedHealthcare. 2011. *Essential health benefits: Summary.* http://www.uhc.com/united_for_reform_resource_center/health_reform_provisions/essential_health_benefits.htm (accessed June 28, 2011).

U.S. Department of the Treasury, DOL, and HHS. 2010. Patient Protection and Affordable Care Act: Preexisting condition exclusions, lifetime and annual limits, rescissions, and patient protections. *Federal Register* 75(123):37188-37241.

Walter-Dumm, A. 2010. Online questionnaire responses submitted by Ashley Walter-Dumm, Health Policy Director, WellPoint, Inc. to the IOM Committee on the Determination of Essential Health Benefits, December 6.

Wojcik, S. 2010. Online questionnaire responses submitted by Steve Wojcik, Vice President, Public Policy, National Business Group on Health to the IOM Committee on the Determination of Essential Health Benefits, December 6.

Zollar, C., and M. Kendrick. 2010. Online questionnaire responses submitted by Carolyn Zollar, Vice President for Government Relations and Policy Development and Martie Kendrick, External Council, American Medical Rehabilitation Providers Association to the IOM Committee on the Determination of Essential Health Benefits, December 6.

6

Public Deliberation

Beginning with an overview of public engagement and the venues through which it is sought, the committee highlights the need for the public's role in making sure that the essential health benefits (EHB) are responsive to user needs and in identifying the core societal values to guide priority setting. The unique features of "public deliberation" and its suitability for decision making around the EHB, per the committee's Recommendations 1, 3, 4b, and 5, are explored. Examples of the use of a public deliberation process in both the private and the public sectors are presented. A set of guidelines for public deliberation is offered that the Secretary could use for informing the Department of Health and Human Services (HHS) about priorities and in directing states for their own application.

The purpose of this chapter is to provide the rationale for the committee's support of the general public having a meaningful role in the design, implementation, evaluation, and updating of the EHB package through two important functions: (1) oversight of the EHB and (2) identification of social values to help guide decisions on what and how coverage is provided within the EHB. Most of the information here relates to this second function.

THE PUBLIC VOICE

In considering how best to capture the public voice in meaningful ways for the determination of the EHB package, this section explores the potential roles of the public, offers guidance to ensure that public processes are reasonable, and defines the value of public deliberation as a distinct approach that incorporates choices among covered benefits and benefit design in a prioritized fashion.

In recent years there has been growing emphasis on patient engagement in health care—helping individual patients become more active in health promotion and self-care, and encouraging a partnership with their physicians and other providers in planning for the services they receive. These efforts are especially important for managing chronic illness and facilitating sound treatment decisions that depend on informed patient preference. Individuals have also been encouraged to become informed consumers when making decisions about their health plans, health care services, and benefit design alternatives. Given the dramatic expansion of health care options, these types of patient or consumer engagement are important and necessary.

The Consumer Adviser

Less evident is the role of the public in advising about health care policy decisions that affect society as a whole. As health care has grown in complexity, appointments of patients, consumers, and advocates to boards, committees, task forces, and other advisory bodies are a testament to the recognition that an array of stakeholder perspectives is needed on issues that profoundly affect people's lives.

There are numerous examples in which national and state bodies provide opportunities for consumers to comment, respond to, and offer suggestions that may affect health policy. Medicare has a public process for reviewing specific technologies individually. The Medicare Evidence Development and Coverage Advisory Committee (MEDCAC) meets in an open forum approximately four to eight times a year to review submitted evidence, listen to testimony, and deliberate about the quality of the evidence. Of the 94 at-large member positions, selected by the Secretary, 6 are reserved for patient advocates (HHS, 2010), with one participating in *every* meeting (HHS, 2010). Further opportunities for public input in the service coverage determination process exist, as illustrated in the case of health technology assessment for Medicare decisions as well as in Oregon and Washington State (Table 6-1), and other venues (Menon and Stafinski, 2011).

Although opportunities for input are essential, they are not a substitute for formal representation on governing and advisory bodies. The committee believes formal representation will be important for the EHB package if it is to attain and maintain the trust and confidence of those it serves (e.g., on the National Benefits Advisory Council; see Chapter 9).

The Citizen Deliberator

There is a third role for the public, distinct from the others: helping to reconcile the tension between comprehensiveness and affordability. Finding the balance between them requires strong political and social will, efforts that can be helped with public deliberation: "the use of critical thinking and reasoned argument as a way for citizens to make decisions on public policy" (McCoy and Scully, 2002, p. 117). Deliberation does not assume consensus, but "it brings into consideration knowledge and judgments coming from various perspectives so that participants develop understandings that are informed by other views" (NRC, 1996, p. 74).

A structured interactive process can elucidate the core values by which the public ultimately reaches societal decisions. As long as there are far more ways to spend health care dollars than there are dollars to spend, these core values must play a role in deciding the coverage obligations of insurance and the personal obligations of individual consumers (Fleck, 2009).

These two roles—consumer adviser and citizen deliberator—are not intended to replicate, substitute for, or undermine the work of legislative, regulatory, or professional bodies. The complexity of health care and the uncomfortable financial precipice on which it hangs requires a different level of discussion than those that are typically part of policy formation or rule making. A public deliberative process on tradeoffs among benefits and benefit design can help political and health care leaders arrive at better decisions, and going through the process of gathering input can help garner public support, trust, and buy-in (Wynia and Schwab, 2006).

Accountability for Reasonableness

Using public deliberation as a component of EHB development is wholly consistent with the concept of "accountability for reasonableness" as described in *Setting Limits Fairly* (Daniels and Sabin, 2008) and the literature on "voice" as described in *Exit, Voice and Loyalty* (Hirschman, 1970). In a pluralistic society such as the United States, there are often decisions that cannot be answered by science or logic, where different perspectives are competing. When deeply held values point to different policy decisions, the way in which these decisions are made becomes an ethical imperative. Daniels and Sabin's contention is that if the decision process is fair and transparent, the subsequent results are more likely to be ethically justifiable and accepted as legitimate and fair. Although some may be unhappy with the results, they should nonetheless be satisfied that the process for reaching those results was reasonable, participatory, and transparent.

TABLE 6-1 Summary of Opportunities for Patient or Public Input in Selected Technology Coverage Processes in Different Regions

Adviser and/or Decision Maker	Identification of Technologies		Selection of Technologies for Assessment		Undertaking of HTA[a]		Review of HTA Results and Formulation of Recommendations		Implementation of Recommendations and Decisions		Dissemination of Decisions and HTA Findings	
	Patients	Public	Patients	Public	Patients	Public	Patients	Public	Patients	Public	Patients	Public
National Level USA[b] CMS (decisions) CMS Medicare Evidence Development and Coverage Advisory Committee	Yes — Patients and/or carers may refer technologies for assessment	No	Yes — Anyone may provide additional information and/or comment on potential technology topics identified by CMS staff	Yes	Yes — Anyone may submit information to group preparing HTA	Yes	Yes — Anyone may register to present to the committee	Yes	Yes — Anyone may appeal recommendations	Yes	N/A	N/A — No information found
State Level Oregon, USA[c] State of Oregon Health Resources Commission (recommendations)	Yes — Technologies may be referred by anyone	Yes	No N/A	No	Yes — Anyone may submit information to group preparing HTA	Yes	Yes — Anyone may register to present to the committee; Anyone may provide comments on report and draft recommendations; Committee meetings in public	Yes	No N/A	No	No N/A	No
Washington, USA[d] • Washington State Healthcare Authority (decisions) • Washington State Healthcare Authority Health Technology Clinical Committee	Yes — Technologies may be referred by anyone	Yes	No N/A	No	Yes — Anyone may submit information to group preparing HTA	Yes	Yes — Anyone may provide comments on report and draft recommendations; Committee meetings held in public	Yes	No N/A	No	No N/A	No

[a] CMS = Centers for Medicare & Medicaid Services; HTA = health technology assessment.
[b] Chalkidou et al., 2009; CMS, 2003, 2006a,b,c; ISPOR, 2011; Washington State Health Care Authority, 2007a.
[c] Oregon Health Resources Commission, 1994, 2006.
[d] Washington State Health Care Authority, 2007a,b,c, 2008.
SOURCE: Adapted from Menon and Stafinski (2011) in *Expert Review of Pharmacoeconomics & Outcomes Research*, February 2011, Vol. 11, No. 1, Pages 75-89 with permission of Expert Reviews Ltd.

Four conditions contribute to being accountable for reasonableness:

1. *Publicity*: Decisions that establish priorities in allocating resources for health needs and their rationales must be publicly accessible.
2. *Relevance*: The rationales for priority-setting decisions should aim to provide a reasonable explanation of why the priorities selected were determined to be the best approach. Specifically, a rationale is reasonable if it appeals to evidence, reasons, and principles accepted as relevant by fair-minded people. Closely linked to this condition is the inclusion of a broad range of stakeholder perspectives in decision making. It is crucial that both individual needs and preferences and population needs and preferences should be considered.
3. *Revision and appeals*: There must be mechanisms for challenge and dispute and, more broadly, opportunities for revision and improvement of policies in light of new evidence or arguments.
4. *Regulative*: There must be mechanisms to ensure that conditions 1, 2, and 3 are met. The publicity condition exposes the rationales of decision makers.

These components are reflected in the recommendations of this committee, which also recognizes that the general public must be part of that "broad range of stakeholders in decision making."

Why Public Deliberation?

The usual avenues for citizen input (e.g., petitions, elections, town hall meetings, telephone surveys) capture public *opinion*. However when issues are complex, are multifaceted, and require tradeoffs among desirable (or undesirable) approaches to a problem, understanding the public's informed perspectives cannot be achieved simply by gathering public opinion (Abelson, 2010). Not only does the content of the issue require more background information than a survey can provide, but also the deliberative process itself takes the average citizen to a level of judgment that many have not experienced, moving from *"What is in the best interest of me and my family?"* to *"What is in the best interest of all who are sharing in the cost and the use of these services?"*

There are many reasons for engaging the public on issues such as health care benefits—as a basis for policy development: to educate the public on the challenges of allocating finite resources; to give purchasers information on how their constituents respond to tradeoffs; to study the impact that deliberation has on the public's views; and to motivate individuals to greater civic participation. It is also a powerful tool for conveying the message, "Your values count."

The elements of health care coverage and decision making are broad and deep. Many components fall under the purview of other players, such as professional associations that set standards for ethical practice; expert panels that develop and recommend clinical guidelines; researchers who study clinical effectiveness; and health plan administrators who determine if a treatment falls within the defined benefits package. The players most central to the use of medical care—physicians and patients—also have specific roles. Physicians diagnose the medical conditions and identify potential treatments for their individual patients. Patients determine which of the recommended and available treatments best meet their particular needs.

Yet none of these stakeholders has a unique claim on deciding what insurance should pay for. Insurers, legislators, and purchasers have typically been the ones to define the boundaries of coverage, yet as the options for coverage expand and available dollars do not, their perspectives cannot be assumed to reflect the views of the public, especially those to whom coverage decisions apply. These circumstances call for a societal perspective of how citizens get the most value for their health care dollar (Fleck, 2009).

When coverage is excluded or cost sharing is prohibitive, some will be disadvantaged. People with sufficient discretionary funds still will be able to pay out-of-pocket for uncovered services, while individuals without those resources will not. If the process for determining where the lines for coverage are drawn is reasonable and transparent, the results may be unfortunate for some, but they are not unfair.

COMPONENTS OF PUBLIC DELIBERATION PROCESSES

Productive processes for identifying public values as a component of determining the benefit package require attention to four elements: (1) specifying the issues that the public is being asked to address; (2) developing and conducting an effective process; (3) interpreting and using the findings to inform policy decisions; and (4) integrating transparency and accountability.

Specifying the Issues for the Public to Address

Public deliberation processes can be applied to a wide variety of coverage, policy, and practice issues. For the purpose of the EHB, the committee believes that certain deliberative questions are particularly relevant:

- When considering the many types of medical problems that could be covered by health insurance, what makes some a higher priority than others?
- How should we determine the limits to when, how, and what medical treatments should be covered?
- What is the preferred balance between various cost-controlling measures, such as comprehensiveness of coverage, cost sharing, utilization management, extent of provider network, etc.?
- What role should incentives play in encouraging high value care and discouraging low value interventions?
- If disadvantaged groups have different needs and priorities than others, what is society's responsibility to address those needs?
- When assessing the benefit of a medical treatment, how should the cost of the treatment be factored into coverage policy? When resources are limited, what is considered a "good value"?
- If the costs of life-extending interventions are prohibitive, is it acceptable to insist on lower prices as a condition of coverage inclusion?
- If research shows that some physicians or hospitals deliver lower quality care than others, should this be relevant to benefits design?
- What should we expect of individuals in terms of their personal health care responsibility?
- If some treatments are proven to be ineffective, what impact should this have on coverage policy?

Many of the questions refer to priority setting that directly impacts patients or consumers. There are additional ways to tackle cost inflation that do not involve consumer compromises so directly. However, the issues most appropriate for public deliberation about coverage are those that present tradeoffs affecting consumers directly. In essence, the process is stating that "some choices have to be made about what we are going to pay for using the limited funds in our insurance pool. Because you are part of this pool, we need you to be involved in making these choices."

Although this focus is on consumer tradeoffs, priority setting by the public should not be in lieu of other stakeholders—providers, insurers, pharmaceutical companies, device manufacturers, and others—taking necessary actions to reduce their own costs for the sake of a more efficient and responsible system. The concept of shared responsibility must apply throughout the EHB program, and to expect sacrifice solely by the public is both unrealistic and unfair.

Developing and Conducting an Effective Deliberative Process

There are components of deliberation that distinguish it from focus groups, town hall meetings, and other means of public input. These latter methods elicit public opinion, reflecting general perspectives and level of knowledge at a certain time. However, public opinion does not capture public values—those core beliefs and convictions that surface when people have the time and opportunity to probe their reflexive judgments and weigh difficult options carefully (Abelson et al., 2003).

The credibility of a deliberative process relies on careful attention to its design and execution. A commonly used format for deliberative processes is a group session with multiple interactive segments. Participants learn the issue or dilemma, consider alternative approaches, choose options, voice perspectives, hear the views of others, debate choices, and identify common ground (Abelson, 2010). Because the alternative approaches all have advantages and disadvantages, deliberation means taking the time to weigh and discuss each, uncovering personal and societal convictions about what can and cannot be compromised.

When conducted by skilled, impartial facilitators, deliberation is always interactive, where demographically represented members have a chance to give their own perspectives and hear the views of others. Most important, deliberation deals with explicit tradeoffs, where decisions to accept one course of action invariably mean giving up a different one. Thus, a deliberative process for the EHB must be structured around a finite budget or specific ranking where participants' decisions explicitly reveal a hierarchy of evaluation. It is this hierarchy requirement that encourages participants to consider carefully what has the most value and why.

The discussion process incorporates common vernacular and experiences of the lay public. Seeing how these options apply in real-life situations allows people to grasp their relevance and assess the impact on themselves and on others. Developing the discussion protocol—how participants are introduced to the dilemmas, the examples of situations that illustrate the "conflict," the process of individual and group decisions—is generally done by experts skilled in deliberative methods. The legitimacy of the process hinges on the extent to which these sessions are (and are perceived to be) factually accurate, balanced, unbiased, representative, and designed commensurate with the knowledge and abilities of the lay public (Fleck, 2009). Other parameters that also speak to the credibility of the process include the following:

- *Number of sessions.* These sessions are far more labor-intensive than phone surveys, so the number of participants will likely be smaller. Although 10 small group sessions (totaling about 120 people) can provide the full range of views, some stakeholders may feel that more sessions are needed for the process and results to be credible to the wider public. Available time and funding often dictate the number of groups that can be conducted.
- *Location of sessions.* Geographic diversity is especially important given the variety of populations that reside within states and the nation as a whole.
- *Length of sessions.* Two- to three-hour discussions are common; more extensive meetings (half-day to multi-day) yield more and richer results but are not always practical.
- *Participant sample.* The target population needs to be defined, whether it is those who are expected to use insurance defined by the EHB, the general public, or particular subsets of the population. Diversity of other demographic features (age, gender, insurance status, ethnicity, education, household income, etc.) is also important. Although most groups are heterogeneous, at times homogeneous group discussions (such as all Spanish-language or adult disabled groups) are needed to truly capture some unique perspectives. With fewer participants than in a phone survey, attention to representative sampling will help instill confidence in the integrity of the effort.
- *Recruitment strategies.* These vary from asking the help of local organizations to posting notices, using professional recruitment firms, and other methods. The more professional the recruitment process, the more likely is demographic representation to be achieved.
- *Facilitation.* Sessions should be facilitated by experienced, neutral professionals who have no vested interest in the outcome or ties to stakeholder groups. Although the discussion protocol is the building block for a credible process, it is the facilitation that determines how participants engage and the impartiality with which the sessions are conducted.
- *Respecting privacy of participants.* For participants to feel that they can speak freely and openly, they must know that their words will not be publicly attributed to them. Although the names of all participants and the transcripts should be publicly available, individual comments should not be identified by name or demographic characteristics.
- *Participant feedback.* There are a variety of ways to assess the success of deliberative sessions, including the reactions of the participants themselves. Post-discussion surveys can determine how participants responded to the process and their assessment of whether it met the goals of being inclusive and balanced.

Although the target groups for deliberative participation are typically those most likely to be subject to the coverage limits, other stakeholders can benefit by observing the deliberative sessions or being participants in separate sessions.[1] Policy and health care leaders usually have no more experience in prioritizing health care benefits than does the general public. Experiencing the challenges—and noting where these elites do and do not make decisions differently from others—can be an eye-opener for policy experts.

Interpreting and Using the Findings to Inform Policy Decisions

When deliberative sessions involve larger numbers of participants, quantitative data can be collected and analyzed, but the most meaningful findings from sessions of any size are qualitative: the reasoning and rationale for participants' choices. These qualitative data are derived from transcripts (audio and/or video) of session recordings.

Just as the development of the discussion protocol and the facilitation of the sessions should be objective and nonpartisan, so should the interpretation of the findings and the development of conclusions or recommendations. The group given this task could include different players, those intimately involved with the deliberations, and those who might bring "fresh eyes" to reviewing the transcripts and conclusions.

Most importantly, these findings should be used to inform policy decisions and public education (Sabik and Lie, 2008). This does not mean that everything the public values takes precedence over all other considerations, but the results should not be ignored or given only token attention. The success of the EHB structure will depend to a large extent on trust by the public—as those whose insurance is defined by the EHB, as taxpayers, and as interested and concerned citizens—and this trust will be damaged if deliberation is viewed as window-dressing. Building public deliberation into the EHB process can also contribute to public understanding of the need to make tough choices about the allocation of health care resources.

An effective process will have a public communication plan for both the process and its findings, with targeted audiences including the decision makers, the participants, the general public, and the entities to which the decision makers are accountable. Inattentiveness to the communication plan can jeopardize the acceptance of the findings, but an effective communication plan can help to build consensus.

Integrating Transparency and Accountability

The need for transparency extends beyond a communication plan. Indeed it should be embedded in the deliberative process as a "way of doing work." The three components of public deliberation—specifying the issue, developing and conducting the process, and interpreting and using the findings—each must be fully transparent to those participating and those on the periphery. Transparency and accountability are the responsibility of the authority ultimately charged with making the EHB determination—the Secretary or the designated state unit. Specifically, these may be manifested in actions such as the following:

- Forming an advisory committee—with representatives of various stakeholders, including consumers and consumer advocates—to provide oversight to the public deliberation process;
- Publicizing information on why public deliberation processes are being conducted;
- Providing opportunities for others to offer suggestions for deliberative topics;
- Making available transcripts and qualitative data (redacted to maintain confidentiality of participants' individual comments) to the public on request;
- Making available a draft version of the analysis for review and comment prior to the final version; and
- Conducting a public session to present the results of the analysis and to get feedback from policy leaders.

---

[1] For example, a deliberative prioritization process (CHAT) was conducted as a 2-hour educational program with 18 business and health care groups in 2009-2010 totaling 250 people. In response to this post-discussion question, *Which statement most closely represents your view about participating in this CHAT session,* 32 percent responded, *This will affect how I consider coverage policy in the future*; 63 percent responded, *This has given me something to think about*; 5 percent responded, *No new information but it was enjoyable*; none responded, *This was not a good use of my time* (Center for Healthcare Decisions, unpublished data).

EXAMPLES OF PUBLIC PARTICIPATION AND DELIBERATIVE PROCESSES

For many years, a number of organizations in this country have developed and/or conducted civic deliberation on a wide variety of public policy issues. The academic community also studies civic deliberation—learning how the public reaches informed decisions, the strength of those decisions, and the impact this has on individuals' sense of civic duty. However the most noteworthy use of public deliberation to help inform new health care policy was in Oregon in 1989.

Oregon Health Plan

As part of the Oregon Health Plan to expand Medicaid to more Oregon residents, Oregon's Senate Bill 27 of 1989 required the Health Services Commission to "actively solicit public involvement by a community meeting process."[2] The architects of the plan recognized that defining a "basic" level of care "must be based on criteria that are publicly debated, reflect a consensus of social values, and consider the good of society as a whole" (DHS, 2006, p. 2). Although a variety of tools were used to gain public input, the initial citizen discussion groups provided the commission with a set of core values to help guide the prioritization process. These discussion groups used a vignette approach, illustrating a range of health care situations and the impact they had on individuals. In 47 small group discussions around the state, skilled facilitators asked participants to rank order the vignettes by their importance for health care coverage and then to discuss their rationale for the rankings. The purpose was not to ascertain a numerical score but to identify the reasoning people used in considering their prioritizations. Understanding the relative importance of various states of health and the significance of different medical problems for individuals and for society helped the Health Services Commission craft its initial set of coverage categories.

These community discussions, while thoughtfully and professionally constructed and analyzed, were subject to much criticism because they did not include the necessary demographic diversity. This failure to meet the criterion of an appropriate participant sample was the consequence of insufficient funding to support the effort needed to find, recruit, and provide stipends to those on Medicaid or those who would qualify under the new state health plan. Thus, these meetings were overrepresented by well-educated, higher-income individuals, many of whom were health care professionals.

Nevertheless, Oregon's long-standing commitment to public participation at all stages and organizational levels is well demonstrated. There is consumer representation on the commission, and meetings are held publicly usually every 1 to 2 months, with the opportunity for both public testimony and review of draft reports and recommendations.

One of the most unique aspects of the Oregon Health Plan, however, was not public engagement per se. It was that the Oregon legislation required that a process to identify public values be a component and that the results were incorporated into the structure of the plan. Other known instances where public deliberation was instrumental in effecting coverage expansion plans were in the communities of Muskegon, Michigan (Fronstin and Lee, 2005),[3] and Galveston, Texas (Danis et al., 2010). They both used public prioritization processes in establishing plans for low-income employees of small businesses.

Both of these communities had separate funding to help underwrite the costs of the deliberative processes. To avoid situations like Oregon's where the meetings were conducted on a shoestring budget, national and state leaders may have to ask the philanthropy community to help fund these efforts. In most cases, deliberative sessions are held episodically, so the funding needed is usually short term.

Public Sector Interest

In the past 5 years, prior to the passage of the ACA, several states have sponsored, organized, and conducted public deliberation sessions to help inform coverage expansion plans in their states.

---

[2] State of Oregon S.B. 27 (1989).

[3] Personal communication with Vondie Woodbury, Muskegon County Health Project, February 2007.

The state departments of insurance of Ohio, Oklahoma, Montana, and North Dakota, under the direction of their state commissioners, all sponsored statewide discussion groups to identify core values and priorities for coverage for the uninsured. Although implementation of these health care expansion programs was stalled because of the economic downturn, the results of the deliberative sessions were useful in providing direction for policy leaders (Danis et al., 2010; North Dakota Insurance Department, 2011; Ohio Department of Insurance, 2009; State of Oklahoma, 2009).

In California in 2004, a public deliberation project was conducted with adult disabled Medicaid beneficiaries (Danis et al., 2006; Ginsburg and Glasmire, 2004). This was designed to see how recipients themselves would construct a benefits package that had to incorporate a 15 percent cut in the cost of coverage, the projected size of the proposed Medi-Cal budget reduction that year. State officials watched this project with interest, which provided them with important information and insights regarding recipients' views and priorities.[4]

Private Sector Interest

A deliberative tool called CHAT (see details below) opened up opportunities for employers to engage their employees in priority setting for health plan benefits. The early 2000s brought rapidly rising premiums, and anxious employers were seeking ways both to educate their employees about the challenges of maintaining affordable health coverage and to gain input on the coverage issues that were especially critical to them. Allina Foundation in Minnesota sponsored a statewide project with the Minnesota Chamber of Commerce in 2001 to gain employee input on how to best structure employer-sponsored health benefits (Minnesota Chamber of Commerce and The Allina Foundation, 2001). The Center for Healthcare Decisions conducted two projects in the greater Sacramento region in 2002 (Danis et al., 2007) and 2006 (Ginsburg et al., 2006), engaging diverse groups of employees in decisions on, respectively, what aspects of coverage were most important for their company's health insurance and what constitutes the elements of a basic health plan for the uninsured. Although the primary intent of the first project was to help employees gain knowledge and insights about health plan coverage limits, at least two employers used the results to help inform their own health plan changes (Danis et al., 2010).

CHAT (Choosing Healthplans All Together)

One particular tool for decision making has received considerable attention in the past 10 years. Developed in 1998 by two bioethicists—Drs. Susan Dorr Goold at the University of Michigan and Marion Danis at the National Institutes of Health—CHAT is a simulation exercise for designing a benefits package when there are more options than there are available funds (Goold et al., 2005). This small group process requires participants (as individuals and as a group) to make choices among competing health care priorities. It is typically conducted with each participant using an individual laptop before coverage decisions must be made as a group. The flexibility of the CHAT software allows the options to be modified as needed to expose participants to the specific choices and tradeoffs that are relevant to the policy issues being explored. An actuarial analysis is incorporated into the CHAT model to ensure that choices are a realistic representation of actual costs.

Among the tradeoffs that can be represented are such competing priorities as ranges of provider choice, degrees of cost sharing, types of cost sharing, extent of coverage categories, types of treatment available, utilization oversight, and standards of treatment effectiveness, among others. The descriptions use terms and concepts that are understood by the average consumer. Quantitative data are easy to capture, but the dominant feature of the process is the interactive dialogue, debate, and negotiation that takes place when a group of 12-15 participants seeks agreement on what aspects of coverage are most important and why. In the United States, CHAT has been used in at least 10 states to help inform state and community leaders about covered benefits and benefit design, including those mentioned previously under the section Public Sector Interest (Danis et al., 2010). In California, CHAT has been used with insured employees, Medicaid beneficiaries, the uninsured, health care professionals,

---

[4] Personal communication with Kim Belshe, former Secretary, California Department of Health and Human Services, July 5, 2011.

and policy leaders and as an educational program for health care and business leadership development (CHCD, 2011; Ginsburg and Glasmire, 2007; NIH, 2011).

CHAT is not the only way to conduct public deliberation about benefits. Less time-intensive and technology-dependent formats can be developed, and other processes have been used for topics related to resource allocation decisions (CHCD, 2009; CHCD and Sacramento HealthCare Decisions, 2001, 2006; Gold et al., 2007). Deliberative processes on other aspects of health care (and other public policy issues) are conducted in communities across the country by Public Agenda, National Issues Forum, AmericaSpeaks, Viewpoint Learning, and other organizations.

Participants' Reaction

Policy leaders may wonder if the public might regard its participation in coverage decisions with suspicion or resentment. This was a particular concern when the Center for Healthcare Decisions (CHCD) conducted deliberative sessions with adult disabled Medi-Cal beneficiaries, as referenced earlier in this chapter. CHCD thought that participants would be outraged at the idea of being asked to make decisions that would reduce their own benefits (which, in fact, was their assignment using the CHAT process). Surprisingly, the general response was, *We know the state is talking about cutting Medi-Cal; we'd rather have a say in this than be ignored.* A post-CHAT survey question reflected this sentiment (Table 6-2).

SUMMARY OF GUIDELINES FOR PUBLIC PARTICIPATION

At every step of their work, national and state entities responsible for defining and refining the EHB should ensure meaningful and visible public participation. There are two broad areas in which guidelines regarding public participation are relevant: (1) in the oversight of the EHB program and (2) in the identification of social values to help guide decisions on what and how coverage is provided within the EHB. These guidelines are consistent with the criteria outlined in Figure S-2 in the Summary and include the following:

- The National Benefits Advisory Council (see Recommendation 5 in Chapter 9) and governance of the state health insurance exchanges need to ensure that the consumer or citizen voice is an active one in the development, operations, and evaluation of the EHB. This may be best achieved through public deliberation, advisory committees, and/or other means of public input and participation.
- A credible process for establishing the EHB includes a public deliberation component. These structured, interactive group sessions identify the values and priorities of key constituents (such as people whose insurance is defined by the EHB) and are germane to establishing the EHB.
- A public deliberation process is also encouraged when seeking approval of state variants in an EHB package or waivers (Recommendation 3 in Chapter 8), and at other times when meaningful changes in benefits structure are being considered. When these are conducted at the state level, these processes are under the direction of the governor or his/her designate (e.g., the exchange governing body).

TABLE 6-2 CHAT Results from Medi-Cal Survey of Users' Views (Adults with Disabilities) on Public Input in Areas of Budget Cut

Agree or Disagree: If the Medi-Cal budget is cut, I think it is important for Medi-Cal users to have a role in deciding how the cuts are made (N = 131)	
Agree strongly	89%
Agree somewhat	5%
Disagree somewhat	2%
Disagree strongly	2%
Not sure	1%

SOURCE: Ginsburg and Glasmire, 2004.

- Public deliberation processes follow protocols that ensure they will be nonpartisan, reasonably representative and inclusive, and professionally designed, executed, and analyzed. The deliberative sessions are of sufficient number so as to produce meaningful and trustworthy findings.
- The findings and recommendations of deliberative sessions are made public (and open to public comment) prior to final reporting.
- Development of or changes in the EHB are accompanied by an explanation of how they relate to the findings of the relevant deliberative processes.

The values of an informed public are not always determinative. The concerns of public health and legislative leaders and issues of social justice (particularly relating to vulnerable populations) may take precedence over some of the priorities identified by the general public. Ultimately, policy leaders are responsible for balancing the needs and interests of multiple stakeholders with diverse concerns. Yet the inevitability of limit-setting requires a nonpartisan, transparent process for eliciting the core values of key players, including taxpayers and health plan enrollees. Health care has always been steeped in tradeoffs; this fact is simply more apparent now. Incorporating an informed citizen perspective can make these tradeoffs more responsible, responsive, and acceptable to the public.

REFERENCES

Abelson, J. 2010. Using qualitative research methods to inform health policy: The case of public deliberation. In *The SAGE handbook of qualitative methods in health research*. London, UK: SAGE Publications Ltd.

Abelson, J., E. Eyles, C. McLeod, P. Collins, C. McMullan, and P. G. Forest. 2003. Does deliberation make a difference? Results from a citizens' study of health goals priority setting. *Health Policy* 66(203):95-106.

Chalkidou, K., S. Tunis, R. Lopert, L. Rochaix, P. T. Sawicki, M. Nasser, and B. Xerri. 2009. Comparative effectiveness research and evidence-based health policy: Experience from four countries. *Milbank Quarterly* 87(2):339-367.

CHCD (Center for Healthcare Decisions). 2009. *What matters most: Californians' priorities for healthcare coverage*. http://www.chcd.org/whatmattersmost/docs/wmm_report.pdf (accessed July 11, 2011).

_____. 2011. *Center for Healthcare Decisions home page*. http://www.chcd.org (accessed July 11, 2011).

CHCD and Sacramento HealthCare Decisions. 2001. *Cost effectiveness as a criterion for medical and coverage decisions: Understanding and responding to community perspectives*. http://chcd.org/docs/vf.pdf (accessed July 11, 2011).

_____. 2006. *Getting good value: Consumers debate costly treatments—is the gain worth the expense?* http://chcd.org/docs/ggv_report.pdf (accessed July 11, 2011).

CMS (Centers for Medicare & Medicaid Services). 2003. *Guiding principles for when national coverage determination topics are referred for external expertise via a technology assessment and/or the Medicare Coverage Advisory Committee draft guidance—not for implementation*. http://www.cms.gov/FACA/Downloads/guidelines.pdf (accessed August 1, 2011).

_____. 2006a. *Factors CMS considers in opening a national coverage determination*. https://www.cms.gov/medicare-coverage-database/details/medicare-coverage-document-details.aspx?MCDId=6&McdName=Factors+CMS+Considers+in+Opening+a+National+Coverage+Determination&mcdtypename=Guidance+Documents&MCDIndexType=1&bc=BAAIAAAAAAAA& (accessed August 1, 2011).

_____. 2006b. *Factors CMS considers in referring topics to the Medicare Evidence Development & Coverage Advisory Committee*. https://www.cms.gov/medicare-coverage-database/details/medicare-coverage-document-details.aspx?MCDId=10&McdName=Factors+CMS+Considers+in+Referring+Topics+to+the+Medicare+Evidence+Development+%26+Coverage+Advisory+Committee&mcdtypename=Guidance+Documents&MCDIndexType=1&bc=AgEAAAAAAAAA& (accessed August 1, 2011).

_____. 2006c. *National coverage determinations with data collection as a condition of coverage: Coverage with evidence development*. https://www.cms.gov/medicare-coverage-database/details/medicare-coverage-document-details.aspx?MCDId=8&McdName=National+Coverage+Determinations+with+Data+Collection+as+a+Condition+of+Coverage%3A+Coverage+with+Evidence+Development&mcdtypename=Guidance+Documents&MCDIndexType=1&bc=AgEAAAAAAAAA& (accessed August 1, 2011).

Daniels, N., and J. E. Sabin. 2008. *Setting limits fairly: Learning to share resources for health*. 2nd ed. New York: Oxford University Press.

Danis, M., M. Ginsburg, and S. D. Goold. 2006. The coverage priorities for disabled adult Medi-Cal beneficiaries. *Journal for the Health Care for the Poor and Underserved* 17(3):592-609.

Danis, M., S. D. Goold, C. Parise, and M. Ginsburg. 2007. Enhancing employee capacity to prioritize health insurance benefits. *Health Expectations* 10(3):236-247.

Danis, M., M. Ginsburg, and S. D. Goold. 2010. Experience in the United States with public deliberation about health insurance benefits using the small group decision exercise, CHAT. *Journal of Ambulatory Care Management* 33(3):205-214.

DHS (Department of Human Services). 2006. *Oregon health plan: An historical overview*. Salem, OR: Oregon Department of Human Services.

Fleck, L. M. 2009. *Just caring: Health care rationing and democratic deliberation*. 1st ed. New York: Oxford University Press.

Fronstin, P., and J. Lee. 2005. *The Muskegon Access Health "Three Share" Plan: A case history*. http://www.ebri.org/pdf/briefspdf/0605ib.pdf (accessed July 8, 2011).

Ginsburg, M., and K. Glasmire. 2004. *Making tough choices: Adults with disabilities prioritize their Medi-Cal options.* http://www.chcd.org/docs/MediCalCHAT.pdf (accessed July 8, 2011).

_____. 2007. *Designing coverage: Uninsured Californians weigh the options.* http://www.chcf.org/~/media/Files/PDF/D/PDF%20Design CoverageForUninsured.pdf (accessed July 8, 2011).

Ginsburg, M., S. D. Goold, and M. Danis. 2006. (De)constructing basic benefits: Citizens define the limits of coverage. *Health Affairs* 25(6):1648-1655.

Gold, M. R., P. Franks, T. Siegelberg, and S. Sofaer. 2007. Does providing cost-effectiveness information change coverage priorities for citizens acting as social decision makers? *Health Policy* 83(1):65-72.

Goold, S. D., A. K. Biddle, H. Klipp, C. Hall, and M. Danis. 2005. Choosing Healthplans All Together: A deliberative exercise for allocating limited health care resources. *Journal of Health Politics, Policy, and Law* 30(4):563-601.

HHS (Department of Health and Human Services). 2010. *Charter: Medicare Evidence Development & Coverage Advisory Committee.* Washington, DC: U.S. Department of Health and Human Services.

Hirschman, A. O. 1970. *Exit, voice, and loyalty: Responses to decline in firms, organizations, and states.* Cambridge, MA: Harvard University Press.

ISPOR (International Society for Pharmacoeconomics and Outcomes Research). 2011. *ISPOR global health care systems road map: United States—health policy decision process.* http://www.ispor.org/HTARoadMaps/USHP.asp (accessed August 1, 2011).

McCoy, M. L., and P. L. Scully. 2002. *Deliberative dialogue to expand civic engagement: What kind of talk does democracy need?* http://www.ncl.org/publications/ncr/91-2/ncr91-2_article.pdf (accessed July 8, 2011).

Menon, D., and T. Stafinski. 2011. Role of patient and public participation in health technology assessment and coverage decisions. *Expert Review of Pharmacoeconomics & Outcomes Research* 11(1):75-89.

Minnesota Chamber of Commerce and The Allina Foundation. 2001. *Minnesota employees' health care spending priorities: The CHAT project [unpublished].* St. Paul, MN: Minnesota Chamber of Commerce.

NIH (National Institutes of Health). 2011. *Engaging the public in priority setting for health.* http://www.bioethics.nih.gov/research/pubeng/ (accessed July 11, 2011).

North Dakota Insurance Department. 2011. *About us: CHAT.* http://www.nd.gov/ndins/about/chat/ (accessed July 11, 2011).

NRC (National Research Council). 1996. *Understanding risk: Informing decisions in a democratic society.* Washington, DC: National Academy Press.

Ohio Department of Insurance. 2009. *Ohio CHATs about healthcare: Voices of the uninsured.* http://www.insurance.ohio.gov/Legal/Reports/Documents/CHATreport.pdf (accessed July 11, 2011).

Oregon Health Resources Commission. 1994. *Medical Technology Assessment Program [MEDTAP].* http://www.oregon.gov/OHA/OHPR/HRC/docs/HRC.Reports/MEDTAP_09_accepted.pdf?ga=t (accessed August 1, 2011).

_____. 2006. *Medical Technology Assessment Program [MEDTAP]: Adopted by the Health Resources Commission on 2-17-06.* http://www.oregon.gov/OHA/OHPR/HRC/docs/Policy/MedTapPolicy.pdf?ga=t (accessed August 1, 2011).

Sabik, L., and R. Lie. 2008. Priority setting in health care: Lessons from the experiences of eight countries. *International Journal for Equity in Health Research* 7(4):1-13.

State of Oklahoma. 2009. *Oklahoma strategic plan: Oklahoma state coverage initiative.* http://www.ok.gov/oid/documents/July14-2009-SCI -Final.pdf (accessed July 11, 2011).

Washington State Health Care Authority. 2007a. *Health technology selection process.* http://www.hta.hca.wa.gov/documents/selection_process.pdf (accessed August 1, 2011).

_____. 2007b. *Prioritization criteria.* http://www.hta.hca.wa.gov/documents/prioritization_criteria.pdf (accessed August 1, 2011).

_____. 2007c. *Washington health technology assessment program (overview).* http://www.hta.hca.wa.gov/documents/hta_overview.pdf (accessed August 1, 2011).

_____. 2008. *Health technology assessment: Program review.* http://www.hta.hca.wa.gov/documents/program_review.pdf (accessed August 1, 2011).

Wynia, M. K., and A. P. Schwab. 2006. *Ensuring fairness in health care coverage decisions.* New York: AMACOM.

7

Program Monitoring and Research

Anticipating the need for data collection and research to support the process of updating the essential health benefits (EHB), the committee recommends that planning and development of a research strategy begin now. The Department of Health and Human Services (HHS) in collaboration (1) with groups such as the National Association of Insurance Commissioners (NAIC) can help promote standardization to enhance comparisons of state-based data (such as categories of benefits, design elements, medical necessity processes, and appeals) and (2) HHS component agencies, the Department of Labor (DOL), and others can develop a complementary research agenda to enable updates to the EHB to be more specific, evidence-based, and value-promoting. This chapter explores some aspects of data collection for program monitoring and development of a research agenda, with a call for development of the infrastructure to support the strategy and public access to data for analytic purposes.

An effective strategy for updating the essential health benefits (EHB) will require that HHS be prepared to respond to the changing health care environment. Over time, new medical care technologies will be introduced, clinical research will gain new insights, provider practices and patient needs will change, what is affordable will have to be considered, and societal preferences will shift. Furthermore, the design of insurance company products, employer offer rates, and consumer preferences will all affect the future private insurance landscape. An effective EHB updating process must be able to identify the key changes that are occurring and develop approaches to respond to those changes. This will require coordinated and thoughtful monitoring and research.

The Institute of Medicine (IOM) committee draws a distinction between monitoring—efforts to describe what is occurring as the EHB are implemented into insurance offerings—and research—efforts to create generalizable knowledge about the implications of the varied responses in markets across the states. Additionally, emerging evidence on medical advances needs to be evaluated to determine whether specific changes to the EHB definition are warranted, that is, whether new evidence changes the relative value of a particular drug, device, service, or category of care delivery. The committee envisions that this type of monitoring and research will be used directly by the Secretary in considering updates to the EHB. The committee calls on the Secretary to ensure that the necessary infrastructure is in place to answer the key questions.

The committee recognizes that the Patient Protection and Affordable Care Act (ACA) contains numerous elements that require monitoring, research, and oversight, such as the implementation of health insurance exchanges or expansion of the traditional Medicaid program. The EHB are just one of many areas requiring attention by HHS.

Although the committee focuses here on the monitoring and research needs relevant to the EHB, it recognizes that the optimal strategy within HHS is likely to be a coordinated approach across all areas. With respect to the EHB, monitoring and research can

- Provide input into the process of updating the EHB,
- Contribute to addressing questions in the Section 1302(b)(4)(G) required reports to Congress and the public,
- Monitor for discriminatory practices and balance as a result of initial EHB definition and its implementation, and
- Assess the impact of the EHB on consumers, employers, health care providers, insurers, and governments at the state and local levels.

Congress, in Section 1302 of the ACA in particular, calls out an interest in any problems related to access, methods for incorporating evidence of medical advances into the EHB, ideas about how best to close any gaps observed in access or changes to evidence, and assessing the cost implications of potential changes to the EHB. The committee also believes that HHS will want to know whether initial guidance on the EHB is achieving an appropriate balance between cost and coverage; how specific design elements and medical necessity determination processes can affect care delivered, outcomes, and value; whether rates of participation by consumers, employers, and insurers are affected by the EHB; how the EHB package can be updated to become more evidence-based and value-promoting; and what impact the composition of exchange participation has on premiums (e.g., greater or lesser participation by employers and individuals).

SETTING A RESEARCH FRAMEWORK FOR DATA COLLECTION AND ANALYSIS

The committee believes the monitoring and research strategy related to the EHB should be articulated thoughtfully as soon as possible to enhance planning efforts, allocate necessary resources, and align priorities for collecting comparable data among different stakeholders. A systematic pursuit of this strategy is consistent with creating a learning health care system (IOM, 2007, 2011). Such a strategy should engage stakeholders in ensuring that the right questions are being asked, that the purposes for the collected data are clear, that modifications to the EHB are justified and fair, that the EHB are becoming increasingly evidence-based over time, and that the country is spending its tax dollars (and enrollees their premium dollars) effectively and efficiently.

State oversight is important during approval of plan offerings, implementation, and appeals. The state and federal health insurance exchanges are responsible for determining which health plans are qualified to operate in the exchange and can serve as a primary data source for what is happening across states and over time in response to the Secretary's guidance. The EHB are also required for incorporation in all non-grandfathered individual and small employer policies offered outside the exchange; such plan oversight would be outside of exchange operations, but under the aegis of state insurance commissioners. Thus, oversight responsibility cannot lay solely with exchanges. Ideally, state departments of insurance will actively take on the responsibility to protect against adverse selection and discriminatory practices in their jurisdiction; it important that health plans, in and out of the exchanges, are complying with requirements of the EHB package and not using benefit design and administration to risk-select or deny access to care. Additionally, the EHB are to be incorporated in new Medicaid benchmark, benchmark-equivalent, and state basic health insurance instruments; these will be under a separate state agency, also reporting to Centers for Medicare & Medicaid Services (CMS).

Leveraging these potential state-level data resources will require providing clarity and standardization in data collection (e.g., categorization of included benefits; descriptions of plan limits, types of treatments and conditions that are the subject of appeals), which will in turn improve opportunities for the analysis of comparative data. State collection and reporting of data can be a condition of states receiving federal funding to establish the exchanges; notably though, federal funding of state exchanges is time limited. Insurer reporting of plan content, however, will remain a condition of being certified a qualified health plan. This information will also provide insight beyond the exchange because of the requirement for insurers to offer the same plans outside as inside. Insurers will likely be contracting with one or more external independent review organizations; these could be required to report appeals data in specific ways. If state regulatory systems will not already compile and publicly report appeals data in a way that is useful for evaluating EHB implementation and nondiscrimination, then additional support may be necessary for data provided to the Secretary. There is urgency in having guidance on required data collection for exchanges, regulatory agencies, and insurance companies. These expectations must be incorporated into planning in preparation for operations starting on January 1, 2014.

Tradeoffs are inevitable in setting the degree of data mining against the available resources (both cost and administrative burden) to collect and analyze data in order to ensure that implementation is achieving its goals and consumers are protected. Thus, priorities need to be set for available state and federal spending on monitoring and analysis. Some of the data collection and reporting would be part of normal state operations, but others, as noted above, might require additional resources. The exchanges and state insurance regulators will not be the only repositories of pertinent data; other state and federal sources might have to be mined to assess factors such as the size of the uninsured population, consumer satisfaction, health care utilization, quality of care, health status, and employer characteristics.

In Recommendation 2a, the committee calls on the Secretary to establish a framework for data collection and research; this framework should be developed with advice from the National Benefits Advisory Council (Recommendation 5 in Chapter 9).

Recommendation 2a: By January 1, 2013, the Secretary should establish a framework for obtaining and analyzing data necessary for monitoring implementation and updating of the EHB. The framework should account for

- **Changes related to providers such as payment rates, contracting mechanisms, financial incentives, and scope and organization of practice;**
- **Changes related to patients and consumers such as demographics, health status, disease burden, and problems with access; and**
- **Changes related to health plans such as characteristics of plans (inclusions, exclusions, limitations), cost-sharing practices, patterns of enrollment and disenrollment, network configuration, medical management programs (including medical necessity determination processes), value-based insurance design, types of external appeals, risk selection, solvency, and impact of the ACA-mandated limits on deductibles, co-payments, and out-of-pocket spending on the ability of plans to offer acceptable products.**

Creating a Responsive and Efficient Research Infrastructure

Furthermore, the committee recommends that the Secretary establish an infrastructure for this enterprise by engaging appropriate HHS components (e.g., CMS, Agency for Healthcare Research and Quality [AHRQ], Food and Drug Administration [FDA], National Institutes of Health, Office of the Assistant Secretary for Planning and Evaluation, Centers for Disease Control and Prevention) and other federal agencies (e.g., DOL, Office of Personnel Management, U.S. Census Bureau) and coordinating their expertise, data, and resources to fulfill research needs within and outside government (IOM, 2002, 2009a). CMS is the likely repository for exchange data as well as data from benchmark plans. Others such as the Kaiser Family Foundation and HRET Employer Health Benefits Annual Survey monitor employer benefit changes over time (KFF and HRET, 2010). Additionally, these activities will generate many questions of comparative effectiveness (IOM, 2009b). Close collaboration with the Patient-Centered Outcomes Research Institute (PCORI) will help to ensure that its research agenda considers these questions.

The Secretary must make the essential information needed for research by outside parties, including the standardized data collected from the EHB implementation processes as well as utilization and outcomes data from federal payers (Medicare, Medicaid), available in a timely, open, and streamlined way, just as HHS has sponsored access to other departmental data (e.g., http://www.health.data.gov). Private insurers must be encouraged and incentivized to collaborate in a similarly streamlined and open fashion. Strict attention to issues of data security and confidentiality, including compliance with all federal and state laws and regulations, must be maintained throughout the process.

To ensure research is conducted in accordance with the highest scientific standards, the committee suggests that the Secretary charge the Agency for Healthcare Research and Quality with responsibility for managing the processes of soliciting, reviewing, funding, and overseeing this research agenda.

Recommendation 2b: The Secretary should establish an appropriate infrastructure for implementing this framework that engages and coordinates the efforts of all of the appropriate HHS and other federal agencies in producing and analyzing the necessary data in a timely manner. These data should be made easily accessible and affordable for public use.

PROGRAM MONITORING AND RESEARCH

The committee offers some guidance for the implementation of these recommendations in terms of data collection via the exchanges and other sources, as well as some illustrative research questions.

Learning from the Exchanges and State Regulators

The EHB package will become a standard setter for the content of health insurance beyond the health exchange, but HHS can learn from those operating exchanges and from state regulators how the EHB are incorporated into health insurance products, what benefit design components are utilized to meet the coverage and premium requirements, how consumer preferences in the market (e.g., for high deductible plans) would relate to the scope and inclusiveness of the benefit package and its associated benefit design and premiums, and through the benefit determination and appeals process, concerns about access to specific benefits or for diverse segments of the population. Standardized approaches to defining data elements and collecting data from insurers will be essential for HHS to be able to analyze trends. The health insurance exchanges will also be better able to understand and improve the benefit design and administration processes if they can compare their experiences with those of other exchanges.

A second objective for the exchanges is to determine whether consumers understand the choices they are being offered. The ACA calls for designing plan materials that are simple and easy for most people to understand.[1] A key aspect of the information that is to be communicated in these materials is the scope of benefits, inclusions and exclusions, and premiums.

Improving Standardization

The EHB definition process offers HHS an opportunity to lead the standardization of categories of benefits and to increase the specificity with which inclusions and exclusions of services are presented. The methods of data collection and EHB articulation can and will set standards for commercial industry practices—which will be subject to intense scrutiny and pressure. Like the DOL, the committee found it difficult to make side-by-side comparisons among plans because of a lack of consistency in categories and degree of specificity. This is the same challenge faced by consumers who are trying to choose between health plans and was likely part of the impetus for the ACA requiring work to improve consumers' ability to understand their choices.

If reporting by the 10 categories is considered desirable (e.g., utilization or expenditures patterns), then several issues arise. First, the EHB list would have to identify what services fall within each category. Second, the 10 ACA categories do not match other payer methodologies, such as those used by Medicare or commercial providers. For example, insurance contracts, provider agreements, and current data tracking typically are based on location (e.g., inpatient vs. ambulatory) and type of provider (e.g., hospital vs. physician). However, the 10 EHB categories also include treatment-, condition-, and age-based categories; as a result, services and items will bridge

---

[1] Patient Protection and Affordable Care Act of 2010 as amended. § 1001, amending § 2715 of the Public Health Service Act, 111th Cong., 2d sess. [42 U.S.C. 300gg–15].

multiple categories. It may prove difficult within the current coding conventions used by public and private payers to categorize services offered or delivered into the 10 EHB categories reliably.

The Secretary, in conjunction with the National Benefits Advisory Council (NBAC), should engage state insurance commissioners and the National Association of Insurance Commissioners (NAIC) to facilitate setting standards for collection and uniform reporting of state-based data from subscriber (enrollee) contracts approved by states, just as HHS is working with insurance commissioners, health plans, and actuaries to standardize the collection of premium information and the disclosure of insurance contract information to consumers.[2]

Types of State-Based Data for Oversight

States currently review subscriber contracts (or "forms") to ascertain whether licensed health insurers are complying with state laws. The scope and nature of those reviews vary by state. HHS should work with states to standardize and collect information from these contracts, including at a minimum

1. Benefits covered and excluded at the plan level, with particular attention to the level of specificity at which those services and items are described, future approaches to categorization as specificity increases, and how the specificity of coverage varies across insurers now and over time;
2. Objective limits to services within covered categories—usually defined as service limits (e.g., number of office visits) to reveal general norms;
3. Exception language;
4. Coverage of new approaches to prevention, diagnosis, treatment, and management;
5. Categories and levels of cost sharing and state or health insurer innovations such as value-based insurance design;
6. Terms and conditions including medical necessity,[3] network limitation, and prior authorization; and
7. Rates of review and approval related to medical necessity, and specification of types of medical necessity review (e.g., by condition, treatment, coverage categories).

Items 1 through 4 will assist the Secretary in updating the EHB definition and ensuring balance and nondiscrimination by describing current variation in EHB implementation, coverage limits, exceptions, and trends in covering new technologies or other interventions. Items 5 and 6 will make clearer the landscape in benefit design, an important consideration in understanding trends in premium prices related to the EHB and measuring the impact of such benefit designs. Although the Secretary is not to preclude insurers from using various utilization management techniques, there is a requirement in Section 1302 to ensure that coverage decisions, reimbursement rates, incentive programs, or designs of benefits are not discriminatory on the basis of age, disability, or expected length of life, while Section 1557 explicitly pertains to nondiscrimination based on race, national origin, and gender. Furthermore, item 7 uses the strengthened appeals process in the ACA as a source of information for monitoring the various nondiscrimination factors in the required elements for consideration of Section 1302. Finally, to the extent feasible, any information collected in the monitoring and oversight process should include demographic data so that disparities and discrimination can be identified and rectified. Box 2-2 in Chapter 2 additionally elaborates on the type of data that should be collected from plans, including quality, utilization, and outcomes data to fully understand benefit design as implemented.

---

[2] The Center for Consumer Information and Insurance Oversight (CCIIO) oversees ACA Consumer Assistance Program Grants, grants to assist states in establishing, expanding, or supporting consumer assistance programs. These grant funds must be used to support activities such as assisting consumers in filing complaints and appeals, collecting data on problems and inquiries encountered by consumers, educating consumers regarding their rights and responsibilities in health plans and insurance coverage, and resolving problems with obtaining the tax credits specified by the law (CCIIO, 2010). NAIC has an online portal, Insure U, which provides consumers with an array of easily understandable resources for assistance in purchasing health insurance (NAIC, 2011).

[3] Ideally, data collection should include data on all medical necessity determinations, or at least on all denials, not just those that result in an appeal, but that may depend on the willingness of insurers to share such data and state requirements. Insurers elect to have a different number of review levels internally; Colorado requires public reporting on all internal second level reviews (State of Colorado, 2010).

The ACA leaves most oversight of health plans to the states, as is true today. As such, the exchanges and regulators are likely to derive considerable utility themselves from the information collected in each of these items. The Secretary will provide a significant service by collecting and compiling this information and supplying analyses back to these local entities. This work should be closely coordinated with other work set forth by the ACA and currently being done by HHS in two areas:

1. Efforts by the HHS Center for Consumer Information and Insurance Oversight (CCIIO), the NAIC, and state insurance departments to articulate standards for disclosure to consumers of subscriber contract elements. These standards should incorporate elements required for EHB specification.[4]
2. The monitoring of state-based exchanges to be conducted by CCIIO for purposes other than EHB definition, such as governance and administrative operations, certification of qualified health plans, the development of plan levels (e.g., gold, silver metal levels), and risk adjustment. Exchanges should not have to deal with multiple monitoring requests from multiple HHS program areas.

Standardization of terms and classification of services into categories is designed to improve comparisons. The committee anticipates that innovation in insurance products will continue and that classifying and analyzing these changes will be facilitated by the use of standardized definitions. Over time, some innovations may require updates to the nature and detail of the information being collected. As with the EHB, the committee does not believe the research and monitoring enterprises will be static.

External Appeals Information

Although the states are charged with monitoring and taking action with respect to appeals, this information would be useful to the Secretary in signaling whether frequently denied treatments indicate uncertainty due to a lack of evidence, changing medical indications that may require study, or lack of clarity about whether the treatment is included as part of the EHB. In addition, the committee recommends that data on appeals serve as the best approach for monitoring the "required elements for consideration" for nondiscrimination. Given its charge, the IOM committee was most interested in understanding coverage denials and complaints that, in turn, would inform both potential lack of access and questions about the available evidence base for services.

A March 2011 Government Accountability Office (GAO) report evaluated the current national availability of data on coverage denial rates (preauthorizations, denials of payment after service delivered) and found that there is "not yet any comprehensive national information on the extent to which coverage for medical services is being denied when consumers seek care" (GAO, 2011, p. 1). What data were available show that denials are "frequently reversed in the consumer's favor" if appealed (GAO, 2011, p. 16). GAO reported significant variability in denial rates due to methodological issues in what is counted (billing errors, duplicate claims, missing data, eligibility, satisfaction of deductible amount, and necessity of the service) and methods of reporting (i.e., paper-based vs. electronic claims). Aggregate coverage denial rates varied across four states examined in detail (11 percent in Ohio and 24 percent in California for 2009) and across the largest insurers within a single state (4 percent to 29 percent for the seven largest insurers in Connecticut in 2009). About 1 in 10 of the coverage denials, according to American Medical Association (AMA) and NAIC data, dealt with the appropriateness of services (GAO, 2011).

States will be providing greater consumer protections related to how coverage decisions and medical necessity determinations are made and how they may be appealed. Section 2719 of the Public Health Services Act, added by Section 10101(g) of the ACA, seeks to bring more consistency to what consumers can expect with respect to internal and external claims and appeals processes through new requirements for group health plans and health insurance companies.[5] In particular, all subscriber contracts must have a final level of "external appeal" to an

---

[4] § 1001, amending § 2715 of the Public Health Service Act [42 U.S.C. 300gg–15].

[5] The NAIC released a model state law that outlines an approach for responding to ACA requirements on grievances and appeals that will apply to insurers (NAIC, 2010). Interim final rules with request for comment were published July 22, 2010, and amendments issued June 24, 2011 (HHS, 2011b; U.S. Department of Labor et al., 2011).

independent outside party. The GAO report also calls attention to the frequency of reversal of coverage denials when such appeals are undertaken: from 39 to 59 percent of internal appeals across four states, and of those then appealed to an external source across six states, from 23 to 54 percent were overturned or revised (GAO, 2011). The GAO report also referenced an earlier study showing a difference in external appeal overturn rates by type of coverage denial in California managed care (42 percent of medical necessity cases overturned vs. 20 percent of experimental and investigational cases in 2002) (Gresenz and Studdert, 2005); more recent data presented to the IOM committee were not so proportionally disparate, showing 40 percent of medical necessity cases and 37 percent of experimental and investigational cases were overturned on independent external review (see Table 7-1). Overall, 661 decisions (out of 1,452 grievances that proceeded through the Independent Medical Review [IMR] process) were in favor of the enrollee; for each of these, the plan was required to authorize the treatment within 5 days of receiving the decision.

Notably, the Director of the California Department of Managed Health Care (DMHC), when testifying before the committee, pointed out another compelling statistic—the percentage of reversals by health plans of externally appealed cases even before they were reviewed (324 of 1,776 cases): 19 percent of medical necessity cases, 13 percent of experimental and investigational, and 34 percent of emergency room reimbursements. Staff of the DMHC felt these reversals were not the result of new clinical information because the pertinent clinical information should have surfaced during the insurer's internal review (DMHC, 2011). To help visualize the overall degree of claims overturned, one insurer provided a figure with self-reported data showing of 91 million claims in the United States, approximately 99 percent of those were paid without a required preauthorization (Figure 7-1). At intermediate steps, 1 in 10 denials was appealed by patients, and 29 percent of the initial denials that were appealed were overturned as additional clinical information was obtained, and 3 percent were overturned on the same clinical information. Overall, 0.006 percent of total eligible claims were not ultimately approved.[6]

The committee agrees with HHS's observation on the GAO report that "very little information is available to help analysts understand the causes or sources of variation in the data" (GAO, 2011, p. 26). Besides helping consumers shopping for insurance, improved data, including developing a standardized appeals database and requirements for reporting of these data, would facilitate recognition of potential problem areas in EHB definition. Once collected, the information should be analyzed to detect and understand meaningful trends, thus effectively also serving to monitor the changes in insurer behavior as part of the monitoring recommended in this chapter.

Standardization includes classifying individual appeals in a way that facilitates analysis. For example, appeals could be classified by condition and treatment, by groupings such as types of contractual coverage exclusions (e.g., cosmetic, experimental), and by reasons of medical necessity), as well as by characteristics of the individual making the appeal (e.g., age, disability, English language ability, race, income). The California DMHC, which currently classifies and analyzes appeals in multiple ways, showed that most treatment-related appeals in descending order were for pharmacy, mental health, durable medical equipment, autism, cancer care, and surgery. DMHC also gave the committee a report on the frequency of appeals by condition: orthopedic, mental disorders, central nervous

TABLE 7-1 Comparison of 2010 Independent Medical Review (IMR) Results in California Managed Care

	Upheld by Review Number (%)	Overturned by Review Number (%)	Reversed by Plan Before Review Number (%)	Qualified IMRs Total Number
Medical Necessity	467 (41%)	452 (40%)	222 (19%)	1,141
Experimental and Investigational	269 (51%)	195 (37%)	67 (13%)	531
Emergency Room Reimbursement	55 (53%)	14 (13%)	35 (34%)	104
TOTALS	791	661	324	1,776

SOURCE: DMHC, 2011.

---

[6] Personal communication with Jeffrey Kang, Chief Medical, Officer, CIGNA, February 17, 2011.

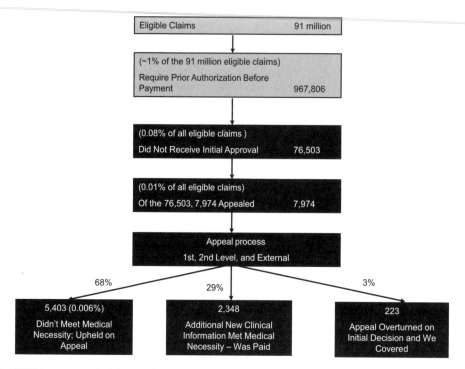

FIGURE 7-1 CIGNA coverage decisions and appeals for preauthorization of health benefits (2010).
SOURCE: Provided to the IOM in response to its question about preauthorization and appeals volume by Dr. Jeffrey Kang, CIGNA's Chief Medical Officer, February 17, 2011.

system or neuromuscular, and cancer (DMHC, 2011). Discussion with other states suggests that the reasons for appeals may vary by state and over time.[7]

Collection of these data can point to the areas of care that are most contentious and require more detailed investigation into the specific services and conditions that need clarification in the EHB set. It is yet unclear the extent to which recent amendments to the interim final external review rules would present a barrier to accessing more detailed diagnostic and treatment code data for analysis of adverse benefit determinations; plans are only required to provide diagnostic and treatment code data for individual cases on request (HHS, 2011a,b; Jost, 2011). Administrative burden and confidentiality concerns were identified as reasons for limiting this specific data. While it would be advisable for insurers to make their clinical policies available in advance, for example, on the Web as multiple insurers do, the committee would support having, at least during the appeals process, the applicable clinical policies be made transparent. Enhanced transparency of clinical policies would allow analysis of whether interpretation of the existing evidence base is similar or different across insurers and what areas need advancement.

Other Types and Possible Sources of Data

Research related to the EHB is likely to include developing explanatory and predictive analyses of the relationship between the nature and characteristics of the benefit package and the decisions made by consumers about which plans to select, which services to use, the cost trends associated with these plans, and the effects on individual and population health. The data mentioned above, if well standardized, provide a necessary starting point for these types of studies. However, many research questions will require linking these data with other sources of information such as claims, hospital discharge data, and enrollee surveys, such as the Consumer Assessment of Healthcare Providers and Systems (CAHPS) survey. For specific questions, researchers may require additional data

---

[7] Personal communication with Mary Kempker, Missouri Department of Insurance, February 18, 2011.

sources such as clinical data from electronic health records or primary data collected via interviews or surveys. These data sources would be more useful if they could be linked at the individual enrollee level. Individual-level data provide greater opportunities to adjust and control for potential case-mix differences between the covered populations being compared. However, if individual-level data are not available or cannot be accessed, analyses relating aspects of EHB definition or benefits design across multiple population units (e.g., exchanges, insurers) to aggregate population measures such as utilization rates, appeal rates, or average costs for those same population units will sometimes be helpful.

New Approaches to Delivering Health Services

New approaches to prevention, diagnosis, treatment, and management are continually emerging. Health insurers have developed greatly varying methods for assessing the safety and efficacy of these interventions. Similarly, many have coverage policies for when they will pay for participation in clinical trials. Although the focus of most current work relates to new technologies, the committee believes it is important to consider the broader range of changes in the ways services are delivered. The committee heard testimony on these coverage components and the importance of developing policies prospectively to guide complex coverage decisions for vulnerable enrollees (Hole-Curry, 2011; Levine, 2011; Nussbaum, 2011). Some evaluations of the effectiveness of new approaches are public—such as the state of Washington's—and some are proprietary. The results of these assessments and the resulting clinical policies may prove useful for the Secretary in updating the EHB, and the committee recommends they be systematically collected for that purpose.

A variety of existing organizations routinely produce systematic reviews of emerging technologies; the comparative effectiveness of alternative approaches to diagnosis, treatment, or management; and the methods for ensuring that care is delivered safely. Using clear and transparent methods for assessment according to a hierarchy of evidence, they provide physicians, health plans, policy makers, and the public with evidence syntheses on which to consider changes in medical practice and coverage policy. However, different insurers, whether private or public, often using the same evidence, after consideration of other criteria may reach different conclusions about whether a specific service should be covered (Figure 7-2). Factors might involve criteria related to the specific population served or to budget constraints, or even different degrees of pressure received from stakeholders depending on the nature of the process employed. HHS can facilitate access to and understanding of a common evidence base for states, insurers, practitioners, and consumers, particularly as it applies to the EHB package.

Medical Cost and Premium Information

In Chapter 9, the committee calls for updates to the EHB to fit within a budget that is defined by the average national silver plan premium for the current EHB package in the next year. In that recommendation, the committee anticipates that the premium costs will increase based on medical inflation, demographic changes in the population, the inclusion of new technologies, and other factors. The Chief Actuary of CMS produces the standard trend data used in tracking these trends. If the Secretary or the Chief Actuary determines that additional, more detailed data can be obtained from the experience of the states with certain elements of the cost calculations that will be required, these data should be specified. In particular, costs associated with new services that are being considered for inclusion in the EHB might be obtained from this process.

BROAD AREAS OF RESEARCH

Here the committee mentions four broad areas of a comprehensive research agenda, recognizing that within each area a rich set of questions will arise.

Understanding EHB definitions and their relationship to benefit design. The committee expects variation in the implementation of the EHB by different insurance companies and in different states, and this variation can be useful for evaluating what is working and what is not.

WA HTA Comparison with Insurer Policies							Reference Sources	
WA HTA			Private Insurer				Medicare	BCBS TEC
Topic	Date	Coverage Decision	Aetna	Group Health	Premera-BS	Regence-BC	NCD	
Upright MRI	May-07	**Not covered**	Less restrictive	No decision	Same	Same	No decision	No decision
Ped Bariatric Surgery <18	Aug-07	**Not covered**	Less restrictive	Less restrictive	Same	Same	n/a	No decision
Ped Bariatric Surgery 18-21		**Conditional**	Same	Same	Less restrictive	Less restrictive	Less restrictive	Same
Lumbar Fusion for DDD	Nov-07	**Conditional**	More restrictive	No decision	Same	Same	No decision	No decision
Discography for DDD	Feb-08	**Not covered**	Less restrictive	Same	No decision	No decision	No decision	No decision
Virtual Colonoscopy (CTC)-Cancer screening	Feb-08	**Not covered**	Same	Same	Same	Same	Same	Less restrictive

Summary Comparison of HTA Decisions and Private Insurers:

- Same as Private (some occur before, some after)   47%
- Private Insurer is Less Restrictive   22%
- Private Insurer is More Restrictive   9%
- Private Insurer Does Not Have Published Policy   18%

FIGURE 7-2 Health Technology Assessment (HTA) program coverage decisions vary between Washington (WA) state and private insurers.
SOURCE: Hole-Curry, 2011.

This may be useful for understanding the impact of variations in the EHB package on subsequent benefit design decisions and costs. Does specifying a more expansive EHB package lead to greater use of limits or caps on visits or other services, to higher premiums and cost-sharing requirements, or to more restrictive networks of care? Are there specific inclusions or exclusions to the EHB that are particularly costly when offered in real-world settings? Is the relationship between benefits and premium costs consistent across settings, or does it vary widely? If it varies, how are some exchanges managing to offer broader benefits without driving prices up? How will the addition or expansion of benefits influence the actuarial value of benefit packages—and the availability of existing covered benefits?

Sources of data for addressing these questions include the standardized data on benefit content and design collected from insurers and from state health insurance exchanges. Information on benefits and benefit design being offered by employers (e.g., DOL survey), from the Medical Expenditures Panel Survey's Insurance/Employer Component (MEPS-IC), and from surveys conducted by Kaiser Family Foundation, Mercer, and others, although currently limited for this purpose, can track changes in employer practices across a wider employer landscape than the exchanges alone unless statewide data are forthcoming on all forms of coverage. Data on costs and utilization patterns could be provided by national insurers active in multiple exchanges and by Medicaid, as well as data collected directly by state exchanges. Additional primary data collection, including patient and provider surveys and qualitative patient interviews in selected settings, would be needed to fully address some questions. In addition to these empirical studies, studies that blend empirical data with modeling approaches may also be valuable.

Relationships of EHB content and benefit design to patient outcomes and cost. Decisions related to the content and administration of the EHB package will affect the care that is offered to enrolled patients and may in turn affect clinical outcomes. A decision by some states or exchanges to include additional types or categories of services to the 10 categories (e.g., adult dental, hospice if they are not in the initially defined package) would create natural experiments that could quantify the costs of adding such coverage for a population, as well as the consequences—both monetary and clinical—to patients. Such information will be needed by the NBAC and the Secretary as refinements to the EHB are contemplated.

In the process of updating the EHB, questions about specific therapies and services within covered categories will arise. Decision making on coverage of specific treatments typically starts with consideration of evidence from randomized controlled trials (RCTs) and syntheses of results when multiple trials have been conducted. Because controlled trials minimize risks of selection bias, they are essential for establishing treatment efficacy, as well as superiority, and are foundational in making coverage decisions. However, RCTs often leave questions remaining about the effect of these treatments in typical patients getting care from community practice settings. Trials generally do not include the entire spectrum of patients who are subsequently offered the treatment. Trials may not include all relevant outcomes, including monetary outcomes or satisfaction for patients, and they may not have followed patients long enough to observe longer-term outcomes. Thus, if insurance exchanges or specific insurers systematically differ in coverage of specific treatments, rigorous evaluation of patient outcomes and costs related to this variation would provide a valuable addition to the public deliberative process.

Many historical benefit design strategies, including cost sharing and restricted provider networks, lower costs to insurers and purchasers. Others, such as pay-for-performance initiatives and centers of excellence, can drive quality improvement efforts. Some of these approaches, however, can adversely affect patients. High prices for needed medications through cost sharing lead to decreases in adherence to chronic medications, with subsequent deterioration of disease control and increased utilization and adverse events. Refinements such as value-based insurance designs endeavor to use evidence on the health benefits of different interventions in designing financial incentives that encourage patients to make the most effective and cost-effective treatment choices by removing financial barriers to those choices and/or by raising these or other barriers to less appropriate options. They hold great promise for improving the effectiveness and efficiency with which health insurance dollars are spent. The emphasis on cost restraints under the ACA will undoubtedly lead to a proliferation of new insurance products with further evolution in benefit design. Systematic evaluation of this variation will ensure that good practices are recognized and spread quickly and that adverse effects are minimized.

Data for studying the impact of EHB content and benefit design on patient outcomes come from the same sources mentioned above. Specific research questions will require augmentation through linkage of these data sources with insurer data on health care utilization (e.g., from Medicaid and private insurers), clinical information from electronic health records and other data sources of health care delivery systems, or data collected from surveys or qualitative interviews with patients selected for specific characteristics such as the presence of a chronic condition.

Possible impact of EHB and benefit design decisions on the required elements for consideration. The ACA includes a number of "required elements for consideration" that must be monitored and may thus require updating of the EHB. These include concerns that there be balance among the covered categories; that there be no discrimination based on age, disability, or expected length of life; that benefits take into account and cover the diverse needs of various population segments; and that emergency care not be restricted (e.g., by requirements for prior authorization).

The monitoring process should include assessing the required elements for consideration specified in the ACA. However, further research will be required to determine whether trends identified in monitoring require action. If variation is found across states or exchanges, not only in appeals but also in other areas, outcomes studies based on utilization and clinical data as well as patient survey data may be needed to establish links between practices and outcomes and to identify best practices.

Attention may focus initially on variation in the absolute and relative expenditures by category across jurisdictions. Outliers, especially on the low side, may signal problematic coverage or implementation. Areas of particular complexity include issues such as mental health services, habilitative services, and orphan diseases. Research approaches of particular value here would include analyses of appeals; the impact of state mandates for services not broadly included in the EHB; and surveys of beneficiaries from various population segments and the providers who care for them.

Comparative effectiveness of specific preventive and therapeutic options. The research discussed above, which uses implementation data to study variation in EHB content and benefits design, will contribute greatly to understanding how inclusion or exclusion of broad categories of services affects patient outcomes and costs. It will also deepen understanding of the effects of various benefits design strategies on these outcomes. However, as the Secretary and the NBAC seek to define EHB more specifically over time, more information will be needed on specific treatments and preventive and diagnostic services, including newly introduced pharmacotherapies, procedures, and devices. These therapies may not yet be covered by any policies in the exchanges, and definitive information on their effectiveness can therefore not come from these data.

The needed information will come from a variety of sources. These include the ongoing publication of original research studies, especially clinical trials; syntheses of previously reported research; recent technology assessments from sources such as BlueCross BlueShield Association's Technology Evaluation Center, AHRQ's Evidence-Based Practice Centers and Developing Evidence to Inform Decisions about Effectiveness (DEcIDE) research program, and the U.S. Preventive Services Task Force (for screening and prevention services), as well as the Medicare Evidence Development and Coverage Advisory Committee (MEDCAC) and professional society guidelines. PCORI is expected to fund comparative effectiveness research (CER) and summaries with a particular emphasis on patient perspectives—yet cannot employ a dollars per quality adjusted life-year threshold in its determinations.[8] These studies will evaluate both specific preventive and therapeutic choices as well as system-level interventions for improving care. The FDA, Department of Defense, CMS, and state Medicaid agencies also generate reports that will deserve consideration. The Secretary and the NBAC will require staffing and a process for ensuring that all relevant data are identified and considered.

In this work, studies that follow the principles of CER will be particularly valuable and should be emphasized. CER principles include comparisons between meaningful therapeutic alternatives, conduct of studies in typical clinical settings and involving a broad range of patients, consideration of multiple outcomes including outcomes of particular importance to patients, and attention to possible differences in treatment effectiveness in patient subgroups.

REFERENCES

CCIIO (Center for Consumer Information and Insurance Oversight). 2010. *The Center for Consumer Information & Insurance Oversight. Initial announcement: Invitation to apply for FY 2010.* http://cciio.cms.gov/resources/fundingopportunities/consumer_assistance_program_grant_foa.pdf (accessed July 22, 2011).

DMHC (California Department of Managed Health Care). 2011. *Independent State Review Processes.* PowerPoint Presentation to the IOM Committee on the Determination of Essential Health Benefits by Cindy Ehnes, Director, Maureen McKennan, Acting Deputy Director for Plan and Provider Relations, and Andrew George, Assistant Deputy Director, Help Center, Department of Managed Health Care, Costa Mesa, CA, March 2.

GAO (Government Accountability Office). 2011. *Private health insurance: Data on application and coverage denials.* Washington, DC: Government Accountability Office.

Gresenz, C. R., and D. M. Studdert. 2005. External review of coverage denials by managed care organizations in California. *Journal of Empirical Legal Studies* 2(3):449-468.

HHS (Department of Health and Human Services). 2011a. *Interim final rules for group health plans and health insurance issuers relating to internal claims and appeals and external review processes under the Patient Protection and Affordable Care Act.* http://www.cq.com/flatfiles/editorialFiles/healthBeat/reference/docs/072301.pdf (accessed September 13 2011).

———. 2011b. Rules and regulations: Group health plans and health insurance issuers: Rules relating to internal claims and appeals and external review processes. *Federal Register* 76(122):37208-37234.

Hole-Curry, L. 2011. *Transforming health care: Using evidence in benefit decisions.* PowerPoint Presentation to the IOM Committee on the Determination of Essential Health Benefits by Leah Hole-Curry, Program Director, Washington State Health Technology Assessment Program, Costa Mesa, CA, March 2.

IOM (Institute of Medicine). 2002. *Leadership by example: Coordinating government roles in improving health care quality.* Washington, DC: The National Academies Press.

———. 2007. *The learning healthcare system: A workshop summary.* Washington, DC: The National Academies Press.

———. 2009a. *HHS in the 21st century: Charting a new course for a healthier America.* Washington, DC: The National Academies Press.

———. 2009b. *Initial national priorities for comparative effectiveness research.* Washington, DC: The National Academies Press.

---

[8] § 6301, amending § 1181 of the Social Security Act.

_____. 2011. *The learning health system series: Continuous improvement and innovation in health and health care.* Washington, DC: The National Academies Press.

Jost, T. S. 2011. *Health Affairs blog.* http://healthaffairs.org/blog/2011/06/23/implementing-health-reform-the-appeals-process-amended-rule/ (accessed September 23, 2011).

KFF (Kaiser Family Foundation) and HRET (Health Research Education Fund). 2010. *Employer Health Benefits 2010 Annual Survey.* Menlo Park, CA and Chicago, IL: Kaiser Family Foundation and Health Research Education Trust.

Levine, S. 2011. PowerPoint Presentation to the IOM Committee on the Determination of Essential Health Benefits by Sharon Levine, Associate Executive Medical Director, The Permanente Medical Group, Costa Mesa, CA, March 2.

NAIC (National Association of Insurance Commissioners). 2010. *Uniform Health Carrier External Review Model Act.* Washington, DC: National Association of Insurance Comissioners.

_____. 2011. *Library: Consumer resources & guides.* http://www.insureuonline.org/ (accessed July 22, 2011).

Nussbaum, S. 2011. *Health insurance plan variance in coverage (inclusions, exclusions, networks) and benefit design for quality improvement.* PowerPoint Presentation to the IOM Committee on the Determination of Essential Health Benefits by Sam Nussbaum, Executive Vice-President, Clinical Policy and Chief Medical Officer, Wellpoint, Inc., Costa Mesa, CA, March 2.

State of Colorado. 2010. *Report of second level appeal and independent external reviews calendar year 2010.* http://hermes.state.co.us/insurance/consumer/2011%20docs/cons2010ReportSecondLevelAndIndependentExternalReviews042111.pdf (accessed November 1, 2011).

U.S. Department of Labor, Treasury, and HHS. 2011. Group health plans and health insurance issuers: Rules relating to internal claims and appeals and external review processes; correction. *Federal Register* 76(143):44491-44493.

8

Allowance for State Innovation

Under Section 1302 of the Patient Protection and Affordable Care Act (ACA), the Secretary of Health and Human Services is granted the authority to define essential health benefits (EHB) provided the definition takes into account and complies with various requirements provided in the statute. This grant of authority would allow the Secretary to approve state-specific variations of the EHB definition, provided that any such state-specific definition complied with the relevant statutory language and was reviewed and approved by the Secretary. The committee provides guidance on the rationale and standards the Secretary should use in approving state-specific definitions of essential health benefits, and recommends that the Secretary consider state-specific definitions as soon as administratively feasible. Such state-specific variations would only be available to states operating their own exchanges.

The insurance provisions in the ACA balance federal and state authority. For example, while federal law will regulate certain aspects of the individual and small group market through various pricing and issuance requirements, states are given relatively broad authority to operate their own health benefit exchanges and to regulate other aspects of health insurance such as premium increases. This balancing of authority is not surprising, given the role that states have traditionally[1] played in regulating health insurance (Pierron, 2008).

AUTHORITY FOR STATE VARIATION

The ACA is clear that the Secretary shall define the EHB, within certain statutory guidelines. The statute is silent, however, regarding whether the Secretary could approve more than one EHB definition, provided that the statutory requirements are otherwise met. The committee believes that the Secretary therefore has the authority to approve refinements of the national EHB definition, if the Secretary chooses to do so, provided such definitions otherwise meet the requirements of Section 1302.

There is also explicit authority in Section 1332 of the ACA for the Secretary to grant *waivers* of the EHB requirements (along with other provisions in the ACA) beginning in 2017. The committee considered and was favorable to this statutory authority as an option for promoting innovation on the EHB as long as the waiver with

---

[1] Traditional was defined in the McCarran-Ferguson Act, which allowed the states to regulate the business of insurance (15 U.S.C. §§ 1011-1015).

respect to the EHB meets the criteria that the committee outlines later in this chapter. There has been some interest expressed in amending this statutory authority to allow waivers to begin before 2017 (HHS, 2011b; The White House, 2011); because it has not passed, waivers are not yet a viable option at this time.[2] As a result, this chapter does not focus on such waivers. Rather, this chapter addresses the ability of the Secretary to approve state-specific variations of the EHB definition that meet each of the requirements set forth in Section 1302.

FLEXIBILITY IN DETERMINING THE EHB

Although the committee notes the deference given to states as they set up their health insurance exchanges (HHS, 2011a) and proceed with rate review enhancement (HHS, 2010), those situations are not analogous to the EHB determination process. The Secretary's responsibilities to lead and define the EHB determination process are clearer, greater, and more direct than those the Secretary has with respect to the health insurance exchanges. For establishment and implementation of health insurance exchanges, the ACA is clear that states have primary responsibility,[3] and it is only if a state opts out or fails to meet the requirements to establish an exchange that the federal government will become involved.[4] Conversely, with respect to defining EHB, the ACA is clear that the Secretary of Health and Human Services (HHS) has sole authority to define the EHB. The authority granted to HHS to define the EHB does not, however, preclude the Secretary from using that authority to approve state-specific variations of the EHB definition.

State Flexibility

The committee believes some state flexibility in defining the EHB package is important from a public policy and practical standpoint. Although informed by clinical evidence and economics, judgments of what constitutes an essential health benefit are social value decisions and reflect, at their core, a set of decisions regarding which medical expenses must be shared within a community. As discussed above, the committee believes that the Secretary has the authority to approve refinements of the EHB definition, and that there will be some circumstances under which the Secretary should approve state-specific EHB definitions that allow states to make their own social value prioritizations and deviate from the federal standard definition of essential health benefits. The committee believes the definition of benefits should become more evidence-based, specific, and value-promoting over time and believes state-based innovation should support these goals, as it charges the Secretary to act (see Recommendation 4a). The committee proposes guiding principles that HHS should consider in determining whether or not to approve a state-specific variation of the federal EHB definition.

The committee's recommendation focuses solely on guidance for when the Secretary should consider state-specific variations of the national EHB definition. It should be noted that nothing in the committee's recommendation negates the direction in Section 1302 for inclusion of the 10 categories of care or observance of the required elements for consideration. Furthermore, the committee believes that the Secretary's approval of a state-specific variation of the EHB definition should be contingent on the state's developing a package with content that is actuarially equivalent to the national package established by the Secretary during initial definition or updating; otherwise, state-specific variations of EHB could either substantially increase aggregate package costs or significantly reduce the intended scope of packages covered by the EHB.

From a practical standpoint, state-specific EHB developed locally and with a credible, accountable public deliberation process are even more likely to gain sustained state-based public support than a single federal definition with no possibility of state-based innovation. The committee suggests guidelines for public deliberation on priorities in Chapter 6.

---

[2] The White House has indicated its support of state empowerment and innovation under the ACA, including support for bipartisan legislation to make waivers available starting in 2014—the "Empowering States to Innovate Act" (HHS, 2011b; The White House, 2011).

[3] Patient Protection and Affordable Care Act of 2010 as amended. § 1311(b), 111th Cong., 2d sess.

[4] § 1321(c).

Additionally, the committee believes that state-specific EHB definitions are appropriate only when a state has made a commitment to operating its own health insurance exchange, as the alternative is a *de facto* agreement to federal involvement[5,6]—which is inconsistent with a desire for a state-specific EHB definition, hence the distinction. In other words, the rationale for not allowing the variation option for states that do not operate their own exchange is that their program would revert to the federal exchange. A state that develops its own definition should be accountable for it; the federal exchange should not have to monitor multiple state-based definitions through the exchange.

Also, in making decisions regarding requests for state-specific EHB definitions, deference should be given to states that have already undertaken significant efforts to establish comprehensive state-based processes for defining a basic health benefit package. Massachusetts has developed a comprehensive process regarding the content of coverage in the individual and small group markets. Several states have also engaged in efforts to define essential health benefits in other market segments—for example, Oregon's Medicaid program (Oregon Health Services Commission, 2011). Provided that these programs and processes meet the minimum requirements set forth below, the committee believes that such preexisting, comprehensive processes with meaningful public input should be afforded deference as the Secretary considers whether to grant a request for a state-specific EHB definition.

Recommendation 3: For states administering their own exchanges that wish to adopt a variant of the federal EHB package, the Secretary should use statutory authority to grant such requests, provided that the state-specific EHB definition is consistent with the requirements of Section 1302 of the ACA and the criteria specified in this report, that they produce a package that is actuarially equivalent to the national package established by the Secretary, and that the request is supported by a process that has included meaningful public input. To best achieve this, the Secretary should encourage a public deliberative process as described in this report and should provide technical assistance to the states for implementing that process.

CRITERIA FOR APPROVING A STATE-SPECIFIC EHB DEFINITION

In determining the more general criteria that must be established in order for a state-specific EHB definition to be approved, the committee focused on two primary goals: (1) clear guidance to the states regarding the circumstances under which a state-specific EHB definition will be considered and (2) ensuring that the state EHB definition is consistent with the broader goals of the ACA. The committee envisions that proposals for state-specific EHB definitions will be proposed and generated by the states themselves, and submitted to the Secretary for approval in accordance with the criteria presented below:

- *Consistency of process and standards.* If the elements of the process and the standards recommended by the committee to be used to develop the EHB are appropriate for the federal definition (see Recommendation 1: coverage of at least the 10 categories of care, scope of typical small employer plan nationally,[7] inclusion of a public deliberative process, and the criteria defined in Figure S-2 in the Summary), then they must also be ensured by HHS to be integral in any state process.
- *State authority.* Such an EHB process must be conducted by an executive or legislative branch office or agency with the legislatively designated authority to make the request to HHS for a state-specific EHB definition and implement the results of the process. The committee takes no position on what state entity is best positioned to do this work, as long as such entities are clearly designated by the legislature.
- *No "race to the bottom."* The Secretary must ensure that state-specific EHB definitions provide coverage that is actuarially equivalent to the national package established by the Secretary—neither significantly higher nor lower. The state-based process should allow for a different set of social values to emerge

---

[5] Patient Protection and Affordable Care Act of 2010 as amended. § 1311(b), 111th Cong., 2d sess.

[6] § 1321(c).

[7] The committee emphasizes that equivalence should be in benefit comprehensiveness; national data to determine state EHB equivalence are a practical consideration and would eliminate cost variances in the determination.

regarding covered benefits, but the overall makeup of that coverage locally should be equivalent to that provided under the federal definition of the EHB. The ACA guarantees both a right and a responsibility for a basic health benefit for all Americans—which should not be significantly compromised depending on the place of one's residence. However, states that can more efficiently offer additional benefits by becoming more evidence-based and value-promoting are encouraged to do so.

*   *Updating.* The state would be held accountable for implementing its state-specific EHB definition, reporting to HHS on the results of implementation, updating the package at least every 2 years, and submitting the results of the updating, along with any requests to modify the state-specific EHB definition at least every 2 years. The goals for state updating should be in accord with the national goals of having the state-specific EHB become more specific, evidence-based, and value-promoting.

*   *Oversight, compliance, and consequences.* HHS shall have the authority to terminate any state-specific EHB definitions where necessary to comply with the requirements of Section 1302, or where the state has failed to comply with any requirements imposed by HHS as a condition of approving a state-specific EHB definition.

*   *Innovation.* Finally, the HHS set of *standards* for a state-based process should encourage state-level innovation in the way those standards are met and require an evaluation plan to document outcomes. HHS could encourage state participation in an HHS evaluation as a condition of granting a state-specific EHB definition. States should be encouraged to learn from one another as they set about creating a proposal for a state-specific EHB definition.[8]

These criteria would form the framework for a set of standards articulated by HHS that a state would have to meet as it embarks on its own process for creating a proposal for a state-specific EHB definition to submit to HHS for approval. In developing these standards, the committee believes HHS would best meet its oversight obligations by recognizing the primary importance of states' demonstrating that they have the structures and processes in place to meet the standards, rather than the degree to which the resultant state package matches the federal package. For example, as HHS develops and applies these standards, the committee, as noted previously, has concluded that if a state already has established comprehensive basic benefit definition processes, as long as the results are consistent with the legislative requirements of Section 1302 and the committee's recommendation, then the state program should be granted deference in the state-specific approval process.

Chapter 6 documents the importance the committee attaches to a public deliberation process to elicit the social values important to developing the EHB definition and to building necessary public trust. The committee believes that HHS should provide technical assistance on public deliberation to states interested in incorporating this process into their application.

POLITICAL IMPLICATIONS

The determination of the EHB is a politically and socially charged endeavor. The committee believes the definition of an EHB package is integral if the ACA is to attain its promise. In meeting this promise, HHS is well advised to develop a process to consider state-specific EHB definitions that maximize the likelihood of success by ensuring the right balance between local engagement, support, and flexibility, and national protection of all citizens and legal residents.

REFERENCES

HHS (Department of Health and Human Services). 2010. Rate increase disclosure and review. *Federal Register* 75(246):81004-81029.
_____. 2011a. Patient Protection and Affordable Care Act; Establishment of exchanges and qualified health plans. *Federal Register* 76(136):41866-41927.

---

[8] There many examples of state-based learning facilitated by federal authorities at the Center for Consumer Information and Insurance Oversight (CCIIO) and the Centers for Medicare & Medicaid Services (CMS) in partnership with private nonprofits such as the National Academy for State Health Policy and Robert Wood Johnson Foundation's State Coverage Initiatives Program.

_____. 2011b. *Preparing for innovation: Proposed process for states to adopt innovative strategies to meet the goals of the Affordable Care Act*. http://www.healthcare.gov/news/factsheets/stateinnovation03102011a.html (accessed June 30, 2011).

Oregon Health Services Commission. 2011. *The prioritized list*. http://www.oregon.gov/OHA/healthplan/priorlist/main.shtml (accessed June 27, 2011).

Pierron, W., and P. Fronstin. 2008. *ERISA pre-emption: Implications for health reform and coverage*. http://www.ebri.org/pdf/briefspdf/EBRI_IB_02a-20082.pdf (accessed July 11, 2011).

The White House. 2011. *Fact sheet: The Affordable Care Act: Supporting innovation, empowering states*. http://www.whitehouse.gov/the-press-office/2011/02/28/fact-sheet-affordable-care-act-supporting-innovation-empowering-states (accessed June 30, 2011).

9

Updating the EHB

The Secretary is charged to periodically update the essential health benefits (EHB) and to report to Congress and the public whether enrollees have had difficulty accessing needed services, whether advances in medicine and scientific evidence need to be accounted for, and whether updates will increase costs relative to actuarial limitations. With these considerations in mind, the committee sets a goal for the EHB package to become more fully evidence-based, specific, and value-promoting over time. To ensure that updates to the EHB do not accelerate health-spending growth beyond medical inflation, the committee recommends that any changes to the EHB be no more expensive than the actuarially equivalent future year cost of the base-year package. Further, to preserve the intent of Congress in extending coverage for a basic set of benefits to most Americans, the committee recommends that the Secretary, in collaboration with others, develop a strategy to restrain health care spending. A standing multidisciplinary National Benefits Advisory Council (NBAC) is also proposed to be established to advise the Secretary on updating the EHB.

The coming decades will bring advances in medical science, the emergence of new health problems, changes in the way health care services are delivered, changes in the way existing technologies are used, and new insights into how to help patients manage their health problems more effectively. As the environment in which health care services are delivered changes, the EHB will also have to change in order to continue to facilitate access to quality care for a broad population. Responsible stewardship of public funds must be a key consideration during updates to the EHB. Difficult choices will have to be made about the categories and specific services that are eligible for coverage under the EHB. In developing its recommended approach to updating, the committee was guided by the requirements in the Patient Protection and Affordable Care Act's (ACA's) charge for the Secretary to report to Congress and the public.

ACA DIRECTION TO THE SECRETARY ON UPDATING THE EHB

The Secretary is charged to periodically update the EHB to address any gaps in access to coverage or changes in the evidence base that the Secretary identifies during the review of the EHB for the mandated Department of

Health and Human Services (HHS) report to Congress and the public.[1] Section 1302 of the ACA requires that the report contain

- An assessment of whether enrollees are facing any difficulty accessing needed services for reasons of coverage or cost;
- An assessment of whether the EHB need to be modified or updated to account for changes in medical evidence or scientific advancement;
- Information on how the EHB will be modified to address any such gaps in access or changes in the evidence base; and
- An assessment of the potential of additional or expanded benefits to increase costs and the interactions between the addition or expansion of benefits and reductions in existing benefits to meet actuarial limitations.[2]

In Chapter 7, the committee recommends developing a framework to guide the data collection and research infrastructure necessary to identify problems with access and advances in science (the first two required elements of the report to Congress). The information developed through this recommendation provides the starting point for the process of updating the EHB. In this chapter, the committee recommends an approach to updating the EHB, using criteria discussed earlier. The committee also recommends an approach to incorporating costs into the update process (responding to the fourth bullet in the report to Congress).

GOALS FOR UPDATING

In its deliberations, the committee recognized that Congress intended the EHB to be similar in structure to existing employer benefit packages. However, the committee believes that over time, the Secretary will have an opportunity to provide leadership through the EHB updating process to improve the content and structure of the EHB to better reflect the scientific evidence base, to reflect societal priorities in providing a basic set of benefits, to ensure greater clarity about what services are and are not eligible for coverage in those policies covered by the EHB definition, and to promote high-value utilization.

Evidence-Based Science Should Be the Guiding Force

The committee concluded that the scope of benefits eligible for coverage should be guided by scientific evidence about which screening, diagnosis, treatment, management, and monitoring interventions are effective in improving or maintaining people's health and functioning. For example, physician specialty societies, independent research organizations, health plans, and other organizations that focus on particular health problems increasingly incorporate the results of scientific studies into their treatment and payment guidelines. The Institute of Medicine (IOM) has recently released reports on strengthening standards for developing trustworthy clinical guidelines and systematic reviews, and the committee believes that these standards should inform the way medical evidence is used to shape future iterations of the EHB (IOM, 2011a,b). This means that the EHB would make eligible for coverage those interventions that are effective and would not make eligible for coverage those aspects of care that have not been shown to be effective. In Chapters 2 and 3, the committee discusses application of hierarchies of evidence in defining the scope of benefit inclusions and the need to strengthen medical practice to be more evidence-based.

Greater Specificity Required in Defining the EHB

If the EHB are to be guided by scientific evidence in the future, the definitions and descriptions of what is included and excluded must become more specific, consistent with the way scientific evidence is structured. There

---

[1] Patient Protection and Affordable Care Act of 2010 as amended. § 1302(b)(4)(H), 111th Cong., 2d sess.

[2] § 1302(b)(4)(G)(i)-(iv).

are few methods of diagnosis or treatment that are either always or never effective. More commonly, interventions such as medications, surgeries, or screening tests are investigated for their effectiveness with specific groups of patients such as those with a particular diagnosis (e.g., hypertension), a certain level of disease severity (e.g., Class IV heart failure), gender or age (e.g., women over 50), and so on. Thus, the committee concluded that as the EHB evolve, greater specificity than is typical of evidence of coverage documents today will be required along with more transparency in clinical policies.

Most health insurance plan documents today provide general statements about what is covered (e.g., ambulatory services) and what is not covered (e.g., experimental treatments). Increased specificity in defining the EHB (inclusions and exclusions) should be designed to reduce uncertainty for patients and doctors about the likelihood that insurance coverage will be available for a course of diagnosis or treatment (vs. the patient being responsible for paying for a selected therapeutic option).

The committee considered several options for improving the degree of specificity to guide the contents of the EHB package and data collection over time: having the Secretary make an increasingly more specific list of included services, making a more specific list of exclusions and nonessential services, and leaving inclusions more general and dependent on insurers' publication of clinical policies and the application of medical necessity. These options are not mutually exclusive. With regard to specificity on inclusions, the Oregon prioritized list, organized by condition-treatment pairs (e.g., medical therapy for hypertensive disease), is the only one the committee encountered with a high degree of specificity of services that matches the way scientific evidence is structured (Oregon Health Services Commission, 2011). In general, the committee believes that the EHB should evolve toward the level of specificity characterized by the Oregon approach. Additionally, as discussed in Chapter 7, health plans should provide greater specificity and transparency around clinical policies and the operation of medical necessity determination processes.

Structure of Benefits Should Promote High-Value Utilization

Finally, the committee concluded that the financial structure of benefit packages should be consistent with and reinforce the use of high-value, necessary care. Today, it is common for policies to treat all interventions (e.g., medication) within the same cost structure (e.g., co-payments relate to whether the drug is generic or name brand but may not make distinctions between medications for different conditions). The use of value-based insurance design has been growing, and the committee believes that this trend should be incorporated into future EHB packages. The principle of value-based insurance design is to provide financial incentives to encourage people to use what is effective and to discourage people from using services when they are not effective. For example, research has demonstrated that cost sharing is associated with lower utilization of services than no cost sharing (Newhouse and the Insurance Experiment Group, 1993). This is suitable if one is seeking to control utilization, but these incentives affect both appropriate and inappropriate uses of services similarly. Thus, if a service is critical to maintain health (e.g., medications for the treatment of high blood pressure), a policy that creates a disincentive for appropriate use may result in poor adherence to a high-value intervention. Value-based insurance design would reduce or eliminate cost sharing in these instances in order to promote high levels of adherence to the use of necessary medications; in many instances, improved adherence to routinely required medications and other services may contribute to avoiding high cost services such as hospitalization. In implementing value-based insurance design packages, insurers will have to comply with the actuarial value limits specified in the ACA. In this regard, it is important that computation of actuarial value not impede inclusions of some services with high cost sharing (as opposed to excluding them).

Table 9-1 illustrates how these three principles for updating could be incorporated into future versions of the EHB as implemented by health plans in response to guidance from the Secretary. The goals are that over time, the package becomes more evidence-based, defined with greater specificity, and constructed to encourage the use of high-value care. Plans could further these goals by including incentives for consumers to engage in other healthy behaviors.

Recommendation 4a: Beginning in 2015, for implementation in 2016 and annually thereafter, the Secretary should update the EHB package, with the goals that it becomes more fully evidence-based, specific, and value-promoting.

TABLE 9-1 Illustrative Comparison of Current and Future Scope of Benefits for the Essential Health Benefits (EHB)

Scope of Benefits Eligible for Coverage in Typical Policies Today	Illustration of How Scope of Benefits Might Be Described in Future Policies
Ambulatory care	Annual visit to a primary care or specialty physician for monitoring of hypertension
Prescription drugs	Antihypertensive medications for persons with an established diagnosis of hypertension
Cost sharing: $10 for generic, $25 for name brand medications, and $20 for an office visit	No cost sharing for annual visit
	No co-payment for generic medications for treatment of hypertension for patients with JNC stage 1 hypertension or higher

NOTE: JNC = Joint National Committee on Prevention, Detection, Evaluation, and Treatment of High Blood Pressure.

CONSIDERING TYPICAL EMPLOYER IN THE FUTURE

Section 1302 of the ACA also requires that the Secretary of HHS' report to Congress on revising benefits contain a certification from the Chief Actuary of the Centers for Medicare & Medicaid Services (CMS) indicating the essential benefits are equal to the scope of benefits provided under a typical employer plan.[3] The committee's first recommendation includes guidance that the Secretary interpret "typical employer" as a small employer. Because the EHB will be incorporated into individual and small group policies both in and out of the exchanges, the typical small employer plan will be defined by the EHB, making an independent reference to typical employer less meaningful over time. As referenced in Chapter 1, how employers respond to the new options available through the ACA could change the way insurance is offered. In addition to employers, insurers may change their behavior and practices in response to experience with the exchanges and the EHB. It will be important to monitor the changes in insurer behavior and plan offerings as part of the monitoring recommended in Chapter 7. Further, states in the future will have the option to open exchanges to businesses of all sizes, and firms that choose to offer insurance through an exchange will have those policies defined by the EHB. Because the method for updating recommended by the committee is designed to keep the costs of the EHB in line with the expected growth in premiums for small employers, the committee believes that the Chief Actuary will have to rely primarily on the cost of the package to certify that the updated EHB is consistent with the intent of the ACA. The committee believes that in going forward, the cost of the EHB should continue to be built on the scope of benefits and premiums of small employers.

METHODS FOR INCORPORATING COSTS INTO UPDATES TO THE EHB

The committee concluded that the updating process must explicitly consider the cost of the EHB and its potential to escalate over time, whether due to technological advances or other medical price increases. The alternative would have been for the committee to recommend that the Secretary not address cost issues in making changes to the EHB over time. The committee believes that it is unacceptable for the Secretary to ignore the costs associated with proposed updates to the EHB. This section explores various options considered and selected for updating to maintain an affordable and sustainable premium level.

In considering how the costs associated with the EHB could be incorporated into updates, the committee discussed a number of design choices: the level at which costs would be considered, the unit by which costs are characterized, the way in which cost information would be used, the approach to enforcement, and the mechanism for achieving any cost target. The pros and cons of each of these are discussed in turn along with the committee's understanding of the current authority available to the Secretary.

---

[3] § 1302(b)(2)(A)-(B).

Level of Consideration of Costs

The committee considered three potential levels at which costs could be incorporated into decisions in subsequent years: (1) federal, (2) state, or (3) health plan.

At the *federal level*, costs would be considered at an aggregate level—without explicit efforts to address regional variation in wages, prices, population characteristics; variations in the intensity and use of technology; and other potential cost drivers. For example, the Secretary could obtain an actuarial estimate from the CMS Chief Actuary of the expected cost to purchase the EHB package in the coming year based on a national standard population,[4] with explicit assumptions about the degree of medical management, network configuration, and other factors typically included in pricing plans for employers. The committee believes that taking cost into account at a national average level is analogous to the strategy used for setting the initial EHB and is within the purview of the Secretary.

If cost was considered at the *state level*, differences in the cost structure of health care delivery in states would have to be explicitly addressed (Branscome, 2011). For example, an actuarial estimate could be obtained for the cost of offering the EHB in each state based on a standard population that reflects the characteristics of state residents that are eligible to purchase policies defined by the EHB. The committee believes that an assessment of costs at the state level is consistent with the required guidance from the Secretary about rates of premium growth considered to be excessive (HHS, 2010). The committee also concluded that few states today have undertaken such assessments and that it might be difficult for most states to conduct this work.

If costs were considered at the *health plan level*, estimates would have to be derived for plans within states or for types of plans within states. These cost estimates would be designed to make explicit how tradeoffs are made among the prevailing costs of care, comprehensiveness of benefits, medical management, network design, and other factors. Plans might be asked to produce packages to offer on the exchanges that fall within the cost guidance and the required EHB design. Alternatively, the Secretary might consider a competitive bidding process similar to that conducted under Medicare Part D. The committee noted that the Secretary does not currently have clear authority to direct or influence pricing of plans, with the possible exception of plans that might be offered in a national or federally directed exchange.

The committee concluded that costs should be incorporated into updates at the federal level consistent with the level at which the EHB are defined in the committee's first recommendation in this report.

Unit at Which Costs Are Characterized

The committee considered three possible ways in which costs might be characterized: (1) estimated premiums, (2) total federal spending (by category), or (3) rates of change.

The *use of premiums* as a budget mechanism to incorporate costs into updates is consistent with the committee's recommended method for establishing the initial health benefits package. Estimated premiums are also one factor incorporated into the cost estimates produced by the Congressional Budget Office (CBO) during debate over the ACA.[5] Premiums are the unit by which costs are characterized for most purchasers, whether employers or individuals. Premiums are a familiar way to express the average expected cost of a package of benefits being offered and are the "price" at which comparative shopping for plans takes place. There are, of course, many factors (e.g., benefit design, population) besides the EHB that go into actuarial calculations of premiums; the committee determined that all of these inputs should be accounted for to inform policy decisions around incorporating costs into the updates.

Another option the committee considered was to *use the federal budget for subsidies and for Medicaid spending* as the unit of cost focus. Similar to premiums, the total cost to the federal government was a significant element of the debate over the law, and design choices were made in order to achieve an overall spending target set by the

---

[4] The national standard population in this case would be those eligible to purchase policies defined by the EHB, that is, the individual and small group market. This is the group that the RAND microsimulation used for its analyses (Eibner et al., 2010).

[5] The others being the expected number of newly insured and their distribution by type of insurance, including the number eligible for federal subsidies (CBO, 2009).

President and Congress. This federal budget amount accounts both for the unit costs (e.g., premiums) of health insurance and for the number of people opting for Medicaid or public subsidies for private insurance. The committee concluded, however, that because the EHB definition is just one component of determining the total federal budget amount for subsidies and Medicaid, this is a less useful way of characterizing costs in updating the EHB.

A third option is to *use the rates of increase in health care spending or in premiums* in incorporating costs into updates to the EHB package. Because the growth in premium prices has exceeded growth in both the purchasing power of the individual (wages) and the economy (gross domestic product, GDP), health care spending is consuming an increasing share of economic output. To control total costs to firms, employers have introduced new products such as high-deductible health plans and other methods for increasing the share of costs paid by individual employees, have changed provider network design, and have reduced the scope of benefits (Claxton et al., 2010).

Within this option, the committee noted that the Secretary could either use information about trends to establish the new cost target within which the scope of benefits would be defined or establish targets around the rate of growth in premiums that are designed to help slow or reverse the growth in health spending (e.g., limiting the allowable growth of premiums to the growth in GDP plus 1 percentage point). In other parts of the ACA, Congress called for ways to address health spending growth. For example, the ACA requires that between 2014 and 2018 adjustments be made to the calculation of premium subsidies that reflect the relative change in premiums compared to changes in household income (known as the regular indexing approach).[6] After 2018, an additional adjustment factor is included that accounts for the excess in premium growth compared to the growth in the Consumer Price Index in urban areas.[7,8] These indexing methods are designed to ensure that the intent of the original subsidy structure is maintained. The report that the Secretary must deliver to Congress annually includes the impact of changes in the EHB on costs as well as the interaction between additions or expansions to the EHB and concomitant reductions in existing benefits in order to meet actuarial limits required by the law. The ACA also established an Independent Payment Advisory Board (IPAB) to identify mechanisms for keeping the growth in Medicare spending linked to the growth of the economy (GDP plus 1 percentage point).[8]

The committee noted that the Secretary could consider trends on an annual basis or within a longer timeframe but ultimately recommends an annual update. The committee concludes that premiums should be the way in which costs are characterized and that the Secretary should use the estimated premium required to buy the current year package in the next year as the budget constraint within which updates to the EHB are evaluated. In Recommendation 1, the committee recommends that the contents of the initial benefit package be constructed within the national average premium for a silver-level plan. Updates to premiums should account for trends in medical prices, utilization, new technologies, and population characteristics.

Use of Cost Information

The committee considered three ways in which information about cost could be used to inform updates to the EHB package: (1) for guidance, (2) to establish voluntary goals, or (3) as a binding constraint.

If cost information were used for guidance, the Secretary might issue an annual report noting the increased cost to purchase the EHB package and the cost implications of proposed changes to the package of benefits. There would be no explicit incorporation of costs into updates; changes would be based solely on evidence about the effectiveness of new categories of service. The Secretary could provide some guidance about how changes in the EHB package (e.g., the addition of a new category of coverage or a new set of services within an existing category) would affect changes in the premiums, total costs, or rates of change in health care spending.

Using cost information to establish voluntary goals would encourage states and health plans to take action to achieve the goal. For example, the Secretary could justify changes to the EHB in terms of a desire to voluntarily keep premium prices within some limit, to ensure federal spending is capped at a particular level, or to maintain a predetermined rate of growth in health care spending. Voluntary goals could be set for states or for health plans.

---

[6] § 1401 adding § 36B(b)(3)(A)(ii)(I) to the Internal Revenue Code.

[7] § 1401 adding § 36B(b)(3)(A)(ii)(II) to the Internal Revenue Code.

[8] § 3403(c)(6)(C)(ii), amending § 1899 of the Social Security Act.

Voluntary goals have been used many times in the past in an effort to avoid more directed federal action in the area of cost containment. These efforts have largely been unsuccessful in achieving goals in the long run, although they have slowed growth of spending in the short run (Block et al., 1987; Raphaelson and Hall, 1978).

Using cost information as a binding constraint would be done in the context of authority to enforce a consideration of cost in future updates to the EHB package. In this case, the Secretary would impose a cost target as part of the update, and changes to the benefit package would have to fall within the established target. The target could range from one that reflects the current trend in medical spending to one that seeks to decelerate the rate of growth. The impact on the scope of the EHB depends on the extent to which the selected cost target is lower than general medical cost trends. For example, if medical cost trends are increasing at 8 percent annually and the Secretary were to set a goal of a 6 percent increase, then the EHB would have to be scaled back to achieve the target. In this case, a binding constraint should not be interpreted to mean that the Secretary is setting premium prices in local markets but rather that the actuarial price of updates to the EHB cannot exceed a pre-established target.

The committee has concluded that costs should be a binding constraint on updates to the EHB but that the cost target should be linked to the rate of premium increases so as not to create a relative disadvantage for the EHB. The committee recognizes that using cost as a binding constraint is challenging and later suggests some mechanisms to assist the Secretary in implementing this approach.

Approaches to Enforcement

The discussion around the use of cost information then led the committee to consider approaches to enforcement, including none, incentives (rewards), penalties, and a binding constraint.

Guidance and voluntary goals do not require enforcement. These approaches rely on the shared willingness of other actors in the health care system to pursue a joint set of goals; all actors means health insurers, hospitals, physicians, other care providers, manufacturers of drugs and devices, regulators, purchasers, employer sponsors, and consumers. The committee agreed that without enforcement, health care spending would continue to increase at a rate that exceeds growth in the economy.

If costs were incorporated at a level other than the federal level, *using incentives or rewards* would provide some financial benefit to complying with the policy goals. For example, cost-of-living increases could be tied to achieving some target cost growth; this is analogous to the approach taken to public reporting for hospitals under the Medicare "pay-for-reporting" initiative, which was successful in encouraging high rates of participation for a relatively small investment of money. Many pay-for-performance initiatives link annual cost increases to achieving specific performance or activity goals.

A variety of *penalties from financial (fines) to restrictions* (e.g., no new subsidized enrollees in a plan) could be considered to enforce consideration of cost targets at levels other than the federal level. Two key challenges were identified in this area: the statutory authority currently held by the Secretary and balancing an effective enforcement approach against ensuring an adequate number of plans offered in the market. If too few plans are available as a result of strict enforcement practices or if too few providers are willing to contract with these plans over time, people might encounter difficulties in complying with the individual mandate or in accessing care.

Finally, if the Secretary required that *a cost target be a binding constraint* on updates to the EHB at the federal level, this would constitute an effective enforcement mechanism. The committee concluded that this approach is the preferred strategy given its focus on incorporating costs at the federal level although the committee recognizes the political and technical challenges in enforcing this constraint. Further, the committee notes that under this approach the constraint is applied only to the contents of the EHB package.

Mechanism for Achieving the Cost Target

The committee considered three mechanisms by which cost targets could be achieved: (1) no mechanism; (2) change only what is included in the essential health benefits; or (3) allow factors other than the scope of EHB to be adjusted.

The first approach acknowledges that for certain options, *no mechanism* to achieve the target is required.

The second approach is to focus on *making adjustments to the EHB that are "cost neutral."* As updates are considered, in order for a new benefit area or new services to be added within an existing area, some other benefit or service would have to be reduced or eliminated to produce a package that falls within the cost target. In the future, the Secretary may be asked to consider categories other than those initially covered. Such inclusions would have to be considered within the context of the budget constraint. This approach is intended to be consistent with ensuring that the EHB package does not become an ever-expanding entitlement over time, resulting in a price that makes the package increasingly unaffordable. Because a major driver of cost increases is medical technology (Smith et al., 2009), whether new technologies are treated as part of the underlying trend or treated as a new benefit area will significantly affect how much this approach contributes to restraining cost growth. The committee notes that in the next few years, because the EHB is likely to lack specificity, there will be limited opportunities for the Secretary to explicitly consider whether certain new technologies should be included or not. They will likely be included in the general categories that define the EHB at the outset. Going forward, however, the committee intends that the specificity of the EHB will increase such that the Secretary can address the role of new technology more explicitly and require that inclusion of such changes meet the process below. The committee believes that this option is within the authority currently held by the Secretary.

The third approach is to *allow all factors that can influence health care costs to be available for achieving the cost target.* This would allow levers such as network design, value-based purchasing, medical management, and similar tools to be used to achieve a cost target. While benefit design would be one of those tools (although limited by the actuarial value rules), it would not be the only available option. The committee believes that this approach is most effectively executed at the state and health plan levels and would anticipate that the implementation of the EHB by health plans offering products would incorporate these strategies. Nonetheless, in estimating a national average premium, explicit assumptions will have to be made about benefit design and medical management.

The committee concluded that adjustments to the EHB should be cost neutral, that is, any changes could not result in a package that is more expensive than the estimated cost of the existing package in the next year. Putting the design choices together, the committee recommends that costs be incorporated into updates to the EHB at the federal level, using premiums as the unit at which the costs of the EHB are characterized, using cost information to create a binding constraint on the content of future year packages, enforcing a cost-neutral approach to updates, and achieving the premium target only through changes in the EHB. The committee believes that the public deliberative process described previously in this report should be used to inform priorities for making tradeoffs within the cost constraints.

Recommendation 4b: The Secretary should explicitly incorporate costs into updates to the EHB package.

- **The Secretary should obtain an actuarial estimate of the national average premium for a silver-level plan with the existing EHB package in the next year; the estimate will account for trends in medical prices, utilization, new technologies, and population characteristics.**
- **Any changes to the EHB package should not result in a package that exceeds the actuarially estimated cost of the current package in the next year. A public deliberative process should be used to inform choices about inclusions to or exclusions from the updated package, with specific attention to how inclusion of new benefits could affect the availability of existing covered benefits.**

CONSEQUENCES FOR THE EHB AND ACA OF FAILING TO ADDRESS RISING HEALTH CARE COSTS

Congress clearly signaled a concern about the impact of changes to the EHB over time on the costs of the package and on existing coverage by calling these items out as specific required aspects in the annual report to Congress and the public. From the beginning of its deliberations, the committee unanimously agreed that if the country does not address the problem of health care costs growing faster than the GDP, the effectiveness of the ACA in achieving its goal of substantially reducing the number of people without a basic level of health insurance will be undermined. This is necessary to ensure the integrity of the EHB in the future. The committee offers two concrete illustrations of the problem.

As Figure 9-1 shows, U.S. health care spending is increasing in all sectors at an exponential rate. The Chief Actuary for CMS estimates that the ACA will not result in a deceleration in the spending growth rate, but likely will contribute to a small increase (0.9 percent between 2010 and 2019) (CMS, 2010a).

Rapid growth in health spending by itself would not be a problem if the U.S. economy were growing at the same rate, but this is not the case, as shown in Figure 9-2. Since 1990, the growth in national health care spending has generally exceeded the growth in GDP by 2 to 3 percentage points. The effect of this pattern is that an increasing share of national spending goes to health care, which crowds out spending on other goods and services by individuals, businesses, and governments, such as support for public education, investment in infrastructure (e.g., transportation and utilities), and provision of social services for vulnerable populations.

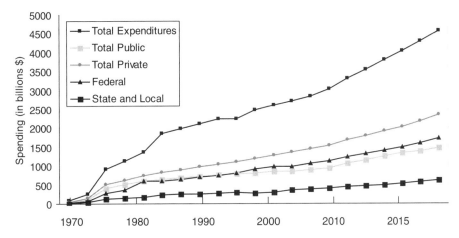

FIGURE 9-1 U.S. health care expenditure trends.
SOURCE: CMS, 2010b.

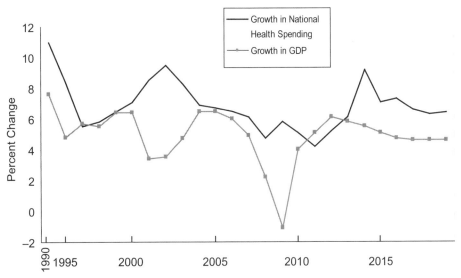

FIGURE 9-2 U.S. national health care spending relative to growth in gross domestic product (GDP).
NOTE: Actual expenditure and GDP figures used 1990-2008; projected figures used 2009-2019.
SOURCE: Adapted from Catlin et al., 2007; CMS, 2010b, 2011.

How does this affect the definition and updating of the EHB? Among other things, it means that each year it will cost relatively more of everyone's income to purchase the same package of benefits, reducing both individual and social capacity to spend and invest in other areas. The committee's Recommendation 4b is designed to ensure that the EHB not accelerate the increase in health spending for the 68 million Americans whose terms of purchase are governed by the EHB definition. However, the committee also recognized that the EHB should not be held to a different standard than the rest of the public and private health care sectors—for example, by limiting the growth in spending on the EHB alone. If the committee had recommended that the growth in the estimated average premium to purchase the EHB be held to a lower rate of growth than increases in premiums in all other sectors, the result would have been to make the EHB cover less and less over time—clearly at odds with the intent of Congress.

Because the committee's Recommendation 4b allows the cost of the EHB to increase with the general increase in health care premiums, this enhances the likelihood of maintaining the initial level of comprehensiveness established by the Secretary. Unfortunately, this also means that the cost of the EHB will likely continue to increase faster than wages and faster than the growth in the economy. In turn, the number of people who will be able to afford to purchase the EHB-defined insurance will decline. As the premiums increase, subsidies will take a larger share of the federal budget. As premiums rise, many more people will choose to enroll in Medicaid, rather than a private plan on the exchange, increasing the strain on state budgets. All of these consequences violate one of the criteria established by the committee: the EHB should be affordable for consumers, employers, and taxpayers. The committee further envisioned that the pressure on federal and state budgets might lead to repeal of the EHB requirement. This threat to the long-term integrity of the EHB caused the committee to consider what could be done in order to mitigate these adverse consequences.

Serious efforts to change the rate of increase in health spending will have to go beyond the definition of essential health benefits—the cost trend cannot be moderated through this mechanism alone. Mindful of its focus on EHB integrity, the committee considered a variety of strategies for addressing this problem and came to some conclusions about desirable attributes of an approach the Secretary might adopt. First, the committee considered whether a Medicare-only strategy for reducing health spending growth might be enough to change the country's health care spending trajectory. Although Medicare represents a significant portion of the U.S. health market (20 percent) (CMS, 2010b; Martin et al., 2011), Medicare is the only sector that is not directly subject to the EHB, and it is not clear that changes in this segment of the market alone would be enough to affect overall spending. The committee was also concerned that Medicare-only strategies might result in responses in other segments that would include higher rates of increase in prices in the non-Medicare market and changes in the quantity and quality of services offered to all patients, which might undermine the effectiveness of this particular cost control strategy. In fact, in a hearing on the 2011 Medicare Trustees Report, representatives from the American Academy of Actuaries indicated that "when evaluating proposals to improve Medicare's financial condition, it is important to recognize that improving the sustainability of the health system as a whole requires slowing the growth in overall health spending rather than shifting costs from one payer to another" (American Academy of Actuaries, 2011, p. 2).

The committee then considered whether a federal-only or government-only strategy would be adequate to control health spending and preserve the intended scope of health benefits. Federal sources of spending (Medicare, Medicaid, Department of Defense, Department of Veterans Affairs, Federal Employees Health Benefits Program [FEHBP], Indian Health Service, community health centers, Title X clinics) combined represent a substantial portion of the health care market (27 percent according to the CMS Actuary). State spending, dominated by Medicaid, adds another 16 percent to the overall share accounted for by the public sector (CMS, 2010b; Martin et al., 2011). Although this approach would contribute to changes in a larger portion of the market, the committee expects that adverse effects on prices in the private sector are possible and that the failure to coordinate strategies with the private sector, which is also affected by the EHB, would limit the effectiveness of this approach.

There are a variety of payers and different payment mechanisms in the market today; changes in one payer can affect the others in many different ways including choices made about which plan to enroll in (Medicaid versus exchange), access to providers willing to take patients with different types of insurance, changes in the site of care (hospital vs. office or stand-alone center), changes in the quantity of services ordered, and changes in the quality of care provided. A private-public strategy can ensure that the approaches in each sector are not in conflict with one another.

Having concluded that a strategy that involves all payers is essential to ensure serious attention to the problem of rising health care costs and a set of strategies that would not result in market distortions, the committee considered whether any existing body could take on this charge. None of the examined entities explicitly engages the private sector although IPAB will ultimately make recommendations that relate to the private sector.

Much of the impetus for establishing IPAB was to provide an alternative to congressional deliberation on technical proposals for improving the sustainability of Medicare and this influenced the structure and function of IPAB. IPAB has not yet been constituted and has a full agenda. Without engagement of the private sector in a meaningful way, the committee believes that it is less likely that actions recommended by IPAB for the private sector will be accepted and acted upon. The committee believes that IPAB's structure (i.e., full-time, federal employees) is not optimal for purposes of engaging the private sector in implementation. Furthermore, IPAB is not required to start making advisory recommendations about spending outside of Medicare until 2015. The committee believes that the legislative language for composition, function, and timeline of activities for IPAB would have to be changed at least in the following ways: (1) have private sector representation, (2) be able to address provider payments before 2020, and (3) have a unified approach addressing both Medicare and the private sector simultaneously (see Ebeler et al., 2011). Because IPAB is seen by some as taking away congressional authority, the committee was concerned that its future might be compromised by ongoing political debate over whether it should exist at all, and the prospect for legislative change is unpredictable at best.

Unless a strategy for containing costs throughout the health care system is adopted, the definition of an essential health benefits package will ultimately fail to achieve congressional intent to establish an appropriate basic package that is affordable and extends coverage to millions.

Recommendation 4c: To ensure over time that EHB-defined packages are affordable and offer reasonable coverage, the Secretary of HHS, working in collaboration with others, should develop a strategy for controlling rates of growth in health care spending across all sectors in line with the rate of growth in the economy.

The committee concluded that any meaningful approach to developing a strategy for controlling cost should include the following attributes: the approach should (1) be nonpartisan, (2) include public and private sector collaboration, (3) integrate activities across all sectors, and (4) be able to ensure action on the recommendations. For example, the Secretary could co-convene a commission with a representative of the private sector experienced in purchasing health services[9] to develop and implement meaningful actions to control costs. Because coordinated federal action would increase the likelihood of success in the public sector, the Secretary of HHS could coordinate federal participation in a commission and oversee federal implementation of such a commission's recommendations.

In summary, while it may appear that addressing the rate of growth in health care spending is beyond the scope of the EHB provisions, the committee views its Recommendations 4b and 4c as necessary complements. The committee's Recommendation 4b is designed to preserve the scope of benefits over time and to ensure that the EHB package itself will not accelerate the increase in spending by keeping the package equivalent in content. But without making concerted progress in stemming rising health care costs (Recommendation 4c), it will cost more to purchase the same package of benefits each year, eroding the purchasing power of the estimated 68 million people who will depend on EHB coverage. Eventually, the EHB package will become a hollow promise of coverage. The committee's charge was to develop a viable approach to defining the EHB that would work now and into the future, and this requires a two-pronged approach.

NATIONAL BENEFITS ADVISORY COUNCIL

Having identified a set of recommendations for updating the EHB and addressing the sector-wide challenges with rising health care costs, the committee next considered whether the Secretary would benefit from forming a new advisory group focused on updates to the EHB. The committee refers to this advisory group as the National Benefits Advisory Council (NBAC). Public respondents to questions posed about updates to the EHB often noted

---

[9] This should not be someone who is a delegate of a lobbying organization.

that this activity should not be solely a staff function within HHS because it requires making tradeoffs based on science, values, and diverse viewpoints and doing so in a transparent and fair manner. This led the committee to agree with numerous commenters that prefer a process to provide the Secretary with ongoing, structured external advice, such as through an advisory body. As envisioned by the committee, the advisory group, would be

- Comprised of a diverse group of stakeholders and
- Free from political influences (e.g., by ensuring that benefit decisions are evidence-based).

Public comments suggested two main advisory body approaches: an HHS panel or "an independent, nonpartisan" advisory body. An HHS panel was variously referred to as an oversight body or standing committee (Borelli, 2010; Keller, 2010; Metz, 2010). Before considering whether any existing entities could serve this function, the committee identified the functions of an external advisory committee.

Functions of the NBAC

The NBAC should advise the Secretary on (1) the research framework and scope of the data collection discussed earlier (Chapter 7), (2) updates to the overall benefit package and related benefit design issues, including assessments for the *Report to Congress* and whether adjustments need to be made for the entry of large employer groups in the exchanges, (3) changes to the premium target, and (4) appropriate mechanisms for evaluating new interventions. The IOM committee considered whether the NBAC should have a role in defining the initial EHB package; although the committee was not opposed to the NBAC having a role, the members thought that it would not be practical to get the NBAC appointed and operational in a timely enough fashion to be useful in the initial definition process. The committee views its own activities as contributing to this initial process and believes the initial EHB package will have to rely more on the scope of the typical employer plan than it will in the future. Additionally, the recommendation for structured public deliberation and making available the actuarial value of possible tradeoffs in rulemaking notices will contribute to a more transparent process during the initial definition of the EHB.

The NBAC approach to updating should conform to the criteria that the committee offers to guide the methods for defining and updating the EHB (Figure S-2 in the Summary). The policy foundations that the committee used to frame its approach reflect the need to find a balance among competing societal goals. The EHB package should ensure that the most vulnerable members of society are protected, the structure of the EHB encourages appropriate use of services, decisions are made on the best available science, available resources are used in the most cost-effective manner, and the process to define and apply decisions about the EHB is fair and transparent. The committee has defined an explicit approach to developing the updated national average premium by incorporating cost into the updating process. This approach is intended to ensure that changes to the EHB are cost-neutral. The NBAC can provide the Secretary guidance on the considerations in updating that premium. Over time, a variety of factors in the private and public health sectors and general economy may require re-examination of the IOM committee's recommended approach. In addition, the NBAC should ensure that a national public deliberative process is conducted periodically to inform debates on tradeoffs. If state-based public deliberations are widespread, sufficient information may be gathered and there may be no need to duplicate the process.

The NBAC is to focus on what is appropriate for *subsidized* coverage in insurance programs that incorporate essential health benefits, not what should be covered in every public or private insurance program. Indeed, Section 1302 points out that the ACA does not prohibit a health plan from providing benefits in excess of the EHB if individuals and/or employers choose to pay the additional costs.

Consideration of Existing Entities

Having identified the functions of the external advisory committee, the IOM committee considered a variety of existing entities to see if they might serve this advisory function as summarized in Table 9-2.

The committee concluded that the U.S. Preventive Services Task Force (USPSTF), Medicare Evidence Development and Coverage Advisory Committee (MEDCAC), and Patient-Centered Outcomes Research Institute (PCORI)

TABLE 9-2 Existing Entities Considered by the Committee to Advise the Secretary on Updates to the Essential Health Benefits (EHB)

Existing Entity	Current Function	Ability to Advise Secretary on Updates to the EHB
U.S. Preventive Services Task Force (USPSTF) (Healthcare Research and Quality Act of 1999 § 915)	The USPSTF identifies preventive services for which there is adequate scientific evidence to recommend routine inclusion in primary care visits.	The USPSTF undertakes scientific evaluations that are consistent with part of the committee's criteria for updating. Focus is solely on preventive services; scope would have to be expanded to take on full range of benefits. Function is not related to benefit coverage. Meetings are not open, and there is no mechanism for considering tradeoffs (services are evaluated independent of one another).
Medicare Evidence Development and Coverage Advisory Committee (MEDCAC) (Public Health Service Act § 222)	The MEDCAC reviews and evaluates medical literature, technology assessments, and examines data and information on the effectiveness and appropriateness of medical items and services that are covered under Medicare, or that may be eligible for coverage under Medicare. The MEDCAC judges the strength of the available evidence and makes recommendations to CMS based on that evidence.	The MEDCAC undertakes evaluations of the science base for making coverage decisions for Medicare. The function is consistent with part of what the committee believes should be considered in updates but does not include a mechanism for making tradeoffs across the entire benefit package and would have to be expanded to consider coverage outside of Medicare.
Patient-Centered Outcomes Research Institute (PCORI) (Patient Protection and Affordable Care Act [PPACA] § 6301)	PCORI is a public-private body that is tasked with developing research on the comparative effectiveness of alternative approaches to screening, diagnosis, treatment, and monitoring, taking account of patients' preferences, values, and experiences in order to inform patient decision making.	PCORI is constituted to develop evidence that might inform updates to the EHB but not to consider coverage issues per se. Focus is more on research and patient (or shared) decision making than on the structure of benefit packages.
Consumer Operated and Oriented Plan (CO-OP) Program Advisory Board (PPACA § 1322)	CO-OP's purpose is to foster the creation of qualified nonprofit health insurance issuers to offer qualified health plans (QHPs) in the individual and small group markets in the states in which issuers are licensed to offer such plans.	CO-OP's focus is on encouraging the development of qualified health plans and not on the benefit packages offered by those plans. Primary advice is on strategies for increasing the number of CO-OP offerings.

would all likely produce scientific information that would be useful in considering updates but that none is constituted to provide the Secretary with the full range of advice required for updating. Thus, the committee recommends that a new body, a National Benefits Advisory Council, be established. The NBAC would be staffed by HHS.

Appointment, Conflict of Interest, and Composition

The IOM committee recommends that the appointment process for membership to this proposed NBAC be coordinated through a nonpartisan entity, such as the Comptroller General of the U.S. Government Accountability Office (GAO). As part of any selection process, consultation could take place with a range of stakeholders on possible nominees, including Congress and the White House, and should include a process for disclosure of any real or perceived conflict of interest related to the EHB, particularly any financial interests and professional or intellectual biases (Guyatt et al., 2010; IOM, 2011a,b).[10] The GAO should take potential conflicts into account in the selection process and attempt to select a council as free of conflicts as possible. The council should be balanced with respect to intellectual and professional biases.

The conflict of interest disclosure process should be repeated at the initial meeting of the NBAC and repeated periodically. Members should not participate as representatives of stakeholder organizations, but rather as independent individuals. In general, members should divest financial investments that could be affected by recommendations, but given the breadth of possible EHB recommendations this may not be possible in all circumstances. Allowances can be made for exceptions, such as when the group is not able to perform its work without members who have a conflict of interest. In all cases, members should recuse themselves from voting on selected topics with specific conflicts.

Various health care advisory bodies are appointed by the GAO because of its own nonpartisan status. It provides Congress with reports, testimonies, correspondence, and legal decisions and opinions (GAO, 2011b). At its head, the Comptroller General of the United States has also been mandated to appoint certain health care–related commissions, advisory groups, and governing boards (GAO, 2011a), and such responsibilities have increased substantially with the passage of the ACA. The GAO is responsible for the appointments of members of six different bodies, including the Medicare Payment Advisory Commission (MedPAC), the Medicaid and CHIP (Children's Health Insurance Program) Payment and Access Commission (MACPAC), the PCORI Governing Board, the PCORI Methodology Committee, the National Health Care Workforce Commission, and the Consumer Operated and Oriented Plan (CO-OP) Program Advisory Board. The committee intends the NBAC to be advisory to the Secretary, not an operational body.[11]

The NBAC should be multidisciplinary and balanced, comprising a variety of methodological experts and clinicians, as well as populations expected to be affected. This body will need sufficient expertise to fulfill its functions, including, for example, persons knowledgeable about the concerns of small employers, consumers, health professionals, and the insurance industry and persons with sufficient understanding of technical aspects of the tasks (e.g., economics, health services research, actuarial science). Members' terms of appointment should be staggered to avoid turnover of the entire council at one time.

Timeline

Annual updates of the scope of benefits in health insurance contracts are the norm. Such updates reflect continuous review processes conducted throughout the year by insurers to consider evidence in the peer-reviewed literature, guidelines, and consensus statements; changes in regulatory agency approvals or in medical protocols that may necessitate a modification in benefits; or other information that is material to the status of a medical technology such as the quantity of use and importance of questions that have arisen regarding specific technologies (McDonough, 2011).

Periodicity

The IOM considered whether an annual update or some other interval was preferable. Respondents to the committee's online questionnaire offered a variety of suggestions—that HHS establish a "6-month monitoring process" (Wojcik, 2010), or that the review occur annually (Edgington, 2010; Monahan, 2010), every 2 to 3 years (Bocchino, 2010; Keller, 2010; Mahoney, 2010), or as infrequently as every 5 years (Hafner, 2010). On the one hand, the process needs to be responsive to changes in public priorities and advances in clinical medicine—for example, some noted the importance of any time line for review having "sufficient flexibility to incorporate new

---

[10] Recent IOM standards for conflict of interest (COI) regarding clinical practice guideline development include the following elements: disclosure of potential conflicts prior to appointment, disclosure within the convened group, and divesture of financial investments whose interest could be affected by recommendations, but allowances made for exceptions, such as, when the group is not able to perform its work without members who have a COI; chairs or co-chairs should not have a COI (IOM, 2009, 2011a).

[11] To be in compliance with the Appointments Clause of the U.S. Constitution. See *Buckley v. Valeo*, 424 U.S. 1 (1976).

information/breakthroughs" (Bocchino, 2010; Sacco, 2010). On the other hand, insurers, in particular, raised concerns that the frequency of reviews "should be balanced with administrative burdens related to the incorporation of new services in a benefit package" (Bocchino, 2010). "It will take time for insurers to adopt any new changes made by HHS, and consumers have an interest in stable, predictable benefits and costs. Unnecessarily adjusting benefit packages will only serve to increase costs for insurers and consumers" (Kelmar, 2010).

Other respondents suggested that updates correspond to updates in the FEHBP, which uses an annual contracting process. The committee concluded that an annual update was best to be consistent with standard contracting practices. It is not expected that the entire EHB must be updated annually; however, the Secretary would have the flexibility to update whatever should be updated within a reasonable time after finding credible evidence of the need for change.

The FEHBP cycle illustrates the amount of time required between identifying the need for change and getting that change implemented. In the context of updating, it suggests that 2016 may be the earliest year that a revised benefit package would be offered in exchanges, and annually thereafter. Reporting from states on their operations during 2014 will likely not occur until at least 2 months into 2015, leaving the balance of that calendar year for consideration of revisions. Thus, the first year in which the Secretary would have to identify a package revision within an updated premium target is 2016.

The NBAC provides an important forum for a transparent, public dialogue about how best to update the EHB in light of advances in science, information about the trends in health care spending, current societal assessments about the relative importance of newly available interventions compared to the existing set, and results from research about the effects of the current EHB on access to appropriate care.

Recommendation 5: As soon as is feasible, the Secretary should establish a National Benefits Advisory Council (NBAC), staffed by HHS but appointed through a nonpartisan process, such as the Office of the Comptroller General of the United States. The NBAC should

- **By January 1, 2013, advise the Secretary on a research plan and data requirements for updating the EHB package;**
- **Starting in 2015 for implementation in 2016, make recommendations annually to the Secretary regarding (1) any changes to the EHB package by applying the committee's recommended criteria (see Figure S-2 in the Summary), (2) any changes to the premium target, and (3) any mechanisms that would enhance the evidence base of the EHB package and its potential for promoting value; and**
- **Advise the Secretary on conducting and using the results of a periodic national public deliberative process to inform its recommendations around updates to the EHB.**

CONCLUSION

The ACA provides for a comprehensive set of categories, within which there are many potential services and items eligible to be deemed essential and thereby qualify for public subsidy of coverage using pooled public resources. A tradeoff exists between the inclusiveness of benefits, and the cost of the insurance product for the consumer and the sustainability of subsidies for the taxpayer. If the appropriate balance between comprehensiveness and affordability is not attained, there are tangible repercussions:

- If the benefits are not affordable, fewer people will get adequate coverage.
- If the benefit design puts excessive impediments to access, people will not get the care they need.
- If health care spending continues to rise disproportionately to GDP, the EHB could end up being substantially cut.

The committee concluded that any determination of scope of the benefit package should be thought about within the context of national, state, and consumer budget constraints and public examination of priorities. The committee's aims for the EHB mirror the criteria for assessing the package's content. The EHB must be affordable, maximize the number of people with insurance coverage, protect the most vulnerable individuals, protect against the greatest financial risks, promote better care, ensure stewardship of limited financial resources by focusing on high value services of proven effectiveness, promote shared responsibility for improving our health, and address the medical concerns of greatest importance to the nation.

REFERENCES

American Academy of Actuaries. 2011. *Statement of Thomas F. Wildsmith, Vice President, Health Practice Council and Cori E. Uccello, Senior Health Fellow, American Academy of Actuaries at the Committee on Ways and Means, Subcommittee on Health, U.S. House of Representatives Hearing on 2011 Medicare Trustees Report, June 22, 2011.* http://waysandmeans.house.gov/UploadedFiles/American_Academy_of_Actuaries622.pdf (accessed September 14, 2011).

Block, J. A., D. I. Regenstreif, and P. F. Griner. 1987. A community hospital payment experiment outperforms national experience. *Journal of the American Medical Association* 257(2):193-197.

Bocchino, C. 2010. Online questionnaire responses submitted by Carmella Bocchino, Executive Vice President, America's Health Insurance Plans to the IOM Committee on the Determination of Essential Health Benefits, December 6.

Borelli, C. 2010. Online questionnaire responses submitted by Claire Borelli, Manager, Health Policy, American Diabetes Association to the IOM Committee on the Determination of Essential Health Benefits, December 6.

Branscome, J. M. 2011. *Statistical brief #329: State differences in the cost of job-related health insurance, 2010.* http://www.meps.ahrq.gov/mepsweb/data_files/publications/st329/stat329.shtml (accessed July 22, 2011).

Catlin, A., C. Cowan, S. Heffler, B. Washington, and the National Health Expenditure Accounts Team. 2007. National health spending in 2005: The slowdown continues. *Health Affairs* 26(1):142-153.

CBO (Congressional Budget Office). 2009. Letter to the Honorable Evan Bayh, U.S. Senate from Douglas W. Elmendorf, Director, Congressional Budget Office, November 30.

Claxton, G., B. DiJulio, H. Whitmore, J. D. Pickreign, M. McHugh, A. Osei-Anto, and B. Finder. 2010. Health benefits in 2010: Premiums rise modestly, workers pay more toward coverage. *Health Affairs* 29(10):1942-1950.

CMS (Centers for Medicare & Medicaid Services). 2010a. *Memorandum by Richard S. Foster, Chief Actuary, CMS on the estimated financial effects of the "Patient Protection and Affordable Care Act," as amended.* https://www.cms.gov/ActuarialStudies/Downloads/PPACA_2010-04-22.pdf (accessed July 11, 2011).

———. 2010b. *National health expenditure projections 2009-2019.* http://www.cms.gov/NationalHealthExpendData/downloads/NHEProjections2009to2019.pdf (accessed March 23, 2011).

———. 2011. *Table 1: National health expenditures aggregate, per capita amounts, percent distribution, and average annual percent growth: Selected calendar years 1960-2009.* https://www.cms.gov/NationalHealthExpendData/downloads/tables.pdf (accessed November 2, 2011).

Ebeler, J., T. Neuman, and J. Cubanski. 2011. *The Independent Payment Advisory Board: A new approach to controlling Medicare spending.* Menlo Park, CA: Kaiser Family Foundation.

Edgington, S. 2010. Online questionnaire responses submitted by Sabrina Edgington, Program and Policy Specialist, National Health Care for the Homeless to the IOM Committee on the Determination of Essential Health Benefits, December 6, 2010.

Eibner, C., F. Girosi, C. C. Price, A. Cordova, P. S. Hussey, A. Beckman, and E. A. McGlynn. 2010. *Establishing state health insurance exchanges: Implications for health insurance enrollment, spending, and small businesses.* Santa Monica, CA: RAND Corporation.

GAO (Government Accountability Office). 2011a. *Health care advisory committees.* http://www.gao.gov/about/hcac/ (accessed July 15, 2011).

———. 2011b. *Our products.* http://www.gao.gov/about/products/ (accessed July 15, 2011).

Guyatt, G., E. A. Akl, J. Hirsh, C. Kearon, M. Crowther, D. Gutterman, S. Z. Lewis, I. Nathanson, R. Jaeschke, and H. Schnemann. 2010. The vexing problem of guidelines and conflict of interest: A potential solution. *Annals of Internal Medicine* 152(11):738-741.

Hafner, J. 2010. Online questionnaire responses submitted by Jay Hafner, Clinic Director, Hafner Chiropractic to the IOM Committee on the Determination of Essential Health Benefits, December 2.

HHS (Department of Health and Human Services). 2010. Rate increase disclosure and review. *Federal Register* 75(246):81004-81029.

IOM (Institute of Medicine). 2009. *Conflict of interest in medical research, education, and practice.* Washington, DC: The National Academies Press.

———. 2011a. *Clinical practice guidelines we can trust.* Washington DC: The National Academies Press.

———. 2011b. *Finding what works in health care: Standards for systematic reviews.* Washington, DC: The National Academies Press.

Keller, K. 2010. Online questionnaire responses submitted by Kate Keller, Senior Program Officer, Health Foundation of Greater Cincinnati to the IOM Committee on the Determination of Essential Health Benefits, December 6.

Kelmar, S. 2010. Online questionnaire responses submitted by Steven Kelmar, Senior Vice President, Government Affairs & Public Policy, Aetna to the IOM Committee on the Determination of Essential Health Benefits, December 6.

Mahoney, K. 2010. Online questionnaire responses submitted by Katie Mahoney, Director, Health Care Regulations, U.S. Chamber of Commerce to the IOM Committee on the Determination of Essential Health Benefits, December 6.

Martin, A., D. Lassman, L. Whittle, A. Catlin, and the National Health Expenditure Accounts Team. 2011. Recession contributes to slowest annual rate of increase in health spending in five decades. *Health Affairs* 30(1):11-22.

McDonough, R. 2011. *Determination of essential health benefits.* PowerPoint Presentation to the IOM Committee on the Determination of Essential Health Benefits by Robert McDonough, Director, Clinical Policy Research and Development, Aetna, Washington, DC, January 13.

Metz, R. D. 2010. Online questionnaire responses submitted by R. Douglas Metz, EVP & Chief Health Services Officer, American Specialty Health to the IOM Committee on the Determination of Essential Health Benefits, December 20.

Monahan, C. 2010. Online questionnaire responses submitted by Christine Monahan, Health Policy Advisor, National Partnership for Women & Families to the IOM Committee on the Determination of Essential Health Benefits, December 6.

Newhouse, J. P., and the Insurance Experiment Group. 1993. *Free for all? Lessons from the RAND health insurance experiment.* Cambridge, MA: Harvard University Press.

Oregon Health Services Commission. 2011. *Prioritized list of health services: April 1, 2011.* http://www.oregon.gov/OHA/OHPR/HSC/docs/L/Apr11List.pdf (accessed May 10, 2011).

Raphaelson, A. H., and C. P. Hall, Jr. 1978. Politics and economics of hospital cost containment. *Journal of Health Politics Policy and Law* 3(1):87-111.

Sacco, R. 2010. Online questionnaire responses submitted by Ralph Sacco, President, American Heart Association to the IOM Committee on the Determination of Essential Health Benefits, December 21.

Smith, S., J. P. Newhouse, and M. S. Freeland. 2009. Income, insurance, and technology: Why does health spending outpace economic growth? *Health Affairs* 28(5):1276-1284.

Wojcik, S. 2010. Online questionnaire responses submitted by Steve Wojcik, Vice President, Public Policy, National Business Group on Health to the IOM Committee on the Determination of Essential Health Benefits, December 6.

Appendix A

Patient Protection and Affordable Care Act, Section 1302, and Web Questions for Public Input

This appendix includes: (1) the Section of the Patient Protection and Affordable Care Act that provides the legislative foundation for the essential health benefits,[1] and (2) 10 questions that were posted online for public comment to inform the committee on various perspectives. All responses were placed in the project's public access file, provided directly to HHS, and analyzed for the committee's review along with other materials submitted for the committee's consideration.

PATIENT PROTECTION AND AFFORDABLE CARE ACT, SECTION 1302

SEC. 1302. ESSENTIAL HEALTH BENEFITS REQUIREMENTS. [42 U.S.C. 18022]

(a) ESSENTIAL HEALTH BENEFITS PACKAGE.—In this title, the term "essential health benefits package" means, with respect to any health plan, coverage that—

(1) provides for the essential health benefits defined by the Secretary under subsection (b);

(2) limits cost-sharing for such coverage in accordance with subsection (c); and

(3) subject to subsection (e), provides either the bronze, silver, gold, or platinum level of coverage described in subsection (d).

(b) ESSENTIAL HEALTH BENEFITS.—

(1) IN GENERAL.—Subject to paragraph (2), the Secretary shall define the essential health benefits, except that such benefits shall include at least the following general categories and the items and services covered within the categories:

(A) Ambulatory patient services.

(B) Emergency services.

(C) Hospitalization.

(D) Maternity and newborn care.

(E) Mental health and substance use disorder services, including behavioral health treatment.

(F) Prescription drugs.

(G) Rehabilitative and habilitative services and devices.

---

[1] To access the full text of the law as amended through May 1, 2010: http://docs.house.gov/energycommerce/ppacacon.pdf. In addition, several organizations have published summary documents of the law. One example, published by the Kaiser Family Foundation can be found at: http://www.kff.org/healthreform/upload/8061.pdf.

(H) Laboratory services.

(I) Preventive and wellness services and chronic disease management.

(J) Pediatric services, including oral and vision care.

(2) LIMITATION.—

(A) IN GENERAL.—The Secretary shall ensure that the scope of the essential health benefits under paragraph (1) is equal to the scope of benefits provided under a typical employer plan, as determined by the Secretary. To inform this determination, the Secretary of Labor shall conduct a survey of employer-sponsored coverage to determine the benefits typically covered by employers, including multiemployer plans, and provide a report on such survey to the Secretary.

(B) CERTIFICATION.—In defining the essential health benefits described in paragraph (1), and in revising the benefits under paragraph (4)(H), the Secretary shall submit a report to the appropriate committees of Congress containing a certification from the Chief Actuary of the Centers for Medicare & Medicaid Services that such essential health benefits meet the limitation described in paragraph (2).

(3) NOTICE AND HEARING.—In defining the essential health benefits described in paragraph (1), and in revising the benefits under paragraph (4)(H), the Secretary shall provide notice and an opportunity for public comment.

(4) REQUIRED ELEMENTS FOR CONSIDERATION.—In defining the essential health benefits under paragraph (1), the Secretary shall—

(A) ensure that such essential health benefits reflect an appropriate balance among the categories described in such subsection, so that benefits are not unduly weighted toward any category;

(B) not make coverage decisions, determine reimbursement rates, establish incentive programs, or design benefits in ways that discriminate against individuals because of their age, disability, or expected length of life;

(C) take into account the health care needs of diverse segments of the population, including women, children, persons with disabilities, and other groups;

(D) ensure that health benefits established as essential not be subject to denial to individuals against their wishes on the basis of the individuals' age or expected length of life or of the individuals' present or predicted disability, degree of medical dependency, or quality of life;

(E) provide that a qualified health plan shall not be treated as providing coverage for the essential health benefits described in paragraph (1) unless the plan provides that—

(i) coverage for emergency department services will be provided without imposing any requirement under the plan for prior authorization of services or any limitation on coverage where the provider of services does not have a contractual relationship with the plan for the providing of services that is more restrictive than the requirements or limitations that apply to emergency department services received from providers who do have such a contractual relationship with the plan; and

(ii) if such services are provided out-of-network, the cost-sharing requirement (expressed as a copayment amount or coinsurance rate) is the same requirement that would apply if such services were provided in-network;

(F) provide that if a plan described in section 1311(b)(2)(B)(ii) (relating to stand-alone dental benefits plans) is offered through an Exchange, another health plan offered through such Exchange shall not fail to be treated as a qualified health plan solely because the plan does not offer coverage of benefits offered through the stand-alone plan that are otherwise required under paragraph (1)(J); and

(G) periodically review the essential health benefits under paragraph (1), and provide a report to Congress and the public that contains—

(i) an assessment of whether enrollees are facing any difficulty accessing needed services for reasons of coverage or cost;

(ii) an assessment of whether the essential health benefits needs to be modified or updated to account for changes in medical evidence or scientific advancement;

(iii) information on how the essential health benefits will be modified to address any such gaps in access or changes in the evidence base;

(iv) an assessment of the potential of additional or expanded benefits to increase costs and the interactions between the addition or expansion of benefits and reductions in existing benefits to meet actuarial limitations described in paragraph (2); and

(H) periodically update the essential health benefits under paragraph (1) to address any gaps in access to coverage or changes in the evidence base the Secretary identifies in the review conducted under subparagraph (G).

(5) RULE OF CONSTRUCTION.—Nothing in this title shall be construed to prohibit a health plan from providing benefits in excess of the essential health benefits described in this subsection.

(c) REQUIREMENTS RELATING TO COST-SHARING.—

(1) ANNUAL LIMITATION ON COST-SHARING.—

(A) 2014.—The cost-sharing incurred under a health plan with respect to self-only coverage or coverage other than self-only coverage for a plan year beginning in 2014 shall not exceed the dollar amounts in effect under section 223(c)(2)(A)(ii) of the Internal Revenue Code of 1986 for self-only and family coverage, respectively, for taxable years beginning in 2014.

(B) 2015 AND LATER.—In the case of any plan year beginning in a calendar year after 2014, the limitation under this paragraph shall—

(i) in the case of self-only coverage, be equal to the dollar amount under subparagraph (A) for self-only coverage for plan years beginning in 2014, increased by an amount equal to the product of that amount and the premium adjustment percentage under paragraph (4) for the calendar year; and

(ii) in the case of other coverage, twice the amount in effect under clause (i).

If the amount of any increase under clause (i) is not a multiple of $50, such increase shall be rounded to the next lowest multiple of $50.

(2) ANNUAL LIMITATION ON DEDUCTIBLES FOR EMPLOYER-SPONSORED PLANS.—

(A) IN GENERAL.—In the case of a health plan offered in the small group market, the deductible under the plan shall not exceed—

(i) $2,000 in the case of a plan covering a single individual; and

(ii) $4,000 in the case of any other plan.

The amounts under clauses (i) and (ii) may be increased by the maximum amount of reimbursement which is reasonably available to a participant under a flexible spending arrangement described in section 106(c)(2) of the Internal Revenue Code of 1986 (determined without regard to any salary reduction arrangement).

(B) INDEXING OF LIMITS.—In the case of any plan year beginning in a calendar year after 2014—

(i) the dollar amount under subparagraph (A)(i) shall be increased by an amount equal to the product of that amount and the premium adjustment percentage under paragraph (4) for the calendar year; and

(ii) the dollar amount under subparagraph (A)(ii) shall be increased to an amount equal to twice the amount in effect under subparagraph (A)(i) for plan years beginning in the calendar year, determined after application of clause (i).

If the amount of any increase under clause (i) is not a multiple of $50, such increase shall be rounded to the next lowest multiple of $50.

(C) ACTUARIAL VALUE.—The limitation under this paragraph shall be applied in such a manner so as to not affect the actuarial value of any health plan, including a plan in the bronze level.

(D) COORDINATION WITH PREVENTIVE LIMITS.—Nothing in this paragraph shall be construed to allow a plan to have a deductible under the plan apply to benefits described in section 2713 of the Public Health Service Act.

(3) COST-SHARING.—In this title—

(A) IN GENERAL.—The term "cost-sharing" includes—

(i) deductibles, coinsurance, copayments, or similar charges; and

(ii) any other expenditure required of an insured individual which is a qualified medical expense (within the meaning of section 223(d)(2) of the Internal Revenue Code of 1986) with respect to essential health benefits covered under the plan.

(B) EXCEPTIONS.—Such term does not include premiums, balance billing amounts for non-network providers, or spending for non-covered services.

(4) PREMIUM ADJUSTMENT PERCENTAGE.—For purposes of paragraphs (1)(B)(i) and (2)(B)(i), the premium adjustment percentage for any calendar year is the percentage (if any) by which the average per capita premium for health insurance coverage in the United States for the preceding calendar year (as estimated by the Secretary no later than October 1 of such preceding calendar year) exceeds such average per capita premium for 2013 (as determined by the Secretary).

(d) LEVELS OF COVERAGE.—

(1) LEVELS OF COVERAGE DEFINED.—The levels of coverage described in this subsection are as follows:

(A) BRONZE LEVEL.—A plan in the bronze level shall provide a level of coverage that is designed to provide benefits that are actuarially equivalent to 60 percent of the full actuarial value of the benefits provided under the plan.

(B) SILVER LEVEL.—A plan in the silver level shall provide a level of coverage that is designed to provide benefits that are actuarially equivalent to 70 percent of the full actuarial value of the benefits provided under the plan.

(C) GOLD LEVEL.—A plan in the gold level shall provide a level of coverage that is designed to provide benefits that are actuarially equivalent to 80 percent of the full actuarial value of the benefits provided under the plan.

(D) PLATINUM LEVEL.—A plan in the platinum level shall provide a level of coverage that is designed to provide benefits that are actuarially equivalent to 90 percent of the full actuarial value of the benefits provided under the plan.

(2) ACTUARIAL VALUE.—

(A) IN GENERAL.—Under regulations issued by the Secretary, the level of coverage of a plan shall be determined on the basis that the essential health benefits described in subsection (b) shall be provided to a standard population (and without regard to the population the plan may actually provide benefits to).

(B) EMPLOYER CONTRIBUTIONS.— [*As revised by section 10104(b)(1).*] The Secretary shall issue regulations under which employer contributions to a health savings account (within the meaning of section 223 of the Internal Revenue Code of 1986) may be taken into account in determining the level of coverage for a plan of the employer.

(C) APPLICATION.—In determining under this title, the Public Health Service Act, or the Internal Revenue Code of 1986 the percentage of the total allowed costs of benefits provided under a group health plan or health insurance coverage that are provided by such plan or coverage, the rules contained in the regulations under this paragraph shall apply.

(3) ALLOWABLE VARIANCE.—The Secretary shall develop guidelines to provide for a de minimis variation in the actuarial valuations used in determining the level of coverage of a plan to account for differences in actuarial estimates.

(4) PLAN REFERENCE.—In this title, any reference to a bronze, silver, gold, or platinum plan shall be treated as a reference to a qualified health plan providing a bronze, silver, gold, or platinum level of coverage, as the case may be.

(e) CATASTROPHIC PLAN.—

(1) IN GENERAL.—A health plan not providing a bronze, silver, gold, or platinum level of coverage shall be treated as meeting the requirements of subsection (d) with respect to any plan year if—

(A) the only individuals who are eligible to enroll in the plan are individuals described in paragraph (2); and

(B) the plan provides—

(i) except as provided in clause (ii), the essential health benefits determined under subsection (b), except that the plan provides no benefits for any plan year until the individual has incurred cost-sharing expenses in an amount equal to the annual limitation in effect under subsection (c)(1) for the plan year (except as provided for in section 2713); and

(ii) coverage for at least three primary care visits.

(2) INDIVIDUALS ELIGIBLE FOR ENROLLMENT.—An individual is described in this paragraph for any plan year if the individual—

(A) has not attained the age of 30 before the beginning of the plan year; or

(B) has a certification in effect for any plan year under this title that the individual is exempt from the requirement under section 5000A of the Internal Revenue Code of 1986 by reason of—

(i) section 5000A(e)(1) of such Code (relating to individuals without affordable coverage); or

(ii) section 5000A(e)(5) of such Code (relating to individuals with hardships).

(3) RESTRICTION TO INDIVIDUAL MARKET.—If a health insurance issuer offers a health plan described in this subsection, the issuer may only offer the plan in the individual market.

(f) CHILD-ONLY PLANS.—If a qualified health plan is offered through the Exchange in any level of coverage specified under subsection (d), the issuer shall also offer that plan through the Exchange in that level as a plan in which the only enrollees are individuals who, as of the beginning of a plan year, have not attained the age of 21, and such plan shall be treated as a qualified health plan.

(g) PAYMENTS TO FEDERALLY-QUALIFIED HEALTH CENTERS.—

[*As added by section 10104(b)(2).*] If any item or service covered by a qualified health plan is provided by a Federally-qualified health center (as defined in section 1905(1)(2)(B) of the Social Security Act (42 U.S.C. 1396d(1)(2)(B)) to an enrollee of the plan, the offeror of the plan shall pay to the center for the item or service an amount that is not less than the amount of payment that would have been paid to the center under section 1902(bb) of such Act (42 U.S.C. 1396a(bb)) for such item or service.

WEB QUESTIONS FOR PUBLIC INPUT ON DETERMINATION OF ESSENTIAL HEALTH BENEFITS

What is your interpretation of the word "essential" in the context of an essential benefit package?

How is medical necessity defined and then applied by insurers in coverage determinations? What are the advantages and disadvantages of current definitions and approaches?

What criteria and methods, besides medical necessity, are currently used by insurers to determine which benefits will be covered? What are the advantages and disadvantages of these current criteria and methods?

What principles, criteria, and process(es) might the Secretary of HHS use to determine whether the details of each benefit package offered will meet the requirements specified in the Affordable Care Act?

What type of limits on specific or total benefits, if any, could be allowable in packages given statutory restrictions on lifetime and annual benefit limits? What principles and criteria could or should be applied to assess the advantages and disadvantages of proposed limits?

How could an "appropriate balance" among the 10 categories of essential care be determined so that benefit packages are not unduly weighted to certain categories? The 10 categories are ambulatory patient services; emergency services; hospitalization; maternity and newborn care; mental health and substance use disorders services, including behavioral health treatment; prescription drugs; rehabilitative and habilitative services and devices; laboratory services; preventive and wellness services and chronic disease management; pediatric services, including oral and vision care.

How could it be determined that essential benefits are "not subject to denial to individuals against their wishes" on the basis of age, expected length of life, present or predicted disability, degree of medical dependency, or quality of life? Are there other factors that should be determined?

How could it be determined that the essential health benefits take into account the health care needs of diverse segments of the population, including women, children, persons with disabilities, and other groups?

By what criteria and method(s) should the Secretary evaluate state mandates for inclusion in a national essential benefit package? What are the cost and coverage implications of including all current state mandates in requirements for a national essential benefit package?

What criteria and method(s) should HHS use in updating the essential package? How should these criteria be applied? How might these criteria and method(s) be tailored to assess whether (1) enrollees are facing difficulty in accessing needed services for reasons of cost or coverage, (2) advances in medical evidence or scientific advancement are being covered, (3) changes in public priorities identified through public input and/or policy changes at the state or national level?

Appendix B

Stakeholder Decisions on Health Insurance

This appendix expands upon Figure 1-2 in Chapter 1 through a discussion of how various stakeholder (individual, employer and employee, state, and health insurance company) decisions in the course of the Patient Protection and Affordable Care Act (ACA) implementation might individually, and together, impact the health insurance landscape.

INDIVIDUAL CHOICE

The individual purchaser must decide whether or not to purchase insurance, which type of plan to participate in, and given a choice of plans, what level of out-of-pocket expenditures (premiums, deductible, co-payments) are considered affordable.

Take-up Decisions

Because of the individual mandate, individuals will have to decide whether to purchase insurance or accept the penalty.[1] Depending on their financial circumstances, employment status, and attitudes toward having insurance, they will have choices among employer-sponsored insurance, subsidized coverage through the exchange, Medicaid, or even to remain uninsured. The key dollar triggers for individual take-up are outlined in Box B-1.

With implementation of the ACA, those currently uninsured will have to decide if they want to purchase coverage to obtain the financial protection and access that insurance provides, or violate the mandate and pay the penalty. While some parties have criticized the requirement that everyone has to buy insurance, others have been

---

[1] Those without health insurance coverage will be required to pay a penalty in the form of a tax. This penalty will be the greater of $695 per year up to a maximum of three times that amount ($2,085) per family, or 2.5 percent of household income. It will be phased in: $95 or 1.0 percent of taxable income in 2014, $325 or 2.0 percent in 2015, and $695 or 2.5 percent in 2016. Beginning after 2016, the penalty will be increased annually by the cost-of-living adjustment. Exemptions will be granted for financial hardship and religious objections, to American Indians, those without coverage for less than 3 months, undocumented immigrants, incarcerated individuals, those for whom the lowest-cost plan option exceeds 8.0 percent of an individual's income, and those with incomes below the tax filing threshold (in 2009 the threshold for taxpayers under age 65 was $9,350 for singles and $18,700 for couples) (Patient Protection and Affordable Care Act of 2010 as amended. § 1501 [42 U.S.C. 18091]. 111th Cong., 2d sess.

BOX B-1
Key Dollar Triggers for Individuals (in 2011 dollars)

Medicaid Eligibility
  Eligibility: 138 percent federal poverty level (FPL) ($15,028 for individual, $30,843 for family of four in 2011)

  No premium and nominal cost sharing

Penalty for Not Having Insurance in 2016
  Is greater of

  • $695 per person, up to $2,085 family OR 2.5 percent adjusted gross income share of premium for lowest-cost option

Exemption for financial hardship:

  • Share of premium for lowest-cost option ≥ 8 percent of income ($3,551 for median income), AND
  • Those with incomes below tax filing threshold ($9,350 for single; $18,700 for couples in 2009)

Exchange Subsidy
  Eligibility: 139-250 percent FPL ($15,137-$27,225 for an individual or $31,067-$55,875 for a family of 4 in 2011)

  • Sliding scale tax credits limit premium costs to 3-8.05 percent of income; sliding scale cost-sharing credits

  Eligibility: 251-400 percent FPL ($27,334-$43,560 for an individual; $56,099-$89,400 for a family of four in 2011)

  • Sliding scale tax credits limit premium costs to 8.05-9.5 percent of income; no cost-sharing credits

Exchange Nonsubsidized:
  Eligibility: >400 percent FPL

  • No sliding scale tax credit and no cost-sharing credits. No annual limit on deductibles specified in legislation

NOTE: The FPL ranges are in current 2011 dollars. The triggers will be in 2014 dollars.

---

critical that the imposed penalty amount is too low to motivate many to buy insurance, particularly if the premiums associated with the essential health benefits (EHB) are high (Laszewski, 2010).

Choice of Insurance

Individual consumers desiring to participate in private plans will retain their choice of insurer and type of plan to be purchased, and they are not required to purchase plans through the health insurance exchanges. The

EHB will set a minimum set of standard benefits for health insurance plans offered to individual purchasers, both inside and outside of the exchange. Plans may add additional benefits beyond those in the EHB package, and an individual can choose to purchase the plan that best suits his or her individual or family needs, although purchasing additional benefits can mean a higher premium.

Out-of-Pocket Costs

Out-of-pocket costs include premiums, deductible payments, co-insurance, and co-payments for covered services in addition to all costs for noncovered services (see Chapter 2 for further discussion of benefit design). Just as how insurance currently functions, insurers will offer a variety of consumer plan options in 2014; having a more standardized benefit set should help consumers more easily comparison shop for the best value for themselves and their families.

Besides the initial premium, most plans have a deductible that the consumer must pay before insurance coverage begins. If enrolled in a plan that is a *health maintenance organization* (HMO), the consumer would likely have a primary care physician, be limited to the health care providers in that network, and would need a referral from the assigned primary care physician to see a specialist. If consumers choose a *preferred provider organization* (PPO), they can see those providers within the PPO network and only be responsible for the deductible and co-payment. It is possible to see an out-of-network provider, but it will cost the consumer more if there is a difference between the provider's bill and the approved level of coverage for in-network providers. Prospective patients have to consider, when seeking care, whether the "value of the care exceeds the out-of-pocket costs" (Baicker and Chandra, 2008, p. w536).

Research has shown that individuals without health insurance are more likely to experience financial burdens associated with utilization of health care services or avoid needed care due to cost. Yet, even among the insured, underinsurance has emerged as a barrier to care because out-of-pocket costs take a substantial percentage of income. For the healthy uninsured, those medical out-of-pocket (MOOP) costs may be minimal, but for the less healthy person they can be substantial, whether insured or not. For example, about one-quarter of those with chronic conditions spend more than 10 percent of their family income on MOOP expenses, whether insured or not; 52.9 percent of persons with private non-group insurance coverage spend more than 10 percent of family income on MOOP. Additionally, 29 percent those who are poor (<100 percent federal poverty level [FPL]) spend more than 10 percent on MOOP expenses (Banthin, 2011; Banthin et al., 2008).[2]

About 80 percent of individuals using the exchanges will be lower income and will qualify for subsidies when their income falls between 139 and 400 percent of the federal poverty level (see Box B-1) (KFF, 2011c).[3] The subsidies are designed to hold enrollee spending on premiums at 3.0-9.5 percent of their household income, in the form of an advanceable tax credit available at the time of purchase and paid to the insurer monthly rather than as a refund on a person's tax return after the year is over (KFF, 2011a).[4] Households with incomes from 139-250 percent of the FPL will also receive subsidies for cost sharing. The poorest citizens with incomes up to 138 percent of the FPL will qualify for Medicaid. Persons who buy coverage outside of the exchange will pay the entire premium, as will those buying in the exchange whose income is over 400 percent of the FPL.

The Congressional Budget Office (CBO) estimated the impact of health reform on premiums under bill H.R. 3590, which is similar to the final ACA provisions, based on an average employer premium. The cost for individuals to purchase insurance in the exchange is likely to result in a premium that is 10-13 percent higher than without ACA requirements, given the more comprehensive nature of the required essential health benefits and the constraints on OOP. On the other hand, premiums would be effectively reduced by 56-59 percent for individuals who qualify for premium subsidies (CBO, 2009).

---

[2] Note: Medical Expenditure Panel Survey (MEPS) data include premiums in MOOP calculations (Banthin et al., 2008).

[3] The Medicaid eligibility level is set at 133 percent of the FPL, but a 5 percent disregard effectively raises it to 138 percent (Health Care and Education Reconciliation Act § 1004(e) amendment of ACA).

[4] ACA as amended § 1412(c)(2)(A).

EMPLOYERS AND EMPLOYEES

Employers must decide whether or not to offer insurance, which type of plan to offer, and what level of premiums, deductible, and co-payments are considered affordable for both the firm and its employees.

Decision to Offer

Before deciding to offer health insurance, employers small and large must first consider the value of offering insurance, not only in terms of recruiting and retaining their workforce, but also as a mechanism to meet employee expectations while promoting wellness and productivity. Uninsured employees who do not want to pay a penalty will be required to acquire insurance. Thus, employers must also consider the law's individual mandate requirement, the subsequent increased demand for insurance by their employees, and the impact of requiring the EHB in insurance packages offered by small employers (Eibner et al., 2010).

Similarly, although not explicitly a mandate, beginning in 2014, firms with 50 or more employees that do not offer insurance and have 1 or more employee who obtains a tax credit on the exchange, will have to pay a "fee" (or a penalty) of $2,000 per employee.[5] If employees are a riskier population (i.e., of older age and in poorer health), an employer may find it more financially advantageous to pay the penalty than to offer health insurance. Key dollar considerations for employers and employees are outlined in Box B-2.

Level of Tax Credit

In making decisions to offer health insurance and/or to self-insure, employers will have to take into account tax credits, the applicable fees or penalties for not participating, and the availability of tax credits for employees, currently and into the future. The ACA authorized a temporary tax credit beginning in tax year 2010 for businesses with less than the equivalent of 25 full-time employees with average annual wages of $50,000 or less[6] (IRS, 2011b; Peterson and Chaikind, 2010). These small firms will receive a tax credit up to 35 percent of the employer premium contribution (employers must be contributing at least half of the premium), and this tax credit portion will rise to 50 percent in 2014 at the time employers are required to offer health plan options through the exchange. How small the firm is (e.g., 10 or fewer, or larger), the average salary of the workforce, and whether the firm is a for-profit or nonprofit entity will determine the actual amount of the credit and how long the credit is available.

Self-Insure vs. Fully Insure

Another decision facing employers is whether to self-insure or fully insure. Under the Employee Retirement Income Security Act (ERISA) law, self-insured employers are already exempt from state-mandated benefits, and even following passage of the ACA, they are similarly exempt from EHB requirements. Self-insured means that firms provide health benefits to their employees with their own funds; these are typically, but not always, larger employers. In fully insured employer-sponsored insurance (ESI), on the other hand, an employer contracts for insurance coverage through an insurance company rather than taking the risk directly. About half of the employees participating in fully insured ESI are considered likely to purchase insurance through state-based health insurance exchanges because of a combination of better coverage options and lower costs (CBO, 2010; Eibner et al., 2010).

With the implementation of the ACA, RAND estimates little impact in terms of the proportion of employers that self-fund their health insurance (6 percent) (Eibner et al., 2011). However, the percentage rises to about a third of businesses being inclined to self-insure if very-low-risk stop-loss plans are allowable as a form of self-insurance

---

[5] § 1513. Note: The penalty does not apply to the first 30 employees.

[6] § 1421.

BOX B-2
Key Dollar Considerations for Employers and Employees

Employer "Fees"

- Firms with more than 50 employees that do not offer coverage are subject to a "fee" of $2,000 per employee if 1 or more employees obtains a tax credit on the exchange (excludes first 30 employees).
- Firms with more than 50 employees that DO offer coverage are subject to a "fee" of the lesser of $3,000 per employee receiving a tax credit on the exchange or $2,000 per full-time employee.

Employee Eligibility for Tax Credit

- Employees are eligible for tax credit if actuarial value of employer plan is less than 60 percent OR if employee share of premium exceeds 9.5 percent of income.

Employee Deductible Limit in ESI

- Maximum deductible of $2,000 for individual and $4,000 for others (§ 1302(c)(2)(A)).

Insurer Cadillac Tax

- Excise tax on insurers of employer-sponsored health plans with aggregate values greater than $10,200 for individuals and $27,500 for families starting in 2018.

---

in the market,[7] thus enabling employers to avoid the EHB and other requirements if they so desire. This steep increase in the share of employers self-insuring would be "driven almost entirely by small businesses (100 or fewer workers)" (Eibner et al., 2011, p. 83).

Even though exchanges are not open to large employers initially, the National Business Group on Health, which represents large employers, still expressed concern about the content of the EHB because "many employers will see anything the federal government does to define essential benefits as the floor for all benefits and that will have the effect of driving up costs" (Darling, 2011, p. 2).

Costs

CBO analyses suggest that small firms with fewer than 50 employees could experience a range of premium change by 2016 from a 2 percent decrease to a 1 percent increase without the small business tax credit; however, the tax credit would reduce premiums 8-11 percent for eligible firms (CBO, 2009).

---

[7] Stop-loss insurance is a "form of reinsurance that provides protection for annual medical expenses above a certain limit. It can take the form of specific stop loss, where the insurance coverage reimburses all claims above a certain deductible (such as $100,000 per individual); or aggregate stop loss, where the coverage reimburses a percentage of claims if a group's claims exceed a certain percentage of the expected level (such as 120 percent)" (SOA, 2009, p. 88). Sixteen states have regulations that prohibit insurers from selling stop-loss policies with attachment points below specified limits, which range from $5,000 to $25,000 (Eibner et al., 2011). Jost further comments, "when small employer packages purchase 'self-insured' packages from insurers, including stop-loss coverage with very low attachment points and administrative services, they are essentially purchasing conventional health insurance, except that it is free from state regulation" (Jost, 2011, p. 1).

STATES

States are concerned about their fiscal picture. They must take into consideration the population that will be newly eligible for Medicaid, any impact the scope of the EHB package might have on their state employee benefit programs, and the extent to which the EHB will include current state mandates.

Medicaid Costs

Figure B-1 illustrates how states' current Medicaid coverage levels stack up against the new ACA eligibility standard of 138 percent of the FPL for adults. All states have begun to consider the future proportion and amount of Medicaid spending that they must cover vs. what portion is paid by the federal government; this will vary considerably by state. Although the EHB do not apply to the traditional Medicaid program, they form the backdrop against which other decisions may affect state financial resources.[8] Some states have expressed concern that the Medicaid expansion will be detrimental to their already tight budgets, yet others are finding that there may be choices in how they implement the ACA Medicaid provisions that may be beneficial once they take into account the federal match[9] and other provisions. For example, states will have to decide whether individuals newly eligible because of their financial status should enter traditional Medicaid or a benchmark/benchmark-equivalent program (CMS, 2010; KFF, 2011d).

For states operating a state-based exchange, they will also have to make decisions about how their exchange intersects with any existing or other newly planned state programs, as well as how they can best ensure continuity of administration, continuity of care, and alignment of benefits across programs. This is especially important because individuals and families frequently face eligibility changes—"churning" in and out of Medicaid eligibility and enrollment (Sommers and Rosenbaum, 2011; Washington State Health Benefit Exchange Project Health Care Authority, 2010). Sommers and Rosenbaum (2011) estimated that 35 percent will have their eligibility change from Medicaid to the exchanges or the reverse within 6 months, and 50 percent will experience a change within one year.

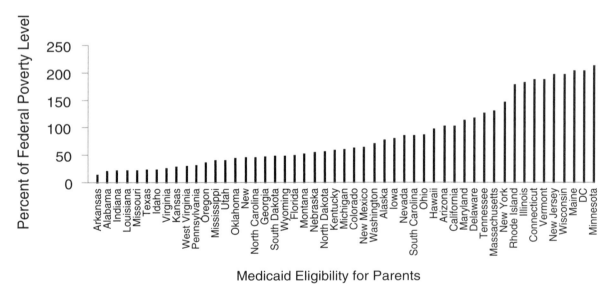

FIGURE B-1 States vary in the potential increase in size of the newly eligible Medicaid population at or under 138 percent of the federal poverty level.
SOURCE: ACA as amended § 2001(a)(1)(C); KFF, 2011b.

---

[8] Title XIX of the Social Security Act (Social Security Act § 1902(a)(10)(A)).

[9] ACA as amended § 2001(y).

EHB Applicability to State Programs

The EHB will apply to the new Medicaid benchmark and benchmark-equivalent plans and state basic health insurance plans for low-income persons not eligible for Medicaid. Traditional Medicaid has its own set of federal mandatory benefits as well as optional benefits states can elect, while benchmark and benchmark-equivalent plans and state basic health insurance plans are modeled more closely on private sector offerings. The EHB will also apply to state employee benefit programs unless states choose to self-insure.

Medicaid benchmark and benchmark-equivalent plans were initiated under the Deficit Reduction Act of 2005 to give flexibility to states to define a different scope of services than those defined in Title XIX. Programs are held to a benchmark (i.e., Federal Employees Health Benefits Program [FEHBP] preferred provider-equivalent coverage, state employee coverage, an HMO with the largest insured commercial population in the state, or any other HHS Secretary's approved benefits coverage). Certain groups of individuals who are "categorically eligible" for Medicaid are exempt from being enrolled in benchmark plans (CMS, 2010; KFF, 2011d).[10]

The State Basic Health Program is an optional insurance plan that states can develop to cover individuals whose income falls between 139 and 200 percent FPL as well as for low-income legal immigrants ineligible for Medicaid. States could receive federal subsidies for this type of program at a level equivalent to 95 percent of the federal subsidy if the person had participated in the exchange. In addition to offering the EHB, Section 1331 of the ACA outlines other requirements for this program: the consumer cannot be charged a premium that would exceed what he/she would have been paid in the exchange; the plan, to the extent available in the area, is a managed care system or like a managed care system; and the plan or provider implements innovations for care coordination and care management, incentives for use of preventive services, and maximizes patient involvement in decision making (Dorn, 2011).

State Mandates

States are also concerned about what the relationship will be between mandates required by each state's own legislature and the EHB. States must pay the cost of mandates that are above and beyond the EHB, thus having repercussions for state budgets when a state has many pre-existing mandates that are not folded into the EHB.[11] On the other hand, if the EHB package was set to mirror the requirements of a state with many mandates, then a state with a history of few mandates would expect that newly resulting commercial insurance products might far exceed what the state thinks is an acceptable premium for its residents. For example, if the EHB package is more comprehensive than that currently offered for state employees, the state will incur additional expenses.

HEALTH INSURANCE COMPANIES

Insurers must decide which markets to enter, which products they will offer, and at what premium price levels.

Products

Insurers participating in the exchanges must offer at least one gold and one silver plan,[12] each of which must meet certain standards regarding benefits,[13] providers (including essential community providers),[14] cost-sharing,[15]

---

[10] These exempt individuals include mandatory categories of pregnant women; blind or disabled individuals; dual eligibles; terminally ill hospice patients; those eligible on basis of institutionalization; medically frail and special needs individuals; beneficiaries qualifying for long term care services; children in foster care receiving child welfare services and children receiving foster care or adoption assistance; TANF (Temporary Assistance for Needy Families) and Section 1931 parents; women in the Breast or Cervical Cancer Program; and limited services beneficiaries (Social Security Act § 1937(2)(B)).

[11] ACA as amended § 1311(d)(3).

[12] § 1301(a)(1)(C)(ii).

[13] § 1302(b)(1)(A)-(J).

[14] § 1311(c)(1)(B)-(C).

[15] § 1402.

premiums,[16] rating restrictions,[17] uniform quality improvement strategy,[18] and measurements of plan performance[19]—the same for new enrollees whether the plan is offered inside or outside of the exchange.[20] Prior to health reform, it has been at the discretion of insurance companies to decide what benefits to offer in their policies or plans and to adjust benefits and prices according to market demand. The ACA requires individual and small group plans to incorporate the EHB and stipulates that nothing prohibits plans from "providing benefits in excess of the essential health benefits."[21]

Pricing

Under the ACA, there is *guaranteed issue*, meaning an individual cannot be turned down based on health or risk status, nor can an employer be turned down for the health status of its employees. That aside, a few demographic characteristics can still be factored into the premium rates, including geographic location, age, and tobacco use (the latter two have restrictions—that is, premiums for older individuals can only be three times higher than the premium for younger individuals and 1.5 times higher for users of tobacco[22]). The ACA still allows insurers to employ utilization management practices in common use by group health plans and health insurance issuers at the time of enactment and bars the issuance of regulations that would prohibit their use.[23]

Deductibles and cost-sharing arrangements are other elements factored into premium prices. For example, when two policies have the same benefits, typically the one with the higher deductible and higher cost-sharing provisions will have a lower premium, although some exceptions exist. The ACA sets limits on deductibles for employer plans ($2,000 for single coverage, $4,000 for others) but not for individual plans, as well as annual limits on cost sharing for both employer and individual plans. Annual cost sharing cannot exceed thresholds applicable to Health Savings Account (HSA)–qualified high-deductible health plans ($6,050 for individuals and $12,100 for families for 2012) (IRS, 2011a). The scope of *benefits* as well as other *benefit design* and administration elements will have an impact on the ultimate premium; these are discussed further in Chapter 2.

REFERENCES

Baicker, K., and A. Chandra. 2008. Myths and misconceptions about U.S. health insurance. *Health Affairs* 27(6):w534.

Banthin, J. S. 2011. *High out-of-pocket financial burdens for health care.* PowerPoint Presentation to the IOM Committee on the Determination of Essential Health Benefits by Jessica Banthin, Economist, Center for Financing, Access and Cost Trends, Agency for Healthare Research and Quality, Costa Mesa, CA, March 2.

Banthin, J. S., P. Cunningham, and D. M. Bernard. 2008. Financial burden of health care, 2001-2004. *Health Affairs* 27(1):188-195.

CBO (Congressional Budget Office). 2009. Letter to the Honorable Evan Bayh, U.S. Senate from Douglas W. Elmendorf, Director, Congressional Budget Office, November 30, 2009.

_____. 2010. Letter to Speaker Nancy Pelosi from Douglas W. Elmendorf with spending estimate of the Reconcilation Act of 2010, March 20, 2010.

CMS (Centers for Medicare & Medicaid Services). 2010. *Re: Family planning services option and new benefit rules for benchmark plans.* https://www.cms.gov/smdl/downloads/SMD10013.pdf (accessed November 14, 2011).

Darling, H. 2011. *Recommendations on criteria and methods for defining and updating individual mandates and packages: Purchaser perspectives.* PowerPoint Presentation to the IOM Committee on the Determination of Essential Health Benefits by Helen Darling, President and CEO, National Business Group on Health, Washington, DC, January 13.

Dorn, S. 2011. *The basic health program option under federal health reform: Issues for consumers and states.* Washington, DC: AcademyHealth.

Eibner, C., F. Girosi, C. C. Price, A. Cordova, P. S. Hussey, A. Beckman, and E. A. McGlynn. 2010. *Establishing state health insurance exchanges: Implications for health insurance enrollment, spending, and small businesses.* Santa Monica, CA: RAND Corporation.

---

[16] § 1401.

[17] § 1311(c)(3).

[18] § 1311(c)(1)(E).

[19] § 1311(c)(1)(D)(i).

[20] Health insurance coverage already in force before January 1, 2014, will be grandfathered and not subject to the restrictions.

[21] § 1302(b)(5).

[22] § 1201, amending § 2701(a)(1)(A)(iii)-(iv) of the Public Health Service Act. [42 U.S.C. 300gg].

[23] § 1563(d)(1). [42 U.S.C. 18120].

Eibner, C., F. Girosi, A. R. Miller, A. Cordova, E. A. McGlynn, N. M. Pace, C. C. Price, R. Vardavas, and C. R. Gresenz. 2011. *Employer self-insurance decisions and the implications of the Patient Protection and Affordable Care Act as modified by the Health Care and Education Reconciliation Act of 2010 (ACA)*. Santa Monica, CA: RAND Corporation.

IRS (Internal Review Service). 2011a. *26 CFR 601.602: Tax forms and instructions*. http://www.irs.gov/pub/irs-drop/rp-11-32.pdf (accessed July 22, 2011).

_____. 2011b. *Small business health care tax credit for small employers*. http://www.irs.gov/newsroom/article/0,,id=223666,00.html (accessed July 5, 2011).

Jost, T. S. 2011. *The Affordable Care Act and stop-loss insurance: Statement to the NAIC ERISA(b) subgroup by Timothy Stoltzfus Jost, NAIC funded consumer representative*. http://www.naic.org/documents/committees_b_erisa_110908_jost.pdf (accessed September 22, 2011).

KFF (Kaiser Family Foundation). 2011a. *Determining income for adults applying for Medicaid and exchange coverage subsidies: How income measured with a prior tax return compares to current income at enrollment. Focus on health reform*. Washington, DC: Kaiser Family Foundation.

_____. 2011b. *Income eligibility limits for working adults at application as a percent of the federal poverty level (FPL) by scope of benefit package, January 2011*. http://www.statehealthfacts.org/comparereport.jsp?rep=54&cat=4&sortc=1&o=a (accessed July 28, 2011).

_____. 2011c. *A profile of health insurance exchange enrollees*. Washington, DC: Kaiser Family Foundation.

_____. 2011d. *Medicaid policy options for meeting the needs of adults with mental illness under the Affordable Care Act*. http://www.kff.org/healthreform/upload/8181.pdf (accessed November 14, 2011).

Laszewski, R. 2010. *Is the individual mandate really a lynchpin in the new health law?* http://www.kaiserhealthnews.org/Columns/2010/December/121410laszewski.aspx (accessed June 30, 2011).

Peterson, C. L., and H. Chaikind. 2010. *Summary of small business health insurance tax credit under PPACA (P.L.111-148)*. Washington, DC: Congressional Research Service.

SOA (Society of Actuaries). 2009. *Glossary*. http://www.soa.org/library/essays/health-essay-2009-glossary.pdf (accessed September 26, 2011).

Sommers, B. D., and S. Rosenbaum. 2011. Issues in health reform: How changes in eligibility may move millions back and forth between Medicaid and insurance exchanges. *Health Affairs* 30(2):228-236.

Washington State Health Benefit Exchange Project Health Care Authority. 2010. *Issue brief #3: Health benefit exchange functions and responsibilities: November 24, 2010*. Olympia, WA: Washington State Health Care Authority.

Appendix C

Examples of Possible Degrees of Specificity of Inclusions in Small Group and Individual Markets

This appendix first provides illustrative information on health plan inclusions as reported through surveys (BLS, 2009; Mercer, 2009, 2011), plan documents (DOL, 2011), and a listing of Maryland's guidance on comprehensive standard health plan requirements for plans offered to small businesses (Table C-1) (MHCC, 2011). Subsequent tables provide detailed inclusion information for standard small group and individual policies for three insurers: CIGNA (Table C-2),[1] UnitedHealthcare (Table C-3),[2] and WellPoint (Table C-4).[3] Each of these insurers responded in their own words and their own understanding of the terms, so the manner in which they responded varies slightly. Also it should be noted that while some services are listed under headings using the 10 categories of care, this does not mean that the other services listed later in the table could not be classified under one of those headings.

---

[1] Personal communication with Rosemary Lester, CIGNA Product, September 9, 2011.
[2] Personal communication with Sam Ho, UnitedHealthcare, September 28, 2011.
[3] Personal communication with Ruth Raskas, WellPoint, September 9, 2011.

TABLE C-1 Reported Frequency of Benefit Coverage

Category (Section 1302 category shaded in grey)[a] [Note: organization of table does not endorse classification of service into category]	DOL 2011 (%)[b]	BLS 2009 Large Employer (%)[c]	BLS 2009 Small Employer (%)[d]	Mercer 2009 Large (%)[e]	Mercer 2009 Small (%)[f]	Mercer 2011 All (%)[g]	Maryland's Standard Health Benefit Plan Requirements for Small Businesses (MHCC, 2011)
Ambulatory patient services							
Kidney dialysis	27%[h]					95%	
Outpatient facility charges						98%	Covered (outpatient hospital services)
Outpatient surgery		97%	98%				Covered
Physician office visits	100%	100%	100%				
Urgent care facility services							
Allergy testing and injections							
Emergency services							
Ambulance services	64%[i]						Covered
Emergency room visits	91%[j]						Covered
Hospitalization							
Hospital room and board	99%	99%	100%				Covered (hospitalization)
Inpatient surgery		98%	99%				
Organ and tissue transplantation	45%[k]					95% (organ transplants)	Covered (for bone marrow, cornea, kidney, liver, lung, heart, heart-lung, pancreas, and pancreas-kidney transplants)
Maternity and newborn care							
Maternity care	66%[l]						Covered (pregnancy and maternity)
Mental health and substance use disorder services, including behavioral health treatment							
Autism services				80%	69%		
Applied behavioral analysis for autism						50%	
Speech, occupational, and physical therapies for autism						61%	

TABLE C-1 Reported Frequency of Benefit Coverage, Continued

Category (Section 1302 category shaded in grey)[a] [Note: organization of table does not endorse classification of service into category]	DOL 2011 (%)[b]	BLS 2009 Large Employer (%)[c]	BLS 2009 Small Employer (%)[d]	Mercer 2009 Large (%)[e]	Mercer 2009 Small (%)[f]	Mercer 2011 All (%)[g]	Maryland's Standard Health Benefit Plan Requirements for Small Businesses (MHCC, 2011)
Mental health and substance abuse[m]							
Inpatient	99%						Covered
Outpatient	85%						Covered
Inpatient substance abuse detoxification	98%						Covered
Inpatient substance abuse rehabilitation	78%						Covered
Outpatient substance abuse rehabilitation	79%						
Prescription drugs							
Pharmacy (full generic + brand coverage)							Covered (generic and brand name drugs)
Pharmacy (generic only to full generic + brand coverage)							
Pharmacy (generic +1 to full generic + brand coverage)							
Specific types of drugs							
Smoking cessation drugs						64% (for nicotine addiction)	
Weight loss drugs							
Infertility drugs							
Contraceptives						88%	
Sexual dysfunction drugs							

continued

TABLE C-1 Reported Frequency of Benefit Coverage, Continued

Category (Section 1302 category shaded in grey)[a] [Note: organization of table does not endorse classification of service into category]	DOL 2011 (%)[b]	BLS 2009 Large Employer (%)[c]	BLS 2009 Small Employer (%)[d]	Mercer 2009 Large (%)[e]	Mercer 2009 Small (%)[f]	Mercer 2011 All (%)[g]	Maryland's Standard Health Benefit Plan Requirements for Small Businesses (MHCC, 2011)
Rehabilitative and habilitative services and devices							
Habilitative services							Habilitative: covered (for children 0-19 for treatment of congenital or genetic birth defects)
Cardiac rehabilitation							
Durable medical equipment	67%[n]					97%	Covered
Early intervention services							
Hearing tests and hearing aids							Covered (audiology screening for newborns)
Hearing aids						43%	Covered (for children 0-18)
Orthotics							
Occupational therapy						92%	Covered (outpatient, short term)
Speech therapy (general)						85%	Covered (outpatient, short term)
Physical therapy	70%[o]					99%	
Prosthetics	46%[p]					86%	
Pulmonary rehabilitation							
Laboratory services							
Laboratory and diagnostic services							Covered (outpatient laboratory and diagnostic services)
Blood and blood products							All cost recovery for blood derivatives, components, biologics, and serums, to include autologous services and albumin
Preventive and wellness services and chronic disease management							
Case management							Program available for medically complex and costly services
Diabetes care management	27%[q]						
Gynecological exams and services	60%[r]						

TABLE C-1 Reported Frequency of Benefit Coverage, Continued

Category (Section 1302 category shaded in grey)[a] [Note: organization of table does not endorse classification of service into category]	DOL 2011 (%)[b]	BLS 2009 Large Employer (%)[c]	BLS 2009 Small Employer (%)[d]	Mercer 2009 Large (%)[e]	Mercer 2009 Small (%)[f]	Mercer 2011 All (%)[g]	Maryland's Standard Health Benefit Plan Requirements for Small Businesses (MHCC, 2011)
Nutritional counseling						53%	Covered (nutritional services for cardiovascular disease, diabetes, malnutrition, cancer, cerebral vascular disease, or kidney disease)
Medical nutritional therapy (diabetes-related)							
Medical nutritional therapy (obesity-related)							
Preventive care services							Covered (services rated by the USPSTF as A or B)
Well child and immunization benefits	77%[s]						Covered (well child visits children 0-24 months and visits including immunizations in children 24 months to 13 years)
Pediatric services, including oral and vision care							
Pediatric dental						46%	
Pediatric vision						44%	
Specific types of services							
Advanced imaging							
Alternative medicine (acupuncture, acupressure, massage therapy, etc.)							
Acupuncture				35%	24%	41%	
Massage therapy				22%	18%		
Bariatric surgery and treatment of morbid obesity						60% (bariatric surgery)	
Biofeedback				7%	6%		
Chiropractic				89%	72%	94%	
Adult dental care—preventive and basic							Covered
Elective abortion							

continued

TABLE C-1 Reported Frequency of Benefit Coverage, Continued

Category (Section 1302 category shaded in grey)[a] [Note: organization of table does not endorse classification of service into category]	DOL 2011 (%)[b]	BLS 2009 Large Employer (%)[c]	BLS 2009 Small Employer (%)[d]	Mercer 2009 Large (%)[e]	Mercer 2009 Small (%)[f]	Mercer 2011 All (%)[g]	Maryland's Standard Health Benefit Plan Requirements for Small Businesses (MHCC, 2011)
Family planning services							Covered
Home health care	73%	71%	75%			93%	Covered
Homeotherapy				12%	11%		
Hospice care	67%	66%	69%			91% (hospice and palliative care)	Covered
Infertility and assisted reproduction services	27%[t]			58%	34%	51%	Covered (after diagnosis of infertility)
Evaluation by specialist				53%	29%		
Drug therapy				35%	20%		
Artificial insemination				24%	9%		
In vitro fertilization				23%	9%		Excluded
Advanced reproductive procedures				12%	3%		
Medical food							Covered (for persons with metabolic disorders)
Orthodontia						49%	
Private duty nursing							
Skilled nursing care	70%	69%	72%			93%	Covered
Skilled nursing facility							
Sterilization	26%[u]						
TMJ treatment and appliances						55%	
Therapy services (radiation, chemo, non-preventive infusion and injection)							
Vision exam, refraction							
Vision therapy						42%	

[a] With the exception of "specific types of services," which is not one of the Section 1302 categories.

175

TABLE C-1 Reported Frequency of Benefit Coverage, Continued

[b] The DOL report (2011) presents data from the National Compensation Survey and a separate plan abstraction exercise as a percentage of workers who are participating in medical care plans. For plan abstraction data, the portion of workers whose plan documents do not mention a service is reported. Many of the services examined are reported by extent of coverage (e.g., coverage in full, subject to overall plan limits or separate limits, co-payment requirements), and the report provides some detail on median co-payments, for example: hospital room and board per admission ($250), physician office visits ($20), ER visits ($50-$150), physical therapy visits ($10-$40), maternity care ($10-$40), and gynecological exams and services ($10-$35).

[c] 100+ workers; the Bureau of Labor Statistics (BLS) National Compensation Survey data reports so that all workers in the medical plans equal 100 percent.

[d] 1-99 workers.

[e] 500+ workers.

[f] 10-499 workers.

[g] The Mercer report presents all data as a percentage of "typical" employer health plans. Most coverage is broken down by percentage offering coverage, percentage with some type of coverage limit in 2010, the median dollar amount for those plans with annual dollar limits in 2010, and of the plans with limits, the percentage making a change due to PPACA for 2011.

[h] 73 percent of workers' plans reviewed by the DOL do not mention coverage.

[i] 35 percent of workers' plans reviewed by the DOL do not mention coverage.

[j] 9 percent of workers' plans reviewed by the DOL do not mention coverage.

[k] 55 percent of workers' plans reviewed by the DOL do not mention coverage.

[l] 33 percent of workers' plans reviewed by the DOL do not mention coverage.

[m] The DOL data predate implementation of the Mental Health Parity and Addiction Equity Act of 2008.

[n] 33 percent of workers' plans reviewed by the DOL do not mention coverage.

[o] 30 percent of workers' plans reviewed by the DOL do not mention coverage.

[p] 54 percent of workers' plans reviewed by the DOL do not mention coverage.

[q] 73 percent of workers' plans reviewed by the DOL do not mention coverage.

[r] 40 percent of workers' plans reviewed by the DOL do not mention coverage.

[s] Well baby care.

[t] 53 percent of workers' plans reviewed by the DOL do not mention coverage, and an additional 20 percent do not have coverage.

[u] 73 percent of workers' plans reviewed by the DOL do not mention coverage, and an additional 2 percent do not have coverage.

SOURCE: BLS (Bureau of Labor Statistics), 2009, Table 14. Medical care benefits: Coverage for selected services, private industry workers, National Compensation Survey, 2008, in *National Compensation Survey: Health plan provisions in private industry in the United States*, 2008, Washington, DC: U.S. Bureau of Labor Statistics; DOL (Department of Labor), 2011, *Selected medical benefits: A report from the Department of Labor to the Department of Health and Human Services*, http://www.bls.gov/ncs/ebs/sp/selmedbensreport.pdf (accessed June 13, 2011); Mercer, 2009, *National survey of employer-sponsored health plans*, New York: Mercer, Inc.; Mercer, 2011, *Health care reform: The question of essential benefits. The third report in Mercer's ongoing series of topical surveys on health reform*, New York: Mercer, Inc., MHCC (Maryland Health Care Commission), 2011, Maryland's comprehensive standard benefit plan for small businesses, http://mhcc.maryland.gov/smallgroup/cshbp_brochure.htm (accessed November 7, 2011).

TABLE C-2 CIGNA Inclusions

In some instances, the plan language in the "Category" column 1 varies slightly from CIGNA's plan language. The information is being provided with the understanding that the intent of the request is to identify service benefits and not to validate plan language. This reflects "typical" individual and small group employer plans and is subject to change.

Category (1302 category shaded in grey[y]) [Note: organization of table does not endorse classification of service into category]	CIGNA Typical Small Group Employer Plan (Includes Limits[w])	CIGNA Typical Individual Benefit Plan (Includes Limits[w])
Ambulatory patient services		
Dialysis/hemodialysis	Benefit	Benefit (facility/professional services)
Outpatient facility charges	Benefit (facility services)	Benefit (facility services)
Outpatient surgery	Benefit	Benefit (facility/professional services)
Physician office visits (primary care, specialist, pre and post natal)	Benefit (PCP/specialist)	Benefit (PCP/specialist)
Urgent care facility services	Benefit	Benefit
Allergy testing and injections	Benefit	Benefit
Outpatient hospital professional services (surgeon, radiologist, pathologist, anesthesiologist)	Benefit	Benefit
Emergency services		
Ambulance services	Benefit	Benefit
Emergency room visits	Benefit	Benefit
Facility charge	Benefit	Benefit
Hospitalization		
Hospital room and board	Benefit (inpatient)	Benefit (inpatient, semi-private room rate)
Inpatient physician services (general medical care, surgery)	Benefit (hospital physician's visits/consultations) and professional services (surgeon, radiologist, pathologist, anesthesiologist)	Benefit (hospital physician's visits/consultations) and professional services (surgeon, radiologist, pathologist, anesthesiologist)
Inpatient surgery	Benefit	Benefit
Organ and tissue transplantation (in network only)	Benefit (with limits)[x]	Benefit (with limits)[x]
Maternity and newborn care		
Maternity care	Benefit	Normal pregnancy/delivery is Not a Benefit unless mandated; ONLY complications of pregnancy as defined in the Policy are Benefit
		Not a Benefit for normal pregnancy/delivery; Benefit ONLY for complications of pregnancy as defined in the Policy
Mental health and substance use disorder services, including behavioral health treatment		
Autism services	Coverage varies by service	Coverage varies by service
Applied behavioral analysis for autism	Not a Benefit, unless state mandates apply	Not a Benefit, unless state mandates apply
Speech, occupational and physical therapies for autism	Not a Benefit, unless state mandates apply	Not a Benefit, unless state mandates apply

TABLE C-2 CIGNA Inclusions, Continued

Category (1302 category shaded in grey[x]) [Note: organization of table does not endorse classification of service into category]	CIGNA Typical Small Group Employer Plan (Includes Limits[w])	CIGNA Typical Individual Benefit Plan (Includes Limits[w])
Mental health and substance abuse		
Inpatient mental health	Benefit	Usually a Benefit, with limits
Outpatient mental health	Benefit	Usually a Benefit, with limits
Inpatient substance abuse detoxification	Benefit	Benefit
Inpatient substance abuse rehabilitation	Not a Benefit, unless state mandates apply	Not a Benefit, unless state mandates apply
Outpatient substance abuse rehabilitation	Not a Benefit, unless state mandates apply	Not a Benefit, unless state mandates apply
Prescription drugs		
Prescription drugs	Benefit, deductible applies	Benefit, deductible applies
Pharmacy (full generic + brand coverage)	Benefit, deductible applies	Benefit, deductible applies
Pharmacy (generic only to full generic + brand coverage)	N/A	N/A
Pharmacy (generic + 1 to full generic + brand coverage)	N/A	N/A
Specific types of drugs		
Smoking cessation drugs	Not a Benefit	Not a Benefit
Weight loss drugs	Not a Benefit	Not a Benefit
Infertility drugs	Not a Benefit, unless state mandates apply	Not a Benefit, unless state mandates apply
Prescribed contraceptives	Policyholder Option	Benefit (with co-payment)
OTC contraceptives	Not a benefit	Not a Benefit
Sexual dysfunction drugs	Not a Benefit	Not a Benefit
Rehabilitative and habilitative services and devices		
Habilitative services	Not a Benefit	Not a Benefit
Cardiac rehabilitation	Benefit (short term, with benefit limits)	Benefit (short term, with benefit limits)
Durable medical equipment	Benefit, with benefit limits	Benefit, with benefit limits
Early intervention services	Not a Benefit, unless state mandates apply	Not a Benefit, unless state mandates apply
Hearing tests and hearing aids	Not a Benefit, unless state mandates apply	Not a Benefit, unless state mandates apply
Hearing aids	Not a Benefit, unless state mandates apply	Not a Benefit, unless state mandates apply
Orthotics	Not a Benefit, unless state mandates apply	Not a Benefit, unless state mandates apply
Occupational therapy	Benefit (short term, with benefit limits)	Benefit (short term, with benefit limits)
Speech therapy (general)	Benefit (short term, with benefit limits)	Not a Benefit, unless state mandates apply
Physical therapy	Benefit (short term, with benefit limits)	Benefit (short term, with benefit limits)
Prosthetics (external prosthetic appliances only)	Benefit	Benefit
Pulmonary rehabilitation	Benefit, with limits	Benefit (short term, with benefit limits)

continued

TABLE C-2 CIGNA Inclusions, Continued

In some instances, the plan language in the "Category" column 1 varies slightly from CIGNA's plan language. The information is being provided with the understanding that the intent of the request is to identify service benefits and not to validate plan language. This reflects "typical" individual and small group employer plans and is subject to change.

Category (1302 category shaded in grey[v]) [Note: organization of table does not endorse classification of service into category]	CIGNA Typical Small Group Employer Plan (Includes Limits[w])	CIGNA Typical Individual Benefit Plan (Includes Limits[w])
Laboratory services		
Laboratory and diagnostic services	Benefit	Benefit
Other diagnostic tests (hearing, EKG)	Benefit	Benefit
Other facility charges (diagnostic lab/x-ray/supplies)	Benefit	Benefit
Advanced imaging (MRI, CT scan, etc.)	Benefit	Benefit
Blood and blood products	Benefit	Benefit
Preventive and wellness services and chronic disease management		
Case management	Not a Benefit	Not a Benefit
Diabetes care management	Not a Benefit	Not a Benefit
Gynecological exams and services	Benefit	Benefit
Nutritional counseling	Benefit for specific conditions	Benefit for specific conditions
Medical nutritional therapy (diabetes-related)	Benefit	Not a Benefit, unless state mandates apply
Medical nutritional therapy (obesity-related)	Not a Benefit	Not a Benefit
Preventive care services	Benefit	Benefit
Well child and immunization benefits	Benefit	Benefit
Pediatric services, including oral and vision care		
Pediatric dental	Not a Benefit	Not a Benefit
Pediatric vision	Not a Benefit	Not a Benefit
Specific types of services		
Advanced imaging	Benefit	Benefit
Alternative medicine (acupuncture, acupressure, massage therapy, etc.)	Not a Benefit	Not a Benefit
Acupuncture	Not a Benefit	Not a Benefit unless mandated
Massage therapy	Not a Benefit	Not a Benefit
Bariatric surgery and treatment of morbid obesity	Not a Benefit, unless state mandates apply	Not a Benefit, unless state mandates apply
Biofeedback	Not a Benefit	Not a Benefit
Chiropractic	Not a separate Benefit	Not a separate Benefit
Adult dental care—preventive and basic	Not a Benefit	Not a Benefit
Dental care—injury to sound natural teeth	Benefit	Benefit
Elective abortion	Policyholder Option	Not a Benefit, unless state mandates apply (non-elective abortion is a Benefit)

TABLE C-2 CIGNA Inclusions, Continued

Category (1302 category shaded in grey^v) [Note: organization of table does not endorse classification of service into category]	CIGNA Typical Small Group Employer Plan (Includes Limits^w)	CIGNA Typical Individual Benefit Plan (Includes Limits^w)
Family planning services (tests/counseling only)	Benefit	Benefit
Home health care services	Benefit, with benefit limits	Benefit, with benefit limits
Home dialysis	Benefit, with limits	Benefit, with limits
Home infusion therapy	Benefit	Benefit, with limits
Homeotherapy	Not a Benefit	Not a Benefit
Hospice care	Benefit	Benefit
Infertility and assisted reproduction services		
Evaluation by specialist	Not a Benefit	Not a Benefit
Drug therapy	Not a Benefit	Not a Benefit
Artificial insemination	Not a Benefit	Not a Benefit
In vitro fertilization	Not a Benefit	Not a Benefit
Advanced reproductive procedures	Not a Benefit	Not a Benefit
Medical food	Not a Benefit, unless state mandates apply	Not a Benefit, unless state mandates apply
Orthodontia	Not a Benefit	Not a Benefit
Private duty nursing	Not a Benefit	Not a Benefit
Residential treatment center	Benefit, with benefit limits	Benefit, with benefit limits
Skilled nursing care	Benefit, with benefit limits	Benefit, with benefit limits
Skilled nursing facility	Benefit, with benefit limits	Benefit, with benefit limits
Sterilization	Benefit	Benefit
TMJ treatment and appliances	Benefit, treatment only (appliances are Not a Benefit)	Benefit, treatment only (appliances are Not a Benefit)
Therapy services (radiation, chemo, non-preventive infusion and injection) (inpatient and outpatient)	Benefit	Benefit
Vision exam/refraction	Not a Benefit	Not a Benefit
Vision therapy	Not a Benefit	Not a Benefit

^v With the exception of "specific types of services."

^w Typical small group employer plans provide broad health care coverage while including limits on certain services, but that would meet the majority of the overall population's health care needs.

^x Also covers for organ transplants—travel, with benefit limits.

TABLE C-3 UnitedHealthcare (UHC) Inclusions

Category (1302 category shaded in grey[y]) [Note: organization of table does not endorse classification of service into category]	UHC Typical Small Group Employer Plan	UHC Typical Individual Plan
Ambulatory patient services		
Dialysis/hemodialysis	Covered	Covered
Outpatient facility charges	Covered	Covered
Outpatient surgery	Covered	Covered
Physician office visits (primary care, specialist, pre and post natal)	Covered	Covered, except pre and post natal excluded
Urgent care facility services	Covered	Covered
Allergy testing and injections	Covered	Covered
Outpatient hospital professional services (surgeon, radiologist, pathologist, anesthesiologist)	Covered	Covered
Emergency services		
Ambulance services	Covered	Covered, ground and air
Emergency room visits	Covered	Covered
Facility charge	Covered	Covered
Hospitalization		
Hospital room and board	Covered	Covered
Inpatient physician services (general medical care, surgery)	Covered	Covered
Inpatient surgery	Covered	Covered
Organ and tissue transplantation	Covered	Covered
Maternity and newborn care		
Maternity care	Covered	Routine maternity and newborn excluded Complications of pregnancy covered
Mental health and substance use disorder services, including behavioral health treatment		
Autism services	Covered, for eligible services	Limited Coverage
Applied behavioral analysis for autism	Covered—only in states where mandated	Limited Coverage
Speech, occupational and physical therapies for autism	Covered	Limited Coverage
Mental health and substance abuse	Covered	Excluded, unless Optional benefit purchased
Inpatient	Covered	Excluded, unless Optional benefit purchased
Outpatient	Covered	Excluded, unless Optional benefit purchased
Inpatient substance abuse detoxification	Covered	Excluded, except for alcohol detox covered
Inpatient substance abuse rehabilitation	Covered	Excluded
Outpatient substance abuse rehabilitation	Covered	Excluded, unless Optional benefit purchased

TABLE C-3 UHC Inclusions, Continued

Category (1302 category shaded in grey[a]) [Note: organization of table does not endorse classification of service into category]	UHC Typical Small Group Employer Plan	UHC Typical Individual Plan
Prescription drugs		
Prescription drugs	Covered if rider purchased	Covered
Pharmacy (full generic + brand coverage)	Generally covered	Covered
Pharmacy (generic only to full generic + brand coverage)	Generally covered	Covered
Pharmacy (generic + 1 to full generic + brand coverage)	Generally covered	Covered
Specific types of drugs		
Smoking cessation drugs	Covered—only in states where mandated	Excluded
Weight loss drugs	Covered—only in states where mandated	Excluded
Infertility drugs	Covered—only in states where mandated	Excluded
Contraceptives	Covered	Covered
Sexual dysfunction drugs	Covered	Excluded
Rehabilitative and habilitative services and devices		
Habilitative services	Not covered	Limited Coverage
Cardiac rehabilitation	Covered	Limited Coverage
Durable medical equipment	Covered	Limited Coverage
Early intervention services	Not covered	Excluded, unless state mandate
Hearing tests and hearing aids	Covered	Covered
Hearing aids	Covered	Excluded, unless state mandate
Orthotics	Varies based on orthotic type	Excluded, except one pair foot orthotics per person
Occupational therapy	Covered	Excluded
Speech therapy (general)	Covered	Excluded
Physical therapy	Covered	Covered
Prosthetics	Covered	Limited Coverage
Pulmonary rehabilitation	Covered	Covered Inpatient, Outpatient, must be covered provider
Laboratory services		
Laboratory and diagnostic services	Covered	Covered
Other diagnostic tests (hearing, EKG)	Covered	Covered
Other facility charges (diagnostic lab/x-ray/supplies)	Covered	Covered

continued

TABLE C-3 UHC Inclusions, Continued

Category (1302 category shaded in grey[y]) [Note: organization of table does not endorse classification of service into category]	UHC Typical Small Group Employer Plan	UHC Typical Individual Plan
Advanced imaging (MRI, CT scan, etc.)	Covered	Covered
Blood and blood products	Covered	Excluded
Preventive and wellness services and chronic disease management		
Case management	Program available	Excluded
Diabetes care management	Program available	Covered
Gynecological exams and services	Covered	Covered
Nutritional counseling	Covered for management of specific clinical conditions	Excluded
Medical nutritional therapy (diabetes-related)	Covered	Excluded
Medical nutritional therapy (obesity-related)	Weight loss programs excluded	Excluded
Preventive care services	Covered	Covered subject to HCR Guidelines[z]
Well child and immunization benefits	Covered	Covered subject to HCR Guidelines[z]
Pediatric services, including oral and vision care		
Pediatric dental	Excluded	Excluded
Pediatric vision	Covered—refractive exams only, every other year	Excluded
Specific types of services		
Advanced imaging	Covered	Covered
Alternative medicine (acupuncture, acupressure, massage therapy, etc.)	Excluded	Excluded
Acupuncture	Excluded	Excluded
Massage therapy	Excluded	Excluded
Bariatric surgery and treatment of morbid obesity	Excluded	Excluded
Biofeedback	Coverage varies by condition	Excluded
Chiropractic	Covered	Covered
Adult Dental care—preventive and basic	Excluded	Excluded
Dental care—injury to sound natural teeth	Covered	Covered
Elective abortion	Covered	Excluded
Family planning services	Covered	Covered
Home health care services	Covered	Covered
Home dialysis	Covered	Covered

TABLE C-3 UHC Inclusions, Continued

Category (1302 category shaded in grey[y]) [Note: organization of table does not endorse classification of service into category]	UHC Typical Small Group Employer Plan	UHC Typical Individual Plan
Home infusion therapy	Covered	Covered
Homeotherapy	Excluded	Excluded
Hospice care	Covered	Covered
Infertility and assisted reproduction services	Covered through to the point of diagnosis. Assisted reproductive services excluded.	Excluded
Evaluation by specialist	Assisted reproductive services excluded.	Excluded
Drug therapy	Assisted reproductive services excluded.	Excluded
Artificial insemination	Assisted reproductive services excluded.	Excluded
In vitro fertilization	Assisted reproductive services excluded.	Excluded
Advanced reproductive procedures	Assisted reproductive services excluded.	Excluded
Medical food	Excluded	Excluded
Orthodontia	Excluded	Excluded
Private duty nursing	Excluded	Excluded
Residential treatment center	Covered for MHSA	Excluded
Skilled nursing care	Covered	Excluded
Skilled nursing facility	Covered	Limited Coverage
Sterilization	Covered	Excluded
TMJ treatment and appliances	Some services excluded	Surgical treatment only, $10,000 limit
Therapy services (radiation, chemo, non-preventive infusion and injection) (inpatient and outpatient)	Covered	Covered
Vision exam/refraction	Covered	Excluded
Vision therapy	Covered	Excluded

[y] With the exception of "specific types of services."

[z] HCR means health care reform.

TABLE C-4 WellPoint Inclusions

Category (1302 category shaded in grey[aa]) [Note: organization of table does not endorse classification of service into category]	Wellpoint Anthem Blue Standard for Small Business	Wellpoint Anthem Blue Standard for Individual Business
Ambulatory patient services		
Dialysis[bb]/hemodialysis	Covered*	Covered*
Outpatient facility charges	Covered*	Covered*
Outpatient surgery	Covered*	Covered*
Physician office visits (primary care, specialist, pre and post natal visits)	Covered*	Covered* except for pre and post maternity visits as maternity not covered in most plans[cc] unless purchase maternity rider or state mandated.
Urgent care facility services	Covered*	Covered*
Allergy testing and injections	Covered*	Covered*
Emergency services		
Ambulance services	Covered*	Covered*
Facility charge	Covered*	Covered*
Emergency room visits	Covered*	Covered*
Hospitalization		
Hospital room and board	Covered*	Covered*
Inpatient surgery	Covered*	Covered*
Organ and tissue transplantation	Covered*	Covered*
Maternity and newborn care		
Maternity care	Covered*	Complications of pregnancy Covered* by most plans; otherwise Not Covered unless purchase maternity rider or state mandated.
Mental health and substance use disorder services, including behavioral health treatment		
Autism services	Autism diagnosis is Covered* according to service type; Coverage criteria may be determined by mandate.	Autism diagnosis is Covered* according to service type; Coverage criteria may be determined by mandate.
Applied behavioral analysis for autism	Covered* by most plans when required by mandate.	Covered* by most plans when required by mandate.

TABLE C-4 WellPoint Inclusions, Continued

Category (1302 category shaded in grey[aa]) [Note: organization of table does not endorse classification of service into category]	Wellpoint Anthem Blue Standard for Small Business	Wellpoint Anthem Blue Standard for Individual Business
Speech, occupational and physical therapies for autism	Covered.* Coverage criteria may be determined by mandate.	Covered.* Coverage criteria may be determined by mandate.
Mental health and substance abuse	Covered*	Covered* by most plans. Coverage criteria may be determined by mandate.
Inpatient	Covered* by most plans	Covered* by most plans. Coverage criteria may be determined by mandate.
Outpatient	Covered*	Covered* by most plans. Coverage criteria may be determined by mandate.
Inpatient substance abuse detoxification	Covered* by most plans	Covered* by most plans. Coverage criteria may be determined by mandate.
Inpatient substance abuse rehabilitation	Covered*	Covered* by most plans. Coverage criteria may be determined by mandate.
Outpatient substance abuse rehabilitation	Covered*	Covered* by most plans. Coverage criteria may be determined by mandate.
Prescription drugs		
Prescription drugs	Covered*	Covered* for all non-grandfathered plans post 9/23/2010
Pharmacy (full generic + brand coverage)	Covered* by most plans (generic + brand)	Covered* by some plans[cc] (generic + brand)
Pharmacy (generic only to full generic + brand coverage)	Covered* by some plans (generic only)	Covered* by some grandfathered plans prior to 3/23/10 (generic only)
Pharmacy (generic + 1 to full generic + brand coverage)	Covered* by very few plans[cc] (generic + at least 1 brand class)	Covered* by some plans (generic + at least 1 brand class)
Specific types of drugs		
Smoking cessation drugs	Covered* by some plans	Covered* by some plans
Weight loss drugs	Not Covered	Not Covered
Infertility drugs	Covered* by some plans as required by mandates	Covered* by some plans as required by mandates
Contraceptives	Covered*	Covered*
Sexual dysfunction drugs	Covered* by most plans	Covered* by most plans

*Covered subject to terms and conditions of the contract. For example, there may be network limitations, medical policy limitations, cost-sharing requirements, dollar caps, visit limits, etc.

continued

TABLE C-4 WellPoint Inclusions, Continued

Category (1302 category shaded in grey^aa) [Note: organization of table does not endorse classification of service into category]	Wellpoint Anthem Blue Standard for Small Business	Wellpoint Anthem Blue Standard for Individual Business
Rehabilitative and habilitative services and devices		
Habilitative services^dd	Covered* by most plans Coverage criteria may be determined by mandates	Covered* by most plans Coverage criteria may be determined by mandates
Cardiac rehabilitation	Covered*	Covered*
Durable medical equipment	Covered*	Covered*
Early intervention services	Covered* by most plans Coverage criteria may be determined by mandates	Covered* by most plans Coverage criteria may be determined by mandates
Hearing tests and hearing aids	Covered* by most plans as required by mandates	Covered* by most plans as required by mandates
Hearing aids	Covered* by some plans as required by mandates	Covered* by some plans as required by mandates
Medical devices	Covered*	Covered*
Medical supplies received from supplier	Covered*	Covered*
Orthotics	Covered* by most plans	Covered* by most plans
Occupational therapy	Covered*	Covered*
Speech therapy (general)	Covered*	Covered*
Physical therapy	Covered*	Covered*
Prosthetics	Covered*	Covered*
Pulmonary rehabilitation	Covered*	Covered*
Laboratory services		
Laboratory and diagnostic services	Covered*	Covered*
Other diagnostic tests (hearing, EKG)	Covered*	Covered*
Advanced imaging (MRI, CT scan)	Covered*	Covered*
Blood and blood products	Covered*	Covered*

TABLE C-4 WellPoint Inclusions, Continued

Category (1302 category shaded in grey[aa]) [Note: organization of table does not endorse classification of service into category]	Wellpoint Anthem Blue Standard for Small Business	Wellpoint Anthem Blue Standard for Individual Business
Preventive and wellness services and chronic disease management		
Case management	Included as member program	Included as member program
Diabetes care management	Included as member program	Included as member program
Gynecological exams and services	Covered* for all non-grandfathered plans post 9/23/2010, and for some grandfathered plans	Covered* for all non-grandfathered plans post 9/23/2010, and for some grandfathered plans
Nutritional counseling	Covered* for all non-grandfathered plans post 9/23/2010, and for some grandfathered plans	Covered* for all non-grandfathered plans post 9/23/2010, and for some grandfathered plans
Medical nutritional therapy (diabetes-related)	Covered* for all non-grandfathered plans post 9/23/2010, and for some grandfathered plans	Covered* for all non-grandfathered plans post 9/23/2010, and for some grandfathered plans
Medical nutritional therapy (obesity-related)	Covered* for all non-grandfathered plans post 9/23/2010, and for some grandfathered plans	Covered* for all non-grandfathered plans post 9/23/2010, and for some grandfathered plans
Preventive care services	Covered* for all non-grandfathered plans post 9/23/2010, and for some grandfathered plans	Covered* for all non-grandfathered plans post 9/23/2010, and for some grandfathered plans
Well child and immunization benefits	Covered* for all non-grandfathered plans post 9/23/2010, and for some grandfathered plans	Covered* for all non-grandfathered plans post 9/23/2010, and for some grandfathered plans
Pediatric services, including oral and vision care		
Pediatric dental	Pediatric oral health screening Covered* for all non-grandfathered plans post 9/23/2010 Full dental coverage offered as Rider	Pediatric oral health screening Covered* for all non-grandfathered plans post 9/23/2010 and for some grandfathered plans Full dental coverage offered as Rider with most plans
Pediatric vision	Pediatric vision screening Covered* for all non-grandfathered plans post 9/32/2010 Vision exam/refraction/eyewear coverage varies across states Full vision coverage offered as Rider	Pediatric vision screening Covered* for all non-grandfathered plans post 9/32/2010 and for some grandfathered plans Vision exam/refraction/eyewear coverage in few plans

*Covered subject to terms and conditions of the contract. For example, there may be network limitations, medical policy limitations, cost-sharing requirements, dollar caps, visit limits, etc.

continued

TABLE C-4 WellPoint Inclusions, Continued

Category (1302 category shaded in grey[aa]) [Note: organization of table does not endorse classification of service into category]	Wellpoint Anthem Blue Standard for Small Business	Wellpoint Anthem Blue Standard for Individual Business
Specific types of services		
Advanced imaging	Covered*	Covered*
Alternative medicine (acupuncture, acupressure, massage therapy, etc.)	Covered* by few plans	Covered* by few plans
Acupuncture	Covered* by some plans	Covered* by few plans
Massage therapy	Covered* by few plans	Not Covered
Bariatric surgery and treatment of morbid obesity	Covered* by some plans mostly as required by mandates	Covered* by some plans mostly as required by mandates
Biofeedback	Covered* by some plans	Covered* by some plans
Chiropractic	Covered* (spinal manipulation)	Covered* (spinal manipulation)
Adult dental care—preventive and basic	Covered* by very few plans / Full dental coverage offered as Rider	Covered* by very few plans / Full dental coverage offered as Rider
Dental services related to an accident	Covered*	Covered*
Elective abortion	Coverage varies across plans	Coverage varies across plans
Family planning services	Covered* (counseling) by most plans	Covered* (counseling) by most plans
Home health care	Covered*	Covered*
Homeotherapy	Not Covered	Not Covered
Hospice care	Covered*	Covered*
Infertility and assisted reproduction services		
Evaluation by specialist	Covered* by most plans to diagnose and to treat underlying cause	Covered* by most plans to diagnose and to treat underlying cause
Drug therapy	Covered* by some plans as required by mandates	Covered* by some plans as required by mandates
Artificial insemination	Covered* by some plans as required by mandates	Covered* by some plans as required by mandates
In vitro fertilization	Covered* by some plans as required by mandates	Covered* by some plans as required by mandates
Advanced reproductive procedures	Covered* by some plans as required by mandates	Covered* by some plans as required by mandates

TABLE C-4 WellPoint Inclusions, Continued

Category (1302 category shaded in grey^aa) [Note: organization of table does not endorse classification of service into category]	Wellpoint Anthem Blue Standard for Small Business	Wellpoint Anthem Blue Standard for Individual Business
Medical food	Covered* by most plans	Covered* by most plans
Orthodontia	Full dental (including orthodontia) offered as Rider	Full dental (including orthodontia) offered as Rider
Private duty nursing	Covered* by some plans	Covered* by some plans
Residential treatment center	Covered* by most plans	Covered* by most plans
Skilled nursing care	Covered* as part of Home Health Care or Inpatient	Covered* as part of Home Health Care or Inpatient
Skilled nursing facility	Covered*	Covered*
Sterilization	Covered* except plans in one state	Covered* except plans in one state
TMJ treatment and appliances	Covered* by some plans	Covered* by some plans
Therapy services (radiation, chemo, non-preventive infusion, including home infusion, and injection)	Covered*	Covered*
Vision exam/refraction	Covered* by some plans	Covered* by some plans
Vision therapy	Not Covered by most plans	Not Covered

* Covered subject to terms and conditions of the contract. For example, there may be network limitations, medical policy limitations, cost-sharing requirements, dollar caps, visit limits, etc.

aa With the exception of "other types of categories/services."

bb Home dialysis is also a covered service.

cc WellPoint defined *few* as generally less than 5; *some* is 5 through 10; and *more* is greater than 10.

dd *Habilitation*: This is a broad category, and there is likely to be variation in what an insurer defines as habilitative. We do not have a specific habilitation benefit or exclusion, but we do have "habilitative" services that may be covered. We were defining habilitative care as a category that include services such as (1) early intervention; (2) autism mandates (i.e., improving language skills); (3) congenital defect mandates; and (4) home health care services provided by a licensed home health agency (i.e., skilled nursing and physical therapy), not services such as meal preparation, bathing, and medication management).

Appendix D

Examples of Benefit Package
Statutory Guidance

This appendix includes a display of benefit categories in statute for various health insurance programs.

	Federal Employees Health Benefits Program (FEHBP)	Medicare	Medicaid	Knox-Keene Health Care Service Plan Act (CA)	Maryland	Massachusetts Exchange
Year Created	1959	1965	1965	1975	1993	2006
Categorization of Benefits	Service Benefit Plan	Part A	Mandatory Services	Basic Health Care Services	Comprehensive Standard Health Benefit Plan (CSHBP)	Minimum Creditable Coverage Standards

Federal Employees Health Benefits Program (FEHBP) — Service Benefit Plan

- Hospital benefits
- Surgical benefits
- In-hospital medical benefits
- Ambulatory patient benefits
- Supplemental benefits
- Obstetrical benefits

Medicare — Part A

- Inpatient hospital
- Skilled nursing facility
- Home health
- Hospice
- Inpatient psychiatric hospital

Medicaid — Mandatory Services

- Physician services
- Lab and X-ray services
- Inpatient hospital services
- Outpatient hospital services
- Early and Periodic Screening, Diagnosis, and Treatment (EPSDT) services for children under 21
- Family planning services
- Federally qualified health center services
- Rural health clinic services
- Nurse midwife services
- Certified nurse practitioner services
- Nursing facility services for those ages 21 and over
- Home health care services

Knox-Keene Health Care Service Plan Act (CA) — Basic Health Care Services

- Hospital inpatient services
- Physician services
- Outpatient and ambulatory care
- Lab and radiology
- Home health
- Preventive health services
- Emergency services (including ambulance and out-of-area coverage)
- Hospice (section 1368.2—only for group coverage)

Maryland — Comprehensive Standard Health Benefit Plan (CSHBP)

- Ambulance service
- Audiology screening for newborns
- Blood and blood products
- Case management program
- Chiropractic services
- Durable medical equipment
- Emergency room
- Family planning services
- Habilitative services
- Hearing aids
- Home health care
- Hospice
- Hospitalization, includes detoxification
- Infertility services
- Medical food
- Mental health and substance abuse
- Nutritional services
- Outpatient hospital services and surgery
- Outpatient laboratory and diagnostic services
- Outpatient short-term rehabilitative services
- Pregnancy and maternity
- Prescription drugs

Massachusetts Exchange — Minimum Creditable Coverage Standards

- Ambulatory patient services (including outpatient day surgery and related anesthesia)
- Diagnostic imaging and screening procedures (including x-rays)
- Emergency services
- Hospitalization (including at a minimum, inpatient acute care services, which are generally provided by an acute care hospital for covered benefits in accordance with the member's subscriber certificate or plan description)
- Maternity and newborn care
- Medical or surgical care (including preventative and primary care)
- Mental health and substance abuse services
- Prescription drugs
- Radiation therapy and chemotherapy
- Doctor visits for preventive care, without a deductible

Federal Employees Health Benefits Program (FEHBP)	Medicare	Medicaid	Knox-Keene Health Care Service Plan Act (CA)	Maryland	Massachusetts Exchange
				• Preventive services rated by the U.S. Preventive Services Task Force as A or B not subject to deductible and no cost sharing if provided in-network • Skilled nursing facility • Transplants • Well child and immunization benefits	
Indemnity Benefit Plan • Hospital care • Surgical care and treatment • Medical care and treatment • Obstetrical benefits • Prescribed drugs, medicines, and prosthetic devices • Other medical supplies and services	**Part B** • Physician and other medical services • Outpatient hospital care • Ambulatory surgical services • Diagnostic tests, x-rays, and lab services • Durable medical equipment • Physical, occupational, and speech therapy • Clinical laboratory services • Home health care • Outpatient mental health services • One-time "Welcome to Medicare" physical exam • Preventive services[a]				

continued

	Federal Employees Health Benefits Program (FEHBP)	Medicare	Medicaid	Knox-Keene Health Care Service Plan Act (CA)	Maryland	Massachusetts Exchange
		Part C (Medicare Advantage^b) Is required to provide all Medicare-covered benefits to enrollees, with at least one plan with basic drug coverage (MA-PD plan) **Part D** • Prescription Drugs				
Optional Services			• Medical care, remedial care by licensed practitioners • Prescription drugs • Diagnostic, screening, preventive, and rehabilitative services • Clinic services • Primary care case management • Dental services and dentures • Physical therapy • Prosthetic devices and eyeglasses • Tuberculosis-related services • Other specified medical and remedial care • Intermediate care facility for the mentally retarded (ICF/MR) services • Institute for mental diseases services for those ages 65 and over	• Outpatient prescription drugs [42.7, Rule 300.67.24] • Chiropractic services • Dental care • Hearing aids		

	Federal Employees Health Benefits Program (FEHBP)	Medicare	Medicaid	Knox-Keene Health Care Service Plan Act (CA)	Maryland	Massachusetts Exchange
			• Inpatient psychiatric care for children under 21 • Home- and community-based care waiver services • Other home health care services • Targeted case management • Respiratory care services for ventilator-dependent individuals • Personal care services • Hospice care			
Statutory Authority	U.S. Code: Title 5—Government Organization & Employees Part III-Employees Subpart G—Insurance & Annuities-Chapter 89—Health Insurance-Section 8904	Title XVIII of the Social Security Act	Title XIX of the Social Security Act	• Section 1345(b) • Section 1367(i), rule 1300.67		Chapter 58—956 CMR 5.00

[a] Flu shot, pneumococcal shot (no coinsurance); limit of one flu shot per flu season; hepatitis B shot, colorectal and prostate cancer screening, pap smear, mammogram, cardiovascular screening, abdominal aortic aneurysm (AAA) screening, bone mass measurement, diabetes screening and monitoring, glaucoma screening, smoking cessation.

[b] Private health plans that receive payments from Medicare to provide Medicare-covered benefits to enrollees.

SOURCE: Families USA, 2006; GPO, 2007; KFF, 2010; O'Malley et al., 2009; State of California, 2011; State of Massachusetts, 2008.

REFERENCES

Families USA. 2006. *Medicaid benefit package changes: Coming to a state near you?* http://www.familiesusa.org/assets/pdfs/DRA-Benefit-Package.pdf (accessed August 4, 2011).

GPO (Government Printing Office). 2007. *Title 5 government organization and employees. Part III—employees. Subpart g—insurance and annuities. Chapter 89—health insurance.* http://frwebgate.access.gpo.gov/cgi-bin/getdoc.cgi?dbname=browse_usc&docid=Cite+5USC8904 (accessed August 4, 2011).

KFF (Kaiser Family Foundation). 2010. *Medicare: A primer.* Menlo Park, CA: Kaiser Family Foundation.

O'Malley, M., M. Moon, and R. W. Cowdry. 2009. *Maryland's Comprehensive Standard Health Plan for Small Businesses.* Annapolis, MD: Maryland Health Care Commission.

State of California. 2011. *Knox-Keene Health Care Service Plan Act of 1975.* http://wpso.dmhc.ca.gov/regulations/11kkap/index.htm (accessed August 4, 2011).

State of Massachusetts. 2008. *956 CMR 5.00: Minimum creditable coverage.* http://www.lawlib.state.ma.us/source/mass/cmr/cmrtext/956CMR5.pdf (accessed August 4, 2011).

Appendix E

Description of Small Group Market Benefits, Provided by WellPoint

The IOM committee found the WellPoint analysis of their products helpful in understanding benefit inclusions and exclusions in the small group market to complement the listing of covered services and exclusions found in Appendix C and F, respectively.

The Determination of Essential Health Benefits

<u>Background</u>

As outlined in our comments submitted to the Institute of Medicine (IOM) on December 6, 2010, WellPoint believes that when determining what benefits are essential, it will be imperative to balance the need for comprehensive, evidence-based coverage with the need to ensure access to affordable coverage for consumers. If "essential" is defined too broadly, such as by including benefits without a sound evidence base or items that are currently not included in many individual or employer benefit packages, consumers' access to affordable coverage will be compromised.

In order to better understand what benefits should be considered essential, WellPoint has undertaken a process to evaluate our fully-insured, small group market (where a small group is defined as one with 1 or 2 to 50 employees) product offerings across the country to identify where there is consistency across our products, where there might be differences, and the cost impacts of these differences. The attached exhibits illustrate our findings. As you will see, there is little variation in our typical small group plans within and across states. However, the cost impact of those benefits that vary can be substantial, especially when taken in sum. We share this information in the hopes that it may be helpful as the IOM makes its recommendations to the Department of Health and Human Services regarding the determination of essential health benefits.

<u>Large Group Benefits</u>

Plans offered in the small group market are standardized and provide little or no flexibility to add or remove coverage for services. These standard plans are offered in all markets, small, mid-size and large, but large groups (those with over 100 employees) have the flexibility to customize their plans. Thus, because large groups also start with the same standard product portfolios in each state as offered to small groups, large group products generally cover the same services as the small group products in any given state. The level of flexibility a large group has to customize their benefits is determined by funding type (fully-insured versus self-insured) and the size of the account. For example, a 150 life fully-insured group has less flexibility to customize benefits than a 1,000 life self-insured group.

Most customization for large groups is around benefit cost share or benefit limits, not coverage/exclusions. Less than 5% of customization requests deal with adding coverage. Examples include requests to add coverage for specific non-covered prescription drugs or over-the-counter medications (majority), coverage for hearing aids, coverage for bariatric surgery, and coverage for infertility. Very few (only about 2%) of the large group customization requests are to remove coverage, and most of these are self-insured groups requesting to remove state mandated coverage (as such mandates generally apply only to fully-insured products).

<u>Helpful Definitions for Exhibit A</u>

- *"Anthem/Blue Standard Coverage/Typical SG Plans"* cover a standard set of medically necessary services including inpatient and outpatient hospital services, diagnostic services, physician visits and medical care, maternity care, surgical services, mental health and substance abuse services, therapy services, skilled nursing facility services, home health care services, preventive care services, and medical equipment and supplies. For more details on inclusions and exclusions to the standard plan, please see Exhibits B and C, respectively.
  - Most variation across these standard plans is driven by differences in cost-sharing, not covered services.

The Determination of Essential Health Benefits

- o There is some variation across these standard plans in the "amount" of benefit provided (for example, the number of visits or services covered).
- o Some variation exists across these standard plans regarding site of care requirements or limitations (for example, coverage may be limited to outpatient setting or coverage only provided if Center of Excellence used).
- o Some variation in medical management exists across these plans across states.
- o While the standard set of covered services in "Typical SG Plans" is generally consistent across plans in each state, regardless of the size of the small group, there are some differences across our plans from state to state resulting from state mandate requirements and/or market demand and competitor standards. The key differences are documented in Exhibit A.
- o As the membership numbers included in the Exhibit A indicate, the majority of WellPoint's small group membership (90%+) are enrolled in standard coverage plans.

- In several states, we offer plans, "*Anthem/Blue Limited Coverage*", in the small group market that provide for a more restricted set of covered services. These plans are low cost options that primarily cover hospital and surgical services, and provide limited or no coverage for other medical services that are generally covered under the more standard plans.

- The response in the "State Mandated Benefit" column indicates whether or not states require coverage of this service under state law and should provide some indication as to why a service may be covered.

The Determination of Essential Health Benefits

Exhibit A: Standard Plan Variances

Benefit	Range of Impact	State Mandated Benefit? (Fully Insured Group Market)	Anthem/Blue Standard Coverage/ Typical Plan in the Small Group and Large Group Markets	Anthem/Blue Limited Coverage Plan
Small Group Membership Allocation (Groups with up to 50 employees for all states)			99.70%	0.30%
Small Group Membership Allocation (Groups with up to 50 employees only for states where Anthem/Blue Limited Coverage is currently marketed)			99.25%	0.75%
Allergy Testing and Injections	0-1%	No	Covered	Not covered
Alternative Medicine (Acupuncture, acupressure, massage therapy, etc.)	0-1%	In few states	Coverage varies across, but not within, states	Not covered
Autism Services	0-1%	In several states	Coverage varies across, but not within, states	Coverage varies across, but not within, states
Bariatric Surgery and Treatment of Morbid Obesity (Rider pricing can be 3 to 10 times higher)	0-1%	In a few states	Coverage varies across, but not within, states Some change to coverage for services related to obesity resulting from PPACA preventive care implementation.	Coverage varies across, but not within, states Some change to coverage for services related to obesity resulting from PPACA preventive care implementation.
Cardiac Rehabilitation	0-1%	No	Covered	Not covered (optional coverage available)
Dental Care - Preventive and Basic (Beyond oral health screening)	1-3%	No	With very few exceptions, offered as optional rider coverage	Not covered
Durable Medical Equipment	1-3%	No	Covered	Not covered except if related to diabetes
Early Intervention Services	0-1%	In several states	Coverage varies across, but not within, states	Coverage varies across, but not within, states
Elective Abortion	0-1%	In a few states the mandate prohibits embedding coverage for fully insured products, but allows coverage to be offered via optional rider	Coverage varies across, but not within, states	Not covered

The Determination of Essential Health Benefits

Benefit	Range of Impact	State Mandated Benefit? (Fully Insured Group Market)	Anthem/Blue Standard Coverage/ Typical Plan in the Small Group and Large Group Markets	Anthem/Blue Limited Coverage Plan
Small Group Membership Allocation (Groups with up to 50 employees for all states)			99.70%	0.30%
Small Group Membership Allocation (Groups with up to 50 employees only for states where Anthem/Blue Limited Coverage is currently marketed)			99.25%	0.75%
Hearing Tests and Hearing Aids	0-1%	In several states	Coverage varies across, but not within, states	Not covered
Infertility and Assisted Reproduction Services	1-3%	In a few states	Coverage varies across, but not within, states	Not covered
Medical Nutrition Therapy (Diabetes-related)	0-1%	In several states	Coverage varies across, but not within, states	Not covered
Medical Nutritional Therapy (Obesity-related)	0-1%	No	Coverage varies across, but not within, states Some change to coverage for services related to obesity resulting from PPACA preventive care implementation.	Not covered
Mental Health and Substance Abuse Services	1-3%	In several states	Covered	Not covered (optional coverage available)
Orthotics and Special Footwear	0-1%	In a few states	Coverage varies across, but not within, states	Not covered
Outpatient Physical Therapy, Occupational Therapy, Speech Therapy and Manipulation Services	3-5%	No	Covered	Not covered
Pharmacy (Full Generic + Brand Coverage)	10+%	No	Generally generic and brand covered	Generic only coverage (with some exceptions)
Pharmacy (Generic Only to Full Generic + Brand Coverage)	10+%	No	Generally generic and brand covered	Generic only coverage (with some exceptions)
Pharmacy (Generic+1 to Full Generic + Brand Coverage)	5-10%	No	Generally generic and brand covered	Generic only coverage (with some exceptions)

The Determination of Essential Health Benefits

Benefit	Range of Impact	State Mandated Benefit? (Fully Insured Group Market)	Anthem/Blue Standard Coverage/ Typical Plan in the Small Group and Large Group Markets	Anthem/Blue Limited Coverage Plan
Small Group Membership Allocation (Groups with up to 50 employees for all states)			99.70%	0.30%
Small Group Membership Allocation (Groups with up to 50 employees only for states where Anthem/Blue Limited Coverage is currently marketed)			99.25%	0.75%
Specific Types of Drugs (Not included in pharmacy impacts above):				
Smoking Cessation Drugs	0-1%	In a few states except contraceptive mandates in most states	Coverage varies across, but not within, states	Coverage varies across, but not within, states
Weight Loss Drugs	0-1%			
Infertility Drugs	0-1%			
Contraceptives	0-1%			
Sexual Dysfunction Drugs	0-1%			
Preventive Care Services Including Specific Screenings (Excludes vision exam cost listed below)	3-5%	All states mandate at least some preventive services	Coverage varies across, but not within, states This has changed to comply with PPACA and standard non-grandfathered plans now include full preventive care coverage	Coverage varies across, but not within, states This has changed to comply with PPACA and standard non-grandfathered plans now include full preventive care coverage
Private Duty Nursing	0-1%	No	Coverage varies across, but not within, states	Not covered
Prosthetics	0-1%	In several states	Covered	Not covered (with some exceptions)
Pulmonary Rehabilitation	0-1%	No	Covered	Not Covered (optional coverage available)
TMJ Treatment and Appliances	0-1%	In several states	Coverage varies across, but not within, states	Coverage varies across, but not within, states

The Determination of Essential Health Benefits

Benefit	Range of Impact	State Mandated Benefit? (Fully Insured Group Market)	Anthem/Blue Standard Coverage/ Typical Plan in the Small Group and Large Group Markets	Anthem/Blue Limited Coverage Plan
Small Group Membership Allocation (Groups with up to 50 employees for all states)			99.70%	0.30%
Small Group Membership Allocation (Groups with up to 50 employees only for states where Anthem/Blue Limited Coverage is currently marketed)			99.25%	0.75%
Urgent Care Facility Services	0-1%	No	Covered	Not covered
Vision Exam/Refraction	0-1%	No	Coverage varies across, but not within, states	Coverage varies across, but not within, states

Actuarial Pricing Assumptions
- All cost impacts were trended to 1/1/2011 based on HAUS or Cost of Care Trends projections through 1/1/2011.
- WellPoint's commercial group pricing model was utilized to value cost impacts where claims experience was not readily available.
- Network discounts used to value claims impacts were averaged across the company.
- Impact estimates are relative to discounted allowed amounts (exclude impacts of member cost-sharing).
- These assumptions are only estimates of the impact and cannot be relied upon for the purpose of setting rates.

The Determination of Essential Health Benefits

Exhibit B: Standard Plan Inclusions

- **Preventive Care**

- **Outpatient Care (In a Clinician's Office)**
  - Primary Care Office Visit
  - Specialist Office Visit
  - Pre and Post Natal Visits
  - Counseling (Family Planning, Nutritional, Other)
  - Allergy Testing
  - Allergy Shots
  - Diagnostic Lab (Non-Preventive)
  - Diagnostic X-Ray (Non-Preventive)
  - Other Diagnostic Tests (Hearing, EKG, etc.) (Non-Preventive)
  - Advanced Imaging (MRI, CT Scan, etc.)
  - Office Surgery
  - PT / OT / ST
  - Chiropractic Care / Spinal Manipulation
  - Therapy: Radiation / Chemo / Non-Preventive Infusion & Injection
  - Prescription Drugs and Administration (For the Drug Itself Dispensed In-Office via Infusion / Injection)
  - Dialysis / Hemodialysis
  - Outpatient Mental Health and Substance Abuse (Psychotherapy, etc.)

- **Emergency Room (ER) Care**
  - Facility ER Charge
  - Other Facility Charges (Diagnostic Lab, X-Ray, Supplies, etc.)
  - Facility Advanced Diagnostic Imaging (CT Scan, etc.)
  - Physician Services (ER Physician, Radiologist, Anesthesiologist, Surgeon, etc.)

- **Outpatient Care in a Hospital, Free-Standing Facility or Urgent Care Facility**
  - Facility Surgery Charge (Surgery Suite)
  - Other Facility Surgery Charges (Diagnostic Lab / X-Ray, Supplies, etc.)
  - Physician Surgery Charges
  - Facility Charge (Charge for Procedure Room, Other Ancillary Facility Services)
  - Physician Charges (Radiologist, Pathologist, Anesthesiologist, etc.)
  - Outpatient Mental Health and Substance Abuse (Facility)
  - Outpatient Mental Health and Substance Abuse (Professional)
  - Diagnostic Lab
  - Diagnostic X-Ray
  - Other Diagnostic (EKG, EEG, etc.)
  - Advanced Diagnostic Imaging (MRI, CT Scan, etc.)
  - PT / OT / ST / Spinal Manipulation
  - Therapy: Radiation / Chemo / Non-Preventive Infusion / Injection
  - Prescription Drugs and Administration (Drug Dispensed in Outpatient Facility via Infusion / Injection)
  - Dialysis / Hemodialysis

 | **The Determination of Essential Health Benefits**

- **Inpatient Care**
  - o Facility Room and Board Charge for:
    - Hospital (Acute Care Facility)
    - Skilled Nursing Facilities (SNF)
    - Mental Health / Substance Abuse Facility
    - Residential Treatment Center
  - o Facility Other Charges (Diagnostics Lab / X-Ray, Supplies, etc.)
  - o Physician Services for:
    - General Medical Care
    - Surgery
    - Maternity
    - Mental Health
    - Substance Abuse

- **Home Care**
  - o Home Health Care Services
  - o Home Dialysis
  - o Home Infusion Therapy

- **Other**
  - o Ambulance (Ground and Air)
  - o Durable Medical Equipment (DME), Prosthetics, Medical Devices, Medical Supplies Received from Supplier
  - o Hospice
  - o Dental Services related to an Accident (Dentist's Office)
  - o Vision Services (Exam)

WELLPOINT.
Health. Care. Value.™

The Determination of Essential Health Benefits

Exhibit C: Standard Plan Exclusions

- **Charges for Administrative Services**
  - Exclude charges for administration or other service fees when not directly providing medical care. This includes, but is not limited to: completion of claim forms, charges for medical records or reports, missed or canceled appointments, storage or other administrative actions.

- **Commercial Weight Loss**
  - Exclude Commercial Weight Loss Programs from core medical benefit.

- **Complications of Experimental Services**
  - Exclude services related to complications resulting or arising from excluded services except where mandated or where DOI agreements have been made to cover.

- **Cosmetic Surgery**
  - Exclude cosmetic surgery or other procedures performed solely for beautification or to improve appearance.

- **Custodial Care**
  - Exclude custodial care (such as feeding, dressing, bathing, transferring, and activities of daily living). Does not apply to hospice.

- **Dental Services**
  - Exclude routine dental services, including topical and oral fluoride preparations, from standard medical and pharmacy benefits except where mandated.
  - This does not apply to products with embedded dental coverage.
  - Exclusion does not apply to:
    - Anesthesia and associated facility charges as a result of age and/or disability criteria.
    - Dental accidents - treatment, sought within 12 months, of an injury to natural teeth and when a treatment plan submitted for prior approval. Injuries resulted from biting and/or chewing are not considered a dental accident.
    - Radiation - dental services to prepare the mouth for radiation therapy to treat head and/or neck cancer.

- **Educational Services; Self-Training; Vocational Services**
  - Exclude educational services, self management / help training services, and vocational services except where mandated for diabetes and asthma, or where explicitly covered by another benefit.

- **Experimental or Investigational Services**
  - Exclude services deemed to be experimental or investigational unless specifically covered (e.g., Clinical Cancer Trials).

- **Food and Dietary Supplements**
  - Exclude benefits for food or food supplements, except formulas and/or food products that are:
    - Prescribed, ordered or supervised by a physician; and
    - Medically necessary as defined by medical policy.

- **Foot Care**
  - Exclude routine or palliative foot care (comfort or cosmetic) unless medically necessary.

The Determination of Essential Health Benefits

- **Gastric Bypass or Bariatric Surgery**
  - Exclude Gastric Bypass and Bariatric surgery except where mandated.

- **Gynecomastia**
  - Exclude surgical treatments of gynecomastia for cosmetic purposes.

- **Health Club Memberships**
  - Exclude Health Club Memberships from core medical benefit.

- **Hearing Aids and Routine Hearing Tests**
  - Exclude coverage for hearing aids. Cover routine hearing screenings as a part of preventive care. Cochlear implants are not included in the exclusion.

- **Infertility Services**
  - Exclude all assisted reproductive technologies (ART) and the associated diagnostic testing and Rx treatments to support ART. Examples include:
    - Artificial insemination
    - In-vitro fertilization
    - ZIFT – Zygote Intrafallopian Transfer
    - GIFT – Gamete Intrafallopian Transfer

- **Legal Liability**
  - Exclude services for which the member has no liability to pay in the absence of this plan's coverage. This includes, but is not limited to: government programs; incarceration; workers compensation; and free clinics.

- **Not Medically Necessary**
  - Exclude services deemed not medically necessary.

- **Oral Surgery**
  - Exclude teeth extractions, surgical removal of impacted teeth, and other oral surgical services (not to include pharmacy services) for care of the teeth or of the bones and gums directly supporting the teeth. These services are dental in nature and not covered under medical.
  - Other Oral Surgical Services are covered, including:
    - Treatment of medically diagnosed cleft lip, cleft palate, or ectodermal dysplasia;
    - Orthognathic surgery that is required because of a medical condition or injury which prevents normal function of the joint or bone and is deemed medically necessary to attain functional capacity of the affected part;
    - Oral/surgical correction of accident related injuries
    - Treatment of lesions, removal of tumors and biopsies
    - Incision and drainage of infection of soft tissue not including tooth-related cysts or abscesses.

- **Private Duty Nursing**
  - Exclude private duty nursing provided in an inpatient setting (acute care or skilled nursing facility).
  - Nursing services in a home or hospice setting are covered as a part of Home Health Care benefits and Hospice benefits.

The Determination of Essential Health Benefits

- **Provider Not Recognized by Plan**
  - o Exclude services, supplies, or devices if they are not prescribed, performed, or directed by a provider or facility not defined by us as such, or not licensed to do so.

- **Reversal of Sterilization**
  - o Exclude reversal of elective sterilization.

- **Services from Relatives or Members of Immediate Family**
  - o Exclude services (applies to medical and pharmacy services) performed by a provider who is a family member by birth, marriage, or adoption, or by the provider to self.

- **Services Related to Surrogacy**
  - o Exclude services related to surrogacy.

- **Sexual Dysfunction**
  - o Exclude drugs and devices used for the treatment of sexual dysfunction.
  - o Exclude services related to sexual transformations.

- **Smoking Cessation Programs**
  - o Exclude smoking cessation programs that are not affiliated with WellPoint.

- **Standby Physician Charges**
  - o Exclude all standby physician service charges.

- **Unlisted Services**
  - o Exclude services not explicitly listed as covered.

- **Vein Surgery**
  - o Exclude treatments of all varicose and spider vein surgeries for cosmetic purposes.

- **Vision Services**
  - o Exclude the following:
    - ▪ Vision Correction Surgery (e.g. Lasik, radial keratotomy, etc.) to correct refractive error, including near sightedness, far sightedness, and/or astigmatism;
    - ▪ Orthoptics and vision therapy/training; and
    - ▪ Prescription and non-prescription eyewear.
  - o Exclusion does not apply to medical and surgical services for the treatment of injuries and diseases affecting the eye (examples include eye exams for diabetics, eyewear/contacts and related services to replace human lenses following surgery or injury, etc.).

Appendix F

General Exclusions

This table presents a sampling of general exclusions, beginning with a set of what was presented as typical of industry-wide practices,[1] followed by a Federal Employees Health Benefits (FEHB) program fee-for-service product,[2] and then exclusions among CIGNA typical small group employer plan,[3] UnitedHealthcare small group plans,[4] Wellpoint Anthem Blue Standard small business plan[5] (see Appendix E for more detail on the latter), and the Medicare program.[6,7] The FEHB program develops a short list of general exclusions for both its fee-for-service and managed care plans (see, for example, Chapter 5, Box 5-2), which individual insurers can expand upon.

---

[1] Personal communication, Charles Bevilacqua, Kaiser Permanente; the list of industry-wide practices are not necessarily specific to Kaiser but identified across many insurers as typical.

[2] These are specific to Blue Cross and Blue Shield (BCBS) fee-for-service benefit plan under the FEHBP program (http://www.fepblue.org/benefitplans/2011-sbp/bcbs-2011-RI71-005.pdf).

[3] Personal communication, Rosemary Lester, CIGNA Product, September 9, 2011.

[4] Personal communication, Sam Ho, UnitedHealthcare, September 13, 2011.

[5] Personal communication, Ruth Raskas, WellPoint, September 9, 2011.

[6] CMS (Centers for Medicare and Medicaid Services) Medicare benefit policy manual: Chapter 16—general exclusions from coverage (http://www.cms.gov/manuals/Downloads/bp102c16.pdf).

[7] Responses were compiled exactly as submitted, explaining any variance in style (e.g., X = excluded; X for Cigna = explicitly excluded or otherwise not a covered benefit; Y = excluded; N = not excluded).

TABLE F-1 General Exclusions of Health Plans

Sample Industry Variation in Exclusion Language	Industry Typical[a]	FEHB-BCBS	CIGNA[b]	United Healthcare	WellPoint[c]	Medicare
General Exclusions						
Service, drugs, or supplies you receive while you are not enrolled in this plan	X	X	X	Y	Not Covered	
Services, drugs, or supplies not required according to accepted standards of medical, dental, or psychiatric practice in the United States		X	X	Y	Not Covered	
Services, drugs, or supplies billed by Preferred and Member facilities for inpatient care related to specific medical errors and hospital-acquired conditions known as never events[d]		X	X	N	Not addressed in contracts	
Services not specifically/explicitly listed as covered		X	X	Y	Not Covered	
All services, drugs, or supplies related to the non-covered service are excluded from coverage, except services we would otherwise cover to treat complications of the non-covered service	X		X	Y	Not Covered	
Services, drugs, or supplies not required to prevent, diagnose, or treat a medical condition	X		X	Y	Not Covered	
Services for conditions that a plan physician determines are not responsive to therapeutic treatment	X		X	Y	Not Covered	
Services or supplies for which no charge would be made if the covered individual had no health insurance coverage		X	X	Y	Not Covered	
Services related to and required as a result of services which are not covered under Medicare				N	Not addressed in contracts	Y
Medical Necessity						
Services deemed not medically necessary			X	Y	Not Covered[e]	
Services, drugs, or supplies that are not medically necessary		X	X	Y		
Services not reasonable and necessary			X	N, eligible expense		Y
Abortion						
Services, drugs, or supplies related to abortions, except when the life of the mother would be endangered if the fetus were carried to term, or when the pregnancy is the result of an act of rape or incest		X	f	Y	Varies across plans	
Active Military Service						
Services, drugs, or supplies you receive without charge while in active military service		X	X	Y	Not Covered	

TABLE F-1 Continued

Sample Industry Variation in Exclusion Language	Industry Typical[a]	FEHB-BCBS	CIGNA[b]	United Healthcare	WellPoint[c]	Medicare
Automobile, No Fault, Any Liability Insurance or Workers' Compensation						
Care for any condition or injury recognized or allowed as a compensable loss through any Workers' Compensation, occupational disease or similar law[g]	X		X	Y	Not Covered by most plans[e]	
Services reimbursable under automobile, no fault, any liability insurance workers' compensation			X	N[h]		Y
Blood						
The cost of whole red blood or red blood cells when they are donated or replaced or billed[i]	X			Y	Not Covered by some plans	
Charges for Administrative Services						
Exclude services, supplies, or devices if they are not prescribed, performed, or directed by a provider or facility not defined by us as such, or not licensed to do so			X	Y	Not Covered	
Clinical Trials						
Research costs (costs related to conducting a clinical trial such as research physician and nurse time, analysis of results, and clinical tests performed only for research purposes)		X	Not a Benefit unless mandated	Y	Not Covered	
Extra care costs related to taking part in a clinical trial such as additional tests that a patient might may need as part of the trial, but not as part of the patient's routine care			Not a Benefit unless mandated	Y	Not Covered	
Cosmetic Services						
Cosmetic services[j]	X		X	Y	Not Covered[e]	
Services, drugs, or supplies you receive for cosmetic purposes		X	X	Y		
Cosmetic surgery or other procedures performed solely for beautification or to improve appearance			X	Y		
Surgical treatments of gynecomastia (male breast reduction) for cosmetic purposes			X	Y		
Cosmetic surgery				Y		Y
Counseling						
Religious, personal growth counseling or marriage counseling including services and treatment related to religious, personal growth counseling or marriage counseling, unless the primary patient has a DSM IV diagnosis	X		X	Y, except DSM diagnosis also Excluded	Not Covered by most plans	

continued

TABLE F-1 Continued

Sample Industry Variation in Exclusion Language	Industry Typical[a]	FEHB-BCBS	CIGNA[b]	United Healthcare	WellPoint[c]	Medicare
Crime						
Treatment of injuries sustained while committing a crime	X		(X in plans for individuals)	Y	Not Covered by most plans	Y
Custodial Care						
Custodial care		X	X	Y	Not Covered[e]	
Custodial care (such as feeding, dressing, bathing, transferring, and activities of daily living)[k]			X	Y		
Custodial care means assistance with activities of daily living (e.g., walking, getting in and out of bed, bathing, dressing, feeding, toileting, and taking medicine), or care that can be performed safely and effectively by people who, in order to provide the care, do not require medical licenses or certificates or the presence of a supervising licensed nurse[l]	X		X	Y		
Dental/Oral Services					Dental services Not Covered with some variation across plans for surgical extraction of impacted teeth and for TMJ treatment and appliances[e]	
Any dental or oral surgical procedures or drugs involving orthodontic care, the teeth, dental implants, periodontal disease, or preparing the mouth for the fitting or continued use of dentures[m]		X	X	Y		
Orthodontic care for malposition of the bones of the jaw or for temporomandibular joint (TMJ) syndrome		X	X	Y		
Dental procedures and appliances to correct disorders of the temporomandibular (jaw) joint (also known as TMD or TMJ disorders)	X		X	Y, except surgery is covered		
Routine dental services, including topical and oral fluoride preparations, from standard medical and pharmacy benefits except where mandated (does not apply to products with embedded dental coverage)[n]		X	X	Y		

TABLE F-1 Continued

Sample Industry Variation in Exclusion Language	Industry Typical[a]	FEHB-BCBS	CIGNA[b]	United Healthcare	WellPoint[c]	Medicare
Teeth extractions, surgical removal of impacted teeth, and other oral surgical services (not to include pharmacy services) for care of the teeth or of the bones and gums directly supporting the teeth. These services are dental and nature and not covered under medical[o]			X	Y		
Extractions, treatment of cavities, care of the gums or structures directly supporting the teeth[p,q]	X		X	Y		
Treatment of periodontal abscess, removal of impacted teeth, orthodontia (including braces), false teeth, or any other dental services or supplies, except as otherwise covered under the plan	X		X	Y		
Items and services in connection with the care, treatment, filling, removal, or replacement of teeth, or structures supporting the teeth[r]			X	Y		Y
Any dental procedures involving orthodontic care, inlays, gold or platinum fillings, bridges, crowns, pin/post reduction, dental implants, surgical periodontal procedures, or the preparation of the mouth for the fitting or continued use of dentures			X	Y		
Educational Services; Self-Training; Vocational Services						
Self-care or self-help training		X	Not a Benefit unless mandated	Y	Not Covered[e]	
Educational services, self management/help training services, and vocational services except where mandated for diabetes and asthma, or where explicitly covered by another benefit			Not a Benefit unless mandated	Y		
Any educational services and programs or therapies for behavioral/conduct problems[s]			Not a Benefit unless mandated	Y		
Coverage does not include services other than self management of a medical condition as determined by the Health Plan to be primarily educational in nature	X		Not a Benefit unless mandated	Y		
Equipment						
Equipment that basically serves comfort or convenience functions or is primarily for the convenience of a person caring for you or your dependent, i.e., exercycle or other physical fitness equipment, elevators, hoyer lifts, shower/bath bench. Air conditioners, air purifiers and filters, batteries and charges, dehumidifiers, humidifiers, air cleaners and dust collection devices	X		X	Y	Not Covered	

continued

TABLE F-1 Continued

Sample Industry Variation in Exclusion Language	Industry Typical[a]	FEHB-BCBS	CIGNA[b]	United Healthcare	WellPoint[c]	Medicare
Experimental/Investigational Procedures						
Experimental or investigational services[t]	X		X	Y	Not Covered[e]	
Experimental or investigational procedures, treatments, drugs, or devices		X	X	Y		
Services related to complications resulting or arising from excluded services except where mandated or where DOI agreements have been made to cover			X	N		
Services deemed to be experimental or investigational unless specifically covered (e.g., Clinical Cancer Trials)			X	Y		
Fees						
Expenses in excess of usual, customary and reasonable fees	X		X	N, eligible expense	Not Covered[e]	
Free care (no charge items)	X		X	Y		
Food and Dietary Supplements						
Benefits for food or food supplements, except formulas and/or food products that are prescribed, ordered or supervised by a physician and medically necessary as defined by medical policy			Not a Benefit unless mandated	Y	Not Covered	
Nutritional supplements and formulae needed for the treatment of inborn errors of metabolism	X		Not a Benefit unless mandated	Y	Covered[u]	
Foot Care						
Foot care[v]	X			N	See below	Y
Routine or palliative foot care (comfort or cosmetic) unless medically necessary			X	Y	Not Covered	
Shoe inserts, orthotics (except for care of the diabetic foot), and orthopedic shoes (except when an orthopedic shoe is joined to a brace)	X		X	N, we cover one pair foot orthotics	Not Covered by most plans	
Furniture						
Furniture (other than medically necessary durable medical equipment) such as commercial beds, mattresses, chairs		X	X	Y	Not Covered	

215

TABLE F-1 Continued

Sample Industry Variation in Exclusion Language	Industry Typical[a]	FEHB-BCBS	CIGNA[b]	United Healthcare	WellPoint[c]	Medicare
Government Programs			X[e]		Not Covered by most plans except as required by mandate[e]	
Treatment where payment is made by any local, state, or federal government (except Medicaid), or for which payment would be made if the Participant had applied for such benefits. Services that can be provided through a government program for which you as a member of the community are eligible for participation. Such programs include, but are not limited to, school speech and reading programs	X			N		
Items and services furnished, paid for or authorized by governmental entities—Federal, state, or local governments			X	N		Y
Health Club Memberships			X[e]		Not Covered by most plans[e]	
Health club memberships from core medical benefit			X	Y		
Membership costs or fees associated with health clubs, weight loss programs	X		X	Y		
Hearing Aids and Routine Hearing Tests					Generally Not Covered by plans unless mandated[e]	
Hearing aids[w]			X	Y		
Hearing aids, hearing devices and related examinations and services	X		X	Y		
Hearing aids and auditory implants				Y		Y
Hypnotherapy						
Hypnotherapy (hypnosis)	X		X	Y	Not Covered	
Infertility Services						
See Reproductive Services					See Reproductive Services	
Legal Liability					Not Covered[e]	
Charges which the enrollee or Plan has no legal obligation to pay, such as excess charges for an annuitant age 65 or older who is not covered by Medicare Parts A and/or B, doctor's charges exceeding the amount specified by the HHS when benefits are payable under Medicare, or State premium taxes however applied		X	X	Y		

continued

TABLE F-1 Continued

Sample Industry Variation in Exclusion Language	Industry Typical[a]	FEHB-BCBS	CIGNA[b]	United Healthcare	WellPoint[c]	Medicare
Services for which the member has no liability to pay in the absence of this plan's coverage. This includes, but is not limited to: government programs; incarceration; workers compensation; and free clinics				Y		
No legal obligation to pay for or provide services			X	N		Y
Location						
Services, other than Emergency Services, received outside the United States whether or not the services are available in the United States	X		X	Y	Covered[e,u]	
Services not provided within the United States				Y		Y
Massage Therapy						
Massage therapy[x]	X		X	Y	Not Covered by most plans	
Medical Reports						
Completion of specific medical reports, including those not directly related to treatment of the Participant, e.g., employment or insurance physicals, and reports prepared in connection with litigation	X		X	Y	Not Covered	
Medical Supplies					Criteria for coverage varies across plans[e]	
Disposable supplies for home use	X		X	Y		
Obesity/Weight Loss Services						
Services, drugs, or supplies for the treatment of obesity, weight reduction, or dietary control, except for office visits and diagnostic tests for the treatment of morbid obesity[y]; gastric restrictive procedures, gastric malabsorptive procedures, and combination restrictive and malabsorptive procedures		X	X	Y	Generally Not Covered by plans unless mandated	
Nutritional counseling when billed by a covered provider such as a physician, nurse, nurse practitioner, licensed certified nurse, nurse practitioner, licensed certified nurse midwife, dietician or nutritionist, who bills independently for nutritional counseling services		X	X	Y	Covered[u] as part of Preventative services for non-grandfathered plans after 9/23/2010 if services are rendered by a covered provider. Otherwise, Not Covered for most plans	

TABLE F-1 Continued

Sample Industry Variation in Exclusion Language	Industry Typical[a]	FEHB-BCBS	CIGNA[b]	United Healthcare	WellPoint[c]	Medicare
Commercial weight loss programs from core medical benefit			X	Y	Not Covered	
Weight reduction programs: fees and charges relating to fitness programs, weight loss, or weight control programs	X		X	Y	Not Covered	
Gastric bypass and bariatric surgery except where mandated			Not a Benefit unless Mandated	Y	Generally Not Covered by plans unless mandated	
Outpatient Prescription Drugs[z]						
Compounded products unless the drug is listed on our drug formulary or one of the ingredients requires a prescription by law	X		X	Y	Compound Covered[u] only if one of ingredients requires a prescription	
Drugs prescribed for cosmetic purposes	X		X	Y	Not Covered	
Drugs that shorten the duration of the common cold	X			N	Covered[u] if a prescription is required	
Drugs used to enhance athletic performance	X		X	Y	Not Covered	
Drugs which are available over the counter and prescriptions for which drug strength may be realized by the over the counter product	X		X	Y	Not Covered by most plans	
Experimental or investigational drugs	X		X	Y	Not Covered	
If a service is not covered, any drugs or supplies needed in connection with that service are not covered	X		X	Y	Not Covered	
Prescription drugs for which there is an over the counter drug equivalent	X		X	Y	Not Covered	
Replacement of lost, damaged or stolen drugs	X		X	N	Not Covered by most plans	
Special packaging (packaging of prescription medications may be limited to standard packaging)	X			N	Not applicable	
Drugs and supplies needed solely for travel	X		X	N	Not Covered by most plans	
Personal Care Items					Not Covered[e]	Y
Personal comfort items			X	Y		
Personal comfort items such as beauty and barber services, radio, television, or telephone		X	X	Y		

continued

TABLE F-1 Continued

Sample Industry Variation in Exclusion Language	Industry Typical[a]	FEHB-BCBS	CIGNA[b]	United Healthcare	WellPoint[c]	Medicare
Personal comfort items such as those that are furnished primarily for your personal comfort or convenience, including those services and supplies not directly related to medical care, such as guest's meals and accommodations, hospital admission kit, barber services, telephone charges, radio and television rentals, homemaker services, travel expenses, over the counter convenience items and take-home supplies	X		X	Y		
Providers/Facilities						
Services, drugs, or supplies you receive from a provider or facility barred or suspended from the FEHB Program		X	X	Y	Not applicable	
Services or supplies furnished by immediate relatives or household members, such as spouse, parents, children, brothers or sisters by blood, marriage or adoption		X	X	Y	Not Covered by most plans	
Services (applies to medical and pharmacy services) performed by a provider who is a family member by birth, marriage, or adoption, or by the provider to self			X	Y	Not Covered by most plans	
Services rendered by a provider who is a close relative or member of your household. Close relative means wife or husband, parent, child, brother or sister, by blood, marriage or adoption	X		X	Y	Not Covered by most plans	
Charges imposed by immediate relatives of the patient or members of the patient's households			X	Y	Not Covered by most plans	Y
Services or supplies furnished or billed by a noncovered facility, except that medically necessary prescription drugs; oxygen; and physical, speech and occupational therapy rendered by a qualified professional therapist on an outpatient basis are covered subject to plan limits		X		Y, except speech and occupational therapy Excluded in most cases	Not Covered	
Services, drugs, or supplies you receive from noncovered providers except in medically underserved areas[aa]		X		Y, except we do not allow in underserved areas either	Not Covered	
Services you receive from a provider that are outside the scope of the provider's licensure or certification		X	X	Y	Not Covered	
Services/service charges of standby physicians		X	X	Y	Not Covered by some plans	
Care by non-plan providers except for authorized referrals or emergencies[bb]				Y	Not Covered under certain plan types	

TABLE F-1 Continued

Sample Industry Variation in Exclusion Language	Industry Typical[a]	FEHB-BCBS	CIGNA[b]	United Healthcare	WellPoint[c]	Medicare
Care by non-plan providers except for authorized referrals, emergencies and out of area urgent care	X			Y	Not Covered under certain plan types	
Private duty nursing			X	Y	Not Covered by some plans	
Private duty nursing provided in an inpatient setting (acute care or skilled nursing facility)[cc]			X	Y	Not Covered by some plans	
Private duty nursing as a registered bed patient unless a plan physician determines medical necessity	X		X	Y	Not Covered by some plans	
Private duty nursing in home or long term facility	X		X	Y	Not Covered by some plans	
Services, supplies, or devices if they are not prescribed, performed, or directed by a provider or facility not defined by us as such, or not licensed to do so			X	Y	Not Covered	
Inpatient hospital or SNF services not delivered directly or under arrangement by the provider				N	Not addressed in contracts	Y
Care in halfway house	X			Y	Not Covered	
Private room unless medically necessary or if a semi-private room is not available	X		X	Y	Generally Not Covered	
Recreational Therapy/Activities						
Recreational or educational therapy and any related diagnostic testing, except as provided by a hospital during a covered inpatient stay		X	X	Y	Not Covered[e]	
Recreational, diversional and play activities	X		X	Y		
Reproductive Services						
Fetal reduction surgery			X	Y	Generally not addressed in contracts	
The reversal of voluntary/elective sterilization	X		X	Y	Not Covered	
Infertility services when the infertility is caused by or related to voluntary sterilization	X		X	Y	Not Covered by most plans except as required by mandate	

continued

TABLE F-1 Continued

Sample Industry Variation in Exclusion Language	Industry Typical[a]	FEHB-BCBS	CIGNA[b]	United Healthcare	WellPoint[c]	Medicare
All assisted reproductive technologies (ART) and the associated diagnostic testing and Rx treatments to support ART (e.g., artificial insemination, in-vitro fertilization, ZIFT [zygote intrafallopian transfer], GIFT [gamete intrafallopian transfer])			X	Y	Not Covered by most plans except as required by mandate	
In vitro fertilization services			X	Y	Not Covered by most plans except as required by mandate	
Infertility services related to advanced reproductive technologies including but not limited to in vitro fertilization (IVF); gamete intrafallopian transfer (GIFT); zygote intrafallopian transfer (ZIFT) and variations of these procedures	X		X	Y	Not Covered by most plans except as required by mandate	
Donor charges and services	X		X	Y	Not Covered by most plans except as required by mandate	
Cryopreservation of donor sperm and eggs	X		X	Y	Not Covered by most plans except as required by mandate	
Any experimental, investigational or unproven infertility procedures or therapies	X		X	Y	Not Covered	
Routine Services					Not Covered under some grandfathered plans[e]	
Routine services and appliances			Unable to determine definition of category, therefore no comment	N		Y

TABLE F-1 Continued

Sample Industry Variation in Exclusion Language	Industry Typical[a]	FEHB-BCBS	CIGNA[b]	United Healthcare	WellPoint[c]	Medicare
Routine services, such as periodic physical examinations; screening examinations; immunizations; and services or tests not related to a specific diagnosis, illness, injury, set of symptoms, or maternity care[dd]		X				N
Sexual Transformations/Dysfunction/Inadequacy						
Sexual reassignment surgery	X		X	Y	Not Covered	
Services related to sexual transformations			X	Y	Not Covered	
Services, drugs, or supplies related to sex transformations			X	Y	Not Covered	
Services, drugs, or supplies related to sex transformations, sexual dysfunction, or sexual inadequacy (except for surgical placement of penile prostheses to treat erectile dysfunction)		X	X	Y	See above and below	
Drugs and devices used for the treatment of sexual dysfunction			X	Y	Not Covered by some plans	
Shift Differentials						
Professional charges for shift differentials		X	X	Y	Not addressed in contract	
Smoking Cessation						
Smoking cessation programs			X	Y,	Programs not affiliated with WellPoint Not Covered in most plans	
Surrogacy					Services provided to an individual not covered under the plan are Not Covered[e]	
Surrogate parenting			X	Y		
Services related to surrogacy			X	Y		
Services related to conception, pregnancy or delivery in connection with a surrogate arrangement. A surrogate arrangement is one in which a woman agrees to become pregnant and to surrender the baby to another person or persons who intend to raise the child[ee]	X		X	Y		

continued

TABLE F-1 Continued

Sample Industry Variation in Exclusion Language	Industry Typical[a]	FEHB-BCBS	CIGNA[b]	United Healthcare	WellPoint[c]	Medicare
Testing						
Testing for ability, aptitude, intelligence or interest	X		X	Y	Not Covered by some plans	
Third-party Requests or Requirements						
Physical examinations and other services, and related reports and paperwork, in connection with third-party requests or requirements, such as those for: employment, participation in employee programs, insurance, disability, licensing, or on court order or for parole or probation	X		X	Y	Generally Not Covered with some nuances across plans	
Topical Hyperbaric Oxygen Therapy (THBO)						
Topical Hyperbaric Oxygen Therapy (THBO)		X	Not a Benefit	N	Not addressed in contract	
Travel or Transportation						
Travel or transportation (other than a state licensed professional ambulance service) expenses even though prescribed by a physician, except as noted under transplants	X		X	Y	Generally not addressed in contract	
Treatment of Dementia, Amnesia, or Mental Retardation						
Treatment of dementia, amnesia or mental retardation, except for treatment of psychological symptoms related to these conditions	X			Y, no mental covered unless optional is purchased	Not Covered by some plans	
Vein Surgery						
Treatments of all varicose and spider vein surgeries for cosmetic purposes			X	Y	Not Covered	
Vision Services					Vision services generally Not Covered with some nuances across plans[e]	
Eye glasses and contact lenses for individuals at least 18 years of age.			X	Y, excluded any age		
Vision correction surgery (e.g., Lasik, radial keratotomy) to correct refractive error, including near sightedness, far sightedness, and/or astigmatism; orthoptics and vision therapy/training; prescription and non-prescription eyewear[ff]			X	Y		

TABLE F-1 Continued

Sample Industry Variation in Exclusion Language	Industry Typical[a]	FEHB-BCBS	CIGNA[b]	United Healthcare	WellPoint[c]	Medicare
Radial keratotomy; and surgery, services, evaluations or supplies for the surgical correction of near sightedness and/or astigmatism or any other correction of vision due to a refractive problem	X		X	Y		
Orthoptics (a technique of eye exercises designed to correct the visual axes of eyes not properly coordinated for binocular vision) or visual training	X		X	Y		
Vision-medical benefits for low vision aids, eyeglasses, contact lenses for prescription or fitting and follow-up care thereof, except that covered expenses will include the purchase of the first pair of eyeglasses, lenses, frames or contact lenses that follows cataract surgery or loss of lens due to eye disease for aphakia or aniridia	X		X	Y		
War					Not Covered by most plans[e]	
Any disease or injury resulting from a war, declared or not, or any military duty or any release of nuclear energy. Also excluded are charges for services directly related to military service provided or available from the Veterans' Administration or military medical facilities as required by law	X		X	Y		
Services resulting from war			X	Y		Y

[a] Approximately 25 percent of customers will accept these exclusions as listed. About 50 percent of customers will add exclusions to the list, while the other 25 percent will remove some exclusions. Those customers who add or remove exclusions typically only make changes to a small number of services. This list of exclusions is typical for both self-funded plans as well as traditionally insured plans. Self-funded plans, however, tend to customize this list more than fully insured plans.

[b] This table reflects exclusions for CIGNA's Typical Small Group Employer Plan.

[c] This table reflects exclusions for Anthem/Blue Standard Coverage/Typical small group and individual plans.

[d] Never events are errors in medical care that are clearly identifiable, preventable, and serious in their consequences, such as surgery performed on a wrong body part, and specific conditions that are acquired during your hospital stay, such as severe bed sores.

[e] Respondents sometimes answered on the gray category line when specific wording choices did not match their own.

[f] Elective abortions are not a benefit in the individual plan products; maternity care is not a typical benefit in individual plans.

[g] Exception: Benefits are provided for actively employed partners and small business owners not covered under a Workers' Compensation Act or similar law, if elected by the group and additional premium is paid. Services or supplies for injuries or diseases related to you or your dependent's job to the extent you or your dependent is required to be covered by a workers' compensation law.

[h] Coordination of benefits provided.

[i] Except expenses for administration and processing of blood and blood products (except blood factors) covered as part of inpatient and outpatient services.

[j] Except as otherwise specified for services covered under "reconstructive surgery."

[k] Does not apply to hospice.

[l] This exclusion does not apply to services covered under "hospice care."

[m] Except as specifically allowable under *Oral and maxillofacial surgery*.

[n] Exclusion does not apply to: anesthesia and associated facility charges as a result of age and/or disability criteria; dental accidents—treatment, sought within 12 months, of an injury to natural teeth and when a treatment plan submitted for prior approval. Injuries resulted from biting and/or chewing are not considered a dental accident; radiation—dental services to prepare the mouth for radiation therapy to treat head and/or neck cancer.

continued

TABLE F-1 Continued

o Other oral surgical services are covered, including treatment of medically diagnosed cleft lip, cleft palate, or ectodermal dysplasia; orthognathic surgery that is required because of a medical condition or injury which prevents normal function of the joint or bone and is deemed medically necessary to attain functional capacity of the affected part; oral/surgical correction of accident-related injuries; treatment of lesions, removal of tumors and biopsies; incision and drainage of infection of soft tissue not including teeth-related cysts or abscesses.

p Structures supporting the teeth mean the periodontium, which includes the gingivae, dentogingival junction, periodontal membrane, cementum of the teeth, and alveolar process.

q This exclusion does not apply to accidental injury to sound and natural teeth.

r Structures directly supporting the teeth mean the periodontium, which includes the gingivae, dentogingival junction, periodontal membrane, cementum of the teeth, and alveolar process.

s This exclusion does not apply to coverage for medication management.

t A Service is experimental or investigational if the health plan, in consultation with the medical group, determines that: generally accepted medical standards do not recognize it as safe and effective for treating the condition in question (even if it has been authorized by law for use in testing or other studies on human patients); it requires government approval that has not been obtained when Service is to be provided; it cannot be legally performed or marketed in the United States without FDA approval; it is the subject of a current new drug or device application on file with the FDA; it is provided as part of a research trial; (see specific section for clinical trials); it is provided pursuant to a written protocol or other document that lists an evaluation of the service's safety, toxicity, or efficacy as among its objectives; it is subject to approval or review of an IRB or other body that approves or reviews research; it is provided pursuant to informed consent documents that describe the services as experimental or investigational, or indicate that the services are being evaluated for their safety, toxicity or efficacy; or the prevailing opinion among experts is that use of the services should be substantially confined to research settings or further research is necessary to determine the safety, toxicity, or efficacy of the service.

u Covered subject to terms and conditions of the contract. For example, there may be network limitations, medical policy limitations, cost-sharing requirements, dollar caps, visit limits, etc.

v Except when medically necessary.

w Cochlear implants are not necessarily included in the exclusion. Cover routine hearing screenings as a part of preventive care.

x Except when provided as a procedure during a covered therapy.

y A condition in which an individual has a BMI of 40 or more, or an individual with a BMI of 35 or more with co-morbidities who has failed conservative treatment.

z Insurer may outline drugs that should be reviewed based on employer selection: drugs used in the treatment of infertility, sexual dysfunction, weight control, smoking cessation, and growth hormone.

aa For 2011, for example: Alabama, Arizona, Idaho, Illinois, Kentucky, Louisiana, Mississippi, Missouri, Montana, North Dakota, Oklahoma, South Carolina, South Dakota, and Wyoming.

bb A medical emergency is the sudden and unexpected onset of a condition or an injury that you believe endangers your life or could result in serious injury or disability, and requires immediate medical or surgical care.

cc Nursing services in a home or hospice setting are covered as a part of home health care benefits and hospice benefits.

dd Certain services are exempted, including those preventive services specifically covered under preventive care (adult and child), preventive screenings specifically listed in the plan brochure; and certain routine services associated with covered clinical trials.

ee The plan might choose alternative wording for this exclusion: in situations where you receive monetary compensation to act as a surrogate, health plan will seek reimbursement of all charges for covered services you receive that are associated with conception, pregnancy and/or delivery of the child. A surrogate arrangement is one in which a woman agrees to become pregnant and to surrender the baby to another person or persons who intend to raise the child.

ff Exclusion does not apply to medial and surgical services for the treatment of injuries and diseases affecting the eye (e.g., eye exams for diabetics, eyewear/contacts and related services to replace lenses following surgery or injury, etc.).

Appendix G

Medical Necessity

The committee's conclusion with respect to medical necessity guidance can be found in Chapter 5. As part of its task, the committee reviewed a variety of definitions of medical necessity identifying key elements, listed here first by individual components solely for comparison purposes, but meant to be combined with other elements. A sampling of complete definitions is given at the end of this appendix.

ELEMENTS OF DEFINITIONS

Significant elements identified in definitions include: who has the authority to decide, what the purpose of an intervention is, what the scope of services would entail, what constitutes acceptable evidence of efficacy, and whether the service has value for potential health gain, is not performed simply for convenience, and is applicable to the individual case.

Authority, Prudent Physician

- Health care services or products that a prudent physician would provide to a patient (AMA, 2005; Harmon, 2011; Maves, 2010)
- "Medically necessary" or "medical necessity" shall mean health care services that a physician, exercising prudent clinical judgment, would provide to a patient (Kaminiski, 2007)
- An intervention is *medically necessary* if, as recommended by the treating physician and determined by the health plan's medical director or physician designee, it is … [meets certain criteria for purpose, scope, evidence, and value] (Singer et al., 1999)

Medical Purpose

- A health intervention for the purpose of *treating* a medical condition—a research project at Stanford further defined a health intervention as an item or service delivered or undertaken primarily to *treat* (i.e., *prevent, diagnose, detect, treat, palliate*) a *medical condition* (i.e., disease; illness; injury; genetic or congenital defect; pregnancy; biological or psychological condition that lies outside the range of normal, age-appropriate human variation) or to *maintain or restore functional ability* (Singer et al., 1999)

225

- Health care services or products … for the purpose of *preventing, diagnosing,* or *treating* an illness, injury, disease, or its symptoms (AMA, 2005; Harmon, 2011; Maves, 2010)
- Health care … for the purpose of *preventing, evaluating, diagnosing,* or *treating* an illness, injury, disease, or its symptoms (Kaminiski, 2007)
- "Medically necessary" is a term for describing a requested service that is reasonably calculated to *prevent, diagnose, correct, cure, alleviate,* or *prevent worsening* of conditions in the client that endanger life, cause suffering or pain, result in an illness or infirmity, threaten to cause or aggravate a handicap, or cause physical deformity or malfunction. There is no other equally effective, more conservative, or substantially less costly course of treatment available or suitable for the client requesting the service. For the purpose of this section, "course of treatment" may include mere observation or, where appropriate, no treatment at all (Washington Administrative Code, 2011)
- To *prevent the onset or worsening of an illness, condition,* or *disability*; to *establish a diagnosis*; to provide *palliative, curative, or restorative* treatment for physical and/or mental health conditions; and/or *to assist the individual to achieve or maintain maximum functional capacity* in performing daily activities, taking into account both the functional capacity of the individual and those functional capacities that are appropriate for individuals of the same age (Dhillon, 2011; NHeLP, 2011)
- To *acquire, retain,* and *improve the self-help, socialization,* and *adaptive skills* necessary to reside successfully in home and community-based settings (Medicaid per [Ford, 2011])
- Screening and diagnostic services to *determine physical or mental defects* in recipients under age 21; and health care, treatment, and other measures to *correct or ameliorate any defects and chronic conditions discovered*[1]
- For the *diagnosis, cure, mitigation, treatment,* or *prevention* of disease or for the purpose of affecting any structure or function of the body[2]
- Health care provided to *correct* or *diminish* the adverse effects of a medical condition or mental illness; to assist an individual in *attaining* or *maintaining* an optimal level of health; to *diagnose* a condition, or *prevent* a medical condition from occurring[3]
- For the *diagnosis* or *treatment of illness or injury* or *to improve the functioning* of a malformed body member[4]
- Necessary to *prevent, diagnose, correct,* or *cure* conditions in the person that cause acute *suffering, endanger life, result in illness or infirmity, interfere with such person's capacity for normal activity,* or *threaten some significant handicap*[5]

Scope

- Clinically appropriate in terms of type, frequency, extent, site, and duration (AMA, 2005)
- Clinically appropriate, in terms of type, frequency, extent, site, and duration, and considered effective for the patient's illness, injury, or disease (Kaminiski, 2007)
- The most appropriate supply or level of service, considering potential benefits and harms to the patient (Singer et al., 1999)

Evidence

- In accordance with generally accepted standards of medical practice (AMA, 2005; Harmon, 2011)
- In accordance with generally accepted standards of medical practice; this means standards that are based on credible scientific evidence published in peer-reviewed medical literature, generally recognized by the

---

[1] Code of Federal Regulations, Title 42, Chapter IV, § 440.40 (current as of August 3, 2011).
[2] Internal Revenue Tax Code, Title 26, Subtitle A, Chapter 1 § 213(d)(1)(A).
[3] Connecticut Agency Regulations, § 17b-134d-63, et seq.
[4] Social Security Act, 42 U.S.C. Title XVIII, Section 1862(a)(1)(a).
[5] New York State Social Services Law, Title 1, Article 5, § 365 (a).

relevant medical community, or otherwise consistent with the standards set forth in policy issues involving clinical judgment (Kaminiski, 2007)

- Generally accepted standards of medical practice—standards that are based on credible scientific evidence published in peer-reviewed medical literature generally recognized by the relevant medical community, physician specialty society recommendations, and the views of physicians practicing in relevant clinical areas and any other relevant factors (Kaminiski, 2007)
- In accordance with standards of medical practice that are based on credible scientific evidence published in peer-reviewed medical literature generally recognized by the relevant medical community, physician specialty society recommendations, and the views of physicians practicing in relevant clinical areas and any other relevant factors (Bocchino, 2010)
- Known to be effective in improving health outcomes. For new interventions, effectiveness is determined by scientific evidence. For existing interventions, effectiveness is determined first by scientific evidence, then by professional standards, then by expert opinion (Singer et al., 1999)

Value

- Not more costly than an alternative service or sequence of services at least as likely to produce equivalent therapeutic or diagnostic results as to the diagnosis or treatment of that patient's illness, injury, or disease (Kaminiski, 2007)
- Cost-effective for this condition compared to alternative interventions, including no intervention; "cost-effective" does not necessarily mean lowest price (Singer et al., 1999)
- That the item or service be the "least costly" alternative course of diagnosis or treatment for which there is adequate "clinical scientific evidence" of its safety and effectiveness[6]
- There is no other equally effective, more conservative, or substantially less costly course of treatment available or suitable for the client requesting the service; for the purpose of this section, "course of treatment" may include mere observation or, where appropriate, no treatment at all[7]
- The least costly among similarly effective alternatives, where adequate scientific evidence exists; and efficient in regard to the avoidance of waste and refraining from provision of services that, on the basis of the best available scientific evidence, are not likely to produce benefit[8]

Not Primarily for Convenience

- Not primarily for the convenience of the patient, treating physician, or other health care provider (AMA, 2005)
- Not primarily for the convenience of the patient, physician, or other health care provider (Kaminiski, 2007)
- Not primarily for the convenience of the patient, physician, or other health care provider (Bocchino, 2011)
- Not primarily for the economic benefit of the health plans and purchasers (AMA, 2005)

Individuality of Application

- Unless the contrary is specified, the term "medical necessity" must refer to what is medically necessary for a particular patient, and hence entails an individual assessment rather than a general determination of what works in the ordinary case. But where, as here, the plan administrator presents sufficient evidence to show that a treatment is not medically necessary in the usual case, it is up to the patient and his or her physician to show that this individual patient is different from the usual in ways that make the treatment medically necessary for him or her (Kaminiski, 2007)

---

[6] Tennessee Code Annotated, § 71-5-144.

[7] Washington Administrative Code, § 388-500-0005.

[8] Connecticut Agency Regulations, § 17b-192-2(14).

SAMPLE COMPLETE DEFINITIONS

Stanford: Model Contractual Language for Medical Necessity

In the late 1990s, a research team at Stanford developed model contract language, as follows: For contractual purposes, an intervention will be covered if it is an otherwise covered category of service, not specifically excluded, and *medically necessary*. An intervention may be medically indicated yet not be a covered benefit or meet this contractual definition of *medical necessity*. A health plan may choose to cover interventions that do not meet this contractual definition of *medical necessity* (as presented in Table G-1) (Singer et al., 1999).

National Settlement Language

A class action court case clarified that medical necessity decisions must be individualized, also affirming that consideration of cost or comparative effectiveness was acceptable. The associated definition agreed to by more than 900,000 physicians and major insurance companies resulted in a definition in widespread practice in the private market (Kaminiski, 2007):

> "Medically Necessary" or "Medical Necessity" shall mean health care services that a physician, exercising prudent clinical judgment, would provide to a patient for the purpose of preventing, evaluating, diagnosing or treating an illness, injury, disease or its symptoms, and that are: a) in accordance with generally accepted standards of medical practice; b) clinically appropriate, in terms of type, frequency, extent, site and duration, and considered effective for the patient's illness, injury or disease; and c) not primarily for the convenience of the patient, physician or other health care provider, and not more costly than an alternative service or sequence of services at least as likely to produce equivalent therapeutic or diagnostic results as to the diagnosis or treatment of that patient's illness, injury or disease. For these purposes, "generally accepted standards of medical practice" means standards that are based on credible scientific evidence published in peer-reviewed medical literature generally recognized by the relevant medical community or otherwise consistent with the standards set forth in policy issues involving clinical judgment.

Selected Medical Definitions

American Medical Association

The AMA defines "medical necessity" as (AMA, 2005):

> Health care services or products that a prudent physician would provide to a patient for the purpose of preventing, diagnosing or treating an illness, injury, disease or its symptoms in a manner that is (a) in accordance with generally accepted standards of medical practice; (b) clinically appropriate in terms of type, frequency, extent, site, and duration; and (c) not primarily for the economic benefit of the health plans and purchasers or for the convenience of the patient, treating physician, or other health care provider.

Medicare

For Medicare, its authorizing legislation defines "medically necessary" rather than "medical necessity":

> Notwithstanding any other provisions of this file, no payment may be made under Part A or Part B for any expenses incurred for items or services, which are not reasonable and necessary for the diagnosis or treatment of illness or injury or to improve the functioning of a malformed body member.[9]

As presented on the Medicare website glossary for patients, "medically necessary" means:

> Services or supplies that are needed for the diagnosis or treatment of your medical condition, meet the standards of good medical practice in the local area, and aren't mainly for the convenience of you or your doctor (CMS, 2011).

---

[9] Social Security Act § 1862 [42 U.S.C. 1395y].

TABLE G-1 Model Contractual Language for Medical Necessity

Authority	Purpose	Scope	Evidence	Value
An intervention is *medically necessary* if, as recommended by the treating physician[a] and determined by the health plan's medical director or physician designee,[b] it is (all of the following):	A health intervention[c] for the purpose of treating a medical condition	The most appropriate supply or level of service, considering potential benefits and harms to the patient	Known to be effective[d] in improving health outcomes.[e] For new interventions,[f] effectiveness is determined by scientific evidence.[g,h] For existing interventions, effectiveness is determined first by scientific evidence, then by professional standards, then by expert opinion[i] and	Cost-effective for this condition compared to alternative interventions, including no intervention[j] "Cost-effective" does not necessarily mean lowest price

[a] *Treating physician* means a physician who has personally evaluated the patient.

[b] *Physician designee* means a physician designated to assist in the decision-making process.

[c] A *health intervention* is an item or service delivered or undertaken primarily to *treat* (i.e., prevent, diagnose, detect, treat, palliate) a *medical condition* (i.e., disease; illness; injury; genetic or congenital defect; pregnancy; or a biological or psychological condition that lies outside the range of normal, age-appropriate human variation) or to maintain or restore functional ability. For the contractual definition of medical necessity, a health intervention is defined not only by the intervention itself, but also by the medical condition and patient indications for which it is being applied.

[d] *Effective* means that the intervention can reasonably be expected to produce the intended results and to have expected benefits that outweigh potential harmful effects.

[e] *Health outcomes* are outcomes that affect health status as measured by the length or quality (primarily as perceived by the patient) of a person's life.

[f] An *intervention* is considered to be *new* if it is not yet in widespread use for the medical condition and patient indications being considered.

[g] *Scientific evidence* consists primarily of controlled clinical trials that either directly or indirectly demonstrate the effect of the intervention on health outcomes. If controlled clinical trials are not available, observational studies that demonstrate a causal relationship between the intervention and health outcomes can be used. Partially controlled observational studies and uncontrolled clinical series may be suggestive, but do not by themselves demonstrate a causal relationship unless the magnitude of the effect observed exceeds anything that could be explained either by the natural history of the medical condition or potential experimental biases.

[h] *New interventions* for which clinical trials have not been conducted because of epidemiological reasons (i.e., rare or new diseases or orphan populations) shall be evaluated on the basis of professional standards of care or expert opinion (as described in footnote a).

[i] For *existing interventions*, the scientific evidence should be considered first and, to the greatest extent possible, should be the basis for determinations of medical necessity. If no scientific evidence is available, professional standards of care should be considered. If professional standards of care do not exist, or are outdated or contradictory, decisions about existing interventions should be based on expert opinion. Giving priority to scientific evidence does not mean that coverage of existing interventions should be denied in the absence of conclusive scientific evidence. Existing interventions can meet the contractual definition of medical necessity in the absence of scientific evidence if there is a strong conviction of effectiveness and benefit expressed through up-to-date and consistent professional standards of care or, in the absence of such standards, convincing expert opinion.

[j] An intervention is considered *cost-effective* if the benefits and harms relative to costs represent an economically efficient use of resources for patients with this condition. In the application of this criterion to an individual case, the characteristics of the individual patient shall be determinative.

SOURCE: Singer et al., 1999.

Medicaid

The Medicaid statute does not define "medically necessary" or "medical necessity," and each state is allowed to develop its own definition (Sindelar, 2002). However, the Early and Periodic Screening, Diagnosis, and Treatment (EPSDT) program's coverage rules, providing guidance for definitions in pediatric cases, are more inclusive of concepts applicable to the Affordable Care Act (ACA) category of habilitation (O'Connell and Watson, 2001):

> Under EPSDT, state Medicaid programs must cover "necessary health care, diagnostic services, treatment and other measures ... to *correct or ameliorate* defects and physical and mental illnesses and conditions." Services must be covered if they correct, compensate for, or improve a condition, or prevent a condition from worsening—even if the condition cannot be prevented or cured.

TennCare adopted, what was controversial at the time, for its Medicaid definition—"including a requirement that the item or service be the 'least costly' alternative course of diagnosis or treatment for which there is adequate 'clinical scientific evidence' of its safety and effectiveness" (Blumstein and Sloan, 2000). Such wording is also now seen in other Medicaid-related programs (e.g., see SAGA below).

A recent examination of Medicaid definitions used by Medicaid programs in Connecticut, Massachusetts, New York, and Rhode Island illustrates the diversity of approaches to definition, with variation even within a single state depending on the applicable population (Cohen, 2010).

For Connecticut Medicaid, as administered through its Department of Social Services (DSS)[10] (State of Connecticut Department of Social Services):

> Health care provided to correct or diminish the adverse effects of a medical condition or mental illness; to assist an individual in *attaining or maintaining* an optimal level of health; to diagnose a condition or *prevent a medical condition or prevent* a medical condition from occurring.

Connecticut's State-Administered General Assistance (SAGA) program (State of Connecticut Department of Social Services, 2009), a cash assistance program for adults without children who are unable to work, uses[11]:

> Health services required to *prevent, identify, diagnose, treat, rehabilitate, or ameliorate* a health problem or its effects, or to *maintain health and functioning*, provided such services are:
>
> 1. Consistent with generally accepted standards of medical practice;
> 2. Clinically appropriate in terms of type, frequency, timing, site, and duration;
> 3. Demonstrated through scientific evidence to be safe and effective and the least costly among similarly effective alternatives, where adequate scientific evidence exists; and
> 4. Efficient in regard to the avoidance of waste and refraining from provision of services that, on the basis of the best available scientific evidence, are not likely to produce benefit.

For MassHealth, a service, regardless of whether in fee-for-service or managed care arrangements, is considered "medically necessary" if[12]:

> 1. It is reasonably calculated to prevent, diagnose, prevent the worsening of, alleviate, correct, or cure conditions in the MassHealth member that endanger life, cause suffering or pain, cause physical deformity or malfunction, *threaten to cause or to aggravate a handicap, or result in illness of infirmity*; and
> 2. There is no other comparable, available, and suitable medical service or site of service that is more conservative or less costly to the MassHealth agency. Services that are less costly to the MassHealth agency including health care reasonably known by the provider or identified by the MassHealth agency pursuant to a prior authorization request to be available to the member through a third party.

It is notable that the Medicaid agency is able to impose sanctions on providers, who (1) provide or prescribe a service or (2) admit a member to an inpatient facility when the services or admission are not medically necessary (Kaminiski, 2007), and Massachusetts publishes on its website specific guidelines for medical necessity for 16 services (e.g., bariatric surgery, organ transplant, physical therapy) (Massachusetts Department of Health, 2011).

Fee-for-service and managed care arrangements through Medicaid in New York define *medically necessary* as[13]:

> Necessary to *prevent, diagnose, correct, or cure* conditions in the person that cause acute suffering, endanger life, *result in illness or infirmity, interfere with such person's capacity for normal activity,* or threaten some significant handicap and which are furnished an eligible person in accordance with state law.

RIte Care, Rhode Island's Medicaid managed health care program uses the national settlement language referenced above (Kaminiski, 2007).

---

[10] Connecticut Agency Regulations, § 17b-134d-63, et seq.

[11] Connecticut Agency Regulations, § 17b-192-2(14).

[12] 130 Massachusetts Code Regulations, § 450.204 (2009).

[13] New York State Social Services Law, § 365-a.

REFERENCES

AMA (American Medical Association). 2005. *Model managed care contract.* http://www.ama-assn.org/ama1/pub/upload/mm/368/mmcc_4th_ ed.pdf (accessed August 5, 2011).

Blumstein, J. F., and F. Sloan. 2000. Health care reform through Medicaid managed care: Tennessee (TennCare) as a case study and paradigm. *Vanderbilt Law Review* 53(1):125-270.

Bocchino, C. 2010. Online questionnaire responses submitted by Carmella Bocchino, Executive Vice President, America's Health Insurance Plans to the IOM Committee on the Determination of Essential Health Benefits, December 6.

_____. 2011. Statement to the IOM Committee on the Determination of Essential Health Benefits by Carmella Bocchino, Executive Vice President, Clinical Affairs and Strategic Planning, America's Health Insurance Plans, Washington, DC, January 13.

CMS (Centers for Medicare & Medicaid Services). 2011. *Medicare glossary.* http://www.medicare.gov/Glossary/a.html?SelectAlphabet =M&Language=English#Content (accessed August 5, 2011).

Cohen, R. K. 2010. *Medical necessity definitions in surrounding states.* http://www.cga.ct.gov/2010/rpt/2010-R-0010.htm (accessed August 1, 2011).

Dhillon, J. 2011. Testimony to the IOM Committee on the Determination of Essential Health Benefits by Jina Dhillon, Staff Attorney, National Health Law Program, Washington, DC, January 14.

Ford, M. 2011. Testimony to the IOM Committee on the Determination of Essential Health Benefits by Marty Ford, Director of Legal Advocacy, The Arc and United Cerebral Palsy Disability Policy Collaboration, Washington, DC, January 13.

Harmon, G. 2011. Statement to the IOM Committee on the Determination of Essential Health Benefits by Gerald Harmon, Retired Major General U.S. Air Force and Member, Council on Medical Service, American Medical Association, Washington, DC, January 14.

Kaminiski, J. L. 2007. *Defining medical necessity.* http://www.cga.ct.gov/2007/rpt/2007-r-0055.htm (accessed April 20, 2011).

Massachusetts Department of Health. 2011. *Guidelines for medical necessity determination.* http://www.mass.gov/?pageID=eohhs2subtopic&L =6&L0=Home&L1=Provider&L2=Insurance+%28including+MassHealth%29&L3=MassHealth&L4=Guidelines+for+Clinical+ Treatment&L5=Guidelines+for+Medical+Necessity+Determination&sid=Eeohhs2 (accessed August 5, 2011).

Maves, M. 2010. Online questionnaire responses submitted by Michael Maves, Chief Executive Officer and Executive Vice President, American Medical Association to the IOM Committee on the Determination of Essential Health Benefits, December 20.

NHeLP (National Health Law Program). 2011. *Medical necessity definition: Model Medicaid managed care contract provisions.* http://www. healthlaw.org/index.php?option=com_content&view=article&id=281:medical-necessity-definition-model-medicaid-managed-care -contract-provisions&catid=42:medicaid (accessed August 5, 2011).

O'Connell, M., and S. Watson. 2001. *Medicaid and EPSDT.* http://www.nls.org/conf/epsdt.htm (accessed July 29, 2011).

Sindelar, T. 2002. *The "medical necessity requirement" in Medicaid.* Boston, MA: The Disability Law Center.

Singer, S., L. Bergthold, C. Vorhaus, S. Olson, I. Mutchnick, Y. Y. Goh, S. Zimmerman, and A. Enthoven. 1999. Decreasing variation in medical necessity decision making. Appendix B. Model language developed at the "Decreasing Variation in Medical Necessity Decision Making" Decision Maker Workshop in Sacramento, CA, March 11-13, 1999.

State of Connecticut Department of Social Services. *Connecticut Medicaid: Summary of services.* http://www.ct.gov/dss/lib/dss/pdfs/medicaid- servicesv3kk.pdf (accessed September 28, 2011).

_____. 2009. *State Administered General Assistance (SAGA): Cash and medical assistance programs.* http://www.ct.gov/dss/lib/dss/pdfs/ sagacashandmedical.pdf (accessed September 28, 2011).

Washington Administrative Code. 2011. *WAC388-500-0005 medical definitions.* http://www.mrsc.org/mc/wac/WAC%20388%20%20TITLE/ WAC%20388%20-500%20%20CHAPTER/WAC%20388%20-500%20-0005.HTM (accessed September 19, 2011).